WITNESS

WITNESS

From the Shah to the Secret Arms Deal

An Insider's Account of

U.S. Involvement in Iran

MANSUR RAFIZADEH
Former Chief of SAVAK

William Morrow and Company, Inc.

New York

Dedicated
to
My Father and My Mother

Library of Congress Catalog Card Number: 87–043087
ISBN: 0–688–07369–7

Printed in the United States of America

First Edition

1 2 3 4 5 6 7 8 9 10

BOOK DESIGN BY MARIA EPES/PANDORA SPELIOS

ACKNOWLEDGMENTS

If I have led anyone to believe that writing this memoir was my own idea, it is a fraud. Credit goes to my brother, Mozafar, who constantly reminded me of the teaching of our father that the truth should be known regardless of the consequences. Had it not been for his continuous persistence, certainly there would be no book at the present time. From the bottom of my heart I want to thank Mozafar, not only as my youngest brother but as my son, and his fiancée, Cheryl Harmony, for their support throughout this ordeal.

This book would not have been completed without my dearest friend, Joan Saccoman. My utmost appreciation goes to her for her assistance in formulating and substantiating the contents of the manuscript. Over the past two decades she has come to know some of the personalities in my book. Her devotion can never be forgotten.

I want to thank Cynthia Low, whose talent and indefatigable efforts were indispensable to this manuscript.

I want to take this opportunity to thank my friend Ted Kruckel, a true gentleman, for his encouragement and invaluable assistance.

I am extremely indebted to Pat Golbitz, my eminent editor at William Morrow, for her superb guidance.

My sincere thanks to Nevins McBride, who introduced me to his daughter-in-law, Margaret McBride, my literary agent. I thank Margaret for paving the road with her wealth of literary knowledge.

I wish to thank John Cox, who did such a commendable job during the original editing of my manuscript.

My sincere thanks go to my friend Raji Samghabadi, whose help was always there when I needed it.

My indebtedness to Professor Agnes Doody and the late Professor Arthur Jeffrey whose advice in writing English cannot be overlooked.

I am particularly appreciative of the legal advice and staunch support of my good friends, attorneys Melvin Gittleman, Raymond Durr, and Teresa Gundersen, especially during the time my life was threatened by the CIA.

I thank Dr. William Lee and Dr. Kendrick Lance, who helped during the crisis when my health was endangered.

Thanks also to Sonia Greenbaum and Jill Hamilton of William Morrow.

I would like to thank the following for their dedicated assistance in this effort—Gail Herlehy, Lois Muniente, Joy Cassano, Linda Tarleton, Kim Keinz, and Michele Hochberg.

Finally, my wholehearted gratitude is extended to all of my sources, especially to those in Iran whose names cannot be revealed.

Contents

PART I

INTRODUCTION

I was a firsthand witness to a reign of terror and played a unique role during a very special time in history. To be precise, I was chief of SAVAK in the United States throughout most of the reign of Shah Mohammad Reza Pahlavi of Iran.

During my lifetime, I evolved from a boy who admired, even worshiped, what he took to be the shah's progressive and enlightened rule into a double agent who willingly functioned as an informer for the CIA and ardently worked to bring about the shah's downfall.

Because of my double role in the shah's secret police, I was to spend my adult life in constant fear of exposure. I still live with fear, but the world deserves to know the truth, and I believe it to be my duty to set the record straight, because I was there. I had personal relationships with the shah and his family for most of my adult life and was able to observe him at close range throughout the various crises that punctuated his reign. During those years, as SAVAK's chief liaison officer with both the CIA and the FBI, I also maintained close personal ties with the hierarchy in the shah's government, including all of the chiefs of SAVAK in Tehran.

Superficially, my life is a paradox. How could I, as the U.S. chief of SAVAK, perhaps the most bloody and diabolical secret police organization in modern history, claim, as I do, to adhere to the principles of nonviolence? How could I know about the shah's legendary atrocities and still work for his regime?

The answers are rooted in my early beliefs and the aspirations of an ambitious young man. As a youth, I truly believed that by working within the system, I, and others like me, would one day see the shah a constitutional monarch, and that we would be the new leaders of Iran's first democratic government.

Destiny didn't grant me that opportunity. Instead, it afforded me a unique chance to study a classic despotism run amok.

In October 1982 I received an urgent call from Washington. "We must see you tomorrow," the caller said. "It's a matter of life and death." When we met in New York City, my contact informed me that the CIA's intelligence sources had discovered that I was one of six persons, including General Gholam Ali Oveissi[1] and Crown Prince Reza Pahlavi, on the hit list of the new revolutionary government in Iran. The Justice Department had already informed the FBI and local police. "Take precautions," the agent warned me. "Don't take unnecessary risks by being seen in public places. You were the chief of SAVAK —you know how to take care of yourself." I accepted the news calmly. "You die only once," I told the man. "It's better to die that once than die of fear a hundred times a day."

The CIA man erupted. "That's your Eastern philosophy, Mansur! But you must realize that this is serious business. They intend to kill you and, with the public life you lead, they will. Mansur, be careful! This intelligence has been confirmed through several channels—we know they are deadly serious."

When I got home after that meeting, my youngest brother, Mozafar, was waiting anxiously to hear about the emergency meeting. "What are you going to do?" he asked.

"What can I do?" I answered. "All they have asked is that I be careful and inform General Oveissi that he is also on the list. The other four people have already been contacted by the CIA."

"But just suppose you were killed," Mozafar protested. "You would be nothing but another victim. Don't let that happen, Mansur. Write down what you know while you can."

Somewhat reluctantly, I decided to write this memoir. Many times thereafter I lost interest and laid the work aside, but Mozafar continued to push me to write, frequently asking what year I was currently writing about.

Then, on the morning of February 8, 1984, less than one and a half years after the CIA warned me of Khomeini's death list, Mozafar came up to my room. "How many pages have you written?" he asked.

"Not many," I responded.

"You had better hurry," he warned me. "They just killed General Oveissi in Paris."

After spending two and a half years at my farm in upstate New York completing this manuscript, I returned to the metropolitan area to meet with publishers, investigate some new business ventures, and finally enjoy a peaceful life surrounded by my family and friends. This brief period of tranquillity was shattered on March 10, 1986.

While traveling from New York to Florida, I called home and was surprised to discover that I had received an urgent phone call from a senior officer of the CIA. I had not seen him since I had severed all of my ties with the CIA in February 1983. What could he want?

I promptly returned his call and asked him what was so urgent. My heart sank when he said, "Am I talking to the about-to-be-world-famous author?"

What the CIA wanted was to prevent me from publishing this book at any cost. After first attempting to bribe me, they threatened to kill me. Their motives will become clear as my story unfolds.

CHAPTER ONE

Childhood: Boundless Injustice; Lasting Hopes

When I was thirteen, in 1944, while I was visiting in one of the villages owned by my mother's relatives, a peasant stole a few pounds of grain from the storage room of the tenant farm on which he lived. The overseer found out about the theft and ordered the peasant to be brought to the village square for trial and punishment. The miscreant confessed his deed, saying he had done it only because he could no longer bear to watch his family starve. His wife and three children swore to the overseer that his account was true. The wife even confessed that she had cooked a meal of the stolen food.

The overseer, a big, burly man with a bushy moustache, ruled out starvation as a sufficient reason for theft. He set the man's punishment at one hundred blows, to be administered with a whip made of a bundle of pomegranate branches that had been tied together and soaked in water. Pliant and strong, the branches cut like a cat-o'-nine tails.

The peasant, stripped to his waist, was spread-eagled on the ground in a position called "the four nails"; the nails in actuality were four heavy stakes driven into the ground to which his arms and legs were tied with ropes. As he sprawled face down, four torturers drove a fifth stake between his legs to keep his body from twisting.

I had seen beggars with missing fingers or missing hands, their punishment for thefts, but I had never witnessed a whipping. I cringed as the first torturer began to beat the man. Slightly built, the peasant wailed and screamed, begging the overseer for forgiveness. His wife fell to the ground, kissing the overseer's feet frantically, beseeching him, "Please, God! He is too weak. He will die! Oh, God, he's taken enough. I beg you, beat me instead. I am the real offender. We were starving. I told him to get the food for us. Oh, by the cut hands of the divine Abbas, I swear to you! Please!"

The children were crying as well, adding their screams to those of their mother. "Oh, God! Help our father. Please help our father." But over their cries rose the overseer's chant, "Beat him! Beat him! Harder! Beat the thief. Beat the thief. Harder!"

Onlookers pressed forward eagerly as the four torturers took turns striking the peasant with all their might. At first the poor man shrieked and blood seeped through his garments. Soon his screams turned to moans; then the moans turned to silence.

At last the overseer ordered him untied. When the man did not move, the overseer shouted at him, "Get up! Don't play dead. You're not fooling me. Get up!" But the peasant had long since surrendered his life. Silence ruled the square. No one protested.

When the provincial gendarmerie in Kerman was informed of the incident by its village outpost, an investigation was launched. The overseer and the men who had beaten the peasant were taken to Kerman for interrogation. But after a few weeks, all of them were released without charge. I saw them after I returned to Kerman. In a holiday mood, they were shopping, buying presents for their families before returning to the village.

Later, I asked my father why the murderers had not been prosecuted.

"Mansur, this is nothing," he answered. "You do not know, but there are far greater injustices than this."

"What could be worse?" The man's cries still echoed in my ears. "They beat him savagely, Father. They beat him until he died."

"Ah, my son, here corruption and injustice begin at the top. It is sad. Those at the top are the ones who should be fair, who are supposed to enforce the law. Should a poor, starving peasant be killed because he steals food? An empty stomach has no beliefs, no principles. Even human beings, who call themselves the lords of creation, will eat each other if they are starving."

"But what happened? Didn't the family protest, Father?"

"The overseer summoned the family to his home and ordered them to keep silent. What could they do? To whom could they appeal? Of course he paid them—blood money—one hundred tomans [the equivalent of fourteen American dollars]."

"Paid! Do you mean after he had killed the man, they took money from him?"

"Of course, Mansur. And they took it because if they hadn't, it would have appeared they intended to seek vengeance. They had no choice."

"And the chief of the gendarmes, the man who was in charge of the investigation? Where is the chief now? What happened to him?"

"Where else? Behind his desk. Investigating the people's complaints, protecting their lives, their property, and their virtue!"

"But what of the family? What can we do for them?"

"Pray." My father's voice was not sarcastic now, it was serious. "Pray!"

"Mansur, if you think there is anything else we can do, you tell me."

For a few moments I was quiet. I could feel a flush of heat on my forehead and ears. "I know what we can do! We can write down the whole tragedy. Then we will go to the villagers, get their signatures on a petition and . . ."

"Signatures? What signatures?" my father interrupted. "They cannot read. They cannot write."

"Isn't there any other way they can sign?"

"Someone could read to them. They could press their fingerprints on the document."

"Fine!" I said excitedly. "Then that's how we'll do it. We'll write it down, the whole tragedy; they'll put their fingerprints on it, and we'll send the petition to the shah! Shadow of the Almighty, Vice-Regent of God! We'll find someone to take the petition to Tehran, to the imperial palace."

At this, my father laughed out loud. "A petition to the shah, the Shadow of God?"

I was offended, thinking that my father was laughing at me. "Then you tell me what to do, my father. What is your solution, besides praying for them?"

"Let's go for a walk," he said.

Outside, to the east, farm fields stretched away to the desert, Kavir-e Lut, and a huge mountain, its peak covered with snow year round, dominated the horizon to the south. My father walked toward the fields. I followed him. Both of us were silent. I heard only the noisy chirping of flocks of sparrows and the droning of locusts that whirred up at our approach.

Finally, my father spoke, looking over his shoulder at me. "You are quiet."

Still hurt, I nodded.

"The truth is, Mansur, that the shah cannot do anything about this injustice."

"Then you believe that even the shah is unjust?"

"Mansur, injustice originates in the ignorance and illiteracy of our people and it will never be abolished until such ignorance and illiteracy are abolished. If our people were educated and informed of such crimes, not only what happened to the peasant, but of our terrible social conditions, our government scandals, our miserable poverty, then things might be different. But here in Kerman, in a city of sixty thousand people, we have only a few weekly newspapers and they are two- or four-page legal notices. How can people learn? How can they become informed? There are too few schools. And even if we had more, how could the parents afford to send their children to them? The children have no clothes for school. Instead, the children, these five- and six-year-old children, are sent to work because their families need the few pennies they can earn."

My father swept his arms open in a wide gesture that included fields, farms, and mountain. "Look at it, Mansur. So quiet, so peaceful. Oh, yes, our town is peaceful. It is also a graveyard. If someone were to raise his voice in protest, who would listen?" He dropped his hands. "But perhaps all is not lost.

"I agree we must do something," he continued. "And you, Mansur, can help. A friend is going to start sending me the Tehran newspaper. You have a social duty. You know how to read and write. I want you to start reading the news to those who cannot read it for themselves. It is only a partial solution. But it can help overcome some ignorance, for the illiterate man is the blind man. He knows neither where he is nor where he is going. By reading to these people you can help to give them their vision."

What my father was proposing was not entirely new. From the age of ten, I had been reading and writing for the people, as had many of my schoolmates. We were held in high esteem, for we were literate. With a page ripped from our notebook and a pencil well licked, we transcribed in large, often clumsy letters the customary phrases "May God protect you [Leilah], your loving mother sends news that she is well." "Beloved daughter, your father is well. Your sisters and brothers are well. Send us a letter to tell us the state of your health." "We give your regards to all who ask for you. God be with you. God protect you. Write us a letter. Don't forget—writing is half of visiting."

Once the letter was finished, or after I had read to them, the family would offer to share whatever food they had or would pour out effusive blessings: "May God protect your soul . . . your heart . . . your brain . . . your family . . ."

For letters or papers of greater significance, the townspeople went to the scribes who stationed themselves in front of the post office and courthouse. There, in positions carefully marked out and jealously guarded, the scribes hunkered all day, their papers held down by stones, pencils at the ready. In winter they pulled heavy wool robes up over their ears and warmed their frozen fingers over small charcoal stoves.

People had favorite scribes, the poetic ones, who could pick the most delicate shade of meaning, the most flourishing phrase suitable for pursuing a lover; the religious scribes, who could console a grief-stricken relative; and another scribe, who was suitable for business transactions. Unfortunately, the scribes' abilities sometimes were not much superior to those of the children. Some could only read, not write, but were not averse to pretending or adding a little extra, just as the children often did, embellishing the letters for the greater pleasure of an eager listener, trying to make a grouchy one more pleasant. My father warned me against the practice. Not only was it not nice to do, but you could be caught. He then told me the story of one scribe who began reading for a customer: "Leilah, may God be with you. We are all . . ." The woman customer broke in, furious: "No, it's a deed. A deed!" Unflustered, the scribe continued without pause, ". . . south, sixty feet, east, twenty-seven feet . . ."

Being literate entailed a social obligation. On occasion, honoring the social obligation was trying, but I usually enjoyed it. Often I helped old Akbar, the grocer, or other shopkeepers tote up their monthly accounts, inscribing the name of each debtor in a ledger as the owner laboriously added up the amounts owed him on his abacus.

These activities had afforded me access of a kind to the daily lives, the homes, the shops of people who lived quite differently from the way we did. I found new friends every day, new adventures. It was exciting, more interesting than the usual pursuits of my schoolmates. I was growing ever more aware of the poverty and misery of Kerman, of the sad deprivations of its townspeople.

But even though I felt my father was right in proposing this new duty for me, even though I shared his sense of obligation, even though I wanted to please him, I felt ill prepared. My father received frequent guests at home, most of them educated, informed, and well traveled. Even to those who spouted nonsense, we listened patiently, picking out and storing every grain of sense or novelty. I was always invited to join these social gatherings, listening to heady talk about ethics, politics, religion. Accordingly, I was aware of my ignorance of foreign lands.

Still, my thirst for learning was great. I was determined to excel in school even though the circumstances were not always congenial. In winter our unheated classroom was so cold that my feet were often frostbitten, but I sat, as did the other children and the teacher, with my feet tucked up beneath my rear, well away from the brick and dirt floor, my long wool jacket tucked in around them. (In the evening I sat with my feet soaking in the hot water saved from cooking turnips, supposedly a healing liquid.)

Frostbitten feet did not, could not, deter me. Nor did my sixth-grade geography teacher, sullen and morose, a great fat toad of a woman. Each morning she marched in, straight to the blackboard (a small four- by four-foot easel) and chalked firmly, in large, bold letters, GOD, SHAH, COUNTRY, with GOD at the apex of the triangle, SHAH to the left, COUNTRY to the right. We all repeated the oath loudly. With our perspective now firmly established, she proceeded. "United States, capital, 'Washeengtoon.' Forty-eight states, many people who have immigrated. Much land. Argentina, capital, Buenos Aires. 'Brazeel,' capital, Rio de Janeiro. Ali! Put up mute map fifteen."

At this, Ali or whoever would pull out one of the mute maps. To this day, I do not know where those maps came from. They were called "mute" because they were not printed in any recognizable language and no one had bothered to mark them in Farsi. We were expected to discern the shapes of individual countries on sight.

I remember one particular occasion. Ali propped the mute map against the blackboard easel, but backwards, so that we could not practice or confer as the teacher left her platform to get a long pointer. Then: "Mansur! France!" I turned the map over and pointed hesitantly, vaguely, then placed my finger firmly on a spot. Whack! "Stupid! With your stupid finger, you travel fast. A one-thousand-mile mistake!" I nursed my stinging hand.

On she droned. Someone was chosen to read. We were asked to write answers to her questions in our notebooks. Necks craned, sighs were muffled. Those who were religious, patriotic or worried about their scholastic standing carefully copied the triangle onto the top of their pages. The teacher knitted. No movement or sound was allowed.

As the class ended and we itched to leave, she addressed us glowingly: "From these very benches will arise the future statesmen, the learned men who will guide our nation's destiny." I permitted myself a glimmer of a smile, thinking of my last composition, which had

proved beyond doubt that the pen outstrips the sword. Wham!! My
head rocked. The monitor, ever watchful, had struck me on the side of
my head and ear with such force that I was momentarily blinded. Hurt,
outraged, I raised my hand and protested. I had done my homework;
I was not a troublemaker. The teacher ignored me and addressed the
class again. "It is obvious that Mansur will not be one of those men.
He is an idiot!"

We filed out. In fact, my punishment had been mild. For such slight
infractions, pupils were often subjected to the *falak,* the equivalent of
Torquemada's fire. The offender was made to remove his shoes, and his
bare feet were forced under the thick rope attached to the middle of a
round stick, held at each end by the janitor and the superintendent. On
his back, with his feet twisted rigidly upward, he was immobilized. The
principal, apparently with great pleasure, then administered blows to
the soles of the offender's feet with the same sort of whip that I had seen
used on the peasant. At the end, feet flayed, legs numb, the student
would be unable to stand. But by the end of the day, he could usually
limp home, shoes tucked under his armpits, his clothes and hair still
covered with the dirt on which he had lain, followed by the jeers of his
fellows, who were only too glad to see another suffer. The violence they
witnessed daily made them violent themselves.

The *falak* was not the only punishment for a student's misbehavior.
Petty misdeeds—laughing out loud in class, for example, or laughing
at or commenting audibly on a teacher's unfortunate habits, such as
nose-picking or, in the case of one teacher, dislodging his false teeth and
clicking them back into place, or being unprepared for a homework
assignment—were punished in several ways. Students were "jailed" in
a dark, dank room, supposedly crawling with snakes and rats. Students
were whipped with wire cables and struck with brass knuckles. Pencils
were placed between a student's fingers and the teacher squeezed the
offender's joints until he screamed. Sometimes the student's earlobe was
folded over a date pit and the thin, hard pit pressed behind the lobe and
squeezed tightly, causing excruciating pain. It was common for teachers to carry date pits in their pockets.

Sometimes one child tormented another by smudging his artwork
or spilling his bottle of ink on completed homework. When the victim
cried out in protest, the suspected offender was forced to stand in front
of the entire class, his hands stretched above his head, one foot raised.
Occasionally, he was innocent, but it was useless to protest. The purpose of the torture was to extract a confession; lowering the raised foot
to the floor was equivalent to confessing one's guilt.

But confession didn't absolve the student. Instead, the *falak* was brought in. The student might receive only a few strokes but he could not escape. The next day, at the end of the assembly that preceded each day of class, after the salute to the shah, the prayer, and the national anthem, the principal called out the names and offenses of every person punished the previous day, and all of them stood in a small group apart. At the principal's command, they were booed loudly three times by the entire student body.

Outside the classroom, the children's lives were often as cruel, if not more so. Stepchildren often suffered greatly at the hands of stepmothers. In my neighborhood a young unmarried girl became pregnant. After a crude attempt to induce an abortion (drinking a large quantity of vinegar and jumping vigorously), the girl was forced to lie down and a heavy stone pestle was ground into her abdomen. She hemorrhaged and died.

Another stepmother, learning that her stepdaughter was going out with a boy, placed a heated pan on the girl's genitals, burning her severely. The girl sought shelter at a neighbor's and became their maid rather than return to her own family. After being burned, the girl stuttered so badly that she was nearly incomprehensible; her stepmother insisted that she had always been retarded.

Understandably, children turned their anger and hostility outward in whatever ways they could. They pursued dogs that had disobeyed, chased them into culverts, trapped them when the frightened animals entered the half-buried pipes, sealed off the ends with rocks and debris, and shouted, "Jailed!" Occasionally, they took pity on the animals and released them after only a short detention; other times the animals were buried alive.

Cats that killed birds or that took food from the neighborhood children were ceremonially judged, found guilty, and hanged. The accusation against the cat was read; its death sentence was pronounced to the attending, approving children; weights were tied to the cat's legs to prevent it from twisting and clawing itself upright; and the rope tightened around its neck. When the cat's bladder relaxed and its body went limp, it was pronounced dead. The burial was carried out with pomp, the sentence read again as the cat was placed in an impromptu grave.

In my hometown the governing authorities frequently announced the impending execution of a robber or murderer. At the first light of dawn, crowds gathered and the victim was led to a scaffold and made to stand on a bench, his hands tied behind his back. The noose was slipped over his head; two men, standing at the rear, held tightly to the rope, which was passed over and behind the scaffold, and yanked hard as the bench was jerked from beneath the victim. The offender's body would not be removed until several hours after daylight, and children on their way to school would gape at the slowly twisting corpse. At times, two or three victims were hanged together.

Several times I heard my father and friends protesting this practice of public execution and, in particular, the prolonged exhibition of the bodies. Violence became part of growing up.

Yet this violence, even the *falak,* couldn't deter me from the pursuit of learning. Nor could the jeers of my schoolmates, who, using my nickname, teased me for my seriousness: " 'Hadji,' 'Son of Baldy.' Always with your nose in a book." After a while I learned to defend myself with "When the test comes, you'll be begging for my notes." My closest friend, Ahmad, who avoided studying at any cost, became even friendlier before each test.

I loved school. Yet I did not hear my teacher's voice so much as my father's. "Mansur, it is possible to become anything—except God," he would say. "And they say God is just. On the contrary, he is most unfair. To some, he gives great intellect; to others, none. But no one complains. No! Heavenly kingdom! Each is sure he possesses more than the next. Try to be a man."

I wasn't sure what this entailed. "What is a man, Father?"

"What is a man? How do you become one? It's very easy and very hard, my son. Once, a man traveling on his mule in winter saw another man standing shivering by the side of the road. 'Are you cold?' he asked. 'Oh, yes,' came the reply. 'Please give me a ride.' The first man instructed him to get up on the mule, to warm his hands on his own belly beneath his robe, to place his feet in his mule's saddlebags. After they had ridden for several miles, they stopped and dismounted. 'Are you hungry?' the man asked. He offered the stranger his cheese and bread. Greedily the man ate. After the meal, the first man fell asleep. Suddenly he awakened to find the stranger mounted on his mule. 'What are you doing?' he asked. 'I'm leaving,' the stranger replied. The good man was shaken, but began to back away, offering no resistance. He stopped a few paces away. 'Please,' he said, 'may I ask you a favor?' 'No,' came the answer. 'No favors. You will ask for your mule back or some food.' 'No, I want nothing,' the good man protested, shaking his head. 'I will tell no one of this incident. Please tell no one either. I do not want people to cease doing good.' " Parables of this sort were the hallmark of my father's teaching.

Thus, because I loved to read, because I felt a strong sense of social obligation, and because I could not disappoint my father, I began the new task of reading to the townspeople.

After a few weeks, the workers requested that I read for twenty minutes or so and then permit them to question me. In no way was I going to agree to this! In the first place, the newspapers I read were out of date. And I knew so little about so much: the foreign lands and the names prominent in the news, who was head of what government, how long that government had existed. But they repeated their entreaties and, daunted, I approached my father. He told me that he would provide me with paper, a scarce and valued commodity, on which I should write down any question I could not answer, and try to find the answer later.

Blank paper had always been rare and expensive in Kerman; it was even more so toward the end of World War II, when I was still in grade school. I did my homework on a despised slate. Once it was seen and corrected by the teacher, I was obliged to wipe it off with a damp cloth, thus destroying my work. Many of the students used the backs of scraps of government stationery for homework. But my father would have none of it. To him it was unethical to use paper intended solely for official use. Besides, it was a punishable offense. But many government employees, hungry and desperate, defied the statutes and traded it to grocers in exchange for food. After the students bought the paper and used it for homework, they traded it back to the grocers, this time for candy. Now the paper was "used," and the grocers were not responsible for "defacing" it.

Scrap paper was also used to protect their scales from contamination by infidel containers. All liquid items—yogurt, oil, date syrup, milk, kerosene—were poured into containers brought by the customers, used and used again. If the customer was Muslim, there was no problem. However, Jews, considered "untouchables," faced real problems. Their containers were viewed as *najess,* or unclean. Refusing to touch the container of an infidel, the shopkeeper would place a piece of paper on the scale; the Jew would place his container on top of the paper, and the measuring began. Unlucky was the Jew if too much liquid was scooped in. He or she had no choice but to accept the quantity and pay for it. The liquid could not be poured back into the common cask, since having now been in the forbidden vessel, it, too, was unclean. The Jew lifted the container gingerly by holding the edges of the paper, taking care not to touch the scale. Once I asked Akbar how he could bring himself to touch the Jew's money: After all, wasn't it, too, unclean? "Oh, no," he assured me. "It has His Majesty the Shah's picture on it!"

Thus, to have my own paper was rare and I cherished it. In addition, my father decided to provide me with a tutor. My tutor was of great help to me; he had been chosen by my father because he worked at the Protestant missionary hospital in Kerman. My father felt that the man's involvement with the staff, mainly British nationals, would give him a world view, helpful to me in gaining a better understanding of the foreign news. Fresh from my sessions with my tutor, I was prepared to face my audience in the shops. They were always eager for any news —the shah's doings, the world's.

One man questioned the way I read the paper, beginning on the first page and flipping through as was necessary to finish each article. "Why do you skip around so?" he asked. "The mirza [the mullah's secretary] comes to our houses every week. He reads straight through like a book. He always does it that way."

Frustrated, baffled, I had no answer. My logic was too weak to prove to him that I was doing it correctly. How could I convince the man?

"Don't try," my father said. "I know the mirza and I know how he reads. He doesn't have much education. But don't make fun of him. He'll get discouraged and stop doing something that is valuable. No matter how small it is, every deed that benefits our people is better than no deed at all. Just tell them you find it correct your way."

Because of the political climate, the people's questions generally concerned the three biggest powers and their leaders.

"How long will Churchill stay in office?"

"Can Roosevelt get along with him?"

"Is Stalin better than Hitler?"

Appearances had an enormous impact on their judgment. Stalin looked fierce, with his uniform, his brimmed hat, that broom of a moustache. Surely he could demand the impossible. Churchill was obviously a politician, deceitful, fat, always smoking a cigar. Roosevelt they saw as thoughtful, a humble man. He must be lucky, too—that high forehead. (In Farsi the word for luck and for forehead is the same —*pishanee*.) He always held his hands quietly in his lap. The Americans were certainly a sensible people to have chosen him!

"If the Americans were aware of our situation, would they keep quiet?"

"No," I answered the questioner. I firmly believed the Americans would continue to help us after the war. Their aid was already apparent.

If the people's questions reflected their old distrust of the British and Russians, they also reflected their affection for the Americans, in whom they saw a principled people, hard working, humanitarian, people who were, above all, generous. American generosity had been shown to the villagers in particular by a gift of bale upon bale of clothing, shipped to Iran and trucked to Kerman by an American rug merchant who had been appalled at the palpable misery and poverty he witnessed firsthand. He had gathered the clothes on his return to America; if they were secondhand, what did it matter?

Such a commotion! A whole warehouse—full—there for the taking! Each inhabitant was permitted one trip through the building to choose his own. There were suits, thousands of suits; ties, which they promptly put to use as belts; overcoats, and dresses. The children, as unobtrusively as possible, searched for coins in the pockets. Each find was spectacular to them. And the results! A man, dressed in a three-piece suit and barefoot, leading his donkey, which wore a tie. Anything from America was a mark of distinction. Some men unwittingly dressed in women's clothes. "Don't laugh, Mansur. The man is clothed," my father would say. "Be thankful for him."

The townspeople's admiration for America grew as the Marshall Plan and Point Four made aid more far-reaching and concrete. Over the postwar years, millions of dollars poured into Iran. Some of the aid reached small towns and villages in the form of food and medicines. The most dramatic benefit was the eradication of the malaria then rampant in Iran. Planes sprayed every field, pond, and ditch. Quinine and other medicines were given to those already suffering from the ravages of the disease and many others common to a population suffering from lack of treatment, hygiene, and good nutrition. This support reached heart, mind, and body.

"These people are good and have helped us. Surely such help will continue," the townspeople said.

I believed in America, too. Moreover, as I read to them, my own knowledge of Americans was broadened as well. My impression of them was in sharp contrast to my knowledge of the atrocities being committed by Russian forces then occupying the north of Iran. I read about those, too.

Learning about what was happening in other countries bewildered me about my own. "Why are we so helpless?" I asked my father.

"Our civilization, once great, had great leaders, people who contributed much to freedom and humanity," he answered. "But today our people suffer. Only a little over a hundred years ago Aga Mohammad Shah put out the eyes of twenty thousand of our people, right here in Kerman! Forty years ago two men who were fighting for freedom had their heads cut off by order of the crown prince and their heads were roasted, cleaned, and stuffed with straw. Then they were sent to the imperial palace as a gift to the shah! Now Russian soldiers rape our women, force our people to dig their own graves, bury them alive! Nothing changes. We suffer under barbarians! We have been barbarians. How can we ever stop it?"

My father was quiet for a moment. Then he continued. "The ocean of injustice has no shores. I know you cannot accept these atrocities, Mansur. But emotion alone cannot serve the people. The only way to help our countrymen is with logic and wisdom."

"And who has that logic and wisdom?" I cried. "To whom should we go?" For the moment there was no answer.

Soon thereafter, my father asked me to accompany him to a lecture, to hear a man he considered great.

"Who is he, Father?" I asked.

"He's Dr. Mozafar Baghai, a man from a very good family in Kerman. His uncle established our first school and his father was very devoted to the cause of freedom. Just like you, he received his early education in Kerman. Then in Tehran he was singled out and sent to France for further studies. There he received a doctorate in philosophy from the Sorbonne University in Paris. Now he teaches ethics at Tehran University—a great man. He is campaigning for Parliament, and for the nationalization of our oil. You are eighteen years old now. Listen carefully to his words, my son."

CHAPTER TWO

Kerman: Poverty and Hospitality

Kerman province, of which the city of my birth was administrative capital, is approximately the size of France, with a population of about 600,000, most of them employed in making the justly famed Kerman carpets, prized for centuries throughout the world. Male members of my father's family had been designers and rugmakers for generations, each a skilled artist producing his own individual design, the signature of his work. My father's shops were scattered throughout several villages in the province, which borders Baluchistan in Iran's extreme southeast.

My mother's family were aristocrats with feudal holdings, including entire villages, property passed down intact from generation to generation. The land was a religious endowment that could neither be sold nor broken up. Proceeds of the major part of the land's profits were donated yearly to a local mosque. At the death of my maternal grandfather, the property, although it belonged to my mother, was administered by her uncle. Women could not participate in such matters.

Our ten-room house in Kerman city had no plumbing or electric power. A charcoal brazier gave us heat and a wood stove in a separate room provided for cooking. The house was lit by kerosene lanterns whose fumes caused us to suffer dreadful headaches and dizziness in winter. In summer the wind relentlessly extinguished the lanterns. Instead of Western chairs and sofas, the rooms were furnished with thick rugs and large cushions. On winter evenings, as a small child, I would snuggle against my father's side, as close as possible, wriggling if I could beneath his heavy wool robe while he told me bedtime stories.

I loved him deeply. I dogged his steps, listened eagerly to his every word. Oh, what horrible-sounding punishments he could threaten me with. "Be good! Or I will place your head between your ears!"

I was the eldest of six children: three brothers and two sisters. My brothers, sisters, and I seldom quarreled. If we did, my mother might tweak an ear here, place a speck of pepper on an offending tongue there.

My father usually disapproved. On one occasion, I recall that he appeared in a doorway, head bent, sad, lower lip pouting. "What shame. Shame upon my head and heart for my raising these children." Reproving my mother for punishing one of us, he added, "There is no need for such measures. As far as I know, he is no animal. Perhaps on your feudal side of the family . . ."

"Don't you know the saying?" she replied. " 'In all, I am my father. My mother was a passer-by.' "

Only once did he cause me great humiliation. One day, coming home from school, I found a small puppy wandering in the street near our home. I called to him and he frisked up to me, his tail wagging wildly. Oh, he was obviously a stray, despite his collar, and he liked me. No doubt about it, he wanted to be mine. I called again, and he followed a few paces and then retreated. Again I called and grabbed at him, but he eluded me. At my younger brother's urging, I slipped off my belt, looped it around the puppy's neck, and dragged the reluctant creature behind me. With a growl and a jerk, he slipped out of my grasp and fled, disappearing into the courtyard of a nearby home. I was heartbroken, but fear quickly erased that. My belt! Now what would I do? How could I explain it? Clutching my pants, I tried to act nonchalant as I passed my mother in the kitchen. No such luck.

"Mansur, come back. What are you doing? Why are you holding your pants that way? Did someone try to touch you?"

I tried to assure her that nothing of the sort had happened, but could not confess the actual story.

"We'll see what your father says about your belt," she said as she exiled me to my room. As soon as my father came home, he questioned me and I blurted out my deed. He insisted that I accompany him to search out the owner of the puppy, who promptly produced my belt. My father accepted it and apologized. "I am deeply grieved to tell you that my son is a thief. On his behalf, I request your gracious pardon and forbearance."

A thief! How I ached in my heart! For my father to call me such a debased human being in front of strangers was humiliation enough, but for him to believe it of me was agony. He left me alone for a time with my grief, and that evening spoke with me further. "My son, you are so fortunate. You have all you need. Why would you take the property of another? If you do not wish to suffer shame, you must not take what is not yours."

I did not try to explain that I had thought the dog was a stray, for he had always told me, "You have two ears to hear with and one tongue with which to speak." If I had only heeded his teachings earlier, nothing would have happened. I resolved never to do anything in the future that would cause him so much pain. His bald head gleamed in the lantern light as he bent to hug me.

My father's total lack of hair was the result of a childhood illness, a ringworm infection. Treatment for this common (today so easily cured) fungal infection consisted of a pastelike salve smeared on the affected region. In his case, a tight cap was then pulled down over his scalp and left in place for weeks. Periodically, it was pulled away from his head, the hair coming away with the cap, the inflamed area smeared once more, the cap replaced. The infection eventually healed, but because of the medieval medical attention he had received, he was hairless. Surely his baldness must have caused him many pangs as a child, for it was the source of my most humiliating nickname, Son of Baldy, but when I asked him about it, he laughed. "Oh, Mansur, one should have something in his head, not on it."

Certainly his case was not unusual or isolated. And far worse diseases were common. Tuberculosis, trachoma, pyorrhea, syphilis, glaucoma, typhus, dysentery, kwashiorkor—the gamut of diseases that result from poor hygiene, poor nutrition—ravaged and decimated the population of Iran. People died in great numbers, victims of influenza and typhoid epidemics. Hosts of other ills plagued them, disease was rife, incessant. There was no plumbing; ignorance of even the most ordinary hygiene contributed to the spread of disease. In a village near us, practically every man, woman, and child was blind. People doctored most ills at home with inadequate or harmful folk remedies. No one sought aid from the local missionary hospital until death was imminent. Even then, because many lived at such a distance or lacked transportation and waited too long to seek aid, they died en route.

Treatment at the hospital was free, but the two British doctors (general practitioners), their orderlies and assistants, and the missionaries, though devoted, were overwhelmed by the inadequate supplies, equipment, and beds, the scope of the afflictions, and the sheer numbers of patients and supplicants—approximately one hundred a day—huddled in misery, filling the courtyard, the road. They labored to provide what care they could, and all they requested in return was that those who could walk attend services in the hospital chapel. For those who could not, a small organ was dragged from ward to ward, and the missionaries sang hymns.

In the courtyard, scattered among the groaning, huddled bodies and their attendant families, were vendors of bottles, their wares strewn about them on old rags. Grimy, of all shapes and sizes, these second-hand bottles could be purchased for a fraction of a cent, to be filled with medicine at the dispensary. If unneeded, they were returned to the vendor, who redeemed them for an infinitesimal sum, and sold them once more, with stout assurances that they had just been washed, but nothing was said about their being sterilized.

One vendor, Churchill, so named for his bald head and chunky body, made his living by dispensing sips of water to the crowd. With a cup attached to his belt by a chain, a once-yellow, now dingy brown, clay cask on his back, barefoot but dressed in a suit whose original material was indistinguishable from innumerable motley patches, the small, bent figure moved from group to group, offering a moment's relief from the intolerable heat, even though the water was warm.

People brought with them their own bedding, and their hopes. But many died. This Protestant missionary hospital was the only fully equipped hospital in Kerman. (The other facility in no way could be classified as a hospital.) The missionary hospital was closed in 1951, when the British were forced to leave Iran after the nationalization of oil.

Aside from health care afforded by the hospitals, there was little recourse for people if they fell ill. It was a miracle that anyone survived childhood. My cousin succumbed to the diphtheria that was so common, as were many of the usual childhood illnesses like whooping cough and chickenpox. These diseases often proved fatal rather than being easily prevented or cured as they are today.

Children who were colicky or persons who suffered from headaches went to see Hassan Khan, the "blade man," a self-described physician, who was a scribe on rainy days or whenever he had no patients. Hassan would make five or six deft cuts on the forehead or the spine of the sufferer, whose cries and moans usually ceased instantly, either because of shock from loss of blood or because the new pain erased the old. Burning cotton was applied to stop the bleeding. For common cuts, someone would urinate on the bleeding area; the force of the stream possibly staunched the blood flow and the chemicals in the urine possibly stopped infection.

(My father had been treated by one such "physician." Later, as a patient at New York Hospital in Manhattan, he was questioned by doctors about his previous "operations," which were in truth the remaining scars of the deft cuts made in his childhood. I had to explain his history to Dr. Walton C. Lillehei, a pioneer of open-heart surgery, who then marked his chart so that no more questions were asked. Most of our "doctors" were just such "permissible" physicians as Hassan Khan, allowed to practice on the strength of the testimony of those they had aided and sometimes cured.)

Despite their frequent failures to cure, these men were faithful, assiduous in the tender, loving care they provided. While real physicians such as those at the hospital might in the end provide better and up-to-date medical care, they were distrusted for their abruptness and their terse prescriptions of tonics and pills. The "permissible" doctors often had some collateral skill or knowledge, even though they were ineffective at times and dangerous at others—many times the cure was far worse than the disease. They persevered, returning again and again to their patients, listening over and over to their complaints, speaking kindly to the family members, reassuring and comforting them, wisely protecting themselves, promising, "I will do my very best but possibly you may need some prayer as well." This stood them in good stead with the religious people. They were at times considered miracle doctors, for their occasional startling or unexpected cures.

One such "doctor," a specialist in broken bones, an "artistic man" named Chini Band Zan, would be called in after a wait of a day or two to judge if the swelling had subsided in the area of a suspected break. Chini Band Zan's usual occupation was the repair of broken dishes and vessels, and he was therefore considered to be the best person to repair the human body, using the same materials he used to mend utensils: an egg-powder mixture that dried to a rock hardness, small splints, and twine. Several strong men immobilized the person to be "mended," and Chini Band Zan manipulated the affected region carefully. When he had determined the location and extent of the break, he pulled and pushed it back together, made his paste, and affixed the splints, tying them fast. At each scream of the patient, a loved one would clap a handful of powdered sugar into his mouth to "sweeten" his suffering, almost smothering the poor patient, who mercifully would often faint. Chini Band Zan was a devoted doctor, arriving conveniently at mealtimes to visit his patients, sometimes even after the break had knitted.

Infections or boils were lanced with a *duk,* a long sliver of polished wood pointed at either end. Again, several strong men held down the sufferer and the doctor pierced the boil. A baked onion with its center removed was used as a poultice.

The ancient art of cupping was performed by lighting a match in a small container to create a vacuum, and applying the container to the skin. Leeches were used to ease swellings or to remove "proud" blood, a source of infection.

Infestations of tapeworms ten to twelve inches in length were common. For these, a large dose of castor oil was administered; the worms were passed, but because of the lack of even rudimentary hygiene (waste from the outhouses poured directly into the water used for drinking, washing, and bathing), the infestation often recurred immediately.

It was not uncommon to see children using, as balloons, the condoms left in some trysting spot by diseased prostitutes and their customers. Thus, the incidence of syphilis was so high that the signboards of doctors advertised: WE TREAT ALL KINDS OF SYPHILIS, EVEN OLD SYPHILIS.

Almost everyone had lice. Sitting outside in the sun, people cracked them in the seams of their clothes. When they finished, their nails were bright with blood. They boiled their clothes, using volcanic ash for soap, to kill the lice, and cut their children's hair short. But they soon caught them again from someone else, in school or in the public baths. Even the wealthiest bathed only once a week, and women were particularly afflicted because of their long hair. Those who suffered from pellagra seldom had lice, and the people who did have them, in shame and self-defense, claimed that lice were a sign of a healthy body.

Many suffered from impetigo, another disease caused by dirt; from dysentery, as a result of the polluted water; from the gamut of afflictions that are handmaidens to poverty, ignorance, and a lack of hygiene and medicines.

The townspeople also patronized the herbalist, whose shelves and several hundred drawers contained all kinds of dried materials, such as eucalyptus, jujube, mints, and various herbs. There were other medicines more exotic, such as the dried excrement of doe and the powdered remains of a stinkbug, for example, which supposedly were unexcelled remedies for whooping cough and croup. The herbalist sang, chanted, and crooned his prescriptions and advice as he mixed and measured for his unending line of clients. "Your mother is sick, my darling? Dizzy? A few teaspoons of this and she will fly like a bird! Give her my regards. And if she's no better tomorrow, come back. Come back! Oh, boil it well now, and, remember, three times a day." To the young women, as he dropped into the packets the small pink dried buds of jujubes that resembled tiny nipples, fingering them lasciviously, he would say, "Be sure to boil these very well." He made a slurping sound with his lips and added a wink. He was, however, far more discreet with the older women.

The herbs were often helpful; magnesium sulfate eased many a stomachache. But the same herbs and ointments were used to no avail for the dread and fatal anthrax rampant among the wool workers.

Glaucoma and trachoma were common. Near us lived an entire family who suffered from trachoma; their eyes, lashless and inflamed, oozed with white pus at the corners. The mother's remedy was to place a fresh-laid chicken egg on the infected eyes. It was useless, of course, and the family was too poor to keep the egg for themselves. It went from eye to market, perhaps to infect some other hapless victim. Trachoma blinded, although it could easily have been cured.

Ironically, the shah gave millions of dollars in donations to universities and medical centers in the United States and Europe. But his touted charity was greatly offset by conditions that prevailed in Iran. As the proverb says, "Why carry a candle to church when your home is unlit?"

My father's baldness, and the ridicule I suffered as a result, never got in the way of our friendship. He was my first mentor, the center of my life. He had not been educated in classrooms, but approached life with immense dignity and common sense. It was he who formed my being, teaching me with gentleness through parables. Richly blessed as he considered himself to be with his four sons and two daughters, he refused to be seen in public with more than one of us at a time. Those who were childless would feel their lack more keenly. Fairly well-to-do in a city of stark poverty, he would not permit us more than one new garment a year and one new pair of shoes. We could not dress for school in anything but the drab clothing worn by all the other children. Once I received a beautiful vest as a holiday gift from a relative and attempted to pass him to show it off outside; he stopped me and removed the vest. I protested, breaking into tears. "But, Mansur," he said, "if you cry over such a thing, do I not know how another father will feel, unable to provide his own child with such a vest? How would Ahmad feel if he were to see it? Would he envy you? How would you feel to provoke such envy?"

A few days later, my father told me of the unearthing of a long-buried grave not far from us. Workers cleaning the gravesites had first turned up the tombstone, still clearly lettered, and then several gold vessels of great antiquity and fragments of elegantly wrought silk. "Why don't you look for his name in the Kerman history book, Mansur? The man must have been very great to have possessed such treasures." I searched diligently but could not find the name and, disappointed, reported back to my father. "Don't feel bad. It wasn't there. I knew you would find nothing. He carried his only riches into his tomb with him, leaving nothing behind that would cause his name to be remembered. Possessions have no value, Mansur. Only the good you do will outlast your grave."

My father supervised all the work in his shops. It was he who designed the patterns of his carpets, decided on the range of colors to be worked into the intricate florals, borders, elaborate figures, mixed the proportions of plants and herbs, hulls and chemicals, and extracted the decoctions for dyeing the long skeins of wool. The moment the skeins had absorbed precisely the desired color, he signaled the workers to lift them, pour cold water over them, and beat out the excess water before spreading them out to dry in the sun.

During carpet weaving, a reader sat between the long rows of weavers, the pattern in front of him, chanting melodiously. "Now, my dear Meloo, insert three cerise . . . and you, my child, Aloo, seven green. Maashoo, if you will be gracious, six beige, ah, lovely . . ." Each shop had such a reader, and his wording was much the same as the others'. His voice soothed and comforted; the workers moved in graceful teamwork, weaving their bodies as they wove the threads. Still, the days were long and the work tedious and heavy.

My father would not permit the employment of young children. But in many of the shops, women came to work with their infants tied to their backs. Often children of five and six worked a full day, from "can see to can't see," right along with the adults. The average pay of a grown man, depending on his task, was three to ten tomans (or one to four dollars) per month. And although workers could bargain with prospective employers to establish terms of production, those terms specified the amount of work to be completed in a certain length of time rather than work conditions. Many shops had brutal overseers with orders to kick or beat workers. My father preferred to oversee his shops himself.

One bitterly cold night, he received a visit from a peddler, a poor man who scavenged the back regions of the country looking for pieces of old rugs, often exquisite and very valuable. "Mr. Rafizadeh," the peddler said, "please come with me this very instant. I discovered two

pieces of such elegant design that only you are worthy of seeing them."
My father was reluctant, for it was late and the night bitter, but the man
persisted. "I cannot wait until morning. You must come with me now."
Persuaded, my father put on his heaviest robe and followed the man
to his small home. Once inside, he drew his robe more closely around
him. There was no heat or light. The man led Father by the hand to
the bed in the corner, lighting one small castor-oil lamp. In its dim light
Father was just able to make out the form of a woman, holding two tiny
forms swaddled to their eyes, twins born that day. The man lit the
kerosene lamp and held it high. "There," he said, "didn't I tell you that
they were magnificent pieces of work?" He turned to my father, his face
twisted. "I have no charcoal and no food for my family. There is no
work. How will I provide for these treasures? I deceived you, but I
hoped you would help us."

Father bent over the infants and placed a coin on each of their
covers. "They are the greatest of treasures," he said. He gave the man
several more coins. "Buy food. Buy charcoal. And in the morning,
come to see me. A father must provide for his family. We will find work
for you."

Always I attempted to follow his precepts, slowly and often pain-
fully acquiring some as my own. And he always reassured me, guided
my knowledge.

"Are you unhappy because they call you names?" he asked on one
occasion. " 'Hadji' or 'Son of Baldy'? What do you want to accomplish
in life? Happiness? Happiness may be found in the interpretation of two
principles. 'Be compassionate with a friend. Be moderate with an
enemy. Then you may find serenity both here and hereafter,' " he
quoted. "I'd add one more: 'You must be a fool for people.' "

"I'm not a fool!" I protested.

He waited to be sure I was finished and continued. "A group of
peasants always consulted the fool in their village if they had problems
they could not solve. Once, they asked him where the center of the earth
was. 'Right here,' he said. 'If you don't believe me, measure it on either
side.' They presented him with another problem. This time he listened,
then laughed. Then he broke into sobs. 'But what is wrong?' they asked.
'Tell us the answer. Why do you behave so?' 'You poor men,' he
answered. 'I'm laughing because even I, a fool, can't answer you, and
I'm crying because if I wasn't here, who else could you ask?' Mansur,
that is the kind of fool you must be. You have to help even when you
have no real answers. People must have confidence in someone. Otherwise they become fearful and lose their ability to solve their own prob-

lems. Always they seek leaders. Always there is someone who is willing and ready to take advantage of that fear. That is a great danger." He paused. "You still don't see. I will tell you another story.

"A man rode his mule into a village. 'Here, you,' he said to the overseer. 'Take my mule's halter. Feed him. Rub him down and see that he is well stabled and warm. And have a room prepared for me. Tell your people to fix me a good dinner. Have them pack me a lunch for tomorrow's journey. Be quick about it! If they don't do as I say, I will do to them just what I did to the peasants in the last village!' Everyone scurried to do his bidding. 'Oh, God, what did he do to them? Not us, please God.' They begged the overseer to ask the man as he was leaving just what the stranger had done. As the man continued to give orders and to issue threats, they trembled and obeyed. In the morning, as he saddled the man's mule, the overseer anxiously asked, 'Please, Your Excellency, how was your stay? Was everything to your satisfaction?' He shook visibly as he waited for the reply. All the villagers, watching, sighed deeply when the answer was yes. 'Then will you please do us a favor and tell us what you did to the people in the last village?' 'Why, nothing at all,' was the answer. 'They wouldn't listen to me so I left and came here.' Now do you understand, Mansur? You must be not only a fool and a wise one, you must learn to recognize the traps that fear can lead to. When you are without fear yourself, when you no longer are swayed by people's opinions of you, perhaps you will be capable of ruling your own emotions and of helping others."

My mother's involvement with my upbringing was less obvious but no less significant. It was she who was responsible for our social conduct; it was she who instructed us in matters of cleanliness, morality, and good behavior, in submission to and respect for elders. I was taught to be humble, not to contradict, not to speak first, and not to lie. I knew how to hold a tray properly and which guest to serve first.

My mother sewed up all my pockets so that I would not be tempted to carry food to school or to accept any. It was not polite to be seen eating in public. When, like all the other children, I wiped my runny nose on my sleeve, she moved my buttons up so that the offending nostrils would be scraped. I protested to my father. "When you are no longer a Russian peasant, you can wear your buttons where they belong," he said, explaining that Russian peasant women had sewn buttons where my mother had sewn mine for the identical reason. They had had the same disgusting habit. "The French, however, moved them down to show that they were gentlemen. Stop wiping your nose on your sleeves and you can be as chic as any Frenchman."

It is a mistake to think that Persian women are relegated strictly
to a secondary position, especially in the matter of raising children,
although I confess my mother's aristocratic background gave her a
certain leverage.

In summer I sometimes visited her relatives, one of whom invited
me to spend a summer vacation with her and her son one year. For
several scorching days, we two walked the fields with her as she checked
on the activities of the workers. The boy was a few years younger than
I, and no sooner did our walk begin than she would thrust a parasol
at me to hold over his head so that the sun would not burn him. She
held another one over her own head. I was very uncomfortable but
unprotesting. When my mother asked me how I had enjoyed myself,
I told her about the parasol. My father overheard. "You see?" he said.
"Your family! Here we go again. You see how they treat our son
because they are aristocrats and I am a businessman. She invites him
for a vacation and makes him hold a parasol."

But if my mother was often the power behind the throne or at least
the equal of my father, outwardly she always deferred to him, refusing
to take any credit.

All of my parents' ancestors had been adherents of Zoroastrianism,
but we were not a religious family. "Religious people can paint any bird
to resemble a canary," my father said, "but they cannot make it sing."
In public we observed custom, for it was not only good sense, but there
was no reason to offend others in their beliefs. For most people, religion
was connected deeply to everyday affairs. In some cases it served the
same function as Western psychoanalysis. At a nearby shrine, those
who wished to talk directly to God could lean over the edge of a well
(covered with boards to prevent people from falling in). The act of
direct appeal to God often assuaged the griefs of the people, and if they
felt the need for an intercessor, they were able to go to another well,
a shrine where, it was said, an imam had disappeared. Believing that
the Mahdi, or Messiah, would return to the place where the most
injustice occurred, the people, perhaps rightly, had decided the place
was holy and a likely place for him to appear. The petitioner donated
a small fee to the mullah, who would write the person's wish on a bit
of paper, then wrap it in a small piece of clay, and return it to the
petitioner, who then threw it into the well—a "letter to God." Perhaps
the supplicant sought rain, the return of a loved one, the recovery of
someone who was ill. Sooner or later, it would rain. The loved one
would return or recover or not. It didn't matter. If things worked out
well, God was beneficent. If not, it was obvious that the petitioner was

lacking in faith or sincerity. When the well clogged, the mullah scooped out the clay, dried it for reuse, and the procedure was repeated.

In a cave in the nearby mountain was a huge boulder with a deep diagonal groove supposedly cut by the sword of Ali, the son-in-law of the Prophet Mohammad, when Ali was in need of water. Although history does not record that he in fact ever traveled in Iran, this did not detract at all from the sacredness of the spot. When the stone was struck, it was said, the water gushed forth to assuage Ali's thirst, and so much burst forth that for years after it was sufficient to irrigate the surrounding fields. Later it dried to a trickle, and it was rumored that evil Zoroastrians had desecrated the sacred ground by drinking forbidden alcohol in the vicinity. But a holy fig tree miraculously grew, and it became a shrine for women who sought relief from the curse of infertility. With a female relative, each woman pilgrimaged to the foot of the mountain, where she stayed. Some removed their shoes for the last one thousand feet in order to suffer more greatly so that God might listen to them with greater pity. Each climbed the mountain alone and tied a coil of bright yellow, pink or blue ribbon to the fig tree, already gaily decorated with the ribbons of the women who had come before. She blew her breath repeatedly on the ribbon as she murmured fervent prayers for a child, preferably male. "Almighty God, grant me the boon of a child. I will fight for your way so that he will be just. Compassionate God, answer my prayer! I swear to Moses, Jesus, and Mohammad, to all holy people known and unknown, to all who walk in your path that I will give him the most humble, the most despised of occupations. If it is a son, I will make him an undertaker! Or an executioner! If it is a daughter, I will make her an undertaker. Only grant me this gift." She would pray over and over in this fashion.

My father told me that a tranced petitioner often heard a voice reverberate from deep within the cave: "You have sought me out, daughter. I will grant your prayer," and the woman would raise her eyes to see a figure dressed in flowing white approaching her.

This apparition was really a local mechanic, a tall man with a beautiful body, who read the Koran with a gorgeous, resonant voice. My father and I knew this man, now dead, who was great fun to be around. He told the most hilarious stories about his outrageous escapades, including what happened at the shrine. He bragged of his contentment. He told of going to the shrine whenever he felt amorous; he had found the perfect solution to his needs. On the occasions when he visited the sanctuary, in resonant tones he would offer the woman her heart's desire. He would have intercourse with the supplicant, and if the fertility problem was not hers, she was likely to have her prayer answered and become pregnant. If she were infertile, her prayer would simply go unanswered.

To atone for his behavior before God, this man would participate in a passion play depicting the events at Karbala, a principal holy city in Iraq. During two days of the reenactment, he would indulge in self-flagellation with two-pound chains. This was a means of cleansing himself, as was the reading from the Koran. During the self-flagellation, he would say that he would not go to the shrine and take advantage of the women anymore, but each time, he decided that he could go through the cleansing rituals again and that God would forgive him.

At shrines scattered throughout the region, believers lit candles in support of their sacred vows, just as do followers of some other faiths. One such shrine near us was so beloved that it was mobbed daily by throngs of the devoted—barefoot, with shoes under their arms. At the smaller shrines, one lone mullah waited patiently with his basket of scented candles. Here, though, a roof covered the last yards to the tomb where the robed mullah was waiting. Rows of shops on either side sold scented candles and religious objects.

After purchasing candles, the people stood patiently as group after group of twenty or so were admitted to the sacred tomb. Once inside, the pious lit the flickering votive candles, touched the silver bars that surrounded the stone tomb, and pressed reverent fingertips to their eyes and to the heads of their children. Sometimes they threw coins, even jewelry into the barred recess. They prayed incessantly, and the mullah added his own continuous invocation: "God will light your house forever! Send a candle to your grave ahead of time. Prepare! Ask forgiveness! Ah, one for my sister, one for my brother. No one will send anything after you've gone. Send it now! God will light your graves. There will be no pressure in your grave on your first night!"

In dread of the companion angels—forces of good and evil who war over possession of souls on the night after death, pressing the skulls until the first drop of mother's milk issued from the nostrils—the devoted poured into the tomb in an unending procession. As one group departed, the door was closed for a moment while, with one quick sweep of his flowing sleeve, the mullah extinguished all but a few candles, dropping the rest into a barrel. Their wicks were trimmed and they were returned to the shops to be sold again. The candle shops, of course, belonged to the mullah.

Religious ritual was a part of daily existence. The pious kept their beads with them, saying prayers as they went about their business. If someone was ill, the beads were told, and a breath was blown several times in succession over the recumbent person after every ten prayers. In the graveyards, mullahs stood around, in fierce competition with one another, awaiting mourners so that they could perform the office for a small fee. As soon as the mourners arrived, several mullahs would rush to the grave, if they knew the family, and have a tug-of-war, and the winner would then sit on the grave in prayer. When the family saw this, they would be so impressed that they would give the mullah some coins. If the mullahs did not know the mourners, they would stay close behind until the family neared the grave and then they would make a mad rush to get to the grave before the family began their prayers. The mullahs would then go through the same ritual.

My father told of a man who was going on a business trip and who had, as was the custom, entrusted his life's savings to the local mullah for safekeeping. As he sat in the mullah's house fingering his hard-earned coins and notes, the mirza carefully inscribed the amount in his ledger.

"Have no fear," said the mullah. "In our hands, your money is as safe as the stars in the hands of God."

The man was gone for several years and, in the meantime, he had lost his business. He returned to his hometown with nothing. He went to the mullah and requested the return of his money.

"Your Holiness, you remember me. I have lost my business and need the money I left with you several years ago. Bless you, Your Eminence, I am in deep need."

"But I am bewildered, my brother," the mullah said. "You have made a great mistake. I have nothing of yours. I do not know you. I know every one of my people in this town. I think of them each day. They are in my dreams each night. You are upset and have confused me with another mullah."

"Oh, no," the man protested. "You must remember me. Oh, God, help me! What am I to do? Oh, please, Your Holiness."

The mullah became annoyed. "Calm yourself. You are mistaken. I am not the one you seek. You are in the wrong place."

Seeing that he would get nowhere, the man left despondently. As he got to the street, he didn't know what to do or where to go.

A woman passing by saw the desperate-looking man wandering aimlessly and felt sorry for him. She went to him and asked, "What's wrong?"

He told her his whole story, adding that he had no witnesses or receipt for the deposit.

After thinking for a few minutes, she told the man, "Return to the mullah's house at the same time tomorrow. I'll be there with the mullah, and when you hear the sound of coins and jewelry being dropped in front of him, walk in and present your request as if for the first time. Don't even mention that you had been there the day before."

"All right. I'll do it."

The next morning the woman filled a box with coins and jewelry. With her maid carrying the box, she entered the mullah's house. She told the mullah, "My husband went on a trip several months ago and has not returned. I am very worried and want to search for him. I don't trust the servants, so I want to deposit these valuables with you. Your name is highly praised. Please be so good as to grant this request."

"All right," the mullah said, "I'll accept the deposit. Let us make an itemized list of the valuables."

After she noisily emptied the box on the carpet, the man, as instructed, walked into the room. "Your Reverence, I have come to request the money I left with you several years ago. I have lost my business and am destitute. Gracious servant of God, thank you for your kindness and patience in keeping it for me."

Avariciously eyeing the woman's large deposit, the mullah compared it with the relatively small deposit that the man had left.

"Do you remember where I told you I would put your deposit?" the religious man asked.

"Yes, on the top left shelf."

The mirza was called in and told to return the money to the man. Confused, the mirza did as he was told.

As soon as the man had his money back, in rushed the woman's husband and his servant. The husband, a party to the charade, told of his returning home after being away for several months. He was anxious to see his wife and asked the servants where she was. When told she was at the mullah's house, he had rushed over to be reunited with her.

Everyone was so happy that they began to dance. The mullah also began to dance. A servant approached him and said, "I can understand why we are happy—the man got his money back, her husband has returned, our master has returned. But why are you so happy?"

The mullah replied, "I have been given the pleasure. She really put one over on me!"

My father ended the story with "You know the old saying, Mansur: 'Find a snake with legs, an ant with eyes, an honest mullah . . .'"

I loved to visit the candle shrine with its bustle, its throngs of the faithful, its colorful shops. But more than anything, I loved to buy freedom for the sparrows. Before the sanctuary stood a wire cage against which hundreds of sparrows beat futile wings, their small bodies struggling furiously. In front of the cage, a mullah implored the pious with a dolorous chant: "Free them, free them. Their song is mute. Oh, how they long to be with their families. God does not mean for them to be caged."

I saved each penny for this purpose. I carefully counted my coins until they added up to a half-toman (fifteen cents). Having saved a half-toman, I knew I would certainly walk in the path of God today! I rushed to the mullah, breathless, and pressed my money on him. He counted it carefully and put it deep into the pocket of his robe. "Well, my little servant of God, one half-toman."

I nearly burst with excitement. "How many sparrows for a half-toman?"

"Four. No, five!" Then, turning to the crowd around us, he shouted, "The poor, pitiful creatures. God created them free. See our brother, our little brother has freed five. Walk in the path of God as he has."

With this, he plunged his hand into the cage and handed me five small, fluttery birds. Each flew rapidly from my hands, with a sharp whirr of wings.

"Ah, see how they fly. Repent your sins, my brothers and sisters. The door of repentance is never closed. You can help them."

Many small bodies lay unmoving on the floor of the cage. They were the ones for whom I felt the most pity. But the mullah never reached for them. They could not have flown.

The people pressed forward eagerly to place their small sums in the mullah's outstretched hand. Over and over. The supply of birds was seemingly endless. "Where do they all come from?" I wondered aloud to my father. He laughed out loud and clapped my shoulder. "Oh, Mansur, think! How do they get in the cage in the first place? Who do you think put them there? Wasn't it that man?"

But the followers of Islam, just like adherents of any faith, gained solace and comfort from these outward manifestations of devotion in their brutal daily existence. The beauty of the shrines, whether tiny and new or majestic and of great splendor, was a sharp relief to their drab hovels. The authority of the mullah lent a sense of order, of divine purpose to the chaos of their lives. And each practice has its direct counterpart in the churches, temples, sanctuaries, statuary, and ceremonies of almost any faith or form of worship.

I am sure that such examples of hypocrisy and religious posing described above helped to diminish any faith my father might have had.

And my own feeling, my credo, was inevitably based on his. Because I knew every thread of my father's thought, of his belief that religious people could rationalize anything and make it right or wrong, I was aware of the reasons for his lack of faith. There was no need to question him on the matter.

Not so with my mother. Although she never spoke much about it, neither did she practice any religion. One day I questioned her about her own noticeable lack of faith, asking her if her beliefs were founded on my father's. She assured me that they had nothing to do with his and that she had her own reasons. Then she told me the following story.

In our hometown of Kerman, there were two ayatollahs, elderly men, brothers. Between them they managed all the religious affairs of the community; the one that was held in higher esteem dealt with doctrinal matters, and the other, not so highly regarded, handled legal matters, such as the duties of a notary public.

The latter ayatollah had a servant, a doorman, who when ill and close to death, begged the ayatollah to take upon himself the guardianship of his beloved daughter, then nine years old. The ayatollah, although seventy-one himself, agreed to do so, and at the man's death took the child under his wing.

She assumed light household chores and at the behest of the ayatollah, who suffered from arthritis, rubbed his aching legs and feet each night.

For several years the situation received scant attention. The ayatollah had several wives, his eldest son was fifty-five, and he had numerous grandchildren. She was one child more, that was all. However, as the girl neared fourteen, a marriageable age, it was suggested to the ayatollah by several families that a match between a girl of such good religious background and one of their eligible sons might be arranged. The ayatollah refused. The girl was so young, too young, and not the slightest burden to him.

Many suitors were turned away.

Finally, one of my mother's cousins, an educated woman and principal of a girls' school in Kerman, approached the ayatollah and suggested that he permit the girl to marry a young man who was a friend of her family. By now the girl was fifteen and quite attractive. The ayatollah, out of respect for my mother's cousin, agreed with reluctance, but insisted that the marriage could not occur until the girl achieved her menses, seeming quite concerned that she not be capable of performing her marital role. But not long after, he announced that the marriage could take place. As was customary in those days, the prospective bride and groom met several times in the presence of both families and were agreeable to the marriage.

Again as was customary in those days, the members of both families were present on the night of the consummation, waiting for the groom to emerge from the bridal chamber and to present to his mother the red-stained napkin that would proclaim his bride's virginity to all. In turn, the mother-in-law would present it to the mother of the bride (not impugning her daughter's virtue), who then would hand it back to the groom, saying, "We give you the bride in her white gown and may only God take her from you again, in her white burial shroud."

The ceremony is important and is taken very seriously. In this case, however, the girl began to cry as soon as the groom approached her, wailing and speaking wildly of shame. The groom, bewildered, asked the members of his family to come and talk with her. He had not yet touched her. What could she be so unhappy about? Him? Their marriage?

Together they calmed her, and her sad story poured out. From the moment he had assumed her guardianship, the ayatollah had taken advantage of her innocence, having intercourse with her since she was ten years old.

After a long discussion, the groom announced his decision. He had compassion for her and would not divorce her. He would be kind. He would treat her as his wife. However, he would also take another wife, a virgin. In this way no shame would be attached to the family name.

That night there was no consummation of the marriage. Everyone, bride and groom foremost, were far too upset. The next morning my mother's cousin went to see the ayatollah. She found him lolling cross-legged on a cushion, and reproached him furiously.

"You, a religious man! You, ayatollah. People trust you. Shame! Her father revered you! A child. Oh, shame."

The ayatollah paled and stammered excuses. She ignored them and continued to abuse him. She informed him of the groom's decision and began her vituperation again.

"Disgraceful! A man of your age. You have grandchildren who are older than she!"

The ayatollah was trembling, desperately shushing her.

"Please," he begged, lifting the corner of his cushion and revealing wads of currency. "Please, please, just take whatever amount the groom paid, but don't tell anyone."

She took the money, counting the precise amount the groom had paid for the wedding expenses, while the ayatollah, his face still ashen, repeated his plea, "Don't tell a soul, I beg you."

The money was duly returned to the family, and eventually the groom married again and children were born of both unions. The ayatollah is long dead, but for many years, his reputation unbesmirched, he was considered one of the finest in the town. Perhaps the judgment of the people should not be discredited. He may have done less evil than others.

Although I was far more fortunate than most people in my economic status, my education, and tutelage, I put no credence in "class." My father was strongly against the concept of class, feeling that only a man's character and actions were an indication of his human worth. But even if he made light of the fact that my mother's family did not consider him on a par with their "aristocratic" standing, it may have been their condescension that caused him to refuse the use of my mother's money for household expenses.

At their wedding, arranged as was customary by a female relative, many family members showed strong opposition to the match. Some started a fire, using kerosene lanterns that had been strung to light the courtyard, disrupting the preparations; they were aided by musicians disgruntled at not having been chosen to entertain. Once the fire was out, the group sang a stinging parody of the usual epithalamium, the wedding benediction. They made it a song of divorce instead. Despite this, and in the face of some continuing hostility, my father and mother remained happily married. Most of her family were eventually resigned to the union, and eight children in all resulted from it; two—twins—died shortly after birth.

My parents lived in Kerman until the early 1960s when they found themselves in a predicament. There were no universities in Kerman, and because they believed in a fine education for *all* of their children, they decided to send my mother and sisters to Tehran. There my sisters could attend Tehran University. After a lonely separation, my father and the rest of the family joined them and continued to live in Tehran until my father's death in 1971. My mother never remarried.

CHAPTER THREE

Political Awakening

Although my father had told me about Dr. Mozafar Baghai's large following, I was not prepared for the crowd I encountered the night I first heard the candidate speak in Kerman. But I soon learned why they were there. I listened, enchanted, to the resonant voice, the modulated tones punctuated with long pauses that held the audience in thrall. He excoriated the British for having brought the dictators to power in Iran. He exhorted Iranians to nationalize their oil, to take back their country and its resources, by voting again and again—until they made their wishes known. But he did not let the Iranians off the hook. "The British are highly civilized," he said. "They have a great history. But they are civilized only in their own island, not here. If your ceiling cracks, if any harm comes to you, it is not the fault of the British. We cannot blame them for our shortcomings, our weaknesses. Look to yourselves. People deserve the government that rules them. No one loves the child like the mother. But if the child does not cry, she will give him no milk."

His anger was apparent not in decibels, but in the way his words quickened, in the way he clipped sentences. "Do not accept injustice! If there are no oppressed, there can be no oppressors! Crying, weeping, beseeching will have no effect. Stand up! Fight for your rights. Vote!"

After the lecture the audience crowded around him and questioned him at length. He answered them patiently, quietly. At the end I did not want to leave. I watched and listened—immobile. I was overpowered by his charismatic presence, his knowledge, his magnificent voice and manner, his style and poise. His ability to answer question after question fascinated me and I begged my father to introduce me to him. He agreed but asked me to be polite: The man might be weary of answering political questions.

I couldn't help myself. My questions spilled out. "Have you heard of the peasant who was beaten?" I asked. "Of the killing?"

"Yes," he said. "Of course."

"But you are in Tehran. Have you told the shah of these things?"

He stared at me for a moment before answering. Then he smiled. "No. I have told him nothing. But what does it matter? It makes no difference if His Majesty the Shah knows about it or not. If they only knew it, villagers have the power in their own hands to change their condition. They are the ones who must punish criminals."

"But when? How long must we wait? When will it happen?"

"When the people awaken."

"But will you promise me that it will happen? Will that overseer and his men be tried? Think of that poor peasant who only wanted to feed his family. Of our people who are tortured now." A torrent of words tumbled out. I could not stop myself.

He was not angry. His calm answer echoed my father's words. "There are so many injustices. You know nothing of them yet. But eventually all who are criminals will receive their punishment. And it will happen in your lifetime. Such criminals are liars, and a lie has a short life. Soon it decays and the decay is the fertilizer from which a truth will grow and blossom, a truth that will last forever."

I believed him. Although I knew little of his reputation, I was mesmerized by his unswerving dedication to principle and by his evident farsightedness. Here was the man I wanted to follow, to be a part of his cause.

After hearing Dr. Baghai lecture a second time, I was determined to join the branch of his political organization in Kerman. His headquarters was located in a small ramshackle building. To me, it was dignified, the embodiment of mankind's struggle against all poverty, injustice, disease, and ignorance. Banners and posters covered its walls, including the organization's motto: "We have arisen to uphold truth and freedom."

Other mottoes included "Those who believe they are all-knowing are either fools or villains," "We despise lying and the liar," and from Voltaire, "I disapprove of what you say, but I will defend to the death your right to say it."

Electrifying! This last had the greatest appeal for me. I asked to join the group.

By 1949 Dr. Baghai's office was a busy one. The nationalization of oil had become a burning issue, and he himself was campaigning for a seat in Parliament. The people wanted all revenues from oil sales to go to the nation rather than continue to line the pockets of the British, who had drained Iran of its black gold, paying almost nothing for it, and had placed in office men who were draining other resources from the country. Most of the key men in office, if not actually puppets of the British, were Anglophiles. Nepotism was so widespread that Iranians called their government the "Thousand Families."

Thus, when Dr. Baghai campaigned with nationalization of oil as his issue, the nation rallied to him. All the same, it was forbidden by police order to wear the buttons imprinted with his slogan, "The Oil industry must be nationalized," although thousands of people in Kerman wore them secretly or carried them in their pockets.

When "the Leader," as Dr. Baghai was affectionately known, arrived in Kerman on his campaign tour, some two hundred members, myself included, marched through the streets, buttons pinned boldly to their jackets. There was no sit-in, no defiance, no organized violence. We simply marched. But the police learned of our demonstration and ordered us to break it up, to take off our buttons and disperse.

When several of us refused, they suddenly fell upon us. Many of us were knocked down, bloodied by rifle butts and nightsticks. Most fled. With five others who had forcefully resisted, I was caught, handcuffed, and taken to the police station. There we were roughed up, strip-searched, clothed in striped prison garb, and, bruised and bleeding, thrown into a dark, dank basement.

As soon as my father learned of my whereabouts, he went to the police station. The next morning we were released to him. Swollen with the importance of what I had experienced, I was shattered to find that he was not at all pleased with my adventure.

When Dr. Baghai later summoned me to his headquarters, I expected a different reaction. Surely he would praise me. Surely he would welcome me as a hero. Hadn't I been beaten and jailed for his cause?

He sat without moving or speaking as I repeated the whole story. Then he said, "You, with your thoughtlessness, have damaged not only the campaign, but our whole movement. If this ever happens again, I will be forced to revoke your membership . . . at least for a time."

Speechless, I stared at him. Then, in a shaking voice, I asked, "But what did I . . . did I really harm the movement?"

"You certainly did."

"But how? Please tell me."

"Mansur, we stand against dictatorship. If our movement is to be successful, if it is to be fruitful for our people, then we must obey the law. We are against violence. Being against violence, how can we be violent? Our every action must be passive. You left headquarters with two hundred people. Now, because of your resistance, at least one hundred and ninety of our followers have run away in fear. You scared the people. What is more, those police are from your hometown. They must obey their orders because it's their job. But how is that their fault?

"On the other hand, if you had offered no resistance at all, more people would have joined you, unafraid. The police would have been forced to request more help. And in the end they would have told their headquarters that there were too many, that they could not fire on their own people—people who were doing no harm. They would not have beaten you. Without fear, the numbers of those who joined our ranks would swell until they encompassed the nation. Faced with such numbers, the government would be helpless. Don't you see? But, instead, through fear, you have driven them away."

At first I could not digest his logic; I was discouraged and hurt. But after a while I realized his reprimand was just. I said that I would do my best in the future to follow his precepts for the good of the organization.

He did not stop with a reprimand. At headquarters the next morning, a large notice pinned to the bulletin board further reproved me. "Violence breeds violence," it proclaimed. "The end stage of violence is war. In war, even the winner is a loser. Nothing gained by violence can result in good for the people."

Dr. Mohammad Mossadegh, a member of Parliament at the time, was in Tehran, likewise campaigning for the nationalization of oil. With the issue of nationalization becoming hotter every day, and with the newspapers strictly controlled by the government, our views had no chance of being published. Therefore, in September 1949, Dr. Baghai began to publish *Shahed* (Witness), a four-page daily broadside, in Tehran. *Shahed* was delivered to Kerman in two-issue bundles by postbus every other day. My friends and I picked them up and took them back to headquarters for distribution. In the October 30, 1949, issue, Dr. Baghai addressed the shah in an open letter:

> Your Majesty, the people of Iran can take no more of your dictatorship masquerading in the name of freedom. The Iranian people have eyes to see, ears to hear, they have common sense. They are not docile sheep, as your advisers tell you. You have often stated that to be king of poor, diseased, hungry people is not an honor.

We'd like to bring to your attention, Your Majesty, that these same poor, diseased, and hungry people will no longer tolerate your false freedom. A few years ago, the world during World War II gave 18,000,000 of its children under the false name of freedom, but today they will not listen to such false proclamations. The world today is a world of frankness. If you tell us we have the dictatorship of Stalin of Russia and Franco of Spain or the democracy of England and America, we will know where we stand.

That day when we went to pick up our papers, a huge policeman, jodhpured and putteed, arms akimbo, and with his enormous belly nearly obscuring the jutting pistol in his holster, greeted us. "Get out, you louse-ridden fools. Get out of here. You can't have these papers."

He threw the bundle onto a pile at the side of the bus, hooked his thumbs into his bullet-filled bandolier, planted his feet apart, and glared at us. We gave him no resistance.

That night my father asked why the policeman had refused to give us the papers. "I don't know," I replied. "Even if he had opened them, he surely couldn't have read them. He just told us he had received orders from Tehran."

My father sighed. "My son," he said, "change is coming. The fight is beginning."

"What do you mean? A fight over our papers?"

"No. I mean revolution."

"I don't understand, Father."

"Mansur, I see chaos ahead. Total destruction. This time, though, the dry wood and the green wood will burn together. In this fight, the guilty and the innocent alike will perish."

That thought disturbed me. Even if I could not prevent what my father foresaw, I resolved to continue with my political efforts. There had to be some way I could help.

Not long thereafter the shah made his first visit to America, to meet with President Truman (November 16, 1949). In that day's issue of *Shahed,* in an article entitled "America Should Know," the American people were addressed directly. The article compared the shah's regime to a government by "deity," or "People of the Heavens." The phrase, however, could be loosely translated from Farsi as "fallen angels" or "devil's henchmen." In fact, although the regime was supposedly a constitutional monarchy, it was a dictatorship. Moreover, the article speculated, was it not a sin for mere mortals, the "people of dirt," to be ruled by such a "deity"? It pointed out that Americans, those

defenders of freedom and protectors of individual rights, who coope-
rated or associated with the dictator shah would be culpable, would
deny those same principles of freedom and individual rights, earning
the unwavering hostility and contempt of the Iranian people. "Do not
stuff cotton in your ears," the article continued, "but hear the words
of the desperate nation that seeks your support."

No sooner was that issue printed than the police raided the printing
plant, confiscated every copy, and jailed Dr. Baghai along with all of
his associates in Tehran. Our office in Kerman meanwhile was "officially closed." On our arrival at headquarters the next day, we found
the door broken and every window smashed. Our furniture, our few
desks and chairs, all now rubble, was lying in the street. Ripped posters
and notices were strewn among the furniture. We learned that some
people who had been discovered in the office had been thrown from the
second-story windows. They were alive, but barely.

I could not bear the destruction, the total loss of all our months of
work. To me, headquarters had been an altar, an assembly, a shrine for
the helpless people. I wept. So did others. We tried to console one
another and began to salvage what we could, but the guards would not
let us. "Great fools," they shrieked. "Puppets of America! Traitors!"

Thereafter we held our meetings secretly in each other's homes,
changing locations each week for discretion. Eventually, however, Tehran relented. The shah had changed his mind once more, perhaps
swayed by the enormous popular vote that had elected Dr. Baghai to
Parliament, even while he was held by the government as a political
prisoner. Of twelve representatives elected from the Tehran district, Dr.
Mossadegh received the largest popular vote. Dr. Baghai came in second. After that we ran our office as before, and resumed distribution
of the paper, but we did not relax entirely. The ways of the shah were
inscrutable.

CHAPTER FOUR

Journey to Tehran

In June 1951 I graduated from high school in Kerman, the top student in the province. My father had written to Dr. Baghai, for I was soon to arrive in Tehran to take the Concours, the preparatory admissions test for Tehran University, where I planned to study law. Getting to Tehran entailed a three-day bus trip, to cover a distance of some 660 miles.

The night before each "scheduled" trip, passengers were required to leave baggage at the bus station so that heavy metal or wooden chests could be tied atop the bus with thick ropes. Bus service was so unpredictable that passengers paid only partial fares in advance, giving the balance to the bus driver's assistant only as they approached their destination. On the morning of my departure, the customary throng of four hundred to five hundred people had gathered at the bus station, either to see their loved ones off or to enliven an otherwise dull day. It was a lucrative occasion for town beggars, who mingled with the passengers and crowd, conferring blessings ("God protect you," "God be with you") in return for some tiny sum of money, always forthcoming from the passengers in the hope of a safe journey.

The rickety bus held some forty passengers and their hand-carried last-minute purchases. Parcels and bags jammed every available space. In meticulous script, outside and inside the bus on every available surface, were admonitions from and supplications to Mohammad. At the front of the bus, above the driver's seat, Mohammad's portrait was displayed in full view of the passengers. Above it, in blue letters, the color of peace and reassurance, was the inscription "If your protector is He whom I know, He shall preserve glass among rolling rocks." Beneath the picture, in red, the color of fear and danger, were the words "If the captain works himself to shreds, God shall take the ship where He wishes."

The passengers boarded, with relatives and friends clutching at them in parting. The hulking driver had apparently been chosen for his physical strength. With a green kerchief knotted at his throat, he took his seat and instructed his assistant to crank up the bus. What a noise that made. The muffler of the bus was always missing! A noisy engine was a sign of power. When it coughed into life, he turned to the assemblage and intoned fiercely, *"Allah-hu akbar* [God is great]. Repeat!" In unison, the crowd shouted back, *"Allah-hu akbar!"*

"Again. Louder."

Three repetitions sounded over the roar of the unmuffled engine. Then the stationmaster, also a large, heavy man, slammed his hand down on the hood. "Go with God," he shouted.

Passengers grabbed at their loved ones one final time through the windows, shrieking, keening, kissing. Then the bus started off in a cloud of smoke and dust at a glorious ten miles an hour. A flock of boys, perched on their high bicycles like elongated, clumsy birds, pedaled furiously alongside for several minutes until, exhausted, they fell away.

We pressed on toward the first day's destination, Yazd, a distance of 240 miles. The passengers, dressed in their best clothing and fresh for their journey, soon were covered with a thick white residue of sand and dust that filtered through every window and crack of the vehicle. As the bus lurched, a container toppled and the floor was awash with liquid butter. Still, the crying died away. People settled down for the trip.

On our arrival in Yazd that evening, we pulled into a "motel," a stark contrast to the beauty of the ancient desert city. Thoroughly shaken up, with faces grimy and eyes red-rimmed, we descended and entered our squalid little rooms with their filthy, infested mattresses. A twenty-gallon container of water in the hallway had to suffice for all of our needs. People passed their hands under the spigot, wiped futilely at their faces, and rubbed them with their sleeves. The desert daytime temperature had been 102°F. Now it was about 80°F. The mattresses were pulled out and we settled down for the night.

Sleep was impossible for me. The mattress was nothing but lumps and other unidentifiable objects, and the day's events had been altogether too exciting. I couldn't wait to reach Tehran. Most of all, I wanted to see the university. At last exhaustion overcame me.

Early the next morning, we boarded the bus for a repeat of the first day's ordeal. An hour out of Yazd we got a flat tire. Although the bus carried several spares, fixing a flat entailed laborious patching, using a metal scraper and glue, and cutting a piece of another old tire. Then, under the searing desert sun, urged on by the raucous cheers of the passengers, the assistant driver struggled for fifteen or twenty minutes, using a bicycle pump, to reflate the tire. Some of the passengers tried to help, but their efforts could not match his. He sweated greatly and had to clutch at his pants to keep them from falling. But God was on his side.

The sun's heat caused a mirage. Although I had never seen a lake or the ocean, the apparition that appeared on the horizon was exactly what I imagined a shimmering sea to be. A few passengers straggled off to relieve themselves, their robes modestly draped, but in view of the others.

All was shortly in order and we resumed our journey. Because the road to Isfahan, our second day's destination, passed through the mos¹ barren and remote stretches of the desert called Kavir-e Lut, we had to make the best possible time. On a narrow stretch of road, the driver pulled over to the shoulder to allow a truck to pass. As it did, its wheels dislodged a rock that hit our windshield, cracking it from one side to the other. Ten minutes more on the rutted road finished the job. The windshield shattered. The bus driver pulled over and stopped. Gloomily, he picked out the remaining shards. There was no point in going back to Yazd. There was no garage, no workshop; no one there could provide us with a windshield. Another bus brought up? No such thing. No. Isfahan was the only hope.

The passengers and the driver conferred. With the grace of God, we would proceed, it was decided. All the men and women began to wrap the driver with scarves, shawls, and oddments of fabric. Out of someone's bag, miraculously, came a pair of goggles. Soon the driver was so swathed that only his nostrils and goggles were seen. He had increased in size by at least half. Together, we hung every available blanket and piece of fabric from the roof supports and tucked the ends under the ropes holding the baggage. We strapped the driver into his seat.

As soon as the bus took off, the wind whipped the blankets away, some of them fluttering off irretrievably into the sands. An older man, seemingly sagacious, assured us that we would equalize the air pressure if we opened all the windows. Unfortunately, we listened. Even though nothing else blew away, the dust increased. It was a disaster. Although our noble driver never faltered in his determination, by the time we arrived in Isfahan, we were only caricatures of human beings—we looked like floured ghosts, dust and sand in every orifice, only our inflamed eyes showing.

Isfahan, even more ancient a city than Yazd, was the capital of Iran during the reign of Shah Abbas and his dynasty (1501–1736). It is a city of magnificent mosques, elaborate architecture, wide streets, and an enormous square. Yet, with all that magnificence, our so-called motel was comparable to the one in Yazd. We were all too weary, however, to be concerned. The driver, indefatigable and devoted, went off in search of a garage. I searched for a night's sleep.

On the third day, with no further misfortune, we neared Tehran. Suddenly the driver called out, "Have any of you ever seen a train?"

"No!" we yelled back.

"Pray then, and chant with me! I will show you a marvel." He stopped the bus and we all got out. Sure enough, to the left, out of nowhere it seemed, an enormous engine loomed; the train's five or six cars sped past us and were gone in a minute. We were astonished. What further marvels would this godly man produce?

We soon found out. As we approached Qom, the holy city, the driver veered sharply onto the shoulder of the road. "A blessing for your eyes! Look at the magnificent holy shrine . . . and give a donation in the name of God." We got out of the bus and stared at the immense blue and yellow domes of the shrine, their gold caps glittering in the sun. We exclaimed, prayed, paid. Next, the driver's assistant stood and, slipping wildly about in the spilled butter, grasping frantically at the backs of the seats, he called out the passengers' names in turn and the amounts still owing.

As the passengers were paying, one old lady did not respond. He called her name again.

"God will give you the money," she cried. "Bless you. You look just like my son. I am going to the holy shrine in Tehran. I will pray for your soul."

"Can't you give me the money? It won't go to my pocket, mother."

"Search my bags." She was despairing. "Search all my belongings. You will see I have nothing. I am only a poor old woman. I have no money. But I will pray. I will beseech God and his prophet, Mohammad, to forgive your sins. I will pray for all your souls." She turned to the passengers in appeal. She pulled a small cookie tin from one of her bags and summoned a small boy to her. "May the sand of the desert become jewels for you, my son. Help me, I beg you."

With this, the boy took the tin and lurched precariously through the bus, approaching each passenger for a little money. As each one dropped a coin, she uttered a blessing, "God will return it to you a hundredfold." Enough was collected to pay her fare with a little left over.

Some twenty miles out of Tehran, we found ourselves on blacktop, the first paved road I had ever seen. The road had been built by American forces during the World War II Allied occupation. However, in Iranian hands, with no technology to repair it, the road was only slightly less bumpy than the dirt one we had left.

Then we entered Tehran itself. A place of magic! Mercedes-Benzes and taxis rubbed fenders with carriages drawn by horses, donkeys, and mules. Pedestrians and bicycles threaded their way through the thronged streets—shouts, horns, general confusion. Tehran was the shah's showplace. It glittered with light. It would show me many new things. But today I had seen my first train! I had traveled on blacktop! And even more amazing, everywhere, in full view, newspapers were spread invitingly on the shelves of kiosks.

I engaged one of the carriages, less expensive than a taxi, to take me to the room rented for me, where, exhausted, I dropped my bags, sank onto the mattress, and promptly fell asleep.

As Dr. Baghai was busy with political affairs, I had days to explore the streets and shops of the city before taking my admissions test for the university. Delighted, I wandered about, chatted with strangers, met with family friends, and found still more marvels. I took the bus that traveled near the imperial palace to see the manner in which our monarch lived.

My letters to my family were several pages long, describing the trip and my new experiences. Against the advice of my friends, I decided to economize and did not buy pails of water, "shah's water," from those who brought it door to door with their old nags, spavined skeletons, pulling water tanks. Instead, I listened to the wife of my landlord, who assured me that it would be safe to drink the tap water, red with tiny parasites, if I strained it first through a cloth. For months afterward, I was afflicted with bloody, amoebic dysentery. Cheap is dear.

Just prior to my arrival in Tehran, in May 1951, Dr. Baghai had established the Iranian Toilers' Party. With my letter of recommendation from the local branch in Kerman in hand, I visited party headquarters, and filled out forms to become a member of the main organization in Tehran. I was making new friends and enjoying new experiences, and would now have the chance to work for my beliefs.

But the bright prospects of my coming classes and my renewed association with Dr. Baghai notwithstanding, I still had to place myself in the context of my past, to sort out the influences that had shaped me, to blend them into the new events in my life, my future.

Some things in Tehran were not so different from home. There was no indoor plumbing, no bathroom. A small outhouse served the needs of all the individuals in my rooming house. Public baths, where one could be doused, scrubbed, and shaved, were available, as they had been in Kerman.

I bought a Coleman stove and kerosene to cook my frugal dinners —soup, eggs, stew. One day I forgot that I had turned on the flame and returned from a visit to a friend to find the stove red hot, the last of the wick sputtering, and the entire room covered with soot, oily and black. After I assured the landlord, who was waiting and hitting his head, that I would pay the cost of repainting, he let me stay. The paint cost more than my entire month's rent, which was four dollars.

Meanwhile, I had presented myself promptly at the university to confirm my registration for the Concours. With great trepidation, I had observed the other students arriving, dressed in beautiful three-piece suits. I felt outlandish in my own heavy suit with its thick shoulder pads and wide lapels. My shoes seemed enormous, and their taps announced my every step. Some students, whose fathers were government officials, arrived in chauffeured cars. Oh, surely, they were better than I, better educated, better prepared, better in every way. The law school accepted only three hundred students of some eight thousand applicants each year. The more I watched the arrivals, the more worried I became. What if I failed?

The four-day Concours covered all subjects: philosophy, the history of civilization, literature, ethics, foreign languages. The questions were tricky and difficult. That first day, I worried myself sick. I sweated through it and through each successive day. The required composition asked the question: "Who serves society better, the teacher or the judge?" I was torn and took several minutes to reflect. I wanted to study law, but it was my firm opinion that a teacher was of far greater benefit to society than a judge. When the test was over, each and every student I spoke to said he had answered that a judge was of greater importance. "Mansur," said one, "you're entering law school. What a fool you are. Of course, they want to hear you say that a judge is more important. You just ruined your chance. They'll put you in the school of education —that is, if you get in at all."

If I had been worried before, that was the last straw. The letter I wrote that night to my father was forty pages long. What advice did he have for me now? I was a failure. It would be a whole month before the results were announced. But what was the use in waiting? I had not passed. What else could I do? Go back home? Useless . . .

I worked at Dr. Bahai's headquarters. I tried to keep busy. But always the composition I had written festered in the back of my mind. Why, oh why, had I answered that way?

In a few days I received a notice asking me to come to the telegraph office to receive a "present or conference telegram" from my father. As I sat next to the wireless operator, the words that were slowly spelled out for me were as comforting as though my father's face were in clear view: "Are you worried, my son?"

"Oh, Father, I have such a small chance of being accepted. If my name is not announced, what then?"

In reassuring taps, his answer came: "Mansur, it would be very unusual for that to happen. If it should, you will spend a year in the Tehran library working with Dr. Baghai, and then you will try again. But why do you think you failed? Because of the composition? Don't you realize that the judges will be looking for your skill in proving your point, not the subject matter you chose? They will look at your argument, your logic. You made the right choice."

"But there is more," I answered. "These people, so well prepared, so, so . . . They have such clothes, they live here, they are accustomed to wealth, to luxury. They have so many books! They were reading until the last minute. Their chauffeurs brought them to the test."

"Keep your head up. A jackass in a suit of clothes is still a jackass. Any person can carry a load of books. If a mule carries books, he is still a mule. Don't worry. Is there anything else? Could you not answer the questions?"

"No, nothing. I just feel that I have failed."

"Remember, head up! But keep your pride in your pocket. Wire me on the day the results are announced. No, never mind. I will hear the results on the state radio. Remember, examiners look at tests; they can't see the suits."

When the results were broadcast, my name was among the first twenty. My elated wire crossed that of my father. His read simply, "Mansur, you are a good merchant." I cried, clutching the telegram, and recalled his story: "Someday your education will serve you well. You will be rich in knowledge. A merchant of goods who gives his property away is soon bankrupt. But he who is a merchant of knowledge can only profit when he gives it away. Neither can anyone steal his riches. His wealth can only increase."

CHAPTER FIVE

Tehran University

Tuition was free for all students. The university furnished me, as it did all of its out-of-town students, free board and a dormitory room.

I was in awe of the spacious marble halls, the marble floors, the luxuriant gardens surrounding the academic buildings, the countless books in the library, the large, well-lit, well-heated classrooms. I took my seat in my first class, Civil Rights, half-expecting to hear an orchestra, to feel a mantle descend on my shoulders. The professor reinforced the effect. "This is the first of your student days in the law school of Tehran University. In the future, who knows? You may be a lawyer, a politician, a judge, and will serve your countrymen. Many great men will arise from these benches." My head swiveled of its own accord. But no monitor stood behind me. I looked back at the professor and grinned broadly.

Our dormitories had been built by the American armed forces for their use during the occupation and had then been donated to the university. Although the rooms were large and sunny, with bathrooms large enough for twenty students at a time at intervals of every twenty rooms, the buildings were not well maintained. In each of the cubicles in the bathrooms there was a basin. As there were no laundries, the poorer students spent hours there, washing their clothes. They festooned their wet belongings over their beds, their doors, and their windows to dry. The stove in the cafeteria did not work properly. Bus service to town consisted of three buses, rusted and in need of repair.

On the day the chancellor of Tehran University visited the dormitories, I joined the crowd to hear his speech. After the address, he asked the students if there were any problems. No one spoke. Without thinking, I raised my hand.

"You. Yes, you." He pointed to me.

I gathered my courage. It was there, but my voice failed.

"What kind of problems do you have?" he asked.

I chose my words carefully. "Chancellor, you are an educated man, a friend of His Majesty the Shah. You are powerful and great. But we are small. Perhaps a man of your stature will not be interested in our small affairs."

"But of course I am interested. That is why I am here. Speak freely. Tell me your problems."

"Chancellor, to the ant in his hill in summer, a few drops of dew is a flood."

"I am deeply concerned with ants," he replied. "Tell me, how are you flooded?"

The chancellor was true to his word. When I had explained the situation, he provided us not only with ten washing machines and a new stove for the cafeteria, but with three new buses. Because I had been the only questioner, he asked me to furnish him a full report on any other existing problems. He further instructed the student body to elect a slate of representatives to oversee the functions of the dormitory. Several students, aware that the Communists were losing no time in choosing their own slate and that they had already proposed a coalition to anyone who ran, approached me and suggested that I run. Was I ready for it? I went to see Dr. Baghai and asked his opinion.

"Why don't you campaign? That was excellent, the 'anthill story.' How did you think of it?"

I told him that I had read it in some old fable. He laughed. "It doesn't matter. You made your point. You have made an impact on the students, too. You were the only one who dared to speak. Go ahead and campaign. But if you disagree with Communist philosophy, you can't agree to any coalition. Go your own way. Chart your own objectives, your goals . . . campaign with those in mind."

Persuaded, I campaigned with four of my friends, one a literature student, two pre-med, and one from the school of engineering. We were all elected. Both my father and Dr. Baghai were pleased. I received a wire from my father.

"Where did you learn to speak like that?"

I wired back: "Where else, my father? I am simply returning your goods."

I put in long hours. Not only was I working hard at my academic subjects, but, as a member of the Toilers' Party, I worked late each night at headquarters, on the campaign, in office affairs, and on the newspaper. Often, when I missed the last bus to campus, I stayed at Dr. Baghai's home. Political issues, particularly the fight for free elections, were reaching a brutal stage. Several prime ministers had toppled or had been assassinated over their stance on this issue.

On July 22, 1951, with a fellow party member, I watched a crowd demonstrating in front of Parliament against Ahmad Ghavam, Prime Minister to His Majesty the Shah. The crowd favored Dr. Mohammad Mossadegh, leader of the National Front.

Suddenly I saw tanks moving toward us. Rapid machine-gun fire followed. Bodies fell all around me, including that of my friend, Amir Bijar, killed instantly. I ducked behind a large wooden crate, a box used by ice sellers. The crowd of demonstrators had raised their hands in immediate surrender, but not before forty-five of them had been killed. It was the first time I had witnessed the full extent of the shah's power.

That night, after the demonstration, Dr. Baghai delivered a speech to a large crowd at our headquarters:

Today as the machine guns stuttered, the emotions of the people boiled over. The stuttering of the guns was saying: "Death! Death! Death!" The poor harmless people welcomed it with open arms, raising their hands to God as the bullets struck. Do not forget, my countrymen, what your brothers and sisters did today for your freedom. They gave their lives for you.

Do not be discouraged. Do not lose your hope. We have a long way to go. Dictators don't give up. Ask your government to punish the criminals who fired on our people. Ask your government to enforce constitutional law. We believe Princess Ashraf, the twin sister of the shah, [because of her involvement] must leave the country and find another home. Enough is enough.

In the fight between the bayonet and thought, the bayonet is always defeated. Today proved it once again. I want to tell them that even if they had been successful, to govern a graveyard is no honor.

The blood of one of the victims remained on the building of our headquarters, where the youth had staggered just before he died.

Our Toilers' Party was strongly in favor of Dr. Mossadegh; he seemed to us not to wear "the uniform of a dictator." Of a good family, aristocrats who had long been active in government, he had served in many posts for many years. Although he lived in a fine house, he dressed simply, usually in a robe. He took no salary and refused to ride in the government car provided for him.

Dr. Mossadegh's greatest appeal for the people was his support for the nationalization of Iranian oil, a cause he backed with great fervor. He drafted the enabling bill and proclaimed that Iran and its resources should be the sole property of Iranians. In his seventies, he didn't seem to be seeking recognition, money or power. With no apparent material desires, this skinny, big-beaked man, often ill and with a doctor (his son) in attendance, emotional, tearful, mocked and caricatured in the international press, frequently fainted dead away in moments of stress. To us, he appeared to be the new Messiah, one possessed of altruism and purity. His following was enormous, his supporters as frenzied as he. The bloody demonstration I had witnessed shortly after my arrival in Tehran was only one of many.

Meanwhile, I continued my work for the party. Its functions, its paper, Dr. Baghai's goals for the nation seemed to be the only positive way. The party consisted of Dr. Baghai, its leader; a central committee; and many subordinate organizations that answered to the Central Committee. Each organization represented a segment of society or a job category: teachers, taxi drivers, carpenters, students, religious groups, youth. One organization consisted of speakers. I was selected to become a speaker. I gave several lectures a day and was well received. Because I had a background in the works of Marx and Engels, I often lectured on communism and explained the party's anti-Communist position to the youth groups to which I had been assigned, groups from the high schools, the university, and the trades. They were strongly against Russia, and still greatly pro-American.

At the same time, I was doing well in school, but in light of the daily political chaos, the university no longer seemed to be in touch with reality. Although I welcomed the opportunity to meet students from all parts of the country, many of them from impoverished towns like my own, the university itself seemed hollow and remote from the problems of the people.

Law school, in fact, offered me little. Lessons were learned by rote, by students who sat in silence with folded hands while the professors lectured. Few, if any, questions were asked or tolerated. Word by word, we learned civil law, criminal law, and constitutional law, from a constitution that had never truly been in effect since its establishment in 1906. I was once reported by undercover agents in the classroom for having asked our professor of Civil Rights just what civil rights he meant, since we had none. At that time, police were not permitted to take custody of a student on the university grounds, and I avoided the agents sent to question me by leaving through another door. I was harassed briefly, but the government had other, bigger quarry to pursue. By placing their agents in classrooms and by questioning students, they sought mainly to instill fear.

Even those who taught us the principles of the Constitution— freedom of speech, of the press, of assembly, the basic human rights— were connected with the government that trampled on those rights. The professor who taught us Introduction to Criminal Law was in charge of the newspaper with the largest circulation in Iran, a country in which all newspapers were censored and all advertising checked by the government. I recalled my first sight of all those newspapers in the kiosk. Now I was aware that all were advertisements for the shah and his family: the shah at the opening of a store, cutting the ribbon; his wife cutting a ribbon; his sister—another ribbon; this one has a cold; that one had gone skiing, attended a concert, gone hunting, gone to the Olympics.

My classes exerted less and less appeal. While many of my professors were intelligent, none became my mentor. Each one had his own weaknesses, with only a few willing to voice the least criticism of the government. After all, they were aligned with it, holding dual posts as professors and members of the cabinet. They were called "doves of the holy shrine," those fortunate birds who escaped being hunted (a national pastime) because they had gained sanctuary, immunity, in the citadel of government.

In private discussions many professors were vehemently antigovernment, but they argued that if they were to state their views in public, they would lose their jobs, both in Parliament and in the university. Furthermore, they argued, no future existed for Iran. Their naysaying only deepened my commitment to work for a better country.

In the economics classes, the teaching was no different. No one swam against the tide. The professors were the equivalent of volunteer firemen, with their main interests lying outside the university. I spent as much time as possible at party headquarters, working on the paper and being a speaker.

As a law student, I could not enroll in Dr. Baghai's classes in the school of education, but I read everything he wrote and received the constant benefit of his teachings. My affinity for him did not lessen. Both the man's philosophy and his personality appealed strongly to me. By then a leader in our Parliament, he was as eloquent in his speeches before that body as he was when addressing the crowds that gathered at headquarters, and as in his *Shahed* editorials. He always advocated a reasoned approach, and the importance of working within the framework of the law. Heavy-jowled, leaning on his cane, he was a striking figure, poised and calm. He lived a spartan life; his home was impressive only for its library. He greatly enjoyed walking and talking with people. His opinions and values were always expressed in the same way, whether in private or public discussion, with friend or foe, with the powerless or the mighty. He listened to all positions, spared no one the full weight of any disapproval, but sought always to make them understand, hearing them out, giving them rope, and then questioning them socratically. "What would you do if you were in the same position?" "Has anyone hurt you directly?" "Are the offenders truly bad?" "Is it the man, the position, the government or the idea?" "Is religion at fault? Or ignorance?"

A follower of Gandhi, he had a firm conviction that the evils that existed in Iran had their roots in the disease of lying, a cancer that had invaded every segment of society, high and low, and that had proliferated through hundreds of years of dictatorship and oppression. A people so suppressed, he believed, with no true leaders, no training, no education, had to learn to lie in order to survive. Like Gandhi, he believed that one must be a guardian of truth, firmly opposed to the lie and to injustice, but always nonviolently.

I was Dr. Baghai's disciplined and devoted follower, carefully adhering to all of his instructions and assignments to me, carrying out my duties as diligently as I could. I looked upon Dr. Baghai not merely as a symbol, or a leader, or a teacher, but more than all of these. He was a man who lived his truth, a man of action. Disillusioned by my professors, by society, by government, by not having accomplished anything with my education other than academic success, I saw in Dr. Baghai's ideas the only hope for the future of Iran. In his estimation, the sickness of Iran could take as long to cure as it had taken to develop. He did not expect to live to see it happen but had the utmost faith in its ultimate occurrence. He waits with the same equanimity still.

Dr. Baghai's prescription to cure Iran's cancer was education of the populace, which would then produce, choose, and support principled and responsible leaders, untouched by the supreme corrupters—concentrated power and money—who would keep the common touch, remaining involved with their constituency and not with factions.

For these reasons I redoubled my work on *Shahed,* in which we continued our strong support of Dr. Mossadegh. I did well enough in

my classes, but within the party I was swiftly promoted and shortly put
in charge of its youth organization. In this capacity, I trained those who
were in high school and at the university; members of trade unions,
such as bakers, grocers, and carpenters; and religious youth. After sessions calculated to determine their level of understanding and to orient
them to party policies and goals, they were placed in party positions or
given duties that would make the best use of their talents and abilities.

In the meantime, in late April 1951, Dr. Mossadegh had become
prime minister. Pleading ill health, he had asked for the authority to
rule by decree—he would become the body of legislators, pass laws
without going to Parliament, and, as chief executive, enforce those laws.
He had said that he would be unable to go frequently to Parliament to
explain what he was doing. Because of the high esteem in which he was
held, the powers he requested were granted.

In the continuing wrangle over the nationalization of oil, meanwhile, the British foreign secretary had refused to concede Iran's rights,
and on May 25, 1951, Norman Richard Seddon, head of the Tehran
office of the Anglo-Iranian Oil Company, had received a communiqué
from the Iranian financial minister demanding compliance with Iran's
orders within one week. On May 28 Britain and Anglo-Iranian had
appealed to the United Nations, which referred the case to the International Court in The Hague for a ruling. At the same time, Anglo-
Iranian offered to continue direct negotiations with the Iranian
government. June 4 was the deadline for any last possible talks between
Britain and Iran, but negotiations continued until July 2 when all talks
broke off.

On that day Mr. Seddon protested to the Iranian State Department
that his office had been raided by a group of men who broke in and
ejected him and all of his employees. The State Department protested
that they knew nothing about the incident. It was quite true.

About two months after Parliament passed the nationalization law
(March 20, 1951), and while negotiations were continuing, Dr. Baghai
formed another organization, called "Expropriation." Some members
of the Toilers' Party were trained to lead the new organization, which
was to watch the offices and employees of the Anglo-Iranian Oil Company. Dr. Baghai was informed that employees were taking documents
from the Office of Advertising and Publication, which was, in fact, the
espionage office of Anglo-Iranian. In a few days Dr. Baghai confirmed
that the documents were being taken from that office, which was under
the supervision of a man named Stakil, to the home of Mr. Seddon.

Dr. Baghai wanted members of the new organization to enter Seddon's house and confiscate the documents, which now belonged to Iran, but he needed the help of the police. At that time, General Fazlollah Zahedi was the chief of police as well as the interior minister. Dr. Baghai told me that he had spoken with General Zahedi in Parliament and asked the general not to reveal the plan to Dr. Mossadegh, because if the prime minister didn't agree to the plan, there would be no way that any action could be taken. General Zahedi agreed to help and placed police officers at Dr. Baghai's disposal. They also obtained a search warrant from the Department of Justice, and the group entered Seddon's house.

When the members of Expropriation broke in and opened the safe, they obtained records of the Anglo-Iranian Oil Company that were of staggering significance. The documents showed payoffs to almost all branches of the Iranian government by the British company. Bribes had spread from the country's leading newspapermen to its highest officials, including Dr. Mossadegh's son-in-law and Shahpur Bakhtiar, who was in charge of all labor at the Abadan refinery, the world's largest. It was discovered that a large number of records—twenty-five suitcases full— had been sent to London. A wire found in Seddon's house, in Stakil's handwriting, stated that the followers of Dr. Baghai were watching the offices and he, Stakil, was afraid they would seize the office. Therefore, he was sending the papers to London. Several copies of all the records were made—one for the library of Parliament, one for the Office of Information, one for Dr. Mossadegh, and one for Dr. Baghai to publish in *Shahed*.

Dr. Mossadegh was enraged with Dr. Baghai over the incident at Seddon's house. Just after the seizure Seddon asked to speak with Dr. Mossadegh. In response to Dr. Mossadegh's criticism of the raid, Dr. Baghai told him to ask Seddon whether the house was Seddon's own personal property or the property of Anglo-Iranian Oil and therefore now the property of Iran. Dr. Mossadegh later laughingly reported that Seddon had had to admit that the house belonged to Anglo-Iranian.

On July 23 Dr. Mossadegh, having seen a way to turn the incriminating documents to his advantage, went with Dr. Baghai and several others to present the evidence to the United Nations in New York, where it was referred to the International Court in The Hague, which was already deliberating on British complaints associated with the nationalization of oil in Iran.

Observing that the startling papers proved beyond a doubt that the Anglo-Iranian Oil Company (and the British Admiralty) was not only a commercial venture but was intricately and illegally involved in subverting the internal government of a foreign nation and in the control of its press, the Court ruled (in 1952), 9 to 5, that because of its meddling in Iran's government, Britain was entitled to no indemnification for its property. The Russian judge, conveniently, was ill and unable to vote. The British judge voted against Britain.

But by then these same people whose names had appeared in the confiscated documents were once again being entrusted by Dr. Mossadegh with some of the highest posts in Iran's government. On Dr. Mossadegh's appointment of Shahpur Bakhtiar as assistant secretary of labor, the speaker of the House, Ayatollah Abolghasem Kashani, challenged Dr. Mossadegh in an open letter: "To whom have you lied? To the International Court in The Hague or to the Iranian people? For what reasons are the same men who have for years defrauded and betrayed the interests of our nation now empowered by you to govern the nation?"

Dr. Mossadegh's answer to the Iranian people sounded naïve. He said publicly that "these men have promised to be good." Further, he claimed, invoking the names of Jesus and Mohammad, who had held themselves above the wrongful acts of their families and followers, that he, Dr. Mossadegh the leader, was not tarnished in any way by the misdeeds of subordinates.

Dr. Mossadegh, in fact, was becoming a dictator himself. He had named himself secretary of defense right after the shah had been forced to bow to the people's choice and make him prime minister. In a visit to the royal palace, he had thrown his power in the shah's face: "You see what I can do. If you want the right to appoint the Secretary of Defense back, I will give it to you." Smarting, the shah said nothing.

Dr. Mossadegh had also used the powers granted him by Parliament to decree martial law. He had done nothing in regard to the promised laws about electoral and social reforms. By 1953, therefore, Dr. Baghai withdrew his support from Dr. Mossadegh; by then there were so many points of disagreement between them that he had no choice.

The National Security Act, which was passed in January 1952, meanwhile had taken away many of the rights of the Iranian people. Under this Act, statements made by the police or the Iranian Justice Department were considered true unless proven otherwise. In other words, a person was guilty until proven innocent; a person could be arrested and jailed without being told the charges; people were no longer free to congregate in groups of more than two, thus precluding demonstrations and strike agitation; it was even considered a crime to admit *thinking* of doing something wrong. Dr. Baghai disapproved of the extension of the power to rule by decree and the extension of martial law, because the government had welshed on the improvements that had been promised when Mossadegh requested these special powers.

Other points of contention centered on the aftermath of the nationalization of oil. The panel Dr. Mossadegh had established to investigate the papers found at Seddon's house was composed of three members —all were Anglophiles. Also, one of the men Dr. Mossadegh had put in charge of the new oil company had been named in the documents and had been spying for the British. After Dr. Baghai had given Dr. Mossadegh the papers, in which Dr. Mossadegh's son-in-law was implicated as being a spy for the British, the prime minister had had the audacity to take his son-in-law to the United States with him as interpreter and adviser at a private discussion with a United States government official. The son-in-law reported on this meeting to London, which caused problems between the United States and Britain. Also at issue was the appointment of Shahpur Bakhtiar. In short, even though Dr. Mossadegh had thrown the British out of Iran, he had given the oil industry to people who were puppets of the British.

Dr. Baghai also objected to a secret coalition Dr. Mossadegh had made with the Communist party.

Having lost Dr. Baghai's support, and fighting threats to his power on several fronts, both national and international, Dr. Mossadegh began to harass Dr. Baghai and the party. Our membership was infiltrated by his undercover agents, and members were jailed on the flimsiest pretexts, without notification of the charges or any right of appeal, under the terms of the National Security Act. Dr. Baghai was accused of having kidnapped General Mahmud Afshartous, the former chief of Iranian police, and of complicity in his murder.

Dr. Mossadegh's political prisons by then were full. The vast differences that now existed between us and the prime minister threatened him greatly. So Dr. Mossadegh was determined to quell all opposition. Soon after his accusation of Dr. Baghai, which was reported in the international press, Dr. Mossadegh's martial-law officers appeared one night at party headquarters. In the melee that followed, some members were able to escape, but some of us, several party executives included, were beaten, kicked, and thrown into an army van. At the military tribunal we were beaten again with wire whips, nightsticks, and fists, and kicked to the floor until we were bleeding and covered with welts and bruises. After that we were thrown into cells.

Because the tribunal was aware of my close connections with Dr.

Baghai, their interrogation of me focused on his whereabouts and connections. The questioners were alternately wheedling and threatening: "You seem to be a nice man, an intelligent man. Why are you connected with such an organization?" When I answered that I believed in its principles, kicks, slaps, and curses followed. "Traitor! Bastard!" Interrogations and beatings took place daily; but with no information forthcoming and no real evidence implicating me, and with growing protest and altercations among the followers and opponents of Dr. Mossadegh, I was released after a week.

Dr. Mossadegh's goons continued their harassment, however, shadowing party members and pelting us with rocks as we attempted to distribute copies of *Shahed*.

But finally Dr. Mossadegh was faced with opposition within Parliament itself, where he was losing the support of religious groups and was strongly resisted by the nationalist groups that had once supported him. He had usurped all the powers of a dictator. His heady defeat of the once all-powerful British Empire had been responsible for his popularity, but that popularity was now seriously eroded. He was losing ground and wanted to remove the parliamentary immunity of his opponents, including Dr. Baghai.

Dr. Mossadegh eventually decided to hold a referendum, ostensibly to see if Parliament was representative of the people's wishes or not. Using wiliness, he had the people vote in two separate places—for the "yes" and "no" votes, respectively. For the supporters of Dr. Mossadegh, there were free buses to the voting place. There, army trucks awaited them, dispensing ice-cold beverages. For "no" voters, such as myself and my friends, a gauntlet awaited. A crowd of thugs fell upon us with rocks, sticks, and knives. "Traitors!" they shrieked at us and struck us as hard as they could as we ran through the group. Again, as we left the polling place, we were attacked. One of the goons seized me by the collar and banged my head against a wall.

It mattered not a bit: I knew my vote was not going to be counted anyway. The effort was all. The vote was further manipulated by the fact that there was no registration. Each person presented his birth certificate to be stamped (or not stamped) and cast an open ballot. If the certificate was not stamped, the person could go to another polling place and vote again. Not surprisingly, there were many who were turned away by Dr. Mossadegh's election officials, and not surprisingly, the returns showed, according to *The New York Times*, that 99.94 percent of the voting populace was squarely behind him. (In a separate referendum, held on January 26, 1963, for the White Revolution, the shah's tally showed the same 99.94 percent to be aligned with the shah!)

Dr. Baghai and Ali Zohari, a friend and fellow member of Parliament (Zohari, a writer, was educated in France, and had originally obtained the permission to publish our newspaper), had predicted the outcome of Dr. Mossadegh's referendum. They realized that it would result in the dissolution of Parliament, effecting the removal of the immunity afforded parliamentary members, including Dr. Baghai and Ali Zohari, thereby leaving all opponents of Dr. Mossadegh vulnerable to Dr. Mossadegh's police.

Prior to the referendum, Ali Zohari, on behalf of the Executive Committee of the Toilers' Party, had written an open letter in *Shahed* (August 1, 1953):

> To Prime Minister Mossadegh: We know you can brook no opposition. We assume you will call a referendum and take away our immunity. We hereby tender our resignation and you can then take us to court personally. But do not abuse the Constitution. There is no provision for such a referendum. And do not dissolve the Parliament. Enforce the Constitution. You will benefit from such enforcement more than anyone else. If you do not, you yourself will become the victim of your illegal actions.

Dr. Mossadegh nevertheless dissolved Parliament in August 1953, claiming the referendum as a mandate for his actions. With Dr. Baghai's and Ali Zohari's immunity thereby removed, he jailed them along with many party members.

Immediately, the shah notified Dr. Mossadegh that because there was no Parliament, he was no longer prime minister. The shah's letter was delivered to Dr. Mossadegh by Colonel Nematollah Nassiri, the commander of the royal guard. Although Dr. Mossadegh acknowledged that he had received the shah's letter, for which he had signed a receipt, he promptly arrested Colonel Nassiri and announced a coup d'état. The shah flew to Baghdad, changed planes, and continued on to Rome, fearing for his life.

Chaos reigned for three days. Huge milling throngs filled the streets. The Tudeh (Communist) party publicly renewed its support of Dr. Mossadegh, although he still denied any affiliation with communism. There were lootings, more jailings, more deaths. Enormous pictures of Lenin now began to appear in public places. In Tehran several statues of the shah and his father were taken down and likenesses of Lenin substituted. Underneath Lenin's pictures appeared the motto

"The only ethical teacher of mankind." Most nationalists were in jail, and the Communists insisted on their innocence, but whoever was responsible for the motto had made a grave mistake. For Muslims, particularly Shiite Muslims, such a title belongs only to Ali, the son-in-law of Mohammad. Religious groups were infuriated and became even more so by inscriptions smeared in excrement on the walls of mosques: "Down with Islam. Up with Communist society."

Street violence continued. Law did not exist.

Our Toilers' Party, in a complete reversal, worked actively to incite demonstrations against the premier. Placards everywhere enjoined NO COMMUNISM IN IRAN! Even soldiers joined the demonstrations. Dr. Mossadegh's government collapsed almost overnight. He escaped from his home and was later arrested by order of the martial-law prosecutor. His home was demolished by the people. After his trial and the completion of his jail term, he was moved to one of his other homes and kept under house arrest until he died in 1967, a powerless and broken man.

With the shah's blessings, General Zahedi became prime minister on August 18, 1953, and thereafter strictly enforced martial law, claiming that conditions necessitated it. We backed him, having little choice and an abundance of hope; but it was foolish hope. Zahedi was just another rubber-stamp dictator.

CHAPTER SIX

Activism and Imprisonment

Because the Toilers' Party soon became outspokenly against the shah's new government, it was blacklisted. In March 1954 we were ordered to cease publication of *Shahed*. Like all opponents of Zahedi, we were once again harassed and jailed.

I was at work in our headquarters in defiance of the latest interdiction against publication of our pamphlets when I was informed that someone was waiting outside to see me, a visitor from Kerman with presents from my family. I stepped out to greet him and consented to accompany him to his car. His accent was not familiar to me and, after walking for several blocks and still not reaching his car, I became suspicious and inquired where he had parked. The reply: a gun leveled at me and two men instantly appearing on either side of me. Thrown into the back of a car, I was taken to police headquarters. There an officer called for my file and ordered his driver to take me to Ghazel-Ghal-eh, a jail in an outlying district. "Well," I thought, "here we go again. Goddamn, this time I'm in trouble."

On my arrival at the jail, the chief of police called me before him. "Traitor—you bastard!" The words were familiar. So was the treatment. I was beaten, kicked, and summarily thrown into yet another damp, gloomy cell.

Soon I was recalled for interrogation. The chief of police made cutting motions with long-bladed scissors, darting them at my face only an inch from my eyes, my lips. "Huh! Want to have your flesh cut, do you? You'd better tell me what I want to know! Who sees Dr. Baghai? Who calls him? Who killed Afshartous? What goes on at party head-quarters? What are you planning?"

I remained silent, trying not to flinch from the maddening, clicking scissors.

"You won't talk? You'll be sorry! Don't make me mad!" A hundred thoughts kaleidoscoped in my mind. His threats were real, my fears hardly groundless. I remembered reading about an early twentieth-century poet who had dared to write of freedom and had had his lips sewn together. Later he was killed. I also remembered having read about resisters who, under Reza Shah, had had ears ripped off their heads by pulling on their earrings, fingers torn from their hands by pulling on their rings. Some prisoners had died of embolisms induced by air being injected directly into their veins. Another chief of police had emptied his pistol into a prisoner who refused to answer. I sweated, but I did not talk.

The police chief touched the points of the blades to my eyelids. "I'm trying to save your life. I tell you, you won't be able to withstand the punishment if you don't tell me everything you know. And believe me, if you ever got to power, you'd do the same to me!"

"I wouldn't."

He pressed harder. "Oh, you think you're in power already, do you? Talk!"

The police chief backed away and raised his hand. From behind the curtains on the fifteen-foot-high windows, several men emerged, knouts in hand, and the beating began. I tried to shield my head with my arms, struggling to keep on my feet. It was useless. The blows rained on me from all directions. Suddenly they stopped, and the police chief ordered me to sit. I wiped my bleeding face, and he held out his handkerchief. "You poor fellow. I feel sorry for you. Talk to me. I am like your brother. Let me help you. Why do you refuse to answer? You mustn't do that. Just tell us what we want to know."

His voice was low, placating; his face registered great sympathy. "Surely you don't wish to be beaten again. What a pity. You are young. Possibly you are misinformed. I want to help you. I certainly don't want to hurt you again."

I took a long breath and assured him I knew nothing, nothing at all.

His voice was sharp again. "Tell me about the relationship between Dr. Baghai and President Nasser of Egypt!"

"I know nothing of such a relationship."

"You do!"

"I don't."

"You are Dr. Baghai's confidant. He tells you everything."

"It's not true. I can't tell you anything."

"Our intelligence says differently. I had mercy on you. Shall I call the soldiers back? They're right outside."

"Call them back. It makes no difference. I know nothing at all."

He smiled at me. "I am a merciful man. I feel great pity for you. Go back to your cell. Think about it. I'm sure you'll feel differently in the morning."

I was returned to my cell, a tiny room with nothing in it except the blanketless bed. With my body aching, I paced and worried. No one knew where I was. In spite of my fears, I thought about what I had heard or read, how all of our officials acted only on what they had learned from a lifetime, many lifetimes, of violence.

Meanwhile, moaning and crying had broken into my consciousness. I was not alone in this jail. I could not sleep. I paced some more. After a while I called the guard and asked to go to the toilet. "Be patient," I was told. I listened at the door for his footsteps; he did not come. Someone called my name. "Mansur, you here, too?" I knew the voice. It was my good friend Abolghasem Sedehi, a party member. "How are you?" he asked. "Did they beat you, too?"

"I'm all right," I answered. "My legs burn, and they're swollen."

Just then the guard reappeared. "Shut up. No talking!" He led me to the toilet and back. I recognized a number of familiar faces.

By morning I had held several brief conversations with the guard. I asked him where he was from, and after he answered that he was from a distant town, I told him, "I'm not a local man either. My home is far away in Kerman and I haven't seen my family in a long time. Have you seen your family recently?"

He suddenly became very sad and told me, "I was snatched from my hometown and my family to serve in the army. [The practice of kidnapping young boys for service in the military was widespread in Iran then as later.] I haven't seen my family in a long time. I wonder if I'll ever see them again."

Because of his situation and his distress, I thought that I might be able to win his sympathy. I spoke of his missing his family and of my missing my family, and I forced a few tears of sympathy from my eyes. Again I told him, "I have no family here. We are in the same predicament, only you are free and I am in jail."

Later in the evening, when we talked some more, I said, "I'm dying for a cigarette." By now he was sympathetic and offered to give me some of his own cigarettes. I declined, saying, "Will you do me a favor? If I give you a letter to my family to let them know where I am, and you deliver it to one of my father's friends, Ali Zohari, I promise he will give you five dollars. If you buy me one dollar's worth of cigarettes, you may keep the other four dollars for yourself. This is a favor between you and me." He agreed.

After breakfast and before he went off duty, the guard brought me a small amount of butter from his breakfast. He told me to rub it on any place that hurt from my beating. I used part of it to rub onto my back and hip. The rest I gave to a friend who had been left lying in the hall, where he had fallen after returning from the toilet. He was in great pain from being beaten, and the guards hadn't bothered to put him back in his cell. After all, he couldn't go anywhere and his moans and cries that he was dying would frighten the other prisoners. He was close enough so that I could pass the butter to him to put on the raw, angry welts on his buttocks.

The guard returned with the cigarettes the next day, and by evening I was called in by the same officer who had questioned me earlier.

"Are you ready to talk to us? We're waiting." His voice was as wheedling, as seductive as ever.

"If your brother was involved in such a matter, what would you do?" I questioned.

"My brother is not that stupid!" He glared at me and continued. "You're trying to get my sympathy."

"No. I am at your mercy."

"I'll call my soldiers again." Positioned right outside, they entered the room at his words. "Take a good look. At the whips, too." The soldiers retreated once more.

"You dirty animal." He was snarling now. "We can tear you to pieces. Talk! Damn you!" He grabbed my collar and whipped my head back against the wall, once, twice. There was blackness for an instant and then a great pounding in the back of my head. "You'll see. No food. No bathroom. Shit in your room like the animal you are!" With that, he pushed the bell and the guards appeared once more.

"Take him back to his hole!" he ordered.

Aching head in hands, I paced my small room once more. The rhythmic tapping of the guard's heels caught my attention, but instead of inspiring fear, it strengthened me. My pain lessened. I looked around me in the gloom. *I am here because I have a mission,* I thought. *What else do I want? This is my room. My place in the scheme.*

I became calmer, but what was happening to my comrades? Had they taken Dr. Baghai? (I did not know then that he was present in Zohari's house when my messenger arrived with my letter.) How many had been killed? Dr. Baghai had told me that during one long imprisonment he would forget where he was as long as he was provided with reading material. When that was removed and all he had left was his imagination, he still managed to sustain himself with thoughts of the sky. I had been in jail less than two days. I was a fighter for our freedom. I believed in our cause. Even my anger against those who had beaten me was dissipating.

Only a few hours had passed when I was roused roughly from my meditations and herded with my fellow party members to the same office, where the same madman addressed us. "Ah," he began, "it seems there has been a mistake. A slight error." Smoothly, he continued, "It is obvious that you are all good people. We apologize for any misunderstanding. I have a temper; it is my great misfortune. I can see that you are sons of the land. You are right to fight for your beliefs and we want to release you. But of course, we must ask you to sign a paper. Nothing much. Please," he said in a pained voice, pointing at Sedehi, "be sure to have a barber fix your hair before you appear in public."

Sedehi's hair had been clipped down to his skull in great swaths on either side by his tormenters. He grinned. "No. I won't. I'm going to the university tomorrow just as I am." The chief sputtered. "We'll fix it here! One of our barbers will take care of you. If you are seen looking like that, people will laugh at you. You look like a nut. They'll say you are crazy."

Sedehi finally consented, and reluctantly we signed the paper. Not too great a price for freedom. With a final lecture, warning us to stay clear of political involvement, the officer released us.

It wasn't until a later conversation with Dr. Baghai at headquarters that we learned of General Hassan Pakravan's call to the chief of police demanding our release.

"General Pakravan was there with us when Zohari read your letter," Dr. Baghai said, referring to an important general in the shah's army, "and he read it, too. 'They treat him well, huh?' said General Pakravan. 'Yes,' Zohari said, 'how about putting up the five dollars?' And General Pakravan did it! He gave the money for you to his own policeman, your messenger! How on earth do you do it, Mansur? You did it beautifully."

Thereafter, we tried as best we could to carry on party activities. Forbidden to distribute party propaganda pamphlets, we procured safe houses, trusted locations where we could pick up and leave our materials.

A safe location was arranged where we could continue to publish party pamphlets. At this time, all printers had been ordered to demand that all documents be signed by government agents authorizing printing jobs, even seemingly innocuous marriage announcements, for there were many coded messages that were promulgated in this fashion. Dr. Baghai ordered me to find two rooms in one of the poorest neighborhoods in Tehran, where we would be able to set up a small manual printing press to continue publication of our pamphlets. Dressed in the shabby clothes of a peasant, I found the rooms, and several of us, in many trips and at odd hours, took our equipment there. Dr. Baghai donated an old wind-up Victrola and a record of a slow march, the sound of its cadences making a noise similar to that of our antiquated pass press. Ours was a dangerous mission. With no such thing as a free press in the shah's Iran, it was enormously difficult and dangerous to print and distribute several hundred copies of a forbidden pamphlet.

Matters came to a head in December 1953, when Vice-President Richard M. Nixon arrived in Tehran on a state visit. As the motorcade taking the vice-president to the imperial palace for his meeting with the shah passed Tehran University's gate, I, with a crowd of other students, tried to rush the cars, holding up banners and posters that we had concealed beneath our clothing: FREEDOM! FREEDOM! THERE IS NO FREEDOM HERE! and NIXON, WE APPEAL TO YOU AS A DOVE OF PEACE.

But the effort was futile. The police forced us back and then fell on us, striking heads and bodies as we ran back to the open door of the college of technology. The police followed us inside and opened fire with machine guns. The bullets ricocheted and echoed in the marble lobby. Three students were killed instantly and others were seriously wounded, some of them as they clawed frantically at the windows in attempts to escape. Many were taken away. I escaped unhurt but sick at heart at the spectacle of the falling bodies, the blood. I ran, crying, to headquarters to find Dr. Baghai. Over and over he questioned me as I wept.

"Mansur, are you sure? They are dead?"

I assured him it was true. Three of them.

He held his head in his hands for a minute. Then he said, "Go to the school tomorrow and see if those same policemen are on duty."

I did. And they were—the same men. I went to the college of technology and was told that workmen were washing the walls and calking the bullet holes. I returned to headquarters to inform Dr. Baghai. He told one of the party members to take all calls. No one was to enter his room.

"Take down this letter, Mansur," he said, pacing back and forth, pipe in hand, as he always did when dictating.

Vice-President Nixon was scheduled to accept an honorary degree of Doctor of Laws on December 14. On December 12, 1953, we published in *Shahed* Dr. Baghai's open letter to Nixon. A copy of the letter was sent simultaneously to the American embassy, care of Ambassador Loy W. Henderson.

The letter read:

> His Excellency, Richard M. Nixon: On your honorary gown, there are three spots of blood.
>
> Here in Iran, we have no freedom—no sign of freedom or democracy. You have been introduced to some imposters, so-called representatives of the people. They kill our students with machine guns inside the university buildings. You, too, are helping them.

The letter went on to say that there was no freedom or justice available to the people of Iran under this government, and that the vice-president of the United States should not feel honored by this visit. The letter urged that Nixon carry home the message that American policy in Iran was committing a grave error in supporting the shah. Dr. Baghai asked that Nixon boycott the ceremony and refuse the honorary Doctor of Laws degree from Tehran University about to be conferred upon him by "dictators and murderers." He concluded that if the American people knew the truth about Iran, "they will think more deeply about future world peace."

Nixon accepted the degree.

In September 1956 I answered the phone in Dr. Baghai's home. It was General Hossein Azmoudeh, the army prosecutor general, asking for Dr. Baghai. After a brief conversation, Dr. Baghai hung up and informed me that he had been asked to present himself at the tribunal the next morning. "They told me if I don't show up myself, they'll come and get me," he said.

"What will you do?" I asked.

"What else?" he replied. "I will go."

The next morning, two other party members and I accompanied Dr. Baghai in a cab to the tribunal. Headquarters had informed the press and, as we left the cab, reporters surrounded Dr. Baghai, snapping his picture and interrupting one another as they questioned him. Several soldiers grabbed at their cameras and notepads, screaming invectives and threats. One soldier ordered Dr. Baghai to accompany him into the courtroom. Dr. Baghai complied, having previously warned us to leave immediately after dropping him off.

He looked back at us as he was led away, making a shooing motion with his hand. But it was too late. A few of the reporters ran, but one of them and the three of us from headquarters were grabbed by the soldiers. We protested in vain that we had only accompanied Dr. Baghai, that no one had ordered our appearance. It was futile. We were pushed and jerked up the stairs and into a room on the second floor. "Stay here!" the soldiers ordered, backing us up against a wall. Dr. Baghai was nowhere in sight.

Just then, General Azmoudeh entered the room. He was about fifty, tall, emaciated, with long, bony arms that almost reached his knees. His lips were black. It was rumored that he was heavily addicted to opium.

General Azmoudeh took several slow steps toward the middle of the room, then turned abruptly and glared at us. Just as abruptly, he began pacing. This was the man who had been the judge of Dr. Mossadegh and his followers for the execution of at least sixty men. We were scared witless.

"You!" He addressed the man on my left. "What's your name? What's your business?"

The man gave his name and told him that he was a businessman.

"Party member?"

"Yes, party member."

At this, General Azmoudeh raised his arm and struck him full in the face, splitting his lip.

I was next.

"Name?"

"Mansur Rafizadeh."

"Business?"

"Student," I answered.

"Party member?"

"Party member."

Wham! He caught me such a blow on my ear that I am partially deaf to this day. My head cleared slowly, but he wasn't through.

"Law school? Free tuition and you become a traitor?" His voice was a shriek. Wham! Same ear. I was silent. I couldn't see. I couldn't hear.

The man on my right answered that he was a farmer and a party member.

"Son of a bitch! Another one! Why are you here? Why aren't you on your farm this morning? Traitor!" He smashed the man's nose. Then he paced from one to another of us, thrusting his furious red face into ours in turn. His shrill voice rose higher and higher.

An adjutant scurried behind the general as he moved, saluting smartly every time the general glanced at him, his face dead serious. Now the general moved to the desk, picked up a heavy club, turned slightly to the saluting adjutant, and strode quickly back to us. The adjutant stepped right behind him.

"Goddammit! Farmer! Merchant! Student! Dammit! Dammit! You bastards. You sons of bitches. You think you can dictate policy in this country." He alternated his words with kicks, slaps, curses, and punches, striking our legs, particularly the kneecaps, with the short, thick club. Whack! "Did you ever serve in the army?" Crack! "You traitors!" An eye. "You filth." A nose again. We were numbed. All of us fought to keep an upright position. It would be even worse if we sank to the floor. The soldiers guarding each exit kept their faces rigidly averted from the scene. He hit the side of my head once again. This time he hurt his hand and stood shaking it, rubbing his wrist. His face twisted. "You think God will hear you here? Even the braying donkey can't be heard here." He turned to his adjutant. "Full description! Put them in jail!"

"Yessir!"

We made no sound. The adjutant saluted, and the general wheeled and left the room. The officers then took our names and addresses, our places of birth, and our fathers' names, and left us sagging against the wall. We could hear them typing and making calls in the adjoining room.

It was three hours before General Azmoudeh reappeared.

"Everything is set," he said. "The driver is here to take you to jail." His tone was much quieter now—calm. "Why did you make me so angry? You, you go wash yourselves. Get that blood off." We did not move.

The adjutant spoke. "His Excellency is ordering you to wash! Don't you understand the language?"

The general was suddenly angry again. "They are fools, jackasses. They don't understand human language."

After being forcibly washed, we were led into General Azmoudeh's inner office. Dr. Baghai was sitting by the window, staring out, seemingly ignoring the process. But he had heard everything.

General Azmoudeh appealed to him, his voice now soft and quavery, with an odd note. "You know, Dr. Baghai, these boys tried to tell me funny stories. One told me he carried your briefcase, another that he . . . he carried your cane! The third said he polished your shoes. Shoes! Why did they try to make a fool of me? Do they think I'm stupid? They refused to say they were members of your party. They made me furious!"

Dr. Baghai shot us a warning look before we could protest. The general continued. "Why, these boys are like my sons." Now his tone was wheedling. "Why do they make me so angry? Why do they make me beat them?"

Dr. Baghai fixed his eyes on the general. "They are not your children. They are my children. You are a good teacher. You teach violence. The same thing will happen to your own son some day. I'm ashamed for your actions against humanity. Deeply ashamed."

At this, the general sagged. He looked suddenly old. His black lips had become gray. "Dr. Baghai, Dr. Baghai . . ." He faltered. "I have no control of my nerves. I'm so tired. So sick of this job. Do you know what happened to me a few days ago?"

Dr. Baghai did not let him finish. "Just look at this young man's face. Swollen. Look at the blood!"

"Please," the general said, "I want to talk to you privately."

"Privately? If you wanted to see me privately, why didn't you come to my home? Why didn't you ask me to come to yours?"

"I wanted the security of my office," he protested. Then, abruptly changing tack, he wailed, "I hate those reporters. Your men here called them. The reporters were out there waiting when you arrived. All they do is cause trouble!" Now he muttered, "I hate this job. I should be home. I should have been home hours ago for lunch. My nerves are shot! Oh, I don't know what to do." His voice lowered. "I'm angry. Oh, I'm angry. But I am sorry for what happened. Very sorry."

He turned to his adjutant and instructed him to bring the papers the officers had typed. The papers were handed to him instantly by one of the officers. He read them to us.

"You should be put in jail for what you did," he declared. "But because you are friends of Dr. Baghai, I'm not going to . . ." In a quiet tone, he said, "Sit. Sit. Sit." He began to mumble again. "Never make me mad. I'm crazy when I'm mad. I'll tell you all what happened to me. You know, one of my own officers . . ." He glared at us ferociously. "I was informed that he had Communist books in his home. I went there myself. I asked him outright if it was true. He denied it. Denied it! But when my men searched, sure enough—they found some! Oh, I banged his head! I tore up those books and I made a tube of those filthy pages. I crammed it down his lousy throat! His family begged. But I didn't listen. That poor bastard! I beat him unconscious. I want truth, don't you see? No lies!" he shrieked. "He could have told me the truth!" Trembling, he darted his eyes from one to another of us, then to Dr. Baghai.

Dr. Baghai had not budged. Slowly, quietly, he replied, "I heard every word that was said here this morning. They told you no funny stories. All I could think of was your actions, your words. If you can't control yourself in your job, what is the future of this land? What will happen to the country?"

Again, the general diminished visibly. "Oh, so much work. So much pressure on me. I can't stand those reporters. If they hadn't called those reporters . . . I'm sorry. I told you I was sorry." Turning to us, he ordered, "Get out of here. Out! Dismissed! Get back to your business, your farm, your school." He glared. "Out! I want to talk to Dr. Baghai privately."

We wasted no time and headed straight for headquarters. Dr. Baghai appeared shortly afterward. We got no sympathy from him.

"You did not listen. The moment I got out of the cab, you should have left. If you hadn't hung around the reporters, you would not have been grabbed. Like to get your picture in the papers, do you? I've told you time and time again what will happen in such circumstances. Did you think he was going to give you chocolate?"

Dr. Baghai called an informal meeting that afternoon and spoke to a few of us. He pulled no punches. "General Azmoudeh is a sick man. He is a sadist. He gets nervous, shaky. He beats people. Why are such people in such positions? Why are our jails in such conditions? Why is the firing squad in daily operation?" Then he added, "He is sick. But he is not the only one. There are many like him. They should put him in the hospital, where he could be treated." He paused. "Some people think that people steal only because they are in need," he continued. "That is a mistake. Some people love the act of stealing. They are sick. General Azmoudeh is sick. He says one thing, then the opposite. He apologizes to someone and then beats him again. I am sorry that such sick people control our destiny. We are at their mercy. There is no logic in such a man. You can't reason with him."

In a matter of days, Dr. Baghai was summoned once again to General Azmoudeh's office. He was summarily rearrested and interrogated about the assassination five years earlier—on March 7, 1951—of General Razmara, the then–prime minister, and then he was jailed for several months.

Unlike most prisoners, many of whom were sadistically tortured, Dr. Baghai was fortunate even after he was sentenced. His previous power and reputation rendered him a degree of safety. Even if he was not currently in favor, what if he were to succeed those who were presently in power? In the hopeless wrangle of Iranian politics, official decisions hinged on just that possibility for many political prisoners. Dr. Baghai was not unaware of this. His commanding presence and his understanding of his opponents—their uncertainties and confusion— rendered him additional immunity. He was released shortly.

By this time, the summer of 1956, I was out of school and spending most of my time in party activities. Because Dr. Baghai feared that my increasing visibility would cause me personal trouble, he advised me to stay away from headquarters, particularly when I was involved in publishing party pamphlets. But one day I disobeyed him and, as I walked in the courtyard of our headquarters, I saw a convoy of army trucks approach. They screeched to a halt, soldiers poured out, and exits were secured. No one was permitted to enter or leave. One officer, swinging his swagger stick, walked up to me. "Where is Rafizadeh?" he asked harshly.

"I don't know," I answered. "He never gets here until five or six o'clock." He walked up to another man, and I yelled out, "Officer, I told you Rafizadeh never gets here until late!"

"Shut up," he said. "I'm not talking to you." I was shaking in my shoes. But the other men had gotten my message. Each one gave the officer the same answer. He demanded to see the leader, and was taken to the second floor of headquarters, where Dr. Baghai promised that I would report to General Teymour Bakhtiar's office that evening. After the officers left, Dr. Baghai spoke to me. "I told you that it was dangerous for you to be seen around here. I had no choice. I didn't really know that you were here, so I didn't really lie. Go to the head- quarters of the military tribunal tonight and introduce yourself."

"Why did you tell him I would come?"

"Listen, do you want to be in jail tonight or free?"

"Free, of course."

"Then do as I say. Take a taxi to the tribunal. Tell the officer that you want to see General Bakhtiar and that you have a message for him from me. He will receive you. Tell him that one of his officers came to me and was looking for you and that, therefore, Dr. Baghai asked you to present yourself to him. You will talk. Then you will take a cab and come back here."

"Are you sure?"

"I know them, I know their mentality. I'm sure."

When I got to General Bakhtiar's office, I waited no more than fifteen minutes before I was received.

"Dr. Baghai sends his regards," I said. "He does not wish to cause any trouble for your officers. He knows that they have a great deal to do and suggested that I come to see you myself. He also says that in the future if you wish to see any of our members, you should notify us and we will be here within fifteen minutes."

"What's your name?" he asked in a gruff tone.

"Mansur Rafizadeh," I replied. He wrote my name on a piece of paper and told his adjutant to bring my file to him. The adjutant returned in a moment and held the file up to General Bakhtiar with both hands, clicking his heels and inclining his head. General Bakhtiar held the file in front of his face, again with both hands, as though singing in a choir.

Then he inquired, "Why do you distribute pamphlets for the party?"

"I only deliver them," I said. "They are written by Dr. Baghai."

"That is true," he replied, "but why should you be involved?"

"I am a party member. I must follow party orders."

"Uh, huh . . . what's your address?"

"I live with Dr. Baghai."

"With Dr. Baghai? Hmmm."

"Yes, at his home."

General Bakhtiar pondered this for a moment. "Well," he said at length, "I would advise you to slow down. Cut down on such activities. How is Dr. Baghai, by the way? Give him my best regards when you see him. And remember, take it easy. You should not get involved. And if we need you, we'll call you."

I walked out. I had not been there an hour.

When I got back to headquarters, Dr. Baghai said, "You see, they don't know what will happen. They have no faith in the government. If I were to get into power, they can't be sure what I would do in their shoes. None of them will take any responsibility." Dr. Baghai suddenly laughed. "How did you make up your mind so fast," he asked, "when that officer asked if you knew where Rafizadeh was?"

"If you had been beaten by their whips, you'd think fast, too."

He laughed again. "Still, I don't think I would have lied. You were really smart today. I wouldn't have thought of it. You were also shrewd enough to say you lived with me. What could he do? But I was pretty sure of what would happen. I know General Bakhtiar the same as I know you. I know his mentality. He has to keep on my good side."

Dr. Baghai was becoming convinced that it would be beneficial— and a politic move—for me to study in the United States, and he shortly summoned me to discuss the prospect.

"It's a good idea, Mansur," he said. "Our people's greatest need is education. You can see that no one here has any faith in the future. No one assumes any responsibility. People continue to place their faith in leaders who have no self-confidence, no faith in themselves. These people are just like card players who don't want to place their cards next to a loser and are always looking around for the next best bet. They want to back a winner. You are clever. You used an ace in your interview with General Bakhtiar. But you must remember—whatever job is yours in the future—you must accept all the responsibilities the job entails, good and bad. We have had so many demagogues. If you are ever in a position to help, you must be deeply involved with all aspects of your work. You cannot make false promises. You cannot live in an ivory tower. You must never become a fellow traveler. You cannot belong to one philosophy today and another tomorrow. Go to America. It is a wonderful opportunity. Listen and learn." He shooed me out.

The more I thought about the possibility of going to America, the more I liked it. I wanted to learn English. I wanted to learn more about democracy in action. I knew that there were Americans who opposed the shah, and I felt that America offered us some hope for change. I would be an eyewitness to the functions of the UN and the American political process, and I would see how the American press operated. Perhaps some day I would be able to apply American ways to Iranian problems.

My father greatly favored this project. If I were to stay in Iran, he said, it was certain I would have to serve in the army and take a position within the government. Such possibilities were anathema to both of us.

After several visits with my cousin Abbas Rafizadeh, a Sufi leader,[2] I was further persuaded to leave. "Here, Mansur, the sun rises and the sun sets. Nothing ever changes. Our people get out of one ditch and immediately fall in another. We are a hopeless case." Abbas made a reference to a kindly but scary-looking maid who was brought into a family to baby-sit. Each time she picked up the child, the child screamed. The maid asked, "What is wrong? What are you afraid of?" "You!" screamed the child.

"Our leaders are just such horrifying maids," said Abbas, "and we have more to fear from them than anything else. Each new 'servant' is worse than the last. Go! See and learn everything you can. See what the

American government is like, the churches, the society, their relations with one another."

Finally on the night before my departure, Dr. Baghai, over drinks in his library, encouraged me again. "You will learn so much . . . economics, the life of the people. You already have a great deal of knowledge. Go there empty, as though you know nothing. Listen to the people. Don't argue. Don't show off. Learn! That is your only task. Learn! Don't teach. Learn! Even if they talk about Iran, don't say that you know more than they. Listen to them instead. Learn!"

PART II

CHAPTER SEVEN

Culture Shock in the United States

I was met at Idlewild Airport by a woman representative of the American Friends of the Middle East, an organization that helped students in Iran to forward papers to American colleges and universities, to apply for visas, and to locate living quarters with American families. The organization also had volunteers at the other end meeting planes and expediting passage through Customs. The woman had been sent my picture, and I had a photograph of her as well. The plane was early, though, and as I had promised my father that I would wire him as soon as I set foot on American soil, I sought and found a policeman. "Telegram, telegram," I said, hoping against hope he would understand. He took me immediately to the Western Union office, where I wrote my message in phonetic Farsi—Farsi transliterated to the Latin alphabet. The operator placed my message with several others, indicating that they had precedence.

"Regular or fast?" he asked.

"Fast," I answered in halting English and gave him five dollars. "Receipt, receipt, please!"

"We don't give receipts, buddy," he said, adding, "Your message will go out in a few minutes. Don't worry."

No receipt! I was incredulous. It did not seem possible. In government offices in Iran, one couldn't do anything without getting a receipt. My family—how could I be sure they would know of my arrival? Now what?

I went to look for the policeman again and, gesturing frantically to reinforce my faltering English, persuaded him to return with me to the Western Union office. The telegraph operator was astonished at my distrust. He assured me that my father would have the message within hours.

In Iran, to be sure, one always distrusted officials; one had to see something tangible. But, on the other hand, I thought of all the advice I had been given. And here I had disobeyed already. Instead of watching, accepting, learning, I had jumped to conclusions.

I realized that my luggage was becoming heavier with every step. I started to put it down, and then I thought, *People—they will steal . . . !* Here we go again! I tried consciously to open my mind to the new experiences, the constant flow of open faces, the well-dressed people who eddied around this skinny, anxious young man. Suddenly I felt a surge of elation. *I am here!* I realized. *What will I find?*

Just then I spotted a middle-aged woman craning her neck to look around her. She held a picture in her hand and brandished a large signboard that read MANSUR! WELCOME TO AMERICA! I hurried over to introduce myself, and she gave me a kiss of welcome. Her husband relieved me of my bag and her first words were "Have you sent a wire to your family?"

"Yes, yes," I told her, "but no receipt!"

She looked puzzled for a moment. "Oh, I see. No. No receipt here. In America, we trust."

My first destination after New York was St. Michael's College in Burlington, Vermont, where I was to study English (as a second language) until I had satisfactorily completed the course. Tentative arrangements had been made for me to go on to Harvard, contingent on my completing the program at St. Michael's.

Soon after my arrival at St. Michael's, a local man drove me into Burlington so that I could send a wire to my father. It was snowing hard and his car skidded, colliding with another on the slippery highway. I jumped out the passenger's side, spoiling for a fight. The two drivers got out, too—and began calmly to exchange small pieces of paper. "You guilty!" I yelled, pointing at the other driver. "You guilty, your fault." The two men began to laugh. A passing policeman stopped to inquire if he could be of help, but the drivers waved him on. "Everything's under control, Officer," one said. The policeman nodded and drove on. The drivers shook hands with each other and the stranger shook mine. I got back in the car, bewildered. In Iran the same incident would have escalated until forty, fifty, a hundred people were involved on both sides—relatives and friends and anyone who happened to be nearby.

Another revelation awaiting me in America was the freedom that existed between the sexes, a far cry from the chaperoned audiences permitted in Iran. Emboldened by the dances given by volunteers at the YWCA, I joined happily in the fox-trot, rhumba, waltz—able for the first time to speak to a girl in public, to embrace a girl on the dance floor without being clobbered by all her male relatives. I couldn't believe it.

Coffee and doughnuts were served after the dances, and one girl invited me to sit with her. She admired my hair, telling me my curls looked like those of an English judge. Before she left me, she handed me her address and phone number.

Mustering all my courage (I had heard this was step one), I called and asked her if she would go with me to a movie.

"Yes!" she answered easily.

On the evening of our date I read and reread the small scrap of paper she had given me: South Airport, number 27. I admired her circumspection. She had obviously chosen an office (number 27) in a public place (the airport). No one she knew would recognize us, and I would be safe from the onslaught of an angry family. It was a smart plan.

Clutching the address, I hailed a cab and pointed at the paper to show the driver where to take me. He nodded. Not long thereafter, he pulled to the curb and I looked out. Surely there must be some mistake, I said. This was a residential street. Where was the airport? He insisted that it was the right place. The door of the house opened and faces appeared at the front window. I grabbed at the driver's sleeve, nearly frantic. "Nope, nope," he said. "This is it, Twenty-seven South Airport Street." He pointed at the house and, sure enough, the whole family was now coming down the walk, smiling genially.

Inside, the father sat me opposite him in the living room, while the girl and her mother went to the kitchen, from which they reappeared with coffee and cake. I chattered nervously. "Your daughter is so kind," I said. "I came here to study English, to learn about America!" I watched his face carefully. What was he going to do?

Presently he and his wife got up to leave. "My wife and I are going out, too," he said pleasantly. "We'll see you later."

What did that mean? I wondered.

In the dark theater, I held myself stiffly aloof. Who was behind us —her brother? Suddenly her hand touched mine. I jumped and looked around me wildly. I put her hand firmly back in her lap. I would lose my visa. I would be deported, beaten, disgraced! I sat rigidly through the rest of the movie, eyes straight ahead, shoulders squared, feet planted firmly, fists clenched at my knees.

In Iran I would have had no acceptable reason to speak to a girl alone, much less visit her in her home, or take her to a public place. On the contrary, I would have been chased by people throwing stones if I did. Even if I had chanced to see the girl and wished to marry her, all arrangements would have had to be made by one of my female relatives, who would have had to visit the prospective in-laws several times before a meeting, overseen by all the family members, took place. After she served me a special delicacy, presumably one that she herself had prepared, and we had had an opportunity to observe each other at close range and feel an empathy, negotiations would resume between the two families. After this stage, we might meet each other in one or the other's home.

Life for teenage boys is complicated all over the world, but life for a boy growing up in Kerman, who was interested in a little sexual experimentation, was extremely so. I had had a whole battery of cultural problems to deal with. As it was unthinkable to approach any girl from a decent family unless I was ready to commit to marriage, I had had only two realistic options. I could try to find a prostitute, which was risky and difficult, or I could locate a willing neighborhood maid.

When I was seventeen, my problem was solved by Fatima, my next-door neighbor's maid. Fatima was a forty-five-year-old widow, fat and ugly. One day she lured me into their dark basement and seduced me. My first sexual experience was frightening because she held me in her viselike fingers and wouldn't release me until she was satisfied. I was totally inexperienced. She had to guide me through it. When it was over, I lived in dread that someone would find out. I vowed never to let it happen again, but I fell victim to a very interesting kind of blackmail. Fatima, a lusty woman, threatened to tell my family about us unless I continued to service her. Later on, I was humiliated to discover that I wasn't the only one taking care of her needs. To say the least, she was not an exclusive lady.

It was quite common for maids in Kerman to make themselves sexually available to the males of a household or even an entire neighborhood. These women were illiterate, came from impoverished backgrounds, and worked seven days a week. There was no opportunity for a normal social life, so they took scraps of affection where they could.

People could actually gauge the power structure of the household by how attractive its maids were. If the male ruled the roost, they were young and pretty. If the wife had control, they would not necessarily be old, but definitely not pretty.

In very religious Muslim homes, where men were forbidden even to look at a woman who was not a family member, there was a special religious ceremony called *Seegeh*. This sanctified the maid's presence and officially made her a part of the family.

When I went to live in Tehran, things didn't change dramatically. "Nice girls" were still off limits. Sure, there were some innocent flirtations, furtive glances, and silly small talk when I was invited to my friends' and relatives' homes, but I knew that if I dared get too close to any desirable young lady, I would become an instant candidate for marriage. I wanted to go to America, so I had to be very careful.

Fortunately, young men in Tehran did have alternatives. Tehran had a large and easily accessible red-light district. It was called New City, but was new in name only. It was located in an old section filled with large rambling houses. These houses were built in classic Middle Eastern style, in which all of the rooms opened onto a courtyard with a reflecting pool in the center. Occasionally, a few friends and I would organize a night out to New City. These outings had a character all their own.

First we would share a taxi to the district. Then, as soon as we had paid our fare, a pimp would latch on to us and follow us through the winding streets, extolling the virtues of the girls he was handling.

"Come with me! Fresh country girls! And even virgins! Clean and sweet! The most beautiful girls in all of Tehran!"

If you went to the brothel he worked for, you would have no problem getting past the burly doorman, who scrutinized each customer through a grate in the massive doors that guarded these places. If you decided to stay, and used one of the girls, the pimp would get a commission.

Inside, the girls would be lounging on benches around the reflecting pool in an assortment of sexy costumes. A customer could take his time and look them over, but there would come a point when the madam decided you had dallied too long and would start screaming at you. "You've seen all that I have! You can't make love with your eyes! Do it or get out!"

These madams were very tough ladies who wore noisy and jingling change makers around their waists. When you made your choice and paid them, they dispensed different-colored tokens. Each color represented a different price category, ranging from twenty-five cents to fifty cents. Some girls were "red," others "blue," and so on. The payment structure was very organized. You simply handed the girl the correct color token and went off to her room.

The rooms in the whorehouses were filled with mirrors, colorful cloth hangings, gaudy little knickknacks, and always had condoms waiting on a table near the bed.

The last time I went to New City I was the guest of honor at a farewell party and I was too excited to use any tokens. I was going to America.

Now in America, I was still slave to the same urges and prohibitions, but in relaxed America, my conduct became ludicrous. After the movie the girl drove me back to her house, where her father was waiting. "Now," I thought, "now he'll confront me"—but no. It was snowing, and at the end of the evening her father, with great affability, proposed that he drive me back to my dorm. The girl and I sat in the backseat, and once again I felt a hand touching my arm. She kissed me! How could I escape? I moved as close to the door as I could, watching the father's reflection in the rear-view mirror. I was scared stiff. As we neared the dormitory and pulled to the curb, *Here we go,* I thought— but no again. He reached back and shook my hand, inviting me to visit them whenever I wished, and assured me of my welcome.

There were many things that impressed me about America, not the least the supermarkets. One day a woman from one of the families to whom I had been introduced took me to a large shopping mall. I followed her into the market. Looking all around, I wondered where the beggars were, the beggar bouncer. None was in sight. I was sure that this marvelous store had just opened. It was immense, with wide clean aisles and shelves stacked high with bright bottles, cans, and boxes; everything was sparkling, colorful. Each price was clearly indicated, such a contrast to the small dingy grocery stores of Kerman.

I wandered up and down the aisles, amazed at the antiseptically clean display of the long cases of milk and dairy products. I thought of the few straggly, rawboned cows in Kerman, of the milk carrier in Tehran who carried his dirty metal cask of watered milk—measured out with a scoop—going from house to house on his rickety bicycle. In Iran only invalids or small children received milk.

Eggs . . . not individual eggs in a basket, but dozens and dozens, crate upon crate of eggs. I looked around to see if I could find the small box for candling the eggs to see if they contained an embryo. Again there was none. None was needed.

Produce . . . it was packed in neat containers: fruit of every kind;

colorful, fresh vegetables, displayed row upon lavish row. In season the markets of Iran held huge displays of vegetables and fruit—pomegranates as big as melons, berries, oranges. Off season, however, the same items could not be had for love or money.

Bread . . . bread and bakery goods had an aisle all their own. This conjured up images of the women who waited daily in line to buy *sangak,* the one- by three-foot staple bread of Iranians, which cost several pennies for the large, flat, pocked sheet. The poorest people purchased it in fragments.

My friend approached the checkout counter with her cart full. I watched as the items rolled past the cashier. There was no scale, and all the food was packed in large paper bags. No scrap paper here! No beggars saying, "God is merciful. Give something to me."

I bombarded my friend with questions as we left. "Did the store close at noon? Would the store shelves be empty by then? Is that why there were so many shoppers with full wagons? Why was it so big? Was it the only one in the city? Could you really buy as much as you wanted? Did people bribe the manager to hide away a piece of meat for them?"

"No," she said. "The store is open every day and the shelves are always full. It really isn't so big; there are many that are bigger and better stocked. Of course, there is no bribery and no need for it. There is no rationing. You can buy anything and as much of it as you want —it isn't considered hoarding."

In Iran the punishment for hoarding had usually been a public whipping. My father had told me that years earlier the governor of our hometown was informed that a local baker was hoarding flour. When the governor searched the premises after the shop had closed for the day, he found the trembling baker—and several hundred pounds of flour. In this case the baker became the loaf and was thrust into his own oven.

I was incapable of expressing the riot of thoughts that this "ordinary" American supermarket had evoked in me. My English was inadequate. All you had to do was pay. You could do it again the next day and the next. This abundance existed every day. I was amazed.

At my friend's home, I pondered as I rinsed the lettuce for our salad. "Where's the permanganate?" I asked.

"What for?"

"You know—to get off the, the . . ." I faltered over the word.

She laughed. "Don't worry. That's against the law here. We use chemical fertilizers. Just wash it."

Several other things impressed me. In a small town in Vermont, all the inhabitants had piped gas in their stoves while the inhabitants of Kerman and Tehran, the capital of Iran, one of the biggest oil-producing nations in the world, used charcoal, wood or dung, and any kerosene used was carried into the house in cans. There was always the possibility of an explosion.

More amazing still for me were the evening news broadcasts. Senators and representatives and the president himself were introduced without fanfare, without effulgent titles. Their words were even interrupted by beer and soap commercials.

But I was impressed, above all, by the pleasantness and friendliness of the ordinary American families who took us on outings, fed and entertained us. Most of the people I met were genuinely concerned and interested in the foreign students. We were asked our food preferences and prohibitions; they seemed happy to learn of our customs. In my poor English, I tried to explain the conditions in my country and what was happening to its government. But by now I was learning to listen to the words of others. I was becoming a closed box at last.

Nevertheless, my first four months in the United States were overwhelming. My English was extremely limited and I wouldn't dare leave my room without my Persian-English dictionary. Still, I wanted to be well liked and didn't discourage any friendly overtures by my new American acquaintances.

I had come to Vermont totally unprepared for the bitter cold winters, so when a nun took pity on my plight and offered to take me shopping for warm clothing, I eagerly accepted. Armed with my dictionary, I arranged to meet her on the highway and spent the next few hours roaming from discount factory outlet to discount factory outlet, buying everything from long underwear to heavy outer clothing.

Sister Mary Elizabeth had a kind and beautiful face. Her vibrant green eyes and flawless white skin were highlighted by the severity of her dark habit. It was difficult to gauge how old she was, but I felt that she might be in her early thirties. After our exhausting shopping expedition, she insisted on taking me to dinner. We had a very pleasant meal, but when we left the restaurant it was snowing heavily. Sister Mary Elizabeth evaluated the situation and told me that the roads were too dangerous for me to return to the school. It would be far preferable for her to take me to her sister's home, which was nearby, and then drop me off at school the next morning before breakfast. Hesitantly, I agreed.

When we arrived at her sister's apartment, no one else was there. Mary Elizabeth casually explained that her sister was skiing. She graciously showed me around, but I felt extremely awkward about being alone with her. She made me coffee and prepared the couch for me to sleep on. As I sat rigidly on the couch, she pointed to her door and explained that it wouldn't be locked. I looked at her blankly. Finally, she realized that I didn't understand what the word "lock" meant. She took my dictionary and we looked up its meaning together. She pointed out the word and I nodded in recognition. "Oh! Lock."

Then she explained that she was going to take a shower and left. After a few minutes, she appeared momentarily in her doorway wearing a diaphanous nightgown. I was startled to see how beautiful and curvaceous her body was. I tried not to stare, and after what seemed an eternity she finally left for the shower. While she was gone, I quickly took off my clothes and slipped under the covers in my underwear. I lay there in the dark, thoroughly confused. I had never known a nun before, but I knew her behavior was certainly strange.

After her shower, Sister Mary Elizabeth returned to the living room and asked, "Do you need anything?" "No," I answered. She approached and sat on the floor next to me and began to stroke my fingers. "You have such beautiful long fingers. Do you play the piano?" She had changed into an even more diaphanous nightgown, and I could see the nipples on her breasts swelling. I was getting extremely excited myself. I had not been with a woman since I left Tehran, and I was a very horny young man, but I was too scared to make any moves. Mary Elizabeth began to caress my neck and I pulled away. Then she took my hand and led me to the bedroom. At last, thinking that she understood the situation, she exclaimed, "You're a virgin!" I stared and she asked, "Are you a virgin?" Getting no response she ran back to the living room and got my dictionary. She fumbled through it and pointed to the word. I recognized "virgin" and started laughing hysterically. Fatima and the countless nights spent at New City flashed through my head. Finally, I stopped laughing and said, "You're the daughter of God." And she said, "You're the son of God, too." Then I said, "I'm not. I'm not a saint." Then I showed her the word for nun in Farsi, clearly describing a nun as the daughter of God. As she began to laugh uncontrollably herself, her beautiful black hair swung from side to side. I didn't know what to do, so I stalled. Then I said, "I don't want marriage or babies. I have no protection." She giggled and said, "Don't worry, I'll take care of that."

With all of these details cleared up, I relaxed and we started to kiss. We began to make love, so frantically that a plant fell down on us. Undaunted, we continued to make passionate love all night long.

That night I learned five new English words—lock, virgin, nun, magnificent, and the four-letter Anglo-Saxon word for fornication.

We began what would become a lengthy and wonderful affair. When I went on to Harvard, Sister Mary Elizabeth came to visit me in Cambridge. She was a beautiful and sensitive person, for whom I shall always reserve a special place in my heart.

By the end of six months at St. Michael's, I spoke English fairly well, and was ready to attend Harvard. There I found new wonders. This famous university was made up of many disparate buildings scattered throughout the town. The structures, neither constructed of marble nor, for the most part, of any magnificence, were not surrounded by walls or iron fences. People wandered freely in and out the many entrances and paths. Such freedom, I thought. Such simplicity . . .

My memory could not rest. As I looked around the quiet Harvard grounds, I recalled the bloody hands of my fellow students in Tehran clutching at the windows as they fell. In this free, friendly, and warm atmosphere I could never be content, I realized; my mind was not at peace. What is a campus? A place of quest, of learning? Or simply an escape?

Mansur's father,
Mohammad Rafizadeh

Mansur's mother,
Malekeh Rafizadeh

Mansur at age fourteen

Mozafar Rafizadeh,
Mansur's youngest brother,
when he visited Mansur in jail
as a six-year-old

Dr. Mozafar Baghai (center) with Mansur (to the right) and other students, arriving at the tribunal in Tehran on September 18, 1956

Mansur (center) with Dr. Manucher Eghbal, the chancellor of Tehran University, to his left

Mansur in 1958 when he was a student at Harvard

Mansur with his father
(seated), his mother, and
his sister Sadri in New York

Dr. Mozafar Baghai in Tehran

Dr. Baghai in 1961 while in
prison in Tehran

Former Chiefs of SAVAK

General Hassan Pakravan

General Nematollah Nassiri

General Nassiri awaiting execution
by a firing squad after being found
guilty by the Islamic Revolution
Court of killing many innocent
people

General Nasser Moghadam

Mansur with his father
(seated), his mother, and
his sister Sadri in New York

Dr. Mozafar Baghai in Tehran

Dr. Baghai in 1961 while in
prison in Tehran

Former Chiefs of SAVAK

General Hassan Pakravan

General Nematollah Nassiri

General Nassiri awaiting execution
by a firing squad after being found
guilty by the Islamic Revolution
Court of killing many innocent
people

General Nasser Moghadam

Prince Reza Pahlavi when he was training in the
United States Air Force in Texas

AZIZ RASHKI

Le Rosey soccer team in Switzerland in 1935. Mohammad Reza Pahlavi, holding the ball, was the captain. Hossein Fardoust is at the upper left, and Richard Helms, also a teammate, is seated to the left of the shah.

The shah
in Tehran with
General Haj Ali Razmara,
whom he later
had killed

CHAPTER EIGHT

Meeting John F. Kennedy; Joining SAVAK

In early 1959 a lawyer, a Democrat from Boston, introduced me to Senator John F. Kennedy at a party. On that occasion I explained Iran's situation again. Kennedy listened carefully and made a promise that if he were elected president in 1960, he would advise the shah to undertake social reforms and enforce the Constitution of Iran. Kennedy also said that several friends of his would be greatly interested in my views and would soon be in touch with me to discuss them. His words were quite convincing.

Not long thereafter, a reporter from *The New York Times* and another from *Time* magazine contacted me and, later that year and in 1960, published several articles critical of the shah. Later still, another individual contacted me, introducing himself as an employee of the U.S. State Department. He was insistently inquisitive, questioning me over and over on the politics of Iran. Only a few years later did I learn that he was a CIA man. Thus in innocence began my first tenuous involvement with American intelligence.

I had recorded my conversation with Senator Kennedy in my diary and, although unable to write directly to or receive a direct letter from Dr. Baghai because of censorship, I found a messenger to carry an account of it to him. He shared this information with his best friend, Ali Zohari, who wrote me a twenty-page letter from Paris.

Zohari did not share my enthusiasm for Kennedy's marked cordiality. "All such men," he wrote, "promise many things when they are not in power, but because such promises are a threat to power, they forget them quickly once they get into office. Going along with a situation is so much easier. He will talk to the shah, certainly," he continued, "—but he will never tell him outright, 'Do as we say or you'll get no help from us.' Mansur, my experience tells me that such a thing would never happen.

"If Kennedy gets to power, all he will do is talk politely to the shah —'We love you. Now, please, don't do this, don't do that.' Then the shah will scare Kennedy with the Communist bogeyman and nothing at all will happen. Don't get your hopes up. If you talk to Kennedy again, don't hold your breath." Zohari's letter ended with: "American foreign policy has a love affair going with the shah. Nothing is going to change."

Later in Washington, after Kennedy's election, I discussed Zohari's letter with a professor who was close to Kennedy. He told me that Zohari was mistaken: The United States would encourage reform in Iran. Again I asked him to use whatever influence he had to make sure that the shah received no aid or moral support in his present course of government.

Meanwhile, I had begun to lose interest in Cambridge and in my classes, as I had earlier at Tehran University. Instead of studying, I focused all my attention on politics. Soon after I had finished my work with a group of researchers at the International Center who were compiling a book on the Farsi and English languages,[3] I moved to New York City.

In New York my first goal was to start a newspaper for Iranians currently in the United States. In order to do this, I solicited funds from Iranians in the States and Europe who were sympathetic to our cause. The result was *Shahab* (Shooting Star), a four-page newsletter published monthly and highly critical of the Iranian government. An "Open Forum" consisting of two columns, one on social reform and one on revolution, invited letters from readers on either topic. As editor in chief, in my editorials I strongly advocated social reform, still believing that revolution would destroy Iran, delaying the advent of freedom. We urged the enforcement of the Constitution, the conferring of human rights and education.

Before I left Tehran for the United States, I had gone to say good-bye to General Pakravan, then the deputy chief of SAVAK,[4] a man whom I had known and respected for many years and a friend of Ali Zohari's. At our late-afternoon meeting, he told me about troubles within his organization, particularly the lack of high-caliber officers. He wanted to recruit men to improve SAVAK.

"We greatly lack good people," he said. "Why don't you join us? You see what these people are—brutal. They have even beaten you up. You could help stop such wrongdoing to some extent if you were working with us."

At that time, I was able to excuse myself gracefully by telling him that I was leaving for the United States. But from the States, I sent him books and kept in communication with him.

In September 1959, when General Pakravan arrived in New York, I went to see him. The newsletter, *Shahab,* and my stand on issues had become known to SAVAK. However, the intelligence organization did not consider me an opponent of the shah, only an opponent of revolution. The general told me that SAVAK was opening branch offices in several countries, including the United States, and proposed once again that I join the organization and establish an office in the States.

I was skeptical. How could I join an organization that I knew from my own experience had suppressed freedom in Iran? But General Pakravan was persuasive.

"Look, Mansur," he said, "we need good people. No one can force you to take this job or to do anything against your principles. But someone will take the job and that someone may be evil. If you believe in good, take the office and do good in your capacity in the office. If you find anything that is repugnant to you, you can resign. But the job will put you in a position of awareness. And if you don't take it, they'll send someone from Iran. Get involved, Mansur."

It was hard to refute his logic. However, I delayed my decision. "I don't think your office will hire me anyway," I told him. "I have a bad record with them."

I sent a message to Ali Zohari, the founder and former editor in chief of *Shahed,* and asked him to discuss the matter with General Pakravan and with Dr. Baghai. "Better you than another," Zohari wrote back, echoing General Pakravan. Dr. Baghai and Ali Zohari both agreed that I should join SAVAK. They wanted to have someone "good" on the inside who could serve as a conduit for them. I was flattered by their faith in my ability, but I knew that I couldn't allow vanity to get in the way of making such an important decision.

Complicating matters even further, at my last meeting with General Pakravan, he had smiled slyly and said, "I have a great future mission for you." What had he meant? Had he singled me out for something special? Did I dare believe it was to get rid of the shah? Or was I reading too much into that remark, and all he really wanted was to raise standards in his organization and merely thought of me as someone who would enhance his staff?

It was after midnight September 1959 and I found myself sitting alone in a Greenwich Village coffee shop trying to peal away the layers of emotion that were preventing me from making a rational decision. The most prevailing feeling was fear. How would my friends respond if I joined the most despised arm of the shah's government? I was placing my future in jeopardy; these people wouldn't hesitate to kill me if they should find it expedient.

Then I began to think of ways to conquer my fear and channel my energies into more positive directions. I remembered my father telling me, "When you are free of fear and you are no longer swayed by people's opinions of you, perhaps then you will be capable of ruling your emotions and of helping others."

At the same time, I still hadn't clarified my feelings about the shah. Was he a barbarian who took away the people's rights or was he a leader who, whatever his faults, was truly interested in bringing his backward country into the twentieth century? I was so confused that I even tried to analyze the shah in percentages. Was he 50 percent bad and 50 percent good, 30 percent bad and 70 percent good, or 80 percent bad and 20 percent good? I finally decided he was 80 percent bad and 20 percent good. Who was I kidding?

I ultimately thought of what I would do. I would work for SAVAK in "another persona." I would wear the mask of the loyal supporter, but I would actually quietly bore from within. Extremely troubled, I turned to my father for advice, and entreated a friend returning to Iran to hand-deliver a letter to him in Kerman.

A week later I received a box of delicacies from Kerman. Secreted under the candy was a letter from my father:

> Think of the shah as a bull. If you take the job you will always have to hold his tail. You can do a great deal of harm to him in the right spot by holding his tail, and no one can harm you with him in front of you. Of course, if the bull finds out who is holding his tail, he will kick you.
>
> I believe you are right. The shah is 80 percent evil and 20 percent good, but I also believe that if you do this, there is a 100 percent chance that you will be a witness to his downfall . . .
>
> If you join SAVAK, don't confide in anyone! No one should know what your true intentions are.

His letter helped me make up my mind. I would join SAVAK, but I would have to formulate a plan immediately.

At the same time, I had a blind faith in the American system of government and honestly believed that if American leaders really knew what was going on inside Iran they would withdraw their support. I would offer my services to the CIA and keep them informed.

I promised myself that I wouldn't work for SAVAK unless I could be based in the United States. That way, I could best accomplish my personal mission and not be involved with any dirty work in Iran. I pledged myself to the removal of the shah. It was as if I had taken a holy vow. Sadly, I also realized that I would have to give up any dreams I had of a normal family life.

Meanwhile, shortly after I was asked to join SAVAK, Ali Zohari died—of heart disease at the age of forty-seven. He had appealed for a passport so he could be treated at Massachusetts General Hospital in Boston, where I had friends. But the shah had denied his appeal, apparently fearing Zohari's impact in America, and the courageous journalist had died in Tehran.

A year later, as was customary on the first anniversary of a death, friends and family gathered at the cemetery for a ceremony. Still undecided, I flew from New York to Tehran in order to attend, and after the ceremony, Dr. Baghai, General Pakravan, and I paused to talk. As General Pakravan and I looked at each other, our tears flowed because of the loss of our friend. Trying to explain what had happened, he said, "Rafizadeh, I asked the shah for the passport, but he refused. And Zohari died." As General Pakravan resignedly threw up his arms, I could see tears in Dr. Baghai's eyes. Even an appeal from the chief of SAVAK for a single passport had been denied by the shah.

So I made the decision that it would be advantageous for all concerned if I took the post, to be within the organization so that Dr. Baghai and his friends would be kept aware of events. I knew these people and the way they thought, and I knew I could be of help— without abrogating my principles.

An application, written entirely in Farsi, was sent to me. It required that I take a physical examination and that the physician stamp the papers.

"How on earth can something stamped 'Top Secret' in Farsi require the signature of an American doctor?" I asked General Pakravan.

"You see?" said the general. "You see why we need you? That's just the kind of work we get from these people. You can get a physical later in Tehran."

General Pakravan submitted my application to the office of General Teymour Bakhtiar, chief of SAVAK in Tehran. Bakhtiar read it, called

for my file, and saw my record. When the application was returned to
Pakravan, the note, in Bakhtiar's handwriting, read, "The said person,
because of record of political activity and imprisonment, is not qualified
to be hired by this office. Rejected."

General Pakravan answered by saying that he had been in communication with "said person," who "promises that he will not get involved with politics again." He requested that Bakhtiar reconsider. The
answer came back: "Okay with this office." So in 1959 I was officially
hired by SAVAK. Station: New York. Duty: Unknown. There was no
interview, nothing. I was SAVAK in the United States.

CHAPTER NINE

SAVAK Assignment

I was completely unequipped for the position. I had had no training in intelligence work. I did not know what to do or how to do it. But to General Pakravan, who shortly became chief of SAVAK in Tehran, I was an invaluable asset. Because we had known each other so long and so well, sharing the same philosophy and opinions about Iran, he had absolute faith in me.

Initially my cover was that of a student and subsequently that of a diplomat assigned to the UN. For the first six months I was given no duties. When at the end of that time General Pakravan returned to New York, I voiced my dissatisfaction. I told him I was representing SAVAK in the United States, but I was doing nothing.

Wagging his finger at me, General Pakravan said, "All I want you to do is to be SAVAK in this country. I do not want anyone else in this job; you must be careful not to do anything that would jeopardize your position. You will have a great mission in the future—just wait and see. I know you will be successful in completing this mission." He paused, then added, "I do not think I, myself, can get along with the inner circle of the shah."

"If you can't get along with them," I wondered aloud, "how can I?"

"Your job is different from mine," General Pakravan said. "I will try to keep my job, but I'm not sure I can."

Again I raised the question, "What should I be doing here?"

"All you have to do, Mansur, is read the newspapers," he answered. "Whenever you find an article about Iran, save it. Do a favor for me also—read *The New York Times Book Review,* and if there are any good books, buy them for me. Then, twice a month, send all the clippings and books to my office in a diplomatic pouch. Do not forget the book reviews. That is what you have to do.

"Also, you know some SAVAK officials have relatives—sons, brothers, cousins—in the United States. We'll introduce these people to you gradually, and they will work for you as agents. Their job will be similar to yours. They will send newspaper clippings to you; then you will send them to us."

"Is that all I have to do in the United States?" I asked.

"Let us hope that is all," General Pakravan responded. "I will talk to the chief of the CIA in Tehran and describe you as our liaison officer in the United States. I will tell him how good you are. This will be your real mission: Little by little, you will inform the CIA about what is happening in Iran—without my knowledge, of course. Be sure to stress our lack of freedom," he emphasized.

Soon some young men were assigned to me as agents. They assumed their duties of collecting newspaper articles and sending them to me. However, I did not send General Pakravan every article I received. I selected only those critical of the shah's regime, as pro-shah articles were already being sent to the Iranian State Department by the press attaché of the Iranian embassy in Washington.

In addition to my official duties, other time-consuming requests were made. SAVAK officials had relatives or friends who came to the United States to obtain medical care. Often I would receive a message from Tehran informing me about ailing family members or friends. When they arrived, I would pick them up, take them to the hospital, and make sure they received proper treatment.

Iranian parents dote on their children and will do anything to ensure their success. An old expression captures this attitude: "A parent is happy to have his child stand on him if it will make the child look taller." The universities in the United States were considered the finest in the world, and Iranian parents believed that if their children had degrees from American universities they would be assured of success.

Many SAVAK officials' children were entrusted to me. Practically every officer and many of their friends had at least one child attending an American college. I had to watch over them like a loving father. I received their grades and reported them to their parents; I doled out their money so they would not squander it; in particular, I monitored their behavior to avoid scandal and prevent heartache. If a child was killed in an automobile accident, I was the one who had to go to the college to attend to the funeral arrangements and send his effects back to Iran. I had so much contact with the students that some of them began to call me "Godfather."

Every high-ranking official in SAVAK had either a child or a sick relative or friend under my care. The Office of the Supervisor of Iranian Students in the United States, attached to the embassy in Washington, was officially in charge of the thousands of Iranian students in the United States, but this office did little or nothing for them. The select group with which I worked gave me a great advantage: I became privy to many family secrets.

When I received an official call from SAVAK in Iran, only the first few minutes were spent on SAVAK business. The remainder of the time —sometimes up to two hours—I would spend listening to a litany of worries and requests: "I haven't heard from my son in three weeks! Please find out what he is doing." "My mother will be coming to New York next month; watch over her." "Is my boy coming home for the summer?" Of the hundreds of communications that were sent to me every year from Tehran, 95 percent concerned personal affairs. No one would risk losing this indispensable service by questioning anything I did.

I gained more satisfaction from my unofficial duties than from my intelligence work. I was able to concentrate on benefits—education and medical care—that the people could not get in Iran. The money that SAVAK spent on these functions was not wasted. My student agents, who came from poor families in most cases, would have unable to complete school if it had not been for their SAVAK employment. At the same time, their American education opened their eyes to the injustices in Iran, and in future years some of them became the "snakes" coming out of the sleeve of the shah to lead the opposition against him. Among these students were children of some of the shah's highest-ranking officials, including the daughter of his prime minister, and children of high-ranking officers in SAVAK.

Even my menial job of sending newspaper clippings was of great value to me. Because, believe it or not, the high-ranking SAVAK officials had no access to American publications and they welcomed the opportunity to see what the United States was printing about the shah's regime. They never saw the clippings sent by the press attaché because those went only to the royal palace and the Iranian State Department. There was no sharing of these materials because SAVAK was looked upon as a sort of stepchild who was not worth the effort. Since the press attaché sent only flattering articles, they were of little use anyway.

In 1963 SAVAK issued a new order. I was to translate the clippings into Farsi and send them and the translations to Tehran. The reason given for this new procedure was a lack of personnel in Tehran to do translations. However, I had the same problem. Because it was impossible to translate all of the articles, I did the important ones myself and had my agents handle some of the others.

When our bimonthly package of clippings and translations arrived in Tehran, General Pakravan would sort them, select those he liked, remove the books I had sent, and forward the remainder of the dispatch to the office for processing. There, each article would be typed, numbered, and filed. At each step, the workers read them as well as filing or numbering them.

However, in 1964 our translating duties stopped abruptly. While I was briefly in Tehran, General Pakravan informed me of a new policy. Banging his fist on his desk, he said, "Mansur, remember what I told you to do? You have done a superlative job. But now His Majesty the Shah has ordered us to establish a new office in SAVAK—one strictly for translation. You won't have to translate articles anymore."

He did not have to tell me that the shah was trying to keep this information from SAVAK employees so that fewer would be able to learn the truth.

From then on, I had less work. I sent the clippings raw to the new office for translation and processing.

For financial reasons, many of my agents sought to curry favor with the shah. Most of them were the sons of SAVAK officials or other bureaucrats, and they did not know that ordinarily I sent only derogatory material about the shah to Tehran. They would write glowing articles about Iran for their college newspapers and send us the published articles. Beforehand, they would have notified their fathers, who awaited the articles eagerly, so that I had no choice but to send them on. As soon as an article reached Tehran, the proud father would put pressure on the office to include it in the bulletin that went daily to the shah. The shah was unaware that many of these college newspapers had a very small circulation—maybe two hundred copies. Assuming that the article had reached a large audience, the shah would send a handsome reward to the student in gratitude for his services. This money was wired to me, and the father would instruct me to parcel it out to his son over a period of months to prevent him from wasting it.

Despite all of these time-consuming activities, I did not neglect

General Pakravan's real purpose for me: to tell Americans the truth about Iran. Among other things, I struck up acquaintances with reporters and tried to convince them to write articles disclosing the shah's suppression of freedom in Iran. General Pakravan knew what I was doing, but the rest of SAVAK did not. Because I was able to inform them of critical articles before they were published, they thought that I had penetrated the hostile publications and could find out what they were planning to publish in the future. I was gaining a reputation for clever intelligence work. The shah was told that SAVAK in the United States could literally read the minds of the reporters before their material was printed!

Indeed, I even used my American press contacts to protect my mentor, as witness the following excerpt from *Time,* February 17, 1961:

> In the rugmaking city of Kerman, anti-government Candidate Mozaffer Baghai had won three times before with large majorities; this time he was credited with only 27 votes against 2,000 for his government opponent. Baghai promptly sent a cable to U.N. Secretary-General Dag Hammarskjold complaining that the government "has suppressed all rights and freedoms." With equal promptness, . . . Baghai was jailed.

The reporters sent me letters of appreciation and complimentary copies of the publications, which I kept in my office safe.

Besides receiving credit from the shah as well as SAVAK for anticipating these articles, I managed to steal some glory from the press attaché in Washington. Whenever I discovered that the attaché had been meeting regularly with a reporter, I would tell the head office that I had met the reporter at a party and convinced him of some accomplishment of the shah. In the future, it was hoped, he would publish the information, which was, of course, fraudulent. The shah loved these articles. Unfortunately, he cared more about having a good image in the eyes of foreigners than about having a good reputation in the eyes of his own people.

To the press attaché's consternation, I frequently obtained the articles and wired them to General Pakravan in Iran before the attaché sent them to the shah. Many times the shah said to General Pakravan: "I don't know to whom I should give the credit—to SAVAK or the press attaché!"

By 1965 I had achieved such prestige with both SAVAK and the shah that I had no detractors. SAVAK officials relied on me to assist

their families in the United States. The shah credited me with responsibility for both positive and negative articles about Iran. Compared with
my accomplishments, the press attaché appeared both disloyal and
dishonest because he submitted only one-sided reports. With agents
all over the country,[5] I could obtain far more information than he
could. I had become invincible—like a god; no one would dare speak
against me.

I used my position as best I could to moderate the cruelties of the
regime in Iran. With the passage of time, the regime exerted increasing
pressure on SAVAK agents for firsthand reports on anti-shah activists
in the United States. As this was official SAVAK policy, I had to
comply. But I made a personal resolution that the reports leaving my
office would be so innocuous that if the person involved ever had an
opportunity to see his own file in SAVAK headquarters, he or she
would be able to say of me, "God bless him."[6]

I also did my best to prevent SAVAK from arresting and torturing
any Iranians who returned to Tehran from the United States. If the
person had come directly from Iran to the States and had not lived in
any other country, protecting him was relatively easy. But if he had
spent time in other countries, such as Germany, there might be incriminating information in the files that I could not refute. Such people were
harder to protect. Still, if I thought that a particular person was in
danger, I would withhold his passport so that he could not return to
Iran. If the prospective trip home was necessitated by illness in the
individual's family or some other pressing personal problem, I would
plead with the SAVAK office in Tehran not to imprison him, asking
that they let him return to the United States as proof that SAVAK did
not take political prisoners. My influence in SAVAK enabled me to
negotiate with them in this way. For the minor offenders, I could easily
obtain immunity, but I did not trust SAVAK when it came to more
serious offenders, such as Mohammad Nakhshab, a student who was
extremely active in the antigovernment movement, especially with the
religious fringe. I accompanied such individuals to and from Tehran to
ensure their safe return to the United States.

In spite of my efforts, there were a few cases in which Iranians were
jailed and tortured after their return to Tehran from the United States.
Two men from California and one from New York were imprisoned
and tortured. The worst case, however, was that of an Iranian, who had
been living in Texas, outspoken in his opposition to the shah. He spent
about one hundred days in jail and was tortured repeatedly. Not even
General Nematollah Nassiri, who succeeded General Pakravan as chief

of SAVAK in 1965, was able to help. The man's American wife vehemently protested to the United States Congress about her husband's imprisonment and torture. Concerned, congressmen approached Ambassador Ardeshir Zahedi, who appealed to me to use my influence with General Nassiri to obtain the man's release. As a last resort, the ambassador appealed directly to the shah. After the shah allowed the man to be released and returned to America, he publicly complained about his torture. The monarch, incensed by negative publicity from the Human Rights Commission and an article in *Playboy* magazine, reprimanded Zahedi for requesting the man's release.

The students who finished their education in the United States and returned to Iran were not imprisoned or tortured; but the reports filed against some of them, even though they had never been acted upon, prevented these young people from obtaining teaching positions in colleges and universities.

Although there were many activist students from the province of Kerman, there were practically no files on them. If a file did exist, it would contain only harmless information. I was shamelessly partial toward those from my own hometown.

Even the people in Kerman relied on me for help. For instance, one man's son had been missing in Iran for several months, and the family asked me to determine what had happened to him. The father was uncertain whether his son had been killed, imprisoned, or simply forced into hiding. On a timely visit to Tehran, I went immediately to General Nassiri, who informed me that the young man had been killed.

In a similar case of a missing son, the father was a physician in my hometown who had taken care of me as a child; the mother was from a respected family. Her father had been active in economic affairs in Kerman and had done much for the city. I contacted General Nassiri about this case as well, and he responded that the son had not been killed, nor was he in SAVAK's custody. When I passed the message on to the family, they did not believe that General Nassiri had told me the truth. Because I knew the mother was literally going insane with worry, I decided that I must find out for certain if General Nassiri was being straight with me. On my next trip to Tehran, I visited the general at his home, where he was playing with his only son, a seven-year-old whom he adored. As soon as the boy ran to me, I caught him by the hand and held on to him. "General," I said, "do you love your son?"

"Mansur," he chided me, "do not even ask a question like that! I love him more than anything in the world!"

I looked him directly in the eye. "I know of a mother and father who are desperately worried because they do not know what has happened to their son. Please tell me the truth: Is the boy dead?"

"Whom do you mean?" he asked.

I told him. I still held firmly to the little boy's hand, preventing him from returning to his father.

"You asked me about him before," the general said. "What did I say? I don't recall."

"You told me that he was neither dead nor in SAVAK's custody, but the family does not believe it."

"It is the truth," General Nassiri said.

"I will not release your son until I am positive that it is." I gripped the boy's hand more tightly.

Suddenly overcome with emotion, the general got up and called the office. "This is General Nassiri. His Majesty demands to know the status of Farzad Dadgar. Return my call immediately!" He hung up.

"Thank you, General," I said, releasing his son.

"They will call back shortly," he said, "and whatever they tell me will be the truth. They would not dare to lie about whether the man is alive or dead, especially when they think the information is intended for the shah."

In less than ten minutes, the news came: The man was a fugitive; he was on SAVAK's "wanted" list. "Intelligence indicates that he is somewhere south of Tehran," the general informed me. "If he is found, he will be killed on the spot."

I trembled. "I hope he is not caught tonight. I will tell his family."

The family again refused to believe me, although I knew SAVAK would not lie to General Nassiri about this, nor would General Nassiri lie to me. After the shah fell, the boy came out of hiding, but it was too late to help his mother, who had already gone insane.

There were other instances when I did succeed in saving lives. One afternoon on one of my trips to Tehran, I visited the chief of students at SAVAK headquarters. During our conversation, the phone rang. He answered it and began to jot down names, repeating them aloud as he did so. My curiosity was aroused when I noted that one of the five names on the list was that of Ahmad Kashani, the brother of Dr. Bager Kashani, a very dear friend of mine (both sons of Ayatollah Abolghasem Kashani).

The chief of students hung up. "There is work to do tonight. I must find the addresses of these people and give explicit directions for finding them to the arresting officers." SAVAK, I knew, always had ready a detailed map of the area and the floor plan of the wanted individual's home, making the arrest practically foolproof if the person had not already escaped.

I realized if I was going to be able to help Dr. Kashani's brother, I would have to work quickly. I hurriedly prepared to leave, bid the chief of students a hasty good-bye, and added, "I have to go home now." Then I rushed to a public phone and called Dr. Kashani.

Later Dr. Kashani told me that SAVAK had come for his brother that night, just as I had predicted, but his brother had eluded them, thanks to my timely warning. (Ahmad Kashani in 1986 was a member of the Iranian Parliament.)

I was assigned other tasks, tasks that I never performed effectively. Although both the shah and SAVAK had ordered me to keep track of all activities of the Iranian diplomats in the United States—gambling, spying, fraternizing with the Soviets—I could not devote much time to this because I had so many other responsibilities. It was a nearly impossible task anyway.

But occasionally the shah did request specific information that I had to supply. When diplomats made reports to His Majesty, the reports were usually sent directly to the royal palace rather than to the Iranian State Department. Sometimes the shah would ask SAVAK for confirmation of a particular report.

For example, Ambassador Zahedi sent a wire to the shah noting that at the monarch's birthday celebration at the Iranian embassy there had been two thousand people in attendance. He listed the number of congressmen, senators, newsmen, and movie stars who had been present, and provided a few names. The shah requested that I confirm the numbers of senators and congressmen in the ambassador's report. Anticipating such a request, I had attended the party and kept a record of the dignitaries and celebrities who were there.

Each time the Iranian secretary of state, the prime minister, or other dignitary came to the United States, it was my routine task to provide the shah with a confidential report on the dignitary's relations with other officials. "Were they cordial to one another?" the shah might want to know. "Did they contact one another while they were there?" "Did one curse the other?" It was to his benefit to promote infighting, and he was wary of possible collusion among his subordinates.

Protocol demanded that I send flowers to visiting Iranian officials. Accordingly, when the secretary of state arrived, I sent him flowers, but the accompanying card read that the sender was Ambassador Zahedi. Surprised, the secretary of state called Ambassador Zahedi to thank him, after which the ambassador called me to ask if I had sent the flowers on his behalf.

"Of course not," I said. "I would never do it unless you asked me."

On the night of his return to Tehran, the secretary of state spent fifteen minutes discussing with me the mystery of the flowers.

"It must have been a mix-up," I said. "Did you receive the bouquet I sent you?"

"No," he responded.

"Then that must have been my bouquet with the wrong name on the card," I concluded.

But the story did not end there. General Nassiri asked me several times on behalf of the shah whether the flowers had been sent by the ambassador or if it had been an honest mistake. The shah was distressed to think that the animosity he had so zealously encouraged might have deteriorated into friendship!

CHAPTER TEN

Exiles and Victims

On March 16, 1961, *The New York Times* reported the following:

Gen. Teimour [sic] Bakhtiar, head of Iran's security service and a vigorous campaigner against Communists, has resigned because of ill health. . . .

In actuality, General Bakhtiar had been dismissed from his position because he represented a serious threat to the shah's security. For seven years he had been one of the shah's top aides, as commander of the Second Armored Division in Tehran, chief of martial law, and finally chief of SAVAK. In such privileged and strategic positions, he had grown increasingly aware of the shah's weaknesses and of his own strengths. Becoming ever more ambitious, he had told the CIA he believed that the shah was an ineffectual despot. General Bakhtiar had suggested that the CIA might do better to support him in an effort to topple the shah and to form a republic of Iran.

The CIA was split on the issue. Those who agreed with General Bakhtiar told President Kennedy that the shah's defeat was imminent and advised a swift and immediate switch of support to General Bakhtiar before the inevitable revolution and chaos occurred. Among these advisers were Senators J. William Fulbright, Hubert H. Humphrey, and Frank Church of the Senate Foreign Relations Committee.[7]

Kennedy was almost convinced to support General Bakhtiar, but the existence of Bakhtiar's plan was leaked to the shah by those CIA officials who were opposed to the general. Immediately the shah chose General Pakravan, the deputy chief, to replace General Bakhtiar, and summoned Bakhtiar to the royal palace for a meeting, later described to me by General Pakravan.

According to Pakravan's account, as soon as General Bakhtiar arrived at the palace, he was disarmed by palace guards. Humiliated, furious, he entered the room where the shah and General Pakravan were awaiting him. The customary polite and formal greetings were exchanged. General Bakhtiar, evidently struggling to control himself, spoke in ordinary tones, and for a while the three men sat talking and drinking.

After a pause in the conversation, the shah addressed General Bakhtiar: "We see that you are building a lovely palace, a presidential mansion, in fact." General Bakhtiar's new and sumptuous home had just been completed at a cost of a million dollars and was situated not far from the royal palace.

There was no mistaking the shah's meaning, nor was General Bakhtiar any longer in doubt about the reason for the meeting. "Your Majesty," he answered, choosing his words carefully, "that house is intended for your heir, the crown prince. I have every faith in the kingdom."

The shah was aware of the significance of General Bakhtiar's choice of words and now administered the coup de grâce. "What you have done for us and for the country, all your help, is deeply appreciated. However, you are to be replaced immediately. General Pakravan will take your place."

General Bakhtiar was speechless for a moment. Then, his face contorted, his hands clenching, he burst out, "Help? My help appreciated! Your Majesty, I am so glad I helped!" He rose from his chair, breathing hard, and moved toward the shah.

Alarmed, General Pakravan interposed himself between the two as the shah and General Bakhtiar continued their angry exchange. "We know your intentions, Bakhtiar. We're aware of your connections with the CIA. Thank you."

"It's not true, Your Majesty," Bakhtiar protested. "I am your obedient servant."

"We know what's in your mind. At any rate, you are replaced!"

The shah seemed frightened. General Pakravan pushed him gently, urging him toward the doorway to an adjoining room; General Bakhtiar was right on his heels. The shah once again addressed him: "We thank you for what you have done for the security of this country."

"Your Majesty, it . . ."

General Pakravan gave the shah a final push, closed the door behind him, and turned to General Bakhtiar.

"Please, General, no more, no more." He led a protesting Bakhtiar to the other entrance.

"That damn coward! That bastard! He had me disarmed. He has no mercy. I've worked for him for so long. I wish to God I'd spilled his filthy blood before."

"General Bakhtiar! Please, be quiet, General! Don't say those things!"

General Bakhtiar thrust his face into General Pakravan's. "You're the fool. Your day will come, too. I've taken people out of the palace just like this." And, having said so, he jerked away from Pakravan and stormed out.

Thus was the man who had approved hiring me as chief of SAVAK in the United States summarily dismissed from his office, and my friend, General Pakravan, responsible for my position, now made chief of SAVAK. In June I was called to Tehran, where General Pakravan told me of my new task: to persuade the CIA officials who had supported Bakhtiar to withdraw that support.

"It would be the worst thing in the world to overthrow the shah and bring Bakhtiar to power in his place," General Pakravan said angrily. "General Bakhtiar would be a far worse dictator. You must convince the CIA. Tell them that for now, the shah is the best possible candidate to rule Iran." He got up from his chair and walked to a map hanging on his office wall. He stabbed his finger hard at Iran. "Here we are. You go back and tell them that if they continue to help General Bakhtiar, we will no longer be an independent country. We'll be just another little state in the Soviet Union."

General Bakhtiar, who had been traveling the length and breadth of Iran seeking support, particularly among members of the Bakhtiari tribe from which he originated, was ordered out of the country on January 26, 1962, for an "extended tour in Europe." In exile in Switzerland, he resumed plotting against the shah, holding meetings there in his home with like-minded men. Ardeshir Zahedi, the ambassador to the United States, suggested to the shah that it might be more politic to attempt to win General Bakhtiar back to the regime by offering him the position of ambassador to Switzerland. The shah opposed the plan, feeling that it would enhance General Bakhtiar's prestige and afford him greater opportunities to work against the throne, but Ambassador

Zahedi was able to overcome the shah's objections and won his consent
to approach Bakhtiar. He flew to Switzerland shortly thereafter for a
private meeting with the general. As he entered Bakhtiar's living room,
according to his account, he saw what were obviously preparations for
guests—rows of chairs lining the room. Ambassador Zahedi was
abrupt.

"General," he said, gesturing toward the chairs, "I have come to
you with a proposal from His Majesty. But I must advise you—this
business must stop. We've heard about your meetings. You should
know better. These people that visit you and denounce His Majesty are
SAVAK agents. They are provocateurs."

General Bakhtiar was puzzled for a minute. Ambassador Zahedi
led him to the corner of the room, an unmistakable signal to a Persian
that important and confidential matters were to be discussed. He told
Bakhtiar of the shah's offer. "Take it, General. Stop this childish business. Be smart. You won't get anywhere with these schemes."

General Bakhtiar stared at him. Then his hand moved to his fly.
He unzipped it slightly. "Here's my answer. You tell him he knows
what he can do. To hell with his ambassador's job."

Ambassador Zahedi claimed that he had slapped the general, who
did not retaliate in any way. Zahedi continued: "You are a fool, General. You're going to die here," to which the general replied, "You tell
him I'll get him first. That bastard. Coward. He won't last much longer.
The end is near."

The shah instructed General Nassiri, who had replaced General
Pakravan as chief of SAVAK in 1965, to give the same orders to
Departments 2 and 3: Seek out General Bakhtiar in Iraq and kill him.
Despite the competition, results were neither swift nor smooth. Over
the next several years, the two departments sent agents to Iraq, and
made many attempts to kill General Bakhtiar by bullet and bomb. He
escaped unscathed and continued as virulent as ever in his broadcasts
and activities against the shah.

In 1968, in a plan of entrapment, SAVAK agents supplied sufficient
arms to General Bakhtiar to overthrow the shah's government; most
of the arms and financial aid came through the SAVAK station in
Kuwait.

Then, while General Bakhtiar was traveling in Lebanon, authorities
there were informed by SAVAK that he was carrying illegal arms. At
a checkpoint, General Bakhtiar's car was searched, the arms were
found, and he was arrested and jailed for a term of nine months.

The shah put pressure on the Lebanese government to extradite

Bakhtiar, first using suasion, then diplomatic negotiations, in a desperate attempt to get back his general and former chief of SAVAK, his right-hand man of fifteen years, cousin of his second wife, Soraya. The shah's plan was to bring him back as a prisoner, meet with him privately in order to gloat over his capture, try him publicly, and execute him. He could not rest until he had done so. But none of his attempts succeeded—until February 1969 when Bakhtiar's nine-month jail term was over and the Lebanese government, under increasing pressure, grudgingly agreed to surrender Bakhtiar in March during the Iranian New Year holiday.

Then on April 1, 1969, *The New York Times* reported the Lebanese government's announcement that it had changed its mind:

> BEIRUT, Lebanon, March 31 (AP)—The Lebanese Government today decided to free Teymour Bakhtiar, an Iranian general wanted by the Teheran Government.
>
> Justice Minister Chafik Wazzan said that he had decided to reject an Iranian request that the general be extradited.
>
> The Iranian government says that General Bakhtiar, a cousin of former Empress Soraya, is wanted on criminal charges dating from the time when he was Iran's security chief.

"In no way will we accept it," the shah stormed. "We'll get that bastard."

The shah's fervent wish was granted: Finally, on August 23, 1970, *The New York Times* reported:

> BEIRUT, Lebanon, Aug. 22 (AP)—Gen. Taymour [sic] Bakhtiar of Iran, an opponent of Shah Mohammed Riza Pahlevi, has been assassinated while on a hunting trip in Iraq, the newspaper *Al Nahar* reported today.

General Nassiri told me that as soon as he received the news of Bakhtiar's death, he went immediately to the royal palace, where an ecstatic shah broke out his best Scotch in celebration. "Beautiful," he said, touching his glass to General Nassiri's. "That son of a bitch. We finally got him."

CHAPTER ELEVEN

A U.S. Ally Who Drank to Kennedy's Murder

On April 10, 1962, the shah arrived in the United States for his long-scheduled meeting with President Kennedy. At that time, there were two groups of Iranians in the United States, each with a distinct political persuasion. The first group, diametrically opposed to the shah, foresaw only violent revolution in Iran; the second group believed that the prospect of revolution could be forestalled if the shah were willing to enforce the Iranian Constitution and allow orderly and lawful elections and social reforms. It was to the second group that I somewhat hesitantly belonged. Both groups had been in contact with the new Kennedy administration. News of the two factions and their conflicting opinions had reached the shah, who, I later learned, was greatly afraid of President Kennedy, although also contemptuous of him.

The shah was greeted in Washington by a mob of chanting Iranian dissidents and, on his arrival in New York, I was informed by the Iranian ambassador that His Majesty would meet with me privately after the public reception scheduled at the Waldorf-Astoria Hotel.

The press, I was told, would be covering the reception, at which the shah would make some remarks and answer a few questions. "The shah wants to be asked two questions," the ambassador told me, "and it must not look as if they were planted. You are not to ask them yourself but to find someone who will. These are the two questions you must instruct your proxies to ask: 'Your Majesty, be frank with us, please. Are you with the East or the West? Clarify your position.' The second ques-

tioner should say, 'As you are aware, Your Majesty, President Kennedy
is the hope of the world for social reform. Do you find yourself any
different from him or do you follow in his ways?' "

The ambassador hesitated a moment before adding, "Between you
and me, His Majesty will answer the questions in a way he thinks will
please Kennedy. Just be sure that no one suspects the questions are a
put-up job."

As it happened, the shah requested my presence *before* the reception took place. He asked that I stand next to him and introduce each
person to him as he or she arrived.

To overcome my nervousness at being in his presence, I told him
about my arrangements. "Your Majesty, I received your message about
the two questions," I said. "A physician will ask one of them, and an
engineer will ask the other."

He smiled at this. "You picked good people—not experienced
politicians. They won't be polite or easy on me."

"It will be left to Your Majesty to answer in any way you choose."
I had made a slip.

He glared and his eyebrows lifted. "The ambassador said something
to you?"

Now I smiled. "Yes, Your Majesty."

He changed the subject. "Can you tell me which dissidents are in
touch with Kennedy's administration?"

"It would be much easier to tell Your Majesty which ones are not."

"Is that so?"

"Yes. Practically all of them are—every leader of a group."

Again he switched the topic abruptly. "You're from Kerman."

It wasn't a question. "Yes, Your Majesty."

"I know the accent. I will ask you how much rain you have in
Kerman yearly. Be prepared for the question. I'll see you again after
the meeting . . . depending on how it goes."

At the appointed time, those who were scheduled to meet the shah
filed in and were introduced. I delivered a short speech. Then the
questioning began.

When the physician posed his question, His Majesty answered in
ringing tones: "I don't know how you or anyone else feels about the
matter, but let me inform you that my position is squarely with the
West. Anyone who chooses to do so can follow the Soviets' path or any
other path he may choose, but I follow in the path of freedom, of
democracy, of the free world! I am with the West."

When the engineer's turn came, the shah's tone was unctuous. "I am deeply touched to have had the honor of meeting President Kennedy, of talking personally to him. We have achieved several of our mutual goals already. There is going to be a new era of social reform for Iran. And you," he said, looking commandingly around the room, "all of you, your country needs you! When you have finished your schooling here, lift your hands for Iran! Bring your minds and your talents home to your country. It is not a time for talk, but a time for action! Previously, the United States has manifested its power, its military might to the world, but I understand from my recent discussions with President Kennedy that he intends to demonstrate both social reform and freedom to the entire world. We will follow in his footsteps!"

Now he pointed at me. "You have a Kermani accent. What is your name?"

"Mansur Rafizadeh, Your Majesty."

"How much rainfall does Kerman get yearly?"

"A few inches, Your Majesty."

He looked triumphantly around the room again. "There! You see? That's a good example. Even nature is against us. We are cats and the United States is a lion. We look alike. We jump alike. We hunt alike. But they are the United States and we are Iran. If you want the wealth and the comforts of this great United States for yourself and for Iran, you must work to achieve it. Hear me! Put your heads, your hands together! Come back to Iran and once again we will show the world that we are of Iran, once the cradle of civilization, and that we still uphold that torch!"

The press attaché from the embassy of Iran in Washington translated the shah's words as he spoke, and members of the news media took copious notes. As the shah ended his "extempore" remarks and prepared to leave, cameramen called for more pictures. He agreed but, before posing, asked if anyone either wished to present another viewpoint or disagreed with his stand. Naturally, no one did. He made his exit after inviting everyone to enjoy the refreshments. The rest of us chatted for a while and left.

A crowd of thirty or forty screaming demonstrators greeted us at the Park Avenue door as we did so. Held back by police, they pushed against the barricades, holding up their placards, gesticulating. "Traitors! Puppets! Down with the shah!" they yelled as they surged against the police lines and broke through. They fell upon us, raining blows on us with their fists and the sticks that held their posters. In the melee, the police were unable to distinguish us from the demonstrators and hit everyone indiscriminately. Our neat black suits, white shirts, and firmly knotted ties—protocol for our meeting with the shah—were no protection at all in battle.

Just then, out of nowhere, about ten men appeared and the battle was joined in earnest. We had no idea who they were, but obviously they were on our side. Our initial opponents were drubbed, no match whatever for these latest fighters.

The photographers clicked away as fists, feet, and sticks struck wherever they could, but police reinforcements quickly arrived, sirens wailing, and with equal lack of discrimination, a number of us were arrested and herded into vans. At a nearby precinct, the sorting out began.

The group of men who had been our saviors flashed some ID. All but one were released immediately; the last vouched for my group and our release, claiming that he knew us to be friends of the shah and not the initiators of the fight. We, too, were released. Five of those who had attacked us were detained. One of them, Sadegh Ghotbzadeh, was subsequently deported when authorities discovered that he didn't have a valid visa.

Later, Ghotbzadeh lived in Paris, and, on Ayatollah Khomeini's accession to power in 1979, came to Tehran with the Ayatollah, who by then addressed him as his son. He became Khomeini's secretary of state, and by the time of the hostage crisis in late 1979 he was the most powerful man in the government of Iran. When his opponents published a retouched photo of our meeting with the shah in the Waldorf-Astoria, one of the faces was now unmistakably that of Ghotbzadeh. Furious and frightened, he sent me a message begging me to testify that it wasn't so, to send him copies of the original photos so that he could prove it.

"Please, Mansur, you know I wasn't there."

I quickly prepared to send the pictures, knowing that it wouldn't change anything.

Later, accused of plotting against the Khomeini regime, Ghotbzadeh was executed by firing squad on September 15, 1982.

After leaving the police station, I called the Iranian ambassador, who told me that the men who had come to our aid were commandos of the shah's army, Secret Service men assigned as his personal bodyguards.

"We wanted to protect you," the ambassador said. "We were looking out the windows and saw the fight start. The shah felt sorry for you. The group that attacked you were paid by the oil companies. You see how His Majesty's men beat them up? He couldn't stand to see you getting the worst of it. He wants to see you tomorrow, Mansur. Be there at eight A.M."

That night was a confusing and upsetting one for me. Iranians, I thought, will never learn. They fight not only inside their country but everywhere else. I was thoroughly disillusioned—three groups, all ostensibly wanting what was best for Iran, "ironing out" their difficulties on a Manhattan street.

Promptly at 8:00 the next morning, I was received by the shah. He was seated at a large table in his suite at the Waldorf having his breakfast. There was a profusion of flowers, mostly roses, throughout the room and on the breakfast table. The shah looked up from his breakfast and motioned for me to sit down. I pulled out a chair from the breakfast table, set it a short distance away from the table, and sat down.

As the shah began talking about the events of the previous evening, I was glad to be sitting down. I was frightened by the fierce, angry expression on his face, and I was afraid that his penetrating eyes would see my true feelings. That look, especially around his eyes and eyebrows, was so disturbing that I would have been visibly shaking if I had not been seated.

The shah began the conversation by asking, "Are they in jail?"

"Yes, Your Majesty—since last night."

"We spoke to our ambassador. We must do our best to see that these people are deported."

"Your Majesty, may I say I don't feel that it was right for those people to be beaten."

"No! You're wrong. 'Donkey meat needs dogs' teeth.' It served them right! We have followers who love us. They couldn't bear to hear the words those men were chanting. And, after all, how many of our men were beaten?"

"It doesn't matter. They are disappointed. They weren't looking for a fight. They wanted a peaceful demonstration."

"We have no choice. We are fighting barbarians."

"Your Majesty, may I say that all violence is bad."

The shah gave me a pitying glance. "You are naïve. Violence is everywhere. There is no freedom or democracy here either. When you are in power, you must have two things: money and force. Without them, it just doesn't work. It's the same in this country. They beat people up. They have fraudulent elections. In North Carolina and Georgia, dead men vote. Kennedy bought his election with pizza parties. Nixon didn't win because he didn't spend enough money. Don't you believe any differently."

"Your Majesty, with your mighty judgment and your highest intellect, are you content that the report presented to Your Majesty about those elections was accurate?"

"Certainly. Several books have been written about it. We will give you the names of them. [He never did.] It's the same everywhere."

"According to your blessed words, then, a valid election could not occur in Iran?"

"Oh, no, no. We will have valid elections, but they will be guided elections. As soon as I arrive in Tehran, we will instruct General Pakravan to call you to discuss solutions for this sort of problem with the students, to discuss our path to democracy." He paused. "At any rate, we are pleased with you and your actions yesterday."

The shah stood, and I knew the discussion was ended. "Think more, think well, about what we have said," he admonished me.

"Yes, Your Majesty," I said, and left.

Now I was even more confused. Dr. Baghai had told me of meeting the shah in 1954 and of the ensuing argument they had had. After protesting the lack of freedom and democracy in Iran and the brutality of the police and security forces, Dr. Baghai had warned the shah of the consequences he might expect, asked him again to enforce constitutional law, and assured him once more that he would benefit most from it in the end. As the futile debate ended, Dr. Baghai rose. Leaning, as usual, on his cane, he had told the shah that his policies would lead inevitably to revolution.

"One day the people will besiege this very royal palace," he said.

The shah raised both arms as though he were aiming a gun at Dr. Baghai and said, "And when they get here, we will meet them with machine guns."

At this, Dr. Baghai raised his cane and pointed it at the shah. "And those same guns can be turned toward the royal palace. God bless you. May God grant you a pleasant ending, Your Majesty. Good-bye."

The assassination of President Kennedy on November 22, 1963, made the shah jubilant. Kennedy had put pressure on him for social reforms. The shah, as always, had raised the banner of the fight against communism, saying, "Our real enemy is communism."

I learned later through General Pakravan that the shah had had a kind of celebration.

"Can you believe this shah?" General Pakravan said. "When he received the news of Kennedy's death, he asked for a drink to celebrate."

CHAPTER TWELVE

Ties to FBI and CIA

Until 1965 my relationship with the FBI and CIA had been routine. Then in 1965, in Washington, I met with the men assigned to the CIA's Iran desk about some ordinary Iranian business. During the course of the meeting, one of the men commented on the success of the shah's social reforms. "The shah is advancing toward democracy," he said. "The Iranian people have far more freedom than in the past. His opponents are all Communists or reactionaries."

I wondered how these people, who were involved in the policy-making machinery of the United States, could be so unaware. They were concerned with inconsequential matters, like who was a Communist and who was not, whom they should suspect and whom they should not. I could see a storm brewing in Iran; most Iranian politicians were liars, corrupt and unwilling to assume responsibility. No matter what happened to Iran in the future, they would blame it on Moscow, London, or Washington. Foreign governments were always the architects of subversive plans.

I could no longer suppress my feelings. "You know, you Americans are the broadcasters of our lies," I burst out. "Whatever lie we tell you, you believe!"

Taken aback by this sudden outburst, they tried to defend themselves. "We do not!" they averred.

I gave them some examples of the lies they were disseminating—about land reform, freedom in Iran, the benevolence of the shah. I think they thought I was either a fool or an agent of the shah trying to elicit what they really knew or felt. The atmosphere grew hostile. One of the agents remarked that we should discuss only the matters at hand—not the situation in Iran.

"You should be aware of what is going on," I persisted. "You should inform President Johnson and the other policymakers of the facts. Otherwise they will be misled, too."

When the meeting was over, I felt as though I had been communicating with people living in a monastery, so isolated that they had no contact with the reality of the outside world. Their only concerns about Iran were its suspected Communists, how many roads were built, what the rise in individual income was. They did not understand or discuss what was really significant—that the basic rights of the people of Iran were being abolished.

On June 5, 1964, the shah returned to Washington for another visit, this time with President Lyndon B. Johnson. General Pakravan had informed me beforehand that His Majesty foresaw no difficulty in his upcoming discussions with the American president. He reportedly had said, "This time the demonstrators can scream as much as they want."

The shah had despised Kennedy, who constantly advised him to restore human rights to his subjects and insisted that such a course of action was necessary and unavoidable. The shah viewed that course as a decided threat to his power and so had refused. Now the threat posed by Kennedy was gone; the shah's relationship with President Johnson was comfortable and he felt no fear of the United States despite the huge demonstrations mounted against him in New York, Washington, and indeed throughout the country.

On the day of the shah's arrival, according to *The New York Times,* President Johnson toasted him as a "reformist twentieth-century monarch whose leadership has kept Iran free and has modernized an ancient land."

But although the shah and President Johnson were friendly, the shah still had no real trust in the United States or its representatives because of the sea changes that had occurred in American-Iranian relations since the time of his initial friendship with President Eisenhower.

The shah, in fact, trusted no one. He would not permit key posts to be filled by men who had friends in other key posts.

The shah's divide-and-conquer tactics reached into every government office. In every office a constant internecine battle was waged. SAVAK was obliged to inform the monarch of any developing friend-

ships between key people. No commander or officer could enter his office after closing hours without it being reported immediately.

Although the chief of SAVAK was officially deputy to the prime minister, and by law was required to report all SAVAK matters regularly to the chief executive, this was not the case. Not only did the chief of SAVAK not consider the prime minister his superior, but because of the way in which the shah conducted all operations, the two men were bitter enemies.

The shah was supremely happy with his system. It is not hard to understand his purpose in cultivating such enmity between key people. It would keep him informed of dissatisfaction, of conspiracy, of possible treason. It is easy to understand also that such a fragmented system contained not only the seeds of its own destruction but also that of the shah. But for the time being, he was running a one-man show. He had them all suspicious and fearful of one another and competing fiercely to bring him intelligence. He loved it.

CHAPTER THIRTEEN

Fratricide

Although the world press portrayed Shah Mohammad Reza Pahlavi as a progressive and enlightened ruler, in actuality he was completely ruthless and didn't hesitate to murder his political opponents.

In 1951 Iran was thrown into political turmoil when General Haj Ali Razmara, the shah's appointed prime minister, was assassinated by a "religious fanatic" as he entered the Great Mosque. For weeks the newspapers were saturated with stories about the "Muslim fanatic murderer." The shah gave lengthy speeches expressing his anger and outrage over the "Muslim fanatics" who would commit such a monstrous act. Pictures of the shah grieving and comforting the weeping widow and children blanketed the pages.

I was extremely puzzled when his alleged murderer was mysteriously pardoned a few months later. I didn't discover anything new about the assassination until 1955 when Dr. Baghai told me that the shah had orchestrated Razmara's death because he had heard rumors that the prime minister had planned to kill him and thought that he would simply beat him to it.

Two years later, another mysterious assassination occurred—General Mahmud Afshartous, who was chief of national police during Prime Minister Mossadegh's administration. When Mossadegh took office, one of the first things he did to clean house was forcibly retire numerous army officers. These men resented him deeply and formed "a retired officers club." This club became the shah's secret weapon against Mossadegh.

The shah had constantly blocked Mossadegh from putting his cronies in powerful administrative positions. General Afshartous was one of the few men whom Mossadegh had in a sensitive and important position. On April 21, 1953, General Afshartous was kidnapped. The press had a field day discussing "who stole the chief of police?" A few days later, Afshartous's body was found. He had been tortured and mutilated. The real killers were never found, but years later General Nassiri complained to me, "I'm tired of paying these old retired army people forever. I wish they would die already." It seems that, as a reward for these special services, the shah had had some members of the "retired officers club" placed on SAVAK's secret payroll for as long as they lived.

Over the years there were many newsmen who were systematically eliminated by the shah, but Karimpoor Shirazi stands out. In 1953 Shirazi was the editor in chief of a tabloid newspaper called *Shooresh* (Rebellion). *Shooresh*'s specialty was printing stories and cartoons that were extremely critical of the shah's government. Daily it contained very clever cartoons ridiculing the shah, Queen Soraya, Princess Ashraf (the shah's twin sister), and other members of the court. Most of these cartoons focused on their depraved sexual behavior, but some were about their alleged thievery, and still others featured the prevalence of corruption in every facet of court life.

Of all the members of the royal court, Shirazi's favorite target was Princess Ashraf. He singled her out and would constantly print articles and jokes about her numerous lovers, chronic gambling, and role in international drug trafficking.

In 1953, when the shah was briefly driven out of the country and Dr. Mossadegh was the prime minister, the press was free to unleash its most vicious attacks and *Shooresh* was at its most virulent. Then, as soon as he returned to power, the shah wanted Shirazi silenced. Martial law was in effect. He had him arrested and taken to a military prison.

Princess Ashraf vehemently hated Shirazi because he had publicly humiliated her. She wanted revenge. She badgered the shah until she convinced him that the journalist didn't even deserve a trial.

A few days later, the newspapers carried an account of Karimpoor Shirazi's accidental death in a prison fire. They reported that while Shirazi was "playing" with his kerosene heater, it had ignited his clothing and started a fire in his cell. They claimed that, although the guards had risked their lives and rushed to save him, they had been too late.

When SAVAK was established in 1957, many of the people who

were involved in handling the shah's dirty work were given jobs—some because they could still be of value, others because they knew too much, and still others because they were being rewarded for their loyalty to the shah.

Years later, while I was on vacation in Tehran, one of the more notorious of these men ran into me. He knew my position and begged me to speak on his behalf to General Nassiri. I instantly recognized him as one of my former jailers from my student protest days. I seized the opportunity to question him about his past. He boasted to me about his importance and his involvement in "the burning up of the newspaper-man." When I pressed him for details, he told me with great bravado about that night in 1953.

"I was the one who soaked him with kerosene while the others held him down. I couldn't light him because my clothes had too much kerosene on them and I would have burned, too. One of the other guys had to roll up a rag, dip it in kerosene, light a match, and throw it at him as we all ran like hell out of the room."

The man had the deranged look that many of the shah's henchmen seemed to develop. Often, these men had to be removed from service because they went mad. They became a threat to the very people for whom they had committed their heinous crimes.

I never spoke to General Nassiri about him.

On October 30, 1954, Radio Tehran stunned the country with a special news bulletin: Prince Ali Reza Pahlavi's plane had lost radio communication while flying from Gorgān to Tehran.

For days the nation waited breathlessly for news of the shah's thirty-two-year-old younger brother and heir presumptive. Special announcement after special announcement interrupted regular programming to keep a news-hungry public informed about the search party's progress. Finally, word came: "We regret to inform the people of Iran that the remains of His Royal Highness Prince Ali Reza, brother of His Imperial Majesty Shah Mohammad Reza Pahlavi, have been found near the wreckage of the plane in the Alborz Mountains." His plane had crashed under mysterious circumstances.

The entire country went into mourning. The shah seemed inconsolable and grieved openly for his beloved brother. He was photographed comforting the prince's French-born widow and children.

Prince Ali Reza had been the shah's only full brother. Their father had had five wives and many other children, but only the children resulting from his marriage to Taj Almalook could legitimately inherit the throne. The shah still had not produced a son and heir. According to the Iranian Constitution, Prince Ali Reza was next in line. His death left the country without a direct heir to the throne.

The two brothers had been a study in contrasts. The shah was introverted and insecure; Ali had been gregarious and self-confident. The shah was cold and aloof; Ali had been warm and approachable. The shah was uncomfortable with anyone outside his own coterie; Ali had been able to share a joke with privates as easily as with generals. Yet, in spite of the differences in their personalities, they had shared an intimacy known only to brothers. The shah could let his guard down with Ali Reza and trusted him implicitly.

The prince's loyalty had been above reproach. During the 1953 coup d'état, the shah fled the country, but Ali Reza risked his life to stay behind as the army's clandestine chief and defend his brother's interests. But their relationship wasn't entirely smooth.

Ali Reza had control over several army generals and, much to the shah's consternation, had often made administrative and policy changes without consulting him. He had been a skilled soldier who had the military's respect, and the shah had become extremely jealous of the ease with which he influenced his officers. The shah's intense jealousy was also fueled by the fact that his own advisers had never hesitated to side with Ali Reza during important policy meetings.

In addition, their relationship had become strained because of the prince's inability to conceal his true feelings from his brother and his propensity to abuse him verbally with the very special cruelty siblings reserve only for each other. Ali Reza would constantly demean the shah with remarks like "When you're in trouble you wet your pants! I, at least, can keep control." As hostilities began to escalate, Prince Ali Reza's taunts became more frequent. "You're too stupid! You'll never be able to save the throne our father gave us!" The shah's ego was too fragile to withstand Ali Reza's indignities. He began to develop a genuine hatred and fear of his younger brother. The shah viewed him as a threat to his power, and ultimately he dealt with him in the same way he did any other person he felt was in his way—he had him killed. Years later SAVAK had Ali Reza's son, Ali, under surveillance. The CIA recorded several phone conversations in which the young man frequently referred to the shah as "father's murderer."

SAVAK had a secret listening office that routinely tapped phone conversations in the Iranian State Department, the CIA, and the American, British, and Russian embassies. In addition, they also monitored members of the royal court, prominent generals, and political figures. Only the most newsworthy and important tapes were sent to the shah for his listening "pleasure."

The SAVAK officers assigned to monitor the princess Shahnaz's phones were astounded one day by a taped conversation between the shah and his daughter. Princess Shahnaz, the sole offspring of his marriage to Princess Fawzia, sister of King Farouk of Egypt, had been married to Ardeshir Zahedi. Subsequently, with His Majesty's permission, they had been divorced. It was rumored that the shah's relationship with his daughter was strained, and this conversation, which I later listened to, certainly supported this rumor.

"How are you feeling? How is your cold?" the shah inquired politely.

"Why are you calling me, you bastard? Leave me alone. You are a murderer. A pimp. What do you want from me?" responded his daughter.

"I know you're not feeling well. I'll call again."

"Don't ever call me again! Haven't you caused enough trouble for me? What more do you want? I'm not free in this country. I can't do anything I want to do. It's like I'm in a jail! Just leave me alone. Enjoy your life with your whores and your perverts!"

"I know you have a fever. That's why you are talking to me like this. I hope you feel better. I'll call you again."

The officers in the secret listening office were shocked by the princess's language and the manner in which she spoke to her father. They certainly didn't know how to report the contents of this tape to General Nassiri. After long deliberation, they finally decided that they would type the conversation in the customary way, but use dots to represent all expletives.

When the general received the report, the tape, and the typed copy, he angrily ordered, "Omit that one. Certainly His Majesty is aware of his own conversations with Princess Shahnaz."

Later Nassiri told me that he couldn't believe just how stupid these officers were. They didn't have enough sense even to figure out not to send this tape report to the shah.

On January 21, 1965, Prime Minister Hassan Ali Mansur was assassinated, a victim of his own popularity.

Mansur was a young and charismatic leader whose approach to leadership had captured the imagination of Iran's young people and had inspired many of them to enter government service. He had been directly responsible for many reforms that encouraged economic growth. But when he made the mistake of openly taking credit for this economic boon, he incurred the shah's wrath. The monarch could not tolerate sharing his glory. He was the "Shah of Shahs," and he and only he could be responsible for Iran's new growth. He had KOOK[8] and

SAVAK eliminate Mansur in the usual way—"fanatics would kill him."

During Shah Mohammad Reza Pahlavi's reign, thousands of people were killed and the blame was always laid on "Muslim fanatics." In *Answer to History,* the shah sings his familiar tune over and over. "On March 7, 1951, Prime Minister Haj Ali Razmara was assassinated by a member of the Fedayeen Islam, a terrorist group of the extreme right, while attending a religious ceremony in the Great Mosque." And again, "On January 21, 1965, Moslem fanatics shot and killed another one of my Prime Ministers, Hassan Ali Mansur. Later several guards were killed and in the early seventies terrorists murdered three American Colonels in the streets of Tehran." In reality, these people, including the three American advisers to the Iranian Army, were all killed by the shah's directive.

When Prime Minister Mansur was killed, General Pakravan was removed as chief of SAVAK. Extremely frustrated, he shared his feelings with me.

"The shah is so upset," he exclaimed, "that he is crying alligator tears again. He ordered Mansur killed by 'fanatics.' He is publicly blaming me for being lax when, in fact, he arranged for the killing. The shah killed two birds with one stone. He got rid of Mansur—and me! If this doesn't stop—all of us—the innocent and the guilty will fall prey to this madman."

That day, I realized that I could no longer pretend even to myself to be loyal to the shah, whose only method of dealing with his enemies seemed to be to kill them. I was forced to conclude that the shah was himself Iran's greatest problem, and that I could no longer work within the system to influence him to adopt a democratic form of government.

Making that decision was painful. How could I supply intelligence to another country that might one day work against Iran? On the other hand, how could I tacitly agree to allow the intolerable conditions in Iran to go unrecognized. In the last analysis, the commitment to freedom and humanity transcends national boundaries. Robert Frost wrote:

> Two roads diverged in a wood, and I—
> I took the one less traveled by,
> And that has made all the difference.

I picked the road that led to the shah's downfall.

I knew I had no choice. My conscience decreed that I give 100 percent of my strength and cunning to destroy this evil man. And so I began what would become nearly two decades of duplicity.

CHAPTER FOURTEEN

A New SAVAK Chief: My Job Lost and Regained

On January 30, 1965, as I was listening to the radio in my Brooklyn apartment, a newscaster announced that the shah had replaced General Hassan Pakravan with a new chief of SAVAK, General Nematollah Nassiri. I went to the window and watched the red ball of the sun setting. I was extremely upset by the news. General Pakravan, my boss, my friend—that gentle and intellectual man, who might have been of great use and help to Iran—had been removed from the most sensitive job in the country. I didn't know Nassiri, only his reputation as an uneducated and brutal man.

I knew why General Pakravan had lost his job, however. He had opposed the shah's exile of Ayatollah Ruhollah Khomeini, and, aware that the shah meant to kill Khomeini, made his feelings known by telling him: "If you have any hope for the continuation of the monarchy, killing Ayatollah Khomeini will put an end to that hope. What Your Majesty contemplates is dreadful."

In 1964 Khomeini had been one of several prominent Shiite religious leaders in Iran. His preaching in Qom, Iran's religious center, had been a constant irritant to the shah, who had had him exiled to Turkey for that reason. Khomeini shortly left that country and established a base in Iraq, where he was supported by his devout religious followers. Thus, the shah, because of his paranoid need to rid Iran of all possible opposition, had transformed Khomeini into a sympathetic symbol of sectarian oppression. He had created a new heir apparent.

Rumor had it that the new chief of SAVAK intended to call back to Iran all chiefs of foreign stations and replace them with his own men. That wasn't unusual. It was a customary procedure, and I had already overstayed the four-year limit placed on foreign assignments in SAVAK. Soon I received a wire ordering me to present myself at the office of the chief of SAVAK within the next two weeks. I sent a return wire indicating my intention to comply with the order, and arrived in Tehran in July 1965.

Heretofore, because I knew the chief of SAVAK personally, I would go straight to his office. This time, I went to see my immediate superior, Colonel Nasser Moghadam, the man General Pakravan had earlier refused to see; he would set up my appointment with General Nassiri. On my arrival, Colonel Moghadam greeted me graciously.

"Ah, Mansur. You are here to see the chief."

"Yes. That's my intention."

We chatted briefly about mutual friends and acquaintances. Suddenly, gauging my expression, he said, "Let me tell you something. You've lost your job."

I kept my expression impassive but my stomach churned. "So, that's how it goes. Sometimes I sit in the saddle and sometimes they saddle me. Do you have a solution?"

Colonel Moghadam's lower lip jutted out. He pursed his mouth and shook his head slowly from side to side, lifting his hands in a gesture of helplessness.

"Why not, Colonel?" I persisted. "Isn't there anything you can do?"

"You know we're good friends," he said. "You help me. I help you. But General Nassiri asked for a full report on all chiefs of foreign stations, every one outside Iran. Want to see yours? What they said about you?"

"Of course, if you can. If you don't mind."

"Well, you can't say a word about it. It's top secret." He walked to his safe and opened it, bringing me two closely typed pages.

I studied the report—read it through twice. It wasn't good:

Said person has been stationed in the United States for almost six years, two years past the regulations of this office. His production is zero. All that he sends to headquarters are newspaper clippings, inconsequential articles about Iran published in the United States, and those published by Iranian dissidents there. He gives us some information about demonstrations but not a word of information about those individuals who take an active part in them.

Said person was the personal envoy of the ex-chief of SAVAK,

General Hassan Pakravan, and has a good relationship with him. Although it is against all regulations for an employee to be in touch with an ex-chief, tapping of General Pakravan's phone shows that said person called him several times recently from New York. He is a devotee of Dr. Baghai, and we suspect that he is circulating Dr. Baghai's pamphlets and publications in the United States. He is also a good friend of Ambassador Ardeshir Zahedi and is frequently in touch with him. With your blessed permission, we must state that the work which said person has performed in his office amounts to nothing. It is left to your blessed judgment.

It was signed by the chief of stations. Appended at the bottom was General Nassiri's penciled notation:

I need no personal envoy of the ex-chief in the United States. If he is a friend of Ambassador Zahedi, I will convince the ambassador that he should not be sent back to the U.S. Submit the names of four capable candidates. Work must be accomplished, not friendship.

I sat like a stone in my chair, then handed the report back to Colonel Moghadam. "Thank you, Colonel," I said hesitantly, then continued, referring to the chief of stations. "Couldn't you do anything? Couldn't you persuade him not to write a report like this?"

"You know him. He's a favorite hawk of Nassiri's. And you know, too, that he doesn't like either one of us. What could I do?"

I knew he was right.

"God be with us both," I said to Colonel Moghadam. We both sighed. "So, when is my appointment with General Nassiri?"

"You see him tomorrow at ten A.M. You will find a chauffeur waiting. He'll know exactly where to take you."

That night I couldn't sleep. I thought again about the report. There was no denying it was a fair one. The chief of stations had seen his chance and done me in. I thought of how he worked against Colonel Moghadam whenever he could, breaking protocol and seeing officials of the CIA, of MI5, without Colonel Moghadam's permission or knowledge, keeping the content of the meetings from him.

His report could cost me my job! I had accomplished so little of my purpose. I had actually not even begun. The next day, after a night of fitful tossing, I got up early, dressed carefully in the regulation dark suit, white shirt, quiet tie. I combed my unruly hair flat, picked up my briefcase, and walked outside. My car was already waiting, the chauffeur holding the door. A bird flew close over my head, depositing an ample token of its blessing on my lapel. The chauffeur laughed as I tried futilely to scrub it off with my handkerchief.

"Your Excellency, it is the greatest of fortunes. Hmmm. Nice suit. You're on your way to see the big boss."

God! The last thing I needed—a cheerful chauffeur.

He chattered on throughout the ride, turning his head to me constantly, his grin of reassurance widening as he zipped precariously through the traffic. "A good man, General Nassiri. A big man. Big heart. Best. Don't be afraid, I'm telling you."

I tried my best to ignore him. But he didn't let up until we arrived. He held the door as I got out.

"I see 'em come; I see 'em go. Best of luck."

After I had sat for thirty minutes in the waiting room, an adjutant walked in, a half-smile on his face. "Mr. Rafizadeh. Come with me. I will present you to His Excellency, General Nassiri."

I followed on his heels as he led me down the hallway and into General Nassiri's office. He clicked one heel sharply against the other and executed a smart salute. "Mr. Rafizadeh, chief of SAVAK in the United States, to see Your Excellency." He snapped to attention again and left the room.

"Good morning, Your Excellency," I said.

General Nassiri gave a loud snort, "hrrumph," in answer. I stuck out my hand and smiled. With a grim frown, he touched my fingertips reluctantly, stretching forward only slightly from his immense chair. He sank back into its depths, one leg bent, the other extended fully. He leaned on one elbow, cupped his hand over his heavy eyebrows, and glared, mouth clenched.

There were two chairs in front of his large desk. Unnerved, I placed my briefcase on the floor and seated myself.

He hunched forward, put his head down, and began to move the piles of paper on his desk, grumbling to himself as he read first one, then another. I was silent.

He lifted his head suddenly, glared again. "What's your problem?" He sat back, extended his leg, and planted his spread hands on the arms of the chair.

"Your Excellency, no problem, none. I obeyed your blessed order to present myself to you."

"Hah! You're the one who sends the clippings! I'm not running any press attaché in the United States. Six years! Six years is plenty. Introduce yourself to Personnel. They'll find something for you to do inside the country."

The worst had come. "Your Excellency." I fought to get in a few words that might influence him. "His Majesty is well aware of the work, and I have the honor to be known to His Maj . . ."

He cut me off. "Sure, sure. But I need work done. We don't need advisers. New job. New man. And as the new chief, I like to choose my own people."

"I don't know what kind of report you have received about me, Your Exc . . ."

Again he cut me off. "Forget it. I'm the new chief. I have every right to send my own man to the United States. Not Pakravan's envoy." Scornfully, he continued. "I know him! He was always falling asleep in the elevator. That kind of chief has this kind of envoy. Look at you! You're not even polite! Who told you to shake hands with me? Who gave you permission to sit down? Don't you know I'm the one who offers? Who told you you could bring your briefcase into my office?"

He was raging. I jumped up hastily, nearly knocking over the chair, cursing myself silently for my breach of protocol. I stood before him, head down, nodding, murmuring apologies, my hands clasped low in a show of deference.

"Sorry, sorry, Your Excellency, sorry."

"Don't be sorry." His voice was gruffer than before. "You see? You see what you learn in the United States? If I let you go on, in a few minutes you'd have your feet up on my desk!"

"No, no," I protested. "Never. I wouldn't do that."

"Yes, you would. That's American manners." His voice rose. "This is Iran!"

"Your Excellency, I am sorry I sat down. Forgive me." I could feel rivulets of sweat running down my back. I blinked sweat from my eyes.

He grabbed the phone off the hook, yelled one word into the receiver, "Moghadam!" and slammed it down again. He threw up one hand in disgust. All he said to me was "Dismissed!"

There were several sets of double doors. In my nervousness, I opened a closet and bumbled into it.

"Closet!" he roared, just as the phone rang. It was Colonel Moghadam calling back. I stood still. General Nassiri ignored me as he spoke to Colonel Moghadam.

"Rafizadeh believes the report about him is not accurate, but no matter what, I have to send my own man. Talk to me about him when you see me and get me an accurate report, too." He banged the receiver down and called out for his adjutant, who came in immediately. Click went the heels. Snap went the arm. "Yessir!"

"Take him out," General Nassiri said in disgust. "You see what kind of man we have in America. The man doesn't even know a closet when he sees one."

"God be with you, General." I followed the adjutant, his heels click-clicking, my own steps echoing in the empty hall, my head down. I was soaking wet as I stepped outside, every article of my clothing sticking to me.

"Here you are," the chauffeur exclaimed. "My! You don't look so good." He held the door open for me, and I climbed in, sank back, and wiped my face.

"Colonel Moghadam's office," I instructed him. The car crept through the thick noontime traffic of Tehran.

The chauffeur tilted his cap up and looked at me over his shoulder, one hand on the wheel, the other draped loosely over the back of the seat. "Warm, isn't it? Bird didn't help, huh?"

I didn't answer.

He gave me a pitying look, oblivious to horns honking behind us. "Not so good, nope, you don't look good, for sure. You know, I could have your job, but"—here he banged his open palm against the dashboard once, twice—"this right here, this is the life for me. I prefer this damn driving."

Maybe if I ignored him . . . not a chance. He went on.

"You know—those people in high offices in SAVAK, my friend told me they handcuff them and take them to jail. Just like that!" He ran his hands fondly over the steering wheel. "You know, to put your hands on a hot wheel like this is better than to fold your hands to them."

I groaned. "Look, I'm not arrested. Nothing happened!"

"You think I don't know," he said, commiserating. "God is merciful. God will help you. All those people I drove . . . all those men of General Pakravan, sheesh! They all came out like you. But it was just your first talk with him. Come on. Give us a smile."

I could have choked him. "Goddammit, leave me alone. I don't need your advice." I was frantically trying to decide what to do when we arrived at Colonel Moghadam's building.

"It's late," I said to the chauffeur, sorry for my outburst. "Go have lunch."

"No," he answered mournfully, "I'll wait here. I told you, you don't look good. You don't eat lunch, I don't eat lunch! Don't worry. Besides, you'd never get a cab. Take care of your business. I'll be here when you come out." There was no getting rid of him.

I walked into Colonel Moghadam's office, and he was laughing as he greeted me. "Wonderful day for you today!"

"Exactly." I told him the whole story and he laughed even harder.

"Colonel, you've got to help me," I entreated. "He asked you for another report."

"Right—another report. But what could I put in it? The chief of stations was right. My report can't help you because you did absolutely zero in the United States. Let's sit on it awhile. You'll have to find a way to get to him yourself."

"I can't wait. I'm going to see General Pakravan."

"Good. Talk to him. Maybe he'll have some advice."

"If he doesn't, if he can't help, I'll go back to General Nassiri and resign. I won't work inside SAVAK here."

"If that's how you feel, okay. But talk it over with General Pakravan first."

"Any other suggestions?"

"You really lost it, but there's always hope. I'd love to see you go back. I sure can't handle you here. Besides, you don't want it."

I thanked him and left. True to his word, my faithful chauffeur was waiting.

"Looking better," he drawled. "Worst didn't come yet."

"Thanks a lot."

He looked over his shoulder again as he pulled out into the traffic. I covered my face and shook my head.

"I'm very kind to you," he said.

"Thank you again."

"You don't ask why."

"Okay. I'll ask. Why are you so kind to me?"

"The motor-vehicle pool called. They said you didn't rate a car anymore. Chiefs of station who lose their jobs get their cars withdrawn. God knows who I'll drive tomorrow," he added lugubriously. "I shouldn't be here now. But, as I said, I'm kind. I'll take you home. I'm not canceling you, but you're canceled. Motor vehicle has said so."

"Well, thank you for your kindness. You're doing me a favor. What shall I do for you?"

"Oh, nothing. I take dignitaries like you every day. Some, they win, some, they lose. Some get a job, some get the ax. That's my job. Back and forth. Jesus, I'm like a priest. Weddings and funerals. My salary's not very big but I like to look good, like everybody else. Give me a few old ties. Who knows? God bless."

At my home, as he held the door again, I looked closely at him: a big man, his buttons valiantly struggling against his belly, his forehead permanently creased where his cap normally rested. The car gleamed in the sun; he spent his waiting moments rubbing its surface to a sheen.

"Wait here," I told him. "I'll be right down." Upstairs, I grabbed some ties in my room and, running back down, pushed the ties into his hands.

"Thank you, thank you, Your Excellency. Hope to see you again. Now listen!"

"What? More?"

"Keep your head up. Don't give up hope. I see scenes like this every day—worse. Health and happiness; that's the ticket! The hell with the job."

At last, he left. Upstairs in my room again, I strode back and forth. What would I do? What could I say?

Later that evening I went to see Dr. Baghai and explained the story from beginning to end. He laughed louder than Colonel Moghadam had. I was beginning to miss the chauffeur.

"He served you right. The truth finally came out," Dr. Baghai said. "Who's the guy who sent in the report about you? I admire him." He laughed again, hitting the arm of his chair as he did so. "Good to have you back, Mansur. That's the funniest story I've heard in a long time. Do me a favor. Write down the conversation with your chauffeur. Forget the rest."

"Seriously, Doctor, what do I do? I'm going to talk to General Pakravan."

"That's probably the best thing to do right now. Then we'll see."

That same evening I wrote out a report to Colonel Moghadam's office requesting official permission to see General Pakravan because he was a personal friend for whom I had great respect. When I received Colonel Moghadam's answer, it read: "Granted. Concerned offices will be informed of my decision." I was struck by the irony of my position. Only a few years ago, I had been interceding with General Pakravan on behalf of Colonel Moghadam. Well, I thought, those roads you see from a plane, so straight they look as though they were drawn there, are actually made by the slow, patient footsteps of men. One hundred miles cannot be walked quickly and easily.

The next day, I went to see General Pakravan, now demoted to minister of information of radio and television of Iran. He received me in his customary pleasant and friendly way.

"Did you obtain proper permission to see me?"

"Yes."

"Written?"

"Written. Colonel Moghadam granted it."

General Pakravan smiled.

For more than an hour, I explained to him what had happened.

When I finished, he sat quietly for a while, smoking thoughtfully. Then he said, "It would not be a good thing for you to resign. If you make him angry, he'll take away your passport. You won't be able to get out of the country. Forget it. On the other hand, I don't believe you should work here in SAVAK. God knows who they'll send to America. I'd like to see you go back. I'll talk to Nassiri. I see him now and then at parties. Yes, I'll talk to him and I'll talk to the shah about you, too." He paused. "Mansur, there are some things you should understand. The man is a soldier. You have to be more tactful with him. You shouldn't have walked in with your briefcase. He got a bad impression of you. It's not your fault. You're not used to this sort of operation. I'll be in touch with you. Just try to enjoy yourself and don't worry. What kind of relationship do you have with Colonel Moghadam right now?"

"Good. Quite good."

"You sure he's not playing both ends against the middle?"

"I'm pretty sure."

"Good, for your sake. Relax and I'll see what I can do."

Four days passed. I heard that the new chief for the United States had been selected, and I was informed that I had to surrender to him the key to my office safe. My heart sank. I went to see Colonel Moghadam immediately.

"Colonel, if the new man opens my safe, do you realize what he'll find?"

"What are you talking about?"

"My safe! All of Dr. Baghai's literature. All my correspondence with you. All the phone numbers. The names."

"You kept my letters?"

"Everything. General Pakravan's, too! I never dreamed this would happen. We're all in trouble."

"Goddammit! I've got to stall the man's appointment. You work with General Pakravan."

I left his office, running. I had no chauffeur waiting for me now, so I leaped onto a taxibar, one of those flatbed vehicles of Tehran that carry huge loads of vegetables to market, as well as poor people who can afford no other transportation. I perched gingerly on a large watermelon, plucking at the legs of my trousers, trying to keep them creased and clean.

In his office General Pakravan stared unbelievingly at me for a moment after I told him. Then he slammed both palms down hard on the arms of his chair. "My God! You shouldn't have kept such things. What else is in there?"

"Everything. Everything I ever did in the United States."

"Jesus, I don't like parties, but because of you I'm going tonight. I'll see Nassiri. Forget the shah. It's too late for that. We have to move fast. All I can do is get another appointment for you with Nassiri. The rest is up to you. Be at my office tomorrow morning."

Like a headless chicken, I ran straight to Dr. Baghai's home.

"Good. Good for you!" he said when he heard the latest development. "Again the truth comes out. You're a member of my party and you want to deny it. Now you'll go to jail. You'll have plenty of time to read and get more experience. You'll learn not to leave things in your safe." He laughed and we talked together, but I was not relieved a bit. Not only had I lost my job, a job I desperately wanted to keep, but the new man would open my safe and all its contents would be brought back to SAVAK in the diplomatic pouch. I was dead. All my meetings with the CIA, the FBI, all the phone numbers of my contacts. Whom could I call? Was there anyone? Who? The chauffeur? Abbas? My father? Dr. Baghai was still chuckling. After I left him, I spent a miserable night.

I was at General Pakravan's office right on time the next morning, scared and tired.

He rose and shook his index finger at me in triumph. "Aha! Got it! Thursday morning, ten A.M., he'll receive you. I talked a lot about you. He told me he had also asked Colonel Moghadam for another report about you. Make sure he makes a good one."

On Thursday morning I was at General Nassiri's office precisely at ten. When the adjutant led me in, I bowed my head low to the general, said not a word, and kept my hands clasped together in deference. He motioned for me to step forward. I did so, still keeping my hands together, inclining my head again.

Gruffly, General Nassiri began. "Rafizadeh. First, you must understand that no one can stay more than four years in any foreign station. You have already exceeded the limit by almost two years. Second, my new position grants me the privilege of choosing my own man for the United States. Third, I have already appointed someone. That can't be changed. But because General Pakravan asked me to receive you, I did so."

He called the adjutant, who clicked his heels and snapped a salute. "Where is the report from Moghadam on Rafizadeh?" The adjutant bowed and offered the folder to him with open palms. General Nassiri studied it and said, "We can give you a good job inside Iran. You're an intelligent man."

My mind was running in crazy circles. It was the end of the road, he had just told me so bluntly. All that stuff in my safe—no way to get it out. And then I thought of the men in SAVAK and how they had avoided me. Of the sickness of the Iranian people. If an Iranian expert wrote about the problems of Iran, Iranians would not believe a word of it. But if a foreigner—lacking all knowledge—wrote a book about the same subject, they would believe it firmly. If an article is published in Iranian newspapers, they have no faith in it, but if the same article is translated into English or French and published in *The New York Times* or *Le Monde* and translated again into Farsi, they would believe it. Iranians fear foreigners and think the big powers will dictate Iran's destiny. I had one last bullet in my gun.

"Your Excellency, with your gracious permission, I would like to brief the new man to the United States."

"Brief him? About what?"

"About you, Your Excellency."

"About me? What about me? What on earth would you have to tell him about me? I'm sitting behind this desk by the blessed order of His Majesty!"

"Your Excellency, I don't know how to present this to you. It is just that I don't want to be called a liar. You see, General, I have also been acting as liaison officer with the CIA. When you were selected by His Majesty as the new chief of SAVAK, there were rumors that . . ." I stopped.

"Go on!" he roared. "What rumors?"

"Your Excellency, the rumors said . . . that you were not capable, not suited for the job. I denied it, of course. I proved to the CIA that you were the perfect choice. I want to brief your next man."

General Nassiri shrank before my eyes. In a small voice, he said, "Don't you get tired? Sit down."

"I'm fine, Your Excellency. I'm fine like this."

"No. Sit down. Talk. Tell me more about these rumors."

"I really don't . . . you would . . . I mean, I wouldn't want to insult Your Excellency. General, we have a saying in Farsi: 'One who repeats an insult gives insult, too.' "

"Never mind the insult. Tell me what you heard."

"I'm sorry, General, I can't. But with your permission. Just let me brief the next man."

"No! Relax. Coffee? Tea?"

"Anything you're drinking is fine."

Tea was brought. I sipped at mine.

"Now tell me. You want to say something. Say it."

"If you insist, General, but please excuse me. The rumors said you were chief of the royal guard, then chief of national police. They said all you cared about were uniforms, spit and polish."

The phone interrupted. General Nassiri grabbed it.

"I'm busy. No calls unless it's an emergency." He slammed the receiver down. "Go on!"

"They said that when you were made chief, the first thing you did was insist on spotlessness and that you ran your hand over the top of the safe to see if there was any dust. I'm really sorry to tell you this, but the rumor got to the CIA and the FBI that all you care about is cleanliness and not work. I defended you. I told them it was nonsense, that you're extremely capable."

"Hmmm. So the CIA in Washington told you I don't know how to work."

"No. No. It was a report they heard. They asked me about it and I denied it. I said His Majesty chose you because you were the best man for the job. Then they asked me about some other things."

"What?"

"It's insulting. I can't . . ."

"What else?"

"They said you didn't speak any foreign languages."

"Wrong! I'm studying English right now. Tell me, who gave them that report? Who started that stupid rumor that I rubbed my hand over the safe?"

"I don't want to make any enemies. Some fool."

"I want the name of the fool!"

"General, just let me brief the man and I'll be at your disposal— your mercy—here."

"I said, tell me the name."

"Well . . . it was the chief of foreign stations. Even Colonel Moghadam was upset with him."

"I know him. You mean he's in touch with the CIA here in Tehran?"

"Yes. He often meets with them."

General Nassiri picked up the phone. "Get me Moghadam." He put it down. "So. What did you tell them?"

"The CIA? I told them everything I could to show them it wasn't true. I told them you had been our chief of national police for more than a decade. And you know yourself that the national police collected more intelligence than SAVAK ever did. And your bravery in delivering His Majesty's order of dismissal to Mossadegh!"

"Damn, you're right. That's why I'm sitting here."

The phone rang.

"Moghadam! From now on, the chief of foreign stations is not permitted to see any foreign intelligence officer! And bring me that man's personnel file! Instantly!" Bang. He hung up. Done. "Mr. Rafizadeh. How long have you been in touch with the CIA?"

"Oh, a long time. Several years."

"You were aware of General Bakhtiar's mission in the United States?"[9]

"Yes. As a matter of fact, General Pakravan assigned me to that matter."

"Good . . . good." He pondered. "You know, I've been chief for a few months now. I've met a few of the CIA men here, casually. But all their reports go to His Majesty."

"If you like, I can have them come to see you."

"You'll do that?"

"Sure. I'll arrange it with the head office."

"Wonderful! I want to establish good relations with them." After a short pause, he continued. "Also, I'd like to see the *chief* of the CIA in Tehran, not some petty official. I'd like to meet with him frequently. They've been ignoring us."

"They don't ignore you, General. It's just that when all the little people get involved, things get messed up this way. It can all be arranged."

"You know, Mr. Rafizadeh, when I was chief of national police, I was invited to the United States. If they were to invite me now . . . I'm a simple man, just a simple invitation . . . Tell them not to get scared. Even if they ask, I won't go. But you understand. It's respect. A matter of respect. They'd have to send several invitations to get me to go there. When you get back, tell them I'll do everything possible to work against communism in this country. We have one common goal, we and the United States, to fight communism." Now his tone was plaintive. "I want a good relationship with them."

"General, it will be arranged."

"Can you do that? Beautiful!"

"Sure, why not?"

"Naturally the invitation shouldn't come through my office. It should go through the royal court or the Foreign Ministry." After thinking for a moment, he continued. "You were involved when General Pakravan was invited to the United States?"

I smiled and did not answer.

"Hah! Modest, too. Pakravan is right! Good character. How soon do you want to go back?"

"I'm at your mercy, General. Whenever you say. But you said you have chosen someone to replace me."

He clasped his hands together. "Two weeks enough to see your family?"

"Yes. Fine, Your Excellency."

"You'll be my representative in the United States. My envoy." He picked up the phone and snapped, "Chief of Department One!" and hung up. It rang back immediately. "Mr. Rafizadeh is here in my office," he said into the receiver. "By order of His Majesty, by his mighty order, the regulations are waived. Mr. Rafizadeh is to return to the United States in two weeks on a special mission. Ignore last appointee! All privileges of chief of station are restored. First-class ticket to be arranged. Inform Colonel Moghadam!" He hung up. "How about a cold drink?"

I was rejoicing, but managed to get out a few words. "Your Excellency, I'm wasting your time."

"No, no. Stay."

Again drinks were brought.

"Pakravan was right," he said once more. "An intelligent man. Tell me again. What does the CIA think about me right now?"

"General, I explained everything I could to them, but my mission is incomplete. That's what I was trying to tell you before."

"All right. Settled. I'm sorry about that first meeting, that we didn't hit it off."

"My apologies, General. My fault."

"How long have you been in the United States?"

"Since 1957."

"Hmmm. A long time. See you again before you leave."

"Of course, General. At your convenience."

"Twice. All right?"

"Yes, General."

"Do you have a car?"

"No, General. They took it away."

"How do you get around?"

"Taxi, General."

"Took it away, huh?"

"Yes, General. Twice I took the taxibar."

"You?"

"Yes, General, I was in a hurry."

General Nassiri picked up the phone. "Department Six!"

When his call was returned, he yelled into the receiver. "When a chief of station is called back, you don't take his car away until the new man is appointed in his place! Immediately reassign a car to Rafizadeh!" He slammed it down again. "What's your relationship with Ambassador Zahedi?"

"We're good friends."

"You know he's a good friend of mine."

"He admires Your Excellency a lot."

"Good. Now we're all friends. You see him often? Did you tell him you lost your job?"

"No, General."

"Why not?"

"He's outside SAVAK. I shouldn't."

"Only Pakravan, huh?"

"Yes, General."

"Good. Good. Glad you talked to me. Okay. You'll be back to see me before you leave." He rose from his chair and shook my hand heartily.

I was thinking to myself as I left his office what fear and insecurity do to people and how insecure General Nassiri was. Two weeks ago, not only did he not shake hands with me, but he practically threw me out of his office. He had called his adjutant and said, "Take him out. You see what kind of man we have in America. The man doesn't even know a closet when he sees one." Today I was sitting, legs crossed, in his office because of his fear of how he would be judged by the CIA. It made him putty in my hands. I was certain he was happier than I because he felt he had an in with the CIA.

The first face I saw as I stepped outside was that of my faithful chauffeur. He walked up to me.

"Your Excellency. At your service."

I was laughing so hard I couldn't answer.

"Did you notice that I'm wearing your tie?" he asked. "How long is it since I saw you? Two weeks? Remember I told you nobody knows what's going on in this country? You never know what will happen."

"You're here on Department Six orders?"

"Right. And I'll be taking you to the airport in two weeks."

"Two weeks? You know that, too?"

"Sure. News travels fast. I told you General Nassiri had a good heart." He cocked his head and winked. "He believes people. I'm experienced in these things."

CHAPTER FIFTEEN

The National Media Spurn the Shah

When the shah arrived for a two-day visit to the United States on August 22, 1967, SAVAK noticed for the first time that among the protesters who greeted his arrival in New York were religious people carrying posters of Khomeini and large placards calling for his return to Iran. SAVAK was notified to use all the means at its disposal to prove to the American authorities that the new breed of demonstrators were traitors, on the payroll of the Iraqi government, which had extended Khomeini indefinite asylum. SAVAK was also instructed to minimize to the press all activities of the demonstrators.

A press conference with American newsmen and TV networks had been arranged for the shah, again at the Waldorf-Astoria. Cameramen and crews arrived early in the morning to set up their equipment in one room of the shah's huge suite. In an adjoining room, an immense table held hors d'oeuvres, including pounds of golden caviar. Also there were stacks of wrapped presents for all the attendants, an enormous gift for the main representative of the newsmen, and, in descending order of magnificence, coins, books, and paintings as gifts for each newsman, cameraman, and crew member.

Walter Cronkite entered the suite, followed by others, including Dan Rather and Marvin Kalb. When all were present, Cronkite asked one of the Iranian attendants to notify His Majesty they were there. The shah's terse reply was that he had decided against the press conference, and that he would give a speech before he left. He would answer no questions from the newsmen.

The newsmen agreed to listen to his speech, but insisted on asking him questions. Back and forth went the messenger, but the shah was adamant in his refusal. Cronkite conferred with the rest of the newsmen; they decided they would not listen to a prepared speech without the privilege of questioning the shah. "Forget it," Cronkite said to the waiting group of newsmen. Then he said to the messenger, "Tell His Majesty 'good luck.' We're leaving."

The shah still did not budge in his refusal, but instructed the attendants to give the presents to the newsmen as they left. As the reporters waited for the elevator, attendants carrying an enormous parcel approached Cronkite, saying they would carry it to his car.

"What is that?" Cronkite asked. When told it was a gift from the shah, he refused it. "No, no present. If His Majesty will talk with us, we'll eat a bite. But presents? No."

Every member of the group refused the shah's gifts. "Nice meeting you," said Cronkite as he entered the elevator. All the newsmen left.

In his own room, the shah, greatly angered and upset, questioned me and other officers.

"You couldn't get them to take them?"

"No, Your Majesty." I answered. "They refused."

"You have their addresses. Send them to their homes."

"With your blessed permission, Your Majesty, it would not be a good idea. They will send them back."

His Majesty reluctantly gave up. By that evening the reception room, the responsibility for its security in the hands of the lower echelon of embassy officials, was stripped bare. Even the caviar was gone. If the shah was informed of this, he said nothing, but those who had not had sufficient chance to grab something (or perhaps those who had grabbed the most) fixed on a scapegoat and fired him.

Later that day, at a White House dinner given in honor of the shah, President Johnson, again according to *The New York Times,* toasted him as "having made steady progress" toward building a society in which "men may prosper and feel happy and secure," and praised him for his "vital reforms." Johnson reportedly continued:

You are winning progress without violence and bloodshed—a lesson others have still to learn. We Americans challenge every propagandist and demagogue—whether he speaks on the radio waves of the world or in the streets of our own cities—to demonstrate his commitment to progress with the facts and figures. The people of the world cry out for progress—not propaganda. They hunger for results, knowing they cannot eat rhetoric.

That same evening, President Johnson further praised the shah and quoted the words of a Persian poet:

> Dig deep and sow good seed;
> Repay the debt you owe your country's soil;
> You need not then be beholden to any man.

"Our distinguished guest this evening has truly sown good seed." The president concluded. "I ask those of you who have come . . . to join me in a toast to the architect of Iran's future . . ."[10]
The shah took any legitimate opportunity to bestow generous gifts. He liked the Johnson family and gave lavish wedding presents to both Lynda Bird and Luci Johnson.

At commencement exercises on June 13, 1968, Harvard University was to confer an honorary Doctor of Laws degree on the shah. It was my duty to be present in Cambridge on that day to coordinate security, and to protect His Majesty from the demonstrators he was convinced threatened his life. About one hundred dignitaries and many parents and guests were to attend the annual alumni meeting in the afternoon part of the ceremonies, during which the shah was to address the audience.
On my flight from New York to Boston, I read a copy of the speech the monarch would be delivering. As the plane descended toward Logan Airport, I could see Massachusetts General Hospital. Now words from the prepared speech echoed in my mind:

> Why should we put up with the present evils in our society? These consist of privations, discriminations, oppressions, bigotries, hatreds, and hostilities; poverty, ignorance, hunger, and illiteracy . . . all individuals have equal rights at birth. Actually, however, a great number of people die of hunger, while a small minority have so much food at their disposal that they simply do not know what to do with it. . . . We are disturbed to find that our society is unwell . . . that the human race is suffering from various forms of injustice. . . . Let us, for once, create an international legion for the purpose of gaining victory in the fight against the real enemies of humanity;

that is, against poverty, hunger, and social injustice in any form.
. . . Let this legion give objective reality to the great words of the
great classical Persian poet Sa'di when he wrote:

> If thou has no sympathy for the troubles of others
> Thou art unworthy to be called by the name of a man.

All of this fine-sounding rhetoric was a lie.

As I stood and gazed over the lawn on which I had sat ten years
earlier on my arrival at Harvard, the lawn where I had pondered the
fate of my Tehran University friends and the huge differences between
that university and Harvard, I hated the shah's speech. There was not
a particle of truth in it. So many years . . . and still the shah would be
spouting his same old lies to an attentive audience of American scholars, businessmen, and officials.

Security was tight. Standing with campus guards and several Massachusetts state troopers, I watched the arriving crowd. As the ticket
holders pressed forward, I recognized many familiar faces from the
demonstrations that had greeted the shah on his previous visits—his
fervent opponents. Off to one side stood a group of them, one obviously
recognizing me as chief of SAVAK and pointing in my direction,
dismayed. Nevertheless, they came toward us.

I had information that many of the shah's opponents had obtained
commencement tickets and meant to disrupt his speech. I knew too that
they were not armed. Still, they had to pass security. As each of the
known demonstrators presented his or her ticket, the security people
looked at me. Remembering Zohari, I nodded and said, "Good people."

Thus, the demonstrators passed through. Perhaps they thought I
did not recognize them. I knew exactly what was going to happen. And
I knew it was wrong. I was chief of SAVAK in the United States and
I wasn't doing anything to maintain security. All I could think of was
that the shah hadn't granted one little passport to a sick man. I don't
know if it was anger, the desire for revenge or what, but I allowed what
occurred to happen.

The shah seemed nervous. The screaming demonstrations that always met him in America may already have unnerved him. He had
hardly begun his speech when he was greeted by a chorus of boos and
cries of "Butcher! Liar!" He flinched noticeably.

Security forces moved quickly to quiet the demonstrators, and a
husky trooper moved onto the platform to stand to the right of the shah.
His Majesty began once more, only to be interrupted again; this hap-

WITNESS   155

pened time after time. He was furious, embarrassed especially by the presence of the troopes. American students joined the protest, and the shah stumbled through his speech to a continuous uproar; chairs and other objects were hurled toward the podium; some women fled in panic before he finished his speech. Chaos prevailed. Even though I felt bad for the honored guests, who now found themselves suddenly trapped on the podium, I couldn't help enjoying the melee. The sight of the elegant older women, wearing their fanciest hats, and the distinguished older men—some with canes—innocently caught in the middle of the upheaval and panicking as they tried to escape, couldn't prevent me from savoring the moment. Zohari's face was in front of me.

The police couldn't control the demonstration. The security forces ran from one area to another, sirens wailed, more police arrived, several demonstrators were led away. The shah, shaking with anger, went on to a faculty reception.

Later, I went to Logan Airport to check on security for his flight to New York. Prior to departure, His Majesty made a sharp motioning gesture to me, snapping his palm forward. There was blood in his look.

"You are not doing a good job here," he barked. "They lowered our esteem. It was very bad today." He drew his brows together. "When we get to Tehran, we will talk to the chief of SAVAK. There must be an end to these barbarians. You have to buy some of them and get rid of the rest. How many times have we said that?" His voice rose. "Tell your chief of our decision!"

Here he was again, plotting further bribery and slaughter.

I kept my head down, hands clasped, as his tirade continued, and murmured, "Yes, Your Majesty. Of course, Your Majesty," but I was exultant. At last, I had served him right!

PART III

CHAPTER SIXTEEN

Princess Ashraf

A strong rivalry existed between the shah and his twin sister, Princess Ashraf. From childhood on, their father had favored her greatly, and it was rumored that when she was seven, she was told by one of the guards of the royal palace to stop playing in the garden because she was destroying the flowerbeds. Sullenly, she obeyed, but when her father appeared, scooped her up, and kissed her, she asked him to carry her over to where the guard was standing. When he did, the little princess reached up and slapped the guard in the face as hard as she could. Her father asked why, and she explained, adding that she couldn't reach him unaided because "he was too tall."

Her father laughed approvingly. "I just wish you had your brother's balls. Then you could take my place instead of him."

The story may be apocryphal, but it is true not only that the princess in later years had great influence over her brother, but that he feared her wrath and scorn. She was far more decisive than he, and when she wished something done—an appointment to a high position for one of her favorites, a job taken away from an enemy—she plopped herself without ceremony on the edge of his desk and badgered him unmercifully until he acceded to her wishes. Without consulting him, she dismissed the chief of national police over some petty disagreement.

Imperious and gratuitously nasty to anyone she considered her inferior, she was adept at soliciting praise and attention. At large gatherings and receptions, such as those held at the United Nations, to which she was head of delegation for a time, she would insist on having a chair brought for her, sink languorously into it, and hold court, upstaging the honored guest and extending her hand disdainfully to be kissed whenever a dignitary came to greet her.

She lived high and could afford to, as there were few lucrative private enterprises in Iran that she didn't have her fingers into; undoubtedly she outdid even her twin in this respect, as in several others. Manipulative and more commanding than he, she saw to it that her brother regularly promoted her staff of advisers (without exception, young, handsome men) to important positions of wealth and influence —ambassadorships and ministries. One Armenian adviser failed to advise satisfactorily. When his plane crashed soon thereafter, rumors circulated that the princess had rewarded him by placing a surprise gift in his plane.

The princess was reputed to have connections with the Mafia, and it was suggested that at least one assassination attempt was made on her life by their hit men. There were also suggestions in the international press that she was connected to drug smuggling, and in 1972, European newspapers implicated her in a drug transaction conducted by a member of the shah's entourage. On March 5 of that year, *Le Monde* recalled:

> People still remember the incident involving Princess Ashraf, the twin sister of the shah, and her entanglement with customs officials at Geneva's Cointrin Airport in 1967. The customs officials found several kilograms of heroin in a suitcase carrying the label of Princess Ashraf. The princess denied the ownership of the suitcase. The shah came to his sister's assistance, and the case was settled very discreetly.

Another charge, reported by *The Washington Post* in 1979, was, in the princess's own words, "neatly cleared up." Many years earlier, in 1958, the *Post* reported she had been caught by French customs officials attempting to smuggle 800,000 francs through customs after having declared only 10,000; a *Time* magazine article of December 8, 1958, reportedly had added: ". . . many wondered how this could happen to so wealthy a woman. Cracked an old Teheran hand: 'Probably habit.' "

Despite her distinctly unsavory reputation, Princess Ashraf became exceptionally powerful during her brother's reign. At various times, she held the positions of: representative for the forty-second Economic and Social Council; representative and chairman for the eighteenth Status

of Women Council; representative and chairman for the World Conference of Women's Year—1975; representative and chairman of the
Iranian delegation to the General Assembly for the twenty-fifth
through thirty-fourth sessions (1970 through 1979); and, in 1970, representative and chairman of the twenty-sixth session of the Human
Rights Commission. It was this last appointment, offered to Princess
Ashraf despite a well-earned reputation for crimes against humanity,
that sparked the greatest international controversy.

She visited New York shortly after the appointment, and I, as chief
of SAVAK in the United States, was responsible for her security. One
afternoon after she had attended a meeting at the United Nations, I met
her, escorted her to her car, and then joined the Secret Service men in
a tail car. A number of demonstrations had been staged by angry
Iranians protesting her appointment to the Human Rights Commission, but that afternoon she made it to her car without incident.

On First Avenue, however, our cars were halted by a mob. A few
hundred people surrounded her car shouting, "Shame, shame! Criminal!" Several youths jumped onto the hood of the car and sprayed
shaving cream across the windshield. Secret Service men positioned
themselves against the car doors while we radioed for more police.
Meanwhile, the demonstrators covered the entire car with shaving
cream. The more the guards tried to clean it up, slipping and sliding
in puddles of the stuff, the more new cans appeared in the hands of the
crowd. We were all hit in varying degrees, and finally began to laugh
at the absurdity of the scene. At last, the cars were able to pass through
the demonstration and we drove on to the Hotel Pierre, where the
indignant princess stomped off.

Almost immediately I was summoned to her suite. She had seen me
laughing during the demonstration and was in a rage. "That entire
incident was your fault!" she said to me as I entered the room. "You
were in charge of my security. Why did you take me down that street?"

"Your Highness," I said politely, "there's no way to get away from
these people. No matter what street we chose, they would have followed
us."

"And you and those Secret Service men aren't smart enough to
avoid them?"

"These people are all over. And the United Nations is a bad place.
No matter how you leave, they'll be waiting at the exit."

"It happened in the street. It was the wrong street. Don't you
understand? You should have taken a different route."

"It wouldn't have mattered."

"But you seemed to think it was very funny when they covered my windshield with shaving cream."

I didn't answer.

"That's it! The end of the line. We have to do something about the United States. SAVAK isn't doing a good job here. I was humiliated today and I plan to talk to His Majesty about it. Dismissed!" She waved her hand at me and turned away.

I was stopped in the lobby by members of the Secret Service. "What happened up there?" they asked. "Was she upset?"

"Yes, she's very upset. I think I may have lost my job. I don't know."

"No, Mansur. Not over that—a bunch of crazy guys with shaving cream!" We all began to laugh again at the thought of it.

Back at the United Nations, I found all of the members of the delegation—including the ambassador—laughing also. I told them how angry she was, and then sent a wire to SAVAK in Tehran describing the incident. I also mentioned the fact that Her Highness was very upset with our station in the United States and was planning to talk to her brother.

That evening I received a phone call from General Nassiri. He asked me to explain exactly what had happened. After I had finished, he too began to laugh.

"It serves her right," he said. "What business does she have serving as chairman of the Human Rights Commission? She's a saint?"

"But General, I think I'm finished. She said she's going to talk with His Majesty about me."

"Don't worry about that. Just sit tight behind your desk; I'm here. Even His Majesty doesn't like the way she shows off. I'll let you know what his reaction is after I see him."

I was aware of the general's relationship with Princess Ashraf. He had been instructed by the shah to avoid her phone calls and thus avoid having to do favors for her. These instructions had been given to General Nassiri after an Australian businessman, selling meat to Iran, failed to pay the appropriate commission to Princess Ashraf's office. She had called General Nassiri and demanded that he jail the Australian, an impossible request, since he was not an Iranian.

Knowing that General Nassiri would meet with the shah on Wednesday morning, I waited until that evening and then phoned him at home. He told me not to worry. Princess Ashraf hadn't said anything to the shah.

Two days later I received a message from the princess asking me to come to see her at the Pierre. On my arrival at her suite, a guard opened the door for me. She was sitting alone on the sofa in a room filled with flowers. The princess looked, as always, manicured and chic.

I bowed. "Good morning, Your Highness."

"Sit down. Have tea." A platter of cookies sat next to the tea set. I sat in a chair across from her.

"I'm so tired," she said, leaning back into the sofa. "So very tired. What about you? What's new with you?"

"Nothing," I replied, taken aback by her gentle manner.

"Tell me, Mansur," she said, crossing one booted leg over the other, "what is your budget here? Does your office have money?"

"We don't have a budget," I explained politely. "Whatever we spend, we submit to SAVAK for approval and they reimburse us."

"I want to get rid of the leaders of that demonstration," she said, sipping her tea.

I gulped mine. "What do you mean 'get rid of'? How?"

She laughed. "I don't understand a SAVAK chief who talks like that. You hire a few Negroes and you pay them, that's all. And you wouldn't have to go through SAVAK. I'll pay for it personally."

"Your Highness, I'm sorry but I can't do that. Besides, it's not so easy to get away with something like that here."

"Softly, swiftly, you put their heads under water. It's not a big deal." She reached for a cookie.

"I can't. I'm sorry, Your Highness."

"If you need money . . ."

"No, I don't."

"Your problem is you're young and inexperienced, Mansur. Also, you don't have children to worry about. But think it over. I can establish you very comfortably. It'll be worth it to me to get rid of those bastards. And between you and me," she said, smiling, "there are plenty of Negroes who would love to do the job. Think about it. I'll call you again."

I couldn't write the head office about this conversation. Again I phoned General Nassiri.

"Don't pay any attention to her," he repeated. "She's vicious. Stay out of her way or you'll get into trouble. And"—he laughed—"you'd better get married. She's got her eye on you."

Nine days passed without my hearing from Princess Ashraf again. On the tenth day, our consulate in New York phoned to tell me that three black men were there asking to meet with me privately. They wouldn't tell the consulate what they wanted from me, only that it was a private matter.

"Tell them to leave their names and phone numbers and that I'll call them personally," I said. Then I sent an officer to the consulate to pick up the information. I never called back, but instead turned the entire matter over to the FBI in New York.

It was protocol for all heads of Iranian offices to escort Princess Ashraf to the airport when she left the United States. I was sitting in the waiting area of Air France at JFK along with the ambassador, the consul general, and some others when she raised her hand and motioned for me to take the seat next to hers. (I hadn't spoken with her since our last meeting at the Pierre.)

"Did you give any more consideration to my idea?" she asked.

I shook my head.

"Well, do. Think about it. I can have you promoted, you know."

I didn't mention the three black men at the consulate.

Back in Tehran, Princess Ashraf approached General Nassiri at a party and, skipping small talk, requested that he promote me to general.

"But, Your Highness," he protested, "Rafizadeh is a civilian, not an army man. I can't promote him to general. Of course, I'll do whatever you want but he's happy with his rank. He's chief of SAVAK in America. What more could he want? Did he demand something from you? Did he ask to be promoted?"

"No. Just do him a favor," she said.

When I spoke with General Nassiri, he wanted to know if I had gone to bed with her.

"No, General," I said. "I was very polite with her, but I didn't ask for any favors. Listen, this whole thing is making me very nervous. Would you do me a favor and call me to Tehran for a meeting? I want to talk to you in person."

"I can't call you back for business but you have two weeks' vacation; why not take that?"

I sent the obligatory request to SAVAK, and the general wired his approval. In Tehran I shared the entire story with him.

"What kind of woman is she?" he asked, shaking his head. "I'm sick and tired of her. Stay out of her reach." The general paused for a few moments and then continued. "Be honest with me, Mansur. Did you do something? It doesn't feel right—the way she talks about you. If you did, you're not the only one." He looked me straight in the eye.

"No," I answered. "I didn't do a thing."

However, I did tell him what had happened when the princess

called me to her suite at the hotel during one of her earlier visits. On arriving at the suite, I had rung the bell. As there was no answer, I waited a few minutes and rang again. Still there was no answer. I decided to wait a little longer and resolved that if there was no answer to my third ring, I would leave a message that I had been there. But on the third ring she answered the bell. To my astonishment she was half naked; she had on only a demi-bra and blue lace panties. She invited me, excused herself, saying that she was on the phone, and went into the bedroom. When she returned, she was wearing only her night-gown. She said that she was running late that day because she had had so many phone calls. She also apologized for not being properly dressed. She talked of her son, Shahram, and his antique business. She said that there had been a problem over an antique her son had sold. The purchaser had discovered that it was a forgery and was complain-ing to SAVAK. The princess wanted me to scare the man and get him to drop his complaint. I told her that I had been instructed by SAVAK not to become involved in any problems connected with her son. Fortu-nately, she dropped the subject. Then the princess had suggested that, since we were now confidants, I should go to a nightclub with her some evening. I replied that I would be honored. But although I had seem-ingly acquiesced, I never did it.

After I related this to General Nassiri, and assured him that noth-ing had happened between us, he warned me again. "Stay away from her. You'll lose your head." He didn't mean figuratively.

I had been in Tehran for five days when General Moghadam re-quested a meeting. In his office he told me about a phone call he had received regarding me.

"A few officers from the royal palace want to meet with you for a briefing on the opposition in America. They'll pick you up at the front gate of SAVAK tomorrow at five."

"But your office can brief them," I said. "Why should I?"

"They asked for you."

"These officers—they're employees of SAVAK?"

He shook his head.

"General, who are they?"

"That I can't tell you. You'll have to find out for yourself. Just don't get into trouble. Use your judgment."

"I can get into trouble?"

"You're already in trouble. I really don't know any more. Just be there tomorrow at five—alone. Let's find out first how they want to be briefed, all right?"

The following afternoon at five, I met two army officers in uniform, who escorted me to a van. They were polite, and during our conversation it became apparent that they were quite sophisticated. We drove through Tehran, but because I hadn't lived in the city for a long time, I didn't recognize the streets. Even today I don't know where they took me, only that they drove slowly and it was a thirty-five-minute ride. The driver of the van parked in front of an expensive-looking house surrounded by a black iron fence. As we passed through the iron gate, a guard inside the house opened the front door. I saw many more guards as I was led up a staircase to the second floor with one officer in front of me, the other behind.

As we entered a large room off the hall, I panicked. Until this moment I had believed I was actually going to be briefing these men on the state of affairs in the United States. Now I found myself in a room resembling an old pharmacy: shelves and shelves of bottles and jars, all neatly labeled, and barrels filled with varicolored powders. Also a picture of the shah with an inscription underneath: "One thousand times Sa'di advises you, 'Don't take a word from this place to any other place.'" Three more army officers stood behind a counter and introduced themselves to me; I was certain they were using false names. On the right side of the counter stood a pharmacist's scale. They asked if I'd like to remove my jacket. I declined. They removed theirs. Two of the men had permanent creases in their foreheads from their army hats. I sat on a stool by the counter and accepted their offer of tea. An officer perched on the stool beside me motioned to the officer behind the counter.

"Why don't you show Mr. Rafizadeh what kinds of 'goodies' you have? And tell him about their strange powers."

The officer came around the counter and led me to a wall lined with shelves. He pointed to a twelve-inch cast-iron pipe on the floor. Part of the pipe had melted, part was broken and sharp, and it was sprinkled with a powdery substance.

"If you take this," he said, lifting a bottle from the shelf, "and put it in cast iron, that's what will happen." He pulled a drawer from the wall. "Know what this is?"

"No."

"TNT. Do you know what kind of power it has?"

"I've heard that it's powerful."

"We've got all kinds of that stuff here." He lifted another jar. "A few ounces of this will send a car a quarter of a mile into the air; it'll blow it to pieces. We've got everything here, but we don't use it for just anyone. Only for enemies. Traitors." He pointed to a shelf filled with all different types of clocks and watches. "Those—those are the commanders. We set them up and at the appropriate time they go off. Explode. Huge powerful explosions. Sit down, Mr. Rafizadeh. We want to talk business with you."

Three of us sat on stools at the counter; the others stood behind it. One of the officers who had been silent from the time I entered spoke now.

"I don't know how to begin my speech to you," he said. "I'm very jealous. His Majesty knows your name; you are obviously in his favor. Very few people get to that position, you know. I haven't. So I'm jealous of you." He paused to light a cigarette, and I realized with a start the kind of damage a cigarette could do in a room like this. "You're aware of what happened during Her Highness Princess Ashraf's trip to New York." He continued, "The car sprayed with shaving cream, demonstrators jumping on the hood. It was disgraceful. After all, she is the chairman of the Human Rights Commission; it was shameful.

"And we don't have to tell you who was behind the whole thing," he added. "The CIA and the FBI have those traitors on a leash and any time it suits them, they loosen the grip—like that stupid act with the shaving cream."

As soon as he introduced the subject of Princess Ashraf's confrontation with the demonstrators in New York, I was certain that even though he had been using the shah's name, the shah knew nothing of this meeting. It was all her work.

"But I don't think the CIA and FBI are agitating these people," I interrupted him. "I firmly believe it was a security problem. With no warning, those people jumped out of the crowd and onto the car with their cans of shaving cream. That's all."

"Just follow me, Mr. Rafizadeh," he said. "You're not going to tell me that you know better than His Majesty, are you? All the oil companies in America are against him and any time we raise the prices to make money for our people, they unleash these traitors. All who oppose His Majesty are traitors. What is a patriotic man like me, who wishes to preserve the dignity of his nation, supposed to do?" He continued to lecture me in this way for another ten minutes, whereupon it was finally disclosed what the meeting was all about.

"We know that the opposition celebrates the New Year at the Hotel Commodore in New York around March twenty-first. Thousands of people will attend. If you give us a hand, we can blow the place up. All we need from you is some basic information: the layout of the place, what kind of musicians will be playing, the locations of their speakers, and what time the music starts. We can plant one of our commanders and explosives in a speaker and that'll be it. Also, we'll fly into California with forged passports, so you won't have to worry about our getting caught. Just get us into the room before the party starts and make sure the speakers are already set up. That's it." He took a deep drag on his cigarette.

"There's no problem, I can do all of that," I said. "But tell me, when everything is set and the explosion goes off, what will happen?"

"It depends on how powerful the stuff is and how much we decide to use."

"I mean how many could be killed?"

"Depends. A hundred, fifty . . ."

"Do you know these people you're going to kill?"

"No, do you?"

"No, I don't."

"But you do know they are traitors."

"I agree with you on that point, but which are the traitors, do you know? It's a big hotel. Do you know how many floors it has? How many rooms? How many guests in case a fire starts?"

"The hotel shouldn't rent the ballroom to these traitors."

"But that's beside the point. Do you know how many other people could be killed if the fire isn't controlled?"

"There's nothing to argue about. It's the only way to keep these people quiet. Some will get killed, the others will go home and shut up." He paused, then continued in a wheedling tone. "If you help us and we are successful, do you realize how lucky you're going to be? The kind of honor you'll have? It is a great honor that His Majesty will be aware of your services through private channels like us. No one else is going to know about it. We want to teach the opposition a lesson they'll never forget."

"Damn right, they wouldn't forget. They'd all be dead!"

"I don't think you realize how fortunate you are to be in the service of the national interest and His Majesty, Mr. Rafizadeh. Many people don't get that opportunity. SAVAK won't know anything about it. Neither will the ambassador. We'll work with you. We know it'll be a strain, that you'll feel tense throughout this thing, but afterward you'll go out to a nightclub with some beautiful woman and forget all about it. You'll have any amount of money you need. No problem. You'll be on the list of His Majesty's favorite people."

My head was reeling. I thought of where I had started—fighting for freedom—and where I found myself now—in a room with a group of terrorists discussing a mass execution. I thought of General Pakravan: "If you don't do it, someone else will." Of my father: "Corruption starts at the top." Of Dr. Baghai: "Violence breeds violence." I thought of the years spent traveling on a road toward freedom only to find myself in this room, with these people.

The officer was still talking. "It's your choice, Mr. Rafizadeh. Be brave. Traitors must be killed."

"I'm sorry, but you don't know my background, my philosophy, my principles," I said.

"We know you better than you think. That's why you're here. You're being offered the greatest honor, a chance to work through a private channel linking you with His Majesty. What more could you want?"

"I don't want to be a part of this. I'm not the type of man to do it. And besides, anyone who does will eventually get caught. I advise you to think twice about it. It's a game that has no end."

"Possibly we informed you too quickly. You weren't ready; that was our mistake. We should have approached you slowly. But we do want you to work with us."

"I can't. I'm sorry but I can't allow myself to put my hand in someone's blood. Just think, if fifty, twenty or even ten people are killed —who would be responsible for their deaths?"

"They would. They are traitors. Listen—you're tense, you're scared."

"Yes," I said, realizing they weren't going to let up. "Let me go now and I'll think about it."

They agreed but warned me not to speak to either General Moghadam or General Nassiri about our meeting. They took me home.

That night I couldn't sleep, imagining the chaos, the tragedy that would result if these men convinced some crazy person to go along with their scheme. I marveled at how ruthless they were in their determination to suppress the opposition. And I also feared that the SAVAK station in the United States would be implicated were such an act actually carried out.

The next day I went to SAVAK to speak with General Moghadam.

"Sit down," he said as I entered. "Why are you so tense?"

"General, those people are crazy, sick. I can't believe it! They want to blow up the Hotel Commodore in New York!"

"Slow down. Tell me exactly what happened, what they're demanding from you."

I gave him a full account of the meeting. "Can you imagine, General? They're talking about blowing up the New Year's party. Your relatives, your own son goes to that party. Can you imagine your son blinded by these maniacs? You should be sick over this."

"How did you leave it with them?"

"I couldn't get out of there without some answer, so I told them I needed to think it over, and that they should do the same. General, why didn't you tell me about this? Why did you say . . . ?"

"Honestly, I wasn't aware. I suspected it but not to this extent. You know, all of this has to do with Princess Ashraf and that stupid demonstration."

"They asked me not to tell you anything."

"Don't worry, you didn't. If they ask for you again, what should we tell them?"

"Tell them I don't agree."

"That's possible, but I think the best solution is for you to have a party, see your friends and family, and then return to New York as soon as possible."

"General, if something like that happened in the United States and someone was killed, I'd get sick and end up in a mental hospital, and I'd tell the authorities. Tell them that if they call."

"Why tell me that? Why don't you tell the boss, tell General Nassiri?"

So I went to General Nassiri's house and described the meeting once again.

He agreed with General Moghadam; I should leave Tehran as soon as possible. "You see how it is here," he said. "There's government inside of government, SAVAK inside of SAVAK—it's crazy."

"General, they never talked about this with you?"

"I knew they had some plan to blow up a building in America—maybe the embassy or the consulate or one of the commercial offices. But no one was going to be killed and it was going to be blamed on the opposition so that American authorities would revoke their visas and deport them. And I didn't agree with the plan. But I never imagined they would carry it to this extreme. But now . . . don't talk to anyone else. Just see family and friends and get back to New York. And you know, Mansur, there is something wrong with you. You're my representative in the United States. You're not a part of the Secret Service, you're not a policeman. Don't go to the scenes of these demonstrations anymore. Stay behind your desk. You didn't have to go yourself to meet Princess Ashraf. I told you to stay away from her; she's vicious."

"What could I do? She called me."

"You could have sent someone else and none of this would have happened. I know you; you must have enjoyed seeing her cursing and trapped in the car. I would have laughed, too. Maybe if this happens to her a few more times, she'll cut out all those unnecessary trips to America. But she's like enema water—goes and comes back, goes and comes back. Make excuses from now on; don't go."

I followed the advice of both generals and left Tehran within a few days. Then, on October 16, 1971, *The New York Times* reported the following incident:

> SAN FRANCISCO, OCT. 15 (UPI)—An explosion heavily damaged the Iranian consulate here late last night. The police said that the type of explosive used had not been identified.
>
> The explosion, strong enough to bend trees, set off a fire that roared up a dumbwaiter to the roof. No injuries were reported.

Following the explosion, my explanation to the United States authorities was that the Iranian opposition to the shah was not responsible. The explosion was timed so that no one was in the building, the amount of explosives suggested Iranian government involvement, and immediately after the explosion, the government was insisting that those opposed to the shah in the United States be deported.

CHAPTER SEVENTEEN

A Fatal Fantasy

In 1971 the shah decided to celebrate the 2,500th anniversary of the establishment of the kingdom of Persia, and in October of that year, on the site of the ancient city of Persepolis, a huge party was planned.

This celebration was intended to introduce the art and culture of Iran to the heads of foreign countries and have the international press broadcast the glory of Iran's civilization to the whole world. But, unfortunately, every civilization was represented except that of Iran or its people. Instead, by this omission, the shah greatly insulted the Iranian people and it can be seen as another element that contributed to his downfall.

This event piqued my curiosity and I obtained a master list from the purchasing department of SAVAK. The cooking and baking for the feast was left to Maxim's restaurant in Paris. The decoration of the fifty-nine guest tents and three royal tents (all air-conditioned) in the desert was left to the French firm of Jansen of Paris, which, incidentally, had been responsible for redecorating the White House for Jacqueline Kennedy. The furniture was Louis XV, the bathrooms French marble. The chandeliers, the Limoges china, the Baccarat crystal, the fireworks, the 165 chefs, the 400 waiters and waitresses, the 20 tailors, 25 beauticians (men and women), 1,500 toupees, 300 hairpieces, and 400 pairs of eyelashes to be worn with costumes were from France. According to *Time* on October 25, 1971, so "were 7,700 pounds of meat, 8,000 pounds of butter and cheese, 1,100 pounds of cream,"

25,000 bottles of wine, $840,000 worth of colored lightbulbs, the rugs for all the tents, the landscaping—which included several thousand plantings and several thousand bouquets of flowers—all brought from Paris to Iran by Iranian Air Force planes. *Time* commented:

> Providing the trappings kept Paris merchants—who supplied everything—busy for a whole year. Bimonthly flights of aircraft and convoys of trucks that made the overland trip from Paris with relays of drivers transported the wares to the desert.

One Iranian pilot told me, "I've been flying my 707 back and forth from Paris to Iran for more than a year just to bring in rugs, crystal, liquor, and marble for the bathrooms."

Although for centuries Iran has been world famous for its magnificent rugs, nevertheless virtually all of the rugs for the tent city had been ordered from France. This was noted by *Newsweek* on October 25, 1971, as were some ideas expressed by detractors: ". . . the only concession to local industry was an occasional Persian rug plopped over the French carpeting."

But somehow even the moments of glory had a taint to them. Detractors asked why—if the purpose of the celebration was to sing the praise of Iran—the shah imported virtually everything from Europe: food, furnishings, china, and crystal, even the entire tent city itself.

Kholar, the famed wine of Shiraz, is prized by experts, but, in all, 25,000 bottles of wine and 1,000,000 bottles of liquor had been imported for the party. As *Time* said: "Maxim's shopping list included 25,000 bottles of wine—including a Chateau-Lafite-Rothschild, 1945, at $100 a bottle—that were sent to Iran a month early to rest."

Long before the celebration, the shah had ordered SAVAK not to allow any news to be leaked to the press concerning the sums of money being expended on his extravaganza, particularly not to New York reporters or to *Le Monde.* Of course, this order was futile, and when he was badgered by New York reporters about the estimated hundreds of millions the colossal celebration was costing his impoverished country, he answered, according to the same article in *Time:*

> Why are we reproached for serving dinner to 50 heads of state? What am I supposed to do—serve them bread and radishes?

The only Iranian food served was caviar from the Caspian Sea. It can only be assumed that the shah had no choice. If he could have found superior French caviar, it is probable that he would have preferred that Maxim's supply it, too.

Some 500 guests dined with the shah at a 235-foot-long mahogany table—made in France. A cake weighing over 72 pounds, and baked by the most famous chef in Paris, was served in honor of Empress Farah's thirty-third birthday, which occurred during the celebration.

The Iranian ambassador to the United States had told me earlier that the shah wanted the celebration to be broadcast by satellite to the whole world, and that he wanted no one but Barbara Walters to do it.

Shortly before the party took place, I ran into the ambassador at the airport. He looked very morose. "What's the matter?" I asked.

"I don't know what to do," he said. "The shah has told me to make sure that Barbara Walters comes to cover the celebration. She's giving me a hard time. I can't seem to pin her down. I have to get her to come or the shah is going to be very upset."

Before we could finish our conversation, my flight was announced and I dashed off. I couldn't figure out why the ambassador was so upset. I realized the shah wanted the most publicity possible, but I couldn't understand why one journalist more or less would be so important to him.

The next time I saw the ambassador, he was in a jubilant mood. "She's coming! The shah is delighted."

Perplexed, I asked, "Why her? What's the big deal?"

He laughed. "Mansur, you fool, you're so naïve. He really believes that after seeing him she'll broadcast with a 'special' kind of energy."

When I left him, I wondered what the attraction had been—power, curiosity, intellect, or greed? Later on I discovered that the shah had been sending her lavish jewelry through SAVAK.

(SAVAK provided many unique services for the shah, and one of them was to buy gifts for important people. SAVAK had a secret budget that was used exclusively for this purpose. There was even a gift office that was kept stocked with jewelry and antiques in the event something was needed quickly. The agency had it down to a science and kept very accurate records. The responsibility was left to SAVAK because it knew how to use sensitivity and discretion in distributing these often lavish gifts to politicians and celebrities.)

Barbara Walters was often photographed wearing the magnificent jewelry I had seen described in embassy memos. For instance, during her first interview with the empress Farah after the shah's death, on the

TV program *20/20,* the whole world got to see Barbara Walters wearing beautiful large turquoise earrings. These were just a small sample of the shah's tokens of appreciation.

At the reception at Persepolis, in addition to heads of state from various republics, there were nine kings, five queens, and twenty-one princes and princesses. However, as *Newsweek* indicated on October 25:

> You just weren't important if you weren't invited; but you couldn't have been that important if you actually showed up.

Separating the tents from the surrounding desert landscape was a rope, one mile of gold rope enclosing the promenade to the tent city. Before the party, the shah inspected the location and, fondling the rope, remarked, "They all say Americans are so clever—building Disneyland. They should know that I built a Disneyland in a desert. But there is a difference. Our gold rope will still be here tomorrow. In America, they would steal it overnight."

In this bash to end all bashes, if Iranians did not have the honor to be waiters and waitresses instead of the French servants imported for the occasion, they most assuredly did have the "honor" to be in jail. Several months before the party, while I was visiting Tehran, General Moghadam told me: "The expense of the party and the stealing that's going on are so astronomical it would make your head spin. Every ministry has had to publish a book about the royal family and it must be printed in Europe. Tons and tons of books are coming to Iran by plane. What has the family of the shah done besides putting heroin and cocaine and opium in their suitcases as presents for foreign dignitaries? What other help have they ever given to humanity? A few nights ago, an Iranian Air Force cargo plane brought in marble and bricks from Italy for one of the shah's friends who's building himself a home. The air-freight bill of lading said it was for the shah's party. And five thousand people have been arrested so far by SAVAK, the army, and the gendarmerie! The shah's instructions are to jail every person he suspects of being a troublemaker. We don't have any more room in the jails!"

"Well, it's for certain the bricks belong to SAVAK," I joked. "What inner-circle member would dare bring them from Italy for himself? The logic must be that if people start protesting against the shah's party, SAVAK can throw the bricks at them. The next day the Iranian press will report that a bunch of liberal idiots were demonstrating against the national security and the pride of the country, and the poor workers couldn't stand it and bricked them."

"C'mon. Are you saying we throw bricks at people?" Moghadam asked.

"General, how much 'stone' is in your hands already? You have your trucks on alert. Listen. I've got a great suggestion. You have no more room in your jails. Why don't you just make one of the southern states a jail and send all his opponents there?"

"You're crazy!"

"What makes you say that?"

"Believe it. If I made that suggestion to him, he'd take it. The maniac is already mad with power. Just shut up. He might hear you!"

On my return to the United States after that visit, I went to Washington. There I met with a top official of the CIA, and during our talk gave him a full account of the conversation I had had with Moghadam.

"I have no doubt that there is deep friendship between Nixon and the shah," I told him, "but for heaven's sake do something to prevent Nixon from attending this party. Not out of respect for Nixon but for the United States. Why make the Iranians their enemies? Please, in your capacity, use whatever means you can to prevent it. Give your office—those in command—the full details of what's happening."

President Nixon and several other heads of state did decline the shah's invitation. *Time* reported on October 25:

> Regrets were sent by President Nixon (who dispatched Spiro Agnew instead), Queen Elizabeth II (who was represented by Prince Philip and Princess Anne) and, in the unkindest cut of all, French President Georges Pompidou, who sent Premier Jacques Chaban-Delmas. What was particularly grating was the fact that the Shah had given the affair such a heavily French accent. Taking note of this, Pompidou is reported by a Western diplomat to have said: "If I did go, they would probably make me the headwaiter."

About a month later General Moghadam called me.

"Those things we discussed in my room that time—about the army planes, the bricks, the southern state for a jail—did you talk to any reporters in the United States? About the five thousand in jail?"

"No. I didn't talk to any reporters. Why? What's going on?"

"The New York reporters are here and they won't give up. They keep talking about five thousand prisoners. They also know the story about the Italian bricks. I didn't reveal that intelligence to anyone but you. You must have told someone."

"No reporters. But someone. Someone big enough to inform the White House so that the president wouldn't attend."

Moghadam was delighted. He laughed and said, "Right now our business is lying about figures. We repeat the words 'twenty-five-hun-dred-year kingdom' so often that it's becoming second nature. When all those reporters were bothering me and asked me how many political prisoners we had, I automatically said twenty-five hundred. If the shah asks me why, I'll say they said five thousand so I cut their figure in half." Indeed, the figure of 2,500 did appear in print—in *Time:*

> Democracy is less advanced. Iran has political parties and elec-
> tions, but the Shah appoints half the members of the Senate and
> makes all the important decisions. The press is firmly controlled,
> and criticism of the Shah is wholly forbidden. For the celebrations,
> the army clamped tight security around a 60-mile circumference of
> the tent city, and, by ironic coincidence, arrested exactly 2,500
> potential troublemakers.

The overall expenditure for the party was estimated at $300 million, but certainly a great deal more was spent, because most of the expense was borne by the various ministries and none of the ministers dared talk to the shah about money. Each government agency and private business was required to donate. According to a rough estimate by the shah, $800 million was spent on his party.

According to *Newsweek* on September 27:

> No one knows how much all this will cost, but in a land where
> per capita income still amounts to only $350 a year, the conspicu-
> ous consumption has ruffled feathers. "We're spending all this
> money on a handful of heads of state," grouses one intellectual in
> Tehran, "when we should be spending it on the people."

And again:

> And more serious critics found it staggering that the Shah
> would spend $11 million of his country's money on food and liquor
> for some of the wealthiest people in the world when poverty and
> starvation still exist in Iran.

The people of Iran, meanwhile, were dying of disease and starvation, some of them living in holes like animals, or worse, in conditions that any observer would quake to see.

It could be said that the shah himself, on behalf of the Iranian people and at their expense, threw a party celebrating the founding of the ancient Persian monarchy that marked the end of the reign of kings in Iran.

CHAPTER EIGHTEEN

Revisiting the Jail

On a Thursday morning in 1973, my third day back in Tehran after the party, General Moghadam asked me to report to his office forthwith. Because we were close friends, and General Moghadam's two sons were staying with me in New York, I was not nervous about complying with his request. Still, when I arrived I could see that the general was disturbed about something.

He told me that a young Iranian student had come from Germany to Tehran two weeks earlier and, because he was on a list of dissidents, had been arrested at the airport before his family had even had a chance to see him. He was subsequently jailed and beaten, and his belongings were held at SAVAK. "The man has been tortured; it was not severe, but it was torture," General Moghadam told me. "This morning," he continued, "the parents of the boy were waiting on the street in front of my home. The mother wept as she tried to kiss my feet. 'I haven't seen my son in several years,' she sobbed. 'What has happened to him? God protect your son. Do something for my son.' "

General Moghadam told me he knew the family well and was greatly affected by the woman's pleas. He spoke of his own children in the United States, and of how he would feel if they were jailed on their return to Iran. "I promised them that their son would be released late today," the general went on, "and told them to plan a party for him on Friday. Saturday he must return to Germany. If they don't comply with my orders, SAVAK will arrest the young man again when they return to work on Saturday."

I understood General Moghadam's dilemma. He did not legally have the power to release the young man, and yet his compassion demanded that he do something. He knew of a way, but it would work only if he had someone who was totally trustworthy. Most SAVAK officers, if asked to participate in such a scheme, would somehow report the general's interference with the law to the inner circle of the shah. He knew that I, just returned, was his only chance to free the boy.

There was little time to act. This was a Thursday, the end of the Iranian work week, so the release had to be accomplished that day.

"I need General Nassiri's help as well as yours," General Moghadam informed me. "I've already contacted him, and he says he's leaving by helicopter at about two this afternoon for a weekend at the Caspian Sea."

"I know," I said.

"How do you know?"

"I saw him yesterday," I responded, "and he invited me to accompany him. I had to refuse because Dr. Baghai is invited to my house this evening."

With that settled, we returned to the business at hand. We had only five or six hours left in which to free the young man. General Moghadam outlined his plan. I was to go to the jail and tell the young man that he would be released if he would write a letter expressing his remorse for his antiregime activities, and promise to refrain from any such activities in the future. I was to instruct him on the proper way to write the letter so that it would be acceptable to General Nassiri, who must sign it.

"Explain the process to him," General Moghadam urged me. "Tell him that he will be released to go home tonight, that there will be a party for him Friday, and that he must return to Germany on Saturday."

Although General Moghadam was my friend, I had long since resolved not to get mixed up in any SAVAK activity in Tehran. In fact, I had managed up till now to stay entirely clear of such involvement. "General," I began, "you know my policy of not working for SAVAK while I'm in Iran. How many times have I told you?"

"This is not work for SAVAK," he protested. "This is a favor for me, and for the young man's family. You are going to get him discharged today."

"Please," I pleaded. "Get another officer."

"I don't trust them. I trust you." General Moghadam was determined. "This boy is very emotional. He may say something that will get him in trouble—they will beat him again. You are an educated man; if you see him, he will talk to you."

Again I refused. "I can't go to that jail. Why can't you understand that?"

He jumped up from his chair. "You know the problem with you people?" he shouted angrily. "You live in ivory towers. You don't ever want to get involved in dirty things. Iranian politicians take pride in saying the things they didn't do rather than the things they did. Come on, Mansur. Don't you want to release the man? Don't you want to make his family happy? Will you go?"

"My heart says yes; my head says no. I don't want to get involved," I said deliberately.

"Go along with your heart," the general urged.

There was no time to think. My mind was in turmoil. I felt I had to refuse, yet I felt I had to help. General Moghadam was already back at his desk calling the SAVAK officer in charge of the jails. "Give the file of that man to my chauffeur immediately," he ordered. "Have him put it in my car." The matter had been decided for me. I could do nothing. I stood there numbly.

General Moghadam picked up the phone again, and called his security guards. "Mr. Rafizadeh is going to the jail right away to interview a prisoner. Tell my chauffeur to get the car ready immediately." He stood up.

"You said I am going to interview him," I said dazedly. "What am I supposed to say?"

"What did you want me to tell them—that you are going to release the man?" He pushed me toward the door. "Go on! And be sure you warn the man to stay calm."

General Moghadam's white Mercedes-Benz was waiting. When the chauffeur opened the door, I noted the folder lying on the front seat. I got into the car, relieved that I didn't have to put up with that other sagacious chauffeur.

Once in the car, I thought to myself, *Here I am, going to release a "traitor" whose only crime is that he attended a few meetings and participated in some demonstrations in Germany. In that respect, I am more of a traitor than he! What kind of justice is this? I, the greater "criminal," am appointed to judge someone else. I am going to ask him for an expression of remorse so that he can be free, when I have no remorse and yet have total liberty.*

We slowed as we passed the prison guards, who saluted when they recognized General Moghadam's car. The car moved slowly into the courtyard and stopped. The chauffeur jumped out to open the door, and as the soldiers saw me get out, they saluted stiffly. I stared at them blankly. Why was I here? An eerie silence pervaded the courtyard. In my mind it was 1956. I had been a prisoner in that very jail. I could hear the curses, feel the pain of the beatings.

I felt as though I was a figure in a tableau. I was standing beside the general's car, staring at the soldiers, who still held their salutes, waiting for me to dismiss them. I tried desperately to get control of the situation. With an effort I saluted the soldiers and barked, "At ease!" Then, turning to the chauffeur, I shouted angrily, "Where is the man in charge of this jail? Where are we supposed to go?"

The chauffeur snapped to attention. "At your service, sir!" he exclaimed, snatching up the folder. He ran toward the building, beckoning me to follow. Slowly, as if in a trance, I walked after him toward the building.

Once inside, my mind began to clear. I remembered my purpose in being there. The sergeant in charge saluted me. "At your service, general!"

"Give him the folder," I ordered the chauffeur.

The sergeant examined the contents of the folder, and guided me to a room where he requested that I be seated at a desk. I sat down and directed him to bring the young man I was to interview.

"Right away!" He stepped to the door and gave an order for the man to be brought. Then, turning to me with a knowing smile, he inquired, "Will he be released today?"

"I don't know," I parried. "It depends on the interview, and ultimately on the decision of the chief."

The sergeant cleared his throat. "Sometimes they get bruises," he said sympathetically. "I don't know if this young fellow has any, but sometimes they do. I hope they let him go. He is too emotional." The sergeant obviously did not know that I had been a prisoner in this jail myself. Nor did he recognize me—even though for six months I had visited Dr. Baghai daily in another jail where he had been assigned. I, on the other hand, remembered him well. He had always impressed me as a good, kindly man, and others shared my opinion of him. His name was known to practically every prisoner. He spoke Farsi with a Turkish accent, and he had a peculiar way of conversing on the telephone. Whenever he received a call from one of the "important" generals, he would hold the receiver firmly in one hand and salute smartly with the other.

Two soldiers accompanied the young man as he was brought to the room where I waited; one walked in front of him and one behind, each holding a rifle at the ready. I dismissed the sergeant and the soldiers.

The young man was obviously frightened. He stared at me apprehensively. I stared back. He was my height. His shirt and pants were similar in style to mine, but they were wrinkled and stiff with dirt. The stubble on his face and his disheveled hair indicated that he had been deprived even of the most basic amenities. I offered him a seat, and he sat down.

I explained to him Moghadam's request that I speak to him about writing the letter of remorse, and told him that if he agreed, I would help him with the letter. As a result, he would be discharged that day; he could attend the party on Friday, but he must return to Germany on Saturday.

He watched covetously as I smoked. "May I have a cigarette?" he asked. I handed him one. "Does my family know where I am?" he inquired.

"Yes," I replied. "As a matter of fact, your parents will be here this afternoon to take you home."

"Where are my suitcases?" he pressed. "Where are the gifts for my family?"

"General Moghadam told me they are in the SAVAK office. They will be delivered to your home today," I assured him.

"General," he pleaded, "will you tell me why I am here?"

"First of all, I am not a general," I responded. "And, secondly, I have the same question—'Why am *I* here?' "

"What do you mean?" the young man asked, puzzled.

"I am not sure why I came," I said slowly. "I was told to come here and help you."

"Do you work for SAVAK?"

"Yes."

He frowned. "You don't look like a SAVAK man to me."

"What do I look like?" I asked curiously.

"Those bulky shoes—that baggy suit. You look like you are from the United States."

"Yes, I am," I replied.

"What is your name?" he inquired.

Ingenuously I told him.

"May I have another cigarette?" he asked.

I handed him the whole pack; then, reaching into my pocket, I placed another pack in front of him. He smiled, leaned back, completely relaxed. His fear seemed entirely gone. "*You* are from America—these are American cigarettes. I haven't smoked for a long time." He paused. "You know they beat me up here."

"I am not here to discuss that," I said brusquely. "I am only here to ask if you want to be released today. You must write a letter—an expression of your remorse—to His Majesty the Shah, telling him that you attended some meetings and demonstrations. You were brain-washed. When you came back to Iran, you saw the progress that has occurred under the leadership of His Majesty. You realized your mis-take, and now you are sorry for what you did. When you go back to Germany, you will work for the Iranian people under the leadership of His Majesty the Shah. That is all you have to do. Write that letter and you will be released."

The young man suspected a trick. "First of all, how can I lie?" he said. "I came directly from the airport to the jail—how could I have seen any progress?"

I gave him a pitying glance. "All of this is a lie," I said flatly. "But this is the manner in which the letter must be written."

He was stubborn. "How can I say I was brainwashed? I wasn't!"

"I know," I said patiently. "But if you want to be released you must write these things."

He persisted. "If I go back to Germany, I will not act any differ-ently."

"Look, my friend," I addressed him firmly. "I cannot tell you what to do when you are in Germany. General Moghadam asked me to have you write this so that you can be released. If you stay here you will get into real trouble."

"What if I write the letter and SAVAK publishes it in the newspa-per, and I am still kept in jail?" he said, in challenge.

"It is possible, but I think everyone here fully intends to release you today. Please follow my advice and write the letter."

"Right this minute?" he asked.

"Right this minute," I said. "I am waiting."

I let him sit at the desk to write, and I took his chair. As he wrote, I observed the room. I had a sudden, sickening feeling of déjà vu. I had been here before. This was the very room where my mother and youn-gest brother, Mozafar, had come to visit me when I was a prisoner in this jail. In my mind I could see the whole drama reenacted as if I were watching a movie.

When I had first come to Tehran from Kerman, I was considered a country boy. I had no family in Tehran, so my friends would often invite me to their homes for lunch or dinner. In 1956, when my mother was forty-two years old, she came to Tehran for the first time in her life. To reciprocate my friends' hospitality, I asked her to cook a special meal one evening and I would invite them over. The plans were made. I was supposed to bring my friends home with me after we finished our meeting at the Toilers' Party headquarters. That morning I asked my mother if there was anything she needed. "Just bring fresh limes," she replied. "I have everything else."

Neither I nor my friends ever tasted that meal. We were picked up by the police, and put in jail.

On my second night in jail, my mother came with my six-year-old brother to this very room. My mother began to cry. Mozafar, frightened by the soldiers and their guns, asked anxiously, "Are they going to shoot you, Mansur?" He began to sob as he stood between my knees, holding tightly to me.

The colonel in charge of the jail pointed at me. "Traitor!" he shouted. "Be kind to these people. Give up your nonsense! Talk!"

I was deeply offended. "I don't want you to come here anymore!" I said angrily to my mother. I jumped up, pushing Mozafar away as I did so.

"You are my son," my mother replied.

"Don't consider me your son anymore," I said furiously.

All she did was look at me with a stricken expression. Then she cried.

"See," the colonel said, "he has no mercy for his family. How can he have mercy for his country?" He motioned to the soldiers. "Take him away."

As I left the room, I overheard the colonel spit out the words, "Take that young fool back to his cell." I cringed. Mozafar cried even harder. The colonel tried to console my mother: "Don't cry, my sister. If he writes the letter of remorse, he will be discharged."

Today, I was the one asking for the letter of remorse. Other things had changed as well. Mozafar, in New York, was a close friend of General Moghadam's sons. The colonel who had been in charge of the jail in 1956 was now in charge of maintenance at SAVAK; he never recognized me as the prisoner he had denigrated some fifteen years earlier. Now he was big and fat, and had little money. I held no grudge against the man; I pitied him. I knew he had a heart problem, and had asked my cousin, a cardiologist trained in the United States and practicing in Iran, to treat him without charge. Just yesterday the colonel had caught me in the hall of SAVAK, and revealed his desperate financial

situation. He had asked for a fifty-dollar raise for his son, who worked
for me as an agent in the United States. I told him to send a request
to General Moghadam, and if the general agreed, I would grant the
raise.

By this time the young man had finished his letter. I sat down next
to him and read it, making a few corrections throughout the draft.
"Don't use 'shah,' " I advised. "Say 'His Majesty—King of Kings.' "
I made a few more changes to make the letter more acceptable, and at
the end I added some phrases expressing the boy's sorrow and begging
the shah to forgive him.

I told the young man how his mother had cried in front of General
Moghadam's home earlier that morning. "Please rewrite this in your
best handwriting, and when you are finished, knock at the door. Give
the letter to the sergeant. They will take you back to jail, and at about
three or three-thirty they will release you. Your mother and father will
be waiting outside to take you home. Do not change anything in the
letter," I emphasized. "Rewrite it carefully, and then be sure to tear up
this draft."

"Are you sure I will be released?" he asked.

"I am positive. I am very upset today myself, but I can promise you
that I will have you released." I shook hands with him. I was anxious
to get away. I stepped out of the room and closed the door behind me.
Calling the sergeant over, I told him, "In a half hour this man will have
his letter ready. As soon as you get it, give it to one of the drivers and
have him take it to General Moghadam's office immediately. The general will call you and tell you when to release the prisoner. Don't
forget!"

"Yessir!" The sergeant saluted me. "I won't forget."

The sergeant opened the door. "Did you hear that?" he addressed
the prisoner. "As soon as I send the letter to the office, you will be free!
Thank him!"

"He doesn't need to thank me," I said gruffly. "Just be sure that
you send it."

Back at SAVAK, on my way to General Moghadam's room, I
encountered the colonel again. "I am not going to write to General
Moghadam for the fifty-dollar raise," he told me. "You should give it
to my son yourself."

I nodded. "Granted. I will give your son the raise." I realized I had
completely forgiven the man for what he had said to me and my mother
that long-ago day.

I gave General Moghadam a full account. "The boy was beaten,"

I told him. "I could see the bruises. He was also in bad shape mentally."

"What could I do?" General Moghadam shrugged. "Thank you, Mansur, I am grateful to you."

As soon as the prisoner's letter was delivered to him, General Moghadam scanned it. "Beautiful," he beamed. "I'll take it to General Nassiri's office." He got up and took it with him.

At about 1:30, General Moghadam rushed back, called the jail, and told them to release the prisoner. He then called the boy's family to tell them the good news. I reminded him to have the young man's luggage sent to his home.

That night when Dr. Baghai came to our house for dinner I told him the whole story. He praised me. "You did a good job. Don't feel bad. You succeeded in getting the man released. All of these people have been victimized by repression and exploitation. I am glad that you gave the fifty-dollar raise to the colonel's son. That was a magnanimous act. One must always consider the circumstances of another's acts, Mansur."

Dr. Baghai's commendations lifted my spirits. "Go and kiss your mother now," he admonished, "and tell her that you are sorry for insulting her that day."

Ten days later, General Moghadam again summoned me to his office. Uncharacteristically, he was laconic and appeared absorbed in his work. He handed me a folder and said, "Read this." I understood that I was to do my reading while he worked. I sat down. In the folder I found a Persian newspaper that had been published in Frankfurt, Germany. Reproduced in it was the rough draft of the letter I had helped the young man write. He had taken it with him! The article, several pages long, explained his experience in detail, even including my name.

Dumbstruck, I read and reread the article. Finally, I closed the folder. I stood up and approached General Moghadam's desk. He picked up his glasses. "Yes?" he inquired, looking up at me. "Did you give him your real name?"

"Yes," I replied somberly.

"Why didn't you take the rough draft away from him?" he asked.

"I hated to wait there any longer. If I had stayed any longer, he would not have trusted me. I wanted to leave him alone. Besides, I didn't want to stay in that room because it revived so many bad memories from my past. I told him to knock on the door and give the letter to the sergeant when he was finished, and then I left."

"You know that by giving him your name, you have caused trouble.

The State Department will present this paper to His Majesty. We must go to General Nassiri right away and try to salvage your reputation. Sloppy work, Mansur."

"I told you I didn't want to do it!" I said.

To our relief, General Nassiri managed to make sure that the shah never saw the incriminating article. Once again I was saved.

On my flight back to New York, we made a short stopover at Frankfurt. When the plane again took off, I asked for a drink. Looking down on the city where the young man lived, I began to laugh. I couldn't help myself! "Look what he did to me—I can't believe it!" I shook my head. "I'll forgive him, too," I mused.

CHAPTER NINETEEN

SAVAK Chief Under the Gun

In the summer of 1974 General Nassiri and his wife visited Washington as guests of the United States government. During their stay, General Nassiri had surgery performed at Walter Reed Hospital for a prostate condition, and protocol required my presence with him in Washington for the duration of his recovery.

When I visited the hospital on August 10, General Nassiri was not in his room. I found him in the sitting room, intently watching the news. Watergate had ended. Nixon had resigned. The president was boarding Air Force One at Andrews Air Force Base for his flight to California. On the TV screen, a haggard Nixon stood on the last step at the door of the plane, waving to the reporters. The door closed behind him and the plane taxied onto the runway. As it took off, the reporters began their comments on Watergate and the vagaries of political office. I translated some of their comments for General Nassiri.

Still staring at the screen, he hit the chair arm with the flat of his palm. "Damn! Damn! Too bad. Good man."

"Yes, General," I answered. "Good man."

"You know, Mansur, sometimes Americans are stupid. They hound a wonderful man like that out of office. Goddammit! His Majesty the Shah has lost a good friend."

"Well, Ford is in. He'll probably turn out to be just as good a friend as Nixon."

"No," General Nassiri said firmly. "No one will ever be like Nixon

ah. He was a good friend." General Nassiri paused, then added,
The shah helped the man."

"Helped?" I asked. "How? In what way?"

"Don't you know?"

"No, I don't, General. What do you mean?"

General Nassiri smiled slightly. "Our ambassador knows that we
. . . here and there, we donate to a campaign."

I knew the shah liked to give gifts to everyone. The reported
amount of the shah's donation to Nixon's campaign fund was
$60,000,000. Of this money, $8,000,000 was stolen by the Iranian intermediaries; of the $52,000,000 remaining, some was transferred to Mex-
ico for laundering and brought into the United States in the form of
cash. The remainder was deposited in Switzerland in the accounts of
Nixon's best friends.

"It's news to me," I said. "But now there's Ford. They can donate
to him."

"Oh, I don't know." General Nassiri locked his fingers together and
shook them. "Nixon and the shah—they were like that. I'm sure His
Majesty is very upset right now. No one else is like Nixon to him."

After General Nassiri's discharge from the hospital, we toured
Washington. As part of the tour, we were taken to a private museum
that belongs to the intelligence agencies, where we were shown all kinds
of criminal devices, booby traps, gory photographs of various crimes,
and wax figures depicting famous acts of violence. One section, our
hosts pointed out to General Nassiri, consisted of Communist-made
devices, which had been sent to them from SAVAK. SAVAK had
confiscated them before they caused any damage. General Nassiri said
that he remembered the circumstances under which some of these items
had been found. I scrutinized them, considering how remarkable it was
that such small devices could raze entire buildings.

As we walked to our car later, General Nassiri began to laugh.

"What's so funny?" I inquired.

"Those booby traps in there," he said. "They were not made by the
Communists. SAVAK made them! We told the Americans that they
were Communist-made, and they believed us. Now they have put them
in a museum! Can you believe it?"

Before General Nassiri and his wife returned to Iran, toward the
end of their stay, I received a telephone call at my home in New Jersey
from George Bush. "Mansur," he said, "talk to the general and, if it's
all right with him, we'd like to meet them for dinner one evening before
he leaves. I'll come with Barb and a few senior officers and their wives.

If he says yes, just let me know which airport is most convenient for you people. We can fly into New York or New Jersey."

I phoned Bush later that day. "The general accepted the invitation and is delighted. If it's not a problem for you, fly into Teterboro Airport. We'll go from there into Manhattan."

When I picked up the general, he was alone and said nothing at first about his wife not being with him. During the ride to the airport, the general seemed uneasy. "I like the man," he said, referring to Bush. "He's polite and he's respectful. But he's so intellectual. He doesn't seem to care at all about appearances. His socks are always sliding down into his shoes and he doesn't notice. He's too busy thinking, always thinking. And he keeps grinding away at me on the issue of human rights. No one speaks to me as frankly as he does about it. He makes me nervous. By the way," he added, "if they ask, Mrs. Nassiri has a bad cold."

I knew that he hadn't extended the invitation to his wife, though it was clearly intended for both of them. "Why didn't you want her to come with us, General?" I asked.

"Because Zoli is so much younger than I and so beautiful I get embarrassed in front of people like Bush and his wife. I get even more nervous. The goddamn shah, he causes me so many problems."

General Nassiri was among a few select people known to be close to the shah, so I was shocked to hear him curse the man so vehemently, but I said nothing.

During dinner, Bush again steered the conversation to the subject of torture. The general had just said jokingly, "If Mansur is not behaving in the United States, I can call him back from his post."

"Yes," Bush responded. "Good idea, call him back to Iran."

"It will serve him right if we call him back," Nassiri said, still joking. "We know what to do to him."

"What?" Bush demanded. "What will you do to him? Put him in the hands of SAVAK men?"

"Oh, no. Here we go again."

"No, no, General. Tell me what you will do to him."

"Nothing, nothing. I was joking, that's all. Now let's . . ."

"Seriously, General," Bush insisted. "You have to do something about the torturing, the imprisonments."

The general reddened. "We don't do those things."

"Look, I'd like to believe that, but if you don't, why are all those reports coming out? I don't understand, General. They're only reporting these things about a few countries and Iran is one of them. Now

I don't think the people doing the investigating harbor any particular hostility toward SAVAK. So why is it such a problem if people choose to disagree with government policies? Take it easy. Don't be so harsh on them. And somehow you have to convey this idea to His Majesty as well. It doesn't follow that people who oppose the government deserve to be tortured or imprisoned. Let's get this idea across. Learn to accept them. Try to understand them."

"The reports lie," the general said. "Maybe at one time they tortured, but as His Majesty told international reporters, 'There is no more physical torturing, only mental.' "

"You're making it worse." Bush laughed. "I read His Majesty's remarks. Who is to say that mental torture is any better than physical torture?"

During the ride home to New Jersey that evening, General Nassiri said, "None of these people understand my situation. They think we can talk to His Majesty about this matter. It's impossible. Americans don't understand."

The following morning I was having breakfast with the general when Mrs. Nassiri entered the room.

"The guards told me that I was invited to the dinner party last night," she said angrily. "Mrs. Bush and the other wives were there and everyone was expecting me. Why didn't you tell me?"

"I didn't know Mrs. Bush or any of the other wives were coming," General Nassiri said. "Mansur wasn't clear about the invitation, that's all."

"Mansur had nothing to do with it. It was you. You didn't want me there."

"That's not true. It wasn't until we met them at the airport that I realized you were expected."

"So why didn't you call me then?"

"What?" He scoffed. "And wait around the airport for three hours while you got ready?"

I mumbled an excuse and left the room as the argument heated up. Later that day when we were alone again, I asked him about it.

"It was a great mistake for me to marry a young, beautiful girl. The marriage has caused me so much embarrassment and it's the shah's fault. Goddamn the man."

Again, it was incredible to me that he was cursing the shah. "What are you talking about?" I asked. "What does your marriage have to do with him?"

"Before I married her, I was invited almost every evening to dine with the shah's family at the royal court. And at every meal I was seated next to the shah's mother-in-law, a widow about my age. During the meals, she touched my hands and caressed my feet under the table. She would catch my eye and raise her glass to me as if drinking a secret toast. I knew what was happening and tried to avoid her, but it was very difficult. As you know, unless there was an urgent report, I saw His Majesty twice a week, Mondays and Wednesdays.

"One Wednesday I entered his room carrying a great deal of work. He always received me sitting behind his desk. But if he was in a particularly good mood, he would leave his desk and sit on the sofa. That Wednesday when I arrived with this bundle of work in my arms, he left the desk and headed for the sofa. He began asking me very personal questions. 'Do you enjoy the single life? With whom do you spend your leisure time? Do you have an interest in any one person?' The more he questioned me in this friendly, familiar fashion, the less secure I felt. All I could imagine was that someone had told him I was going out with a young girl and he wanted to know why I'd kept it from him. I was about to tell him when he smiled at me and said, 'I'm sure you want to settle down. That doesn't mean if you marry that you can't see other women. No. But a single man in your position is vulnerable to all kinds of accusations. Of course we don't listen—we know what kind of faithful soldier you are. And as you are aware, my mother-in-law finds you very interesting. She is in love with you.' The shah then stood erect with his thumbs in his vest pockets. I obediently stood up. With his back toward me, he stared out the window and continued, 'The empress and I approve of her feelings and I suggest that you propose marriage.' I was stunned, but fear propelled me to speak. I had to offer a reason to refuse without offending.

" 'Your Majesty,' I began, 'for the past few months I have wanted to break the news to you that I am in love with a young girl I've known for some time and I hoped to receive your blessing to marry her. I only wish that I had met Her Highness, the mother of the empress and an exceptional woman, before I became involved with this other girl. Then I would have had the supreme honor of being related to Your Majesty. But it seems to me that honor is not to be mine. The only honor I have is to be your obedient servant.'

"So you see, Mansur, I had been going out with this girl but had absolutely no intention of marrying her. But I did and it has caused me endless grief. I know it's difficult for some people to believe that His Majesty dictates even our personal lives. We don't have the right to choose to marry or remain single. If I had told him outright that I had no interest in his mother-in-law, I would have feared not only his wrath, but that of the empress and her mother. As it is, the empress is thirsty for my blood. I haven't been invited to dine with the royal family since that time. And when I have to attend official dinners at the royal court, the empress always seats me far away from the family table."

That same day we received a wire from the office of His Majesty the Shah. General Nassiri was ordered to return to Tehran as soon as possible for an emergency. He instructed me to wire the following response: ARRANGED TO LEAVE FOR TEHRAN AS SOON AS BLESSED IMPERIAL ORDER RECEIVED. WILL KISS YOUR FEET AT ROYAL PALACE. YOUR OBEDIENT SERVANT. I was also instructed to arrange for his flight from New York that evening and for a SAVAK plane to be waiting for him in Paris. We left my home in New Jersey at four o'clock. He ordered the guards to drive ahead of us and requested that I drive him in my car. He was quieter than usual and seemed distracted.

"Mansur," he said as we reached Route 4, "I know that my wife is still upset. Take her shopping. Let her buy anything she wants. And ask our friend Joan to spend more time with her. [Nassiri loved to indulge his wife's passion for beautiful clothes and jewels. Once he even bought the contents of three Saks Fifth Avenue windows and had them shipped to Tehran, only to discover that everything was the wrong size.] Also, make certain that she doesn't speak to me over the phone while I'm in Tehran unless she's in a very good mood."

"Of course, General," I said. "I'll do my best."

As we approached the George Washington Bridge on our way to Kennedy Airport, he spoke again but in a changed voice. "Rafizadeh, I don't know what to do. My phone is being tapped."

I caught my breath. His phone tapped? The phone of the chief of SAVAK tapped? Did I hear right—that the man millions feared, the all-powerful "second shah," was vulnerable to such a thing? that the man sitting next to me—who had run SAVAK for a decade, served as chief of the national police for another and as commander of the royal guard—could be reduced to such helplessness? By whose order? And who would carry out such an order? I realized dully that he was still talking. ". . . she shouldn't call me unless she's in a pleasant mood," he was saying, his voice sounding like that of a child. "If she's going to talk nonsense about me having girl friends, other women, I don't want those things taped."

"General. General, I can't believe it. Your phone is tapped?"

"Yes."

"By whose order?"

"You know."

"No, I don't."

"His Majesty the Shah."

I turned my head and looked at him. "Are you sure?"

"I listened to my own tape."

At that moment our tail car pulled up beside us and motioned to me that our car was swerving. I struggled to steady myself. "General," I asked, "who would carry out such an order?"

"You know who. Mr. Sabeti. The man who spies for the empress and Prime Minister Hoveyda, my two good friends," he added with bitterness. "You don't believe me?"

"Of course, I believe you. I'm shocked he would go so far as to spy on you, one of his most loyal men."

"He distrusts his own family."

We arrived at Kennedy Airport in good time but because of a technical problem with the plane, the general's flight was delayed for an hour. He instructed me to discharge the guards, and we went to wait in the VIP lounge.

"Mansur, I don't believe the day will ever come when I'll be free of all this," he said, sipping his Scotch. "I don't believe I'll ever be free to live an ordinary life here in the United States."

"Why do you feel that way, General?"

"His Majesty is becoming crazy, mad with power. The only end I see for myself is to be jailed or killed by him."

"But why?"

"The shah has no mercy for anyone. No mercy. He's obsessed with power. The entire world belongs to him or to the crown prince. The rest of his family doesn't mean anything to him. And you know what happened to Bakhtiar, the first chief of SAVAK!"

"Why don't you resign, then?" I asked.

"It is worse to submit a resignation," he told me. "My only hope, what I pray for, is that he will dismiss me peacefully. But I doubt that will happen."

After I saw the general to the gate for his flight, one of my officers drove me back to New Jersey. I sat in the backseat and thought more about my conversation with Nassiri. As a high-ranking officer of SAVAK, I was certainly aware of the possibility that I was being invaded in this way—tapped telephones, bugged cars, and homes. Top-level positions in government or politics did not guarantee any-one immunity. Yet I had believed until that afternoon that the chief of SAVAK enjoys a privileged status, a status that offers a certain security. It wasn't so. SAVAK was tapping its own chief's telephone.

I couldn't sleep that night. I felt overwhelmed by the full impact of the general's disclosure, unfathomable to me. SAVAK, internationally renowned for violating the rights of the Iranian people, was now turning on its leader. General Nassiri, at that moment, flying from New York to Paris, was still in charge of the nation's security, yet how could he be thinking of anything but this bizarre turn of events? Then I took a glass of milk and fell asleep.

CHAPTER TWENTY

The Imperial Court

On every trip the shah made to the United States, he was accompanied by an entourage of at least fifty persons, some of whom were given the title of civilian or military adjutant, although many were taken along only to perform personal services for the monarch. Sometimes the chief of protocol of the royal court would "have the honor of being present," as he did in May 1975 when the shah visited President Gerald Ford. The shah, as usual, was staying at Blair House, the president's guest house next to Lafayette Park, where a demonstration against him was in progress. There were the typical banners and placards with their anti-shah slogans, as well as participants shouting, "Down with the shah! Shame on you, butcher!"

I was sitting in Blair House when the chief of protocol, an older man, slender and of medium height, came and sat down beside me. As always, he was dressed in a very fashionable outfit straight from Paris. It was common knowledge that he was an opium addict.

He opened the conversation by saying, "Every time His Majesty comes to the United States and gives me the honor of being present, I would like to refuse, but I cannot. One cannot refuse the mighty, blessed order of His Majesty."

I stared at him, unable to believe that he would want to turn down what almost any member of the royal court would consider a great honor.

"Do you know why I do not like to come?" he pressed.

I shrugged.

"I cannot tolerate these traitors. Whenever they scream their lies about the shah, I become greatly disturbed. If I were the shah, I would order SAVAK to capture all these demonstrators, take them back to Iran, cut out their tongues, and execute them!"

I shrugged again. "It cannot be done."

"How many of them are there in Lafayette Park?" he wanted to know.

"I am not sure—probably around two hundred," I answered.

"Will you do me a favor?" he asked. "Walk with me down to Lafayette Park. I want to see the faces of these traitors: I cannot believe they are Iranians. No real Iranian would ever say such horrible things about His Majesty."

"There is no doubt about their being Iranians," I said. "It is clear from their accents." I refused his request, knowing that the demonstrators would recognize me, and since I was a SAVAK man, my presence would only stir them up more.

"Please accompany me," he begged. "We do not have to get too close—I only want to see them from a distance."

Finally, I gave in, knowing that there was a police barricade that would keep us at a distance.

As we neared the demonstrators, they did recognize me, and, aiming their bullhorns at me, began cursing SAVAK.

"Have you had enough?" I asked the chief of protocol.

"Yes. Let's walk back." He paused. "I can't believe they are doing this," he said, shaking his head.

As we turned around, he asked that I hold his hand. I did so and noticed that he was trembling. "Please don't walk fast," he pleaded. "I am not at all well." Gradually as we went on, more and more of his weight rested on me until finally I was almost carrying him.

"What is wrong?" I asked him, by now very concerned.

He clutched at his chest. "I have a hard time breathing," he gasped. "Something is wrong with my heart. I am unused to these outrageous insults against His Majesty. How can I continue to come to the United States when these demonstrations make me so ill?"

Seeing our plight as we neared Blair House, the Secret Service men hastened to our aid. Immediately, the chief of protocol collapsed, breathing heavily, and four or five of us carried him inside. He had fainted and white foam trickled from his mouth. We laid him on the sofa where we had previously sat, and someone loosened his tie and unbuttoned his shirt. Blair House servants, very solicitous, asked if there was anything they could do to help. The chief of protocol, reviving slightly, asked for tea with lemon. He could hardly speak and complained that he was still having difficulty breathing.

Members of the shah's entourage gathered around, asking what had happened. I told them briefly about our walk to Lafayette Park. One of them began to reprimand me sharply. "Mr. Rafizadeh, you should not have done this to such a devoted slave of His Majesty. Don't you understand that he is unused to encountering such indignities against His Majesty?"

I tried to explain that he had insisted on going, but no one would listen to me.

Finally, the chief of protocol whispered weakly, "It isn't his fault. Don't blame it on him." A tear slipped down his cheek as he spoke.

I was terribly upset that I had caused the problem, but I did not know what to do about it. The members of the entourage were also in a quandary. They asked whether a physician should be called. The chief of protocol, seeming to gain strength, raised his hand and said, "No, no. Don't call a physician. I am feeling a little better already."

Once the shah's entourage realized that the chief of protocol would be all right, they turned their attention back to me. "You shouldn't have taken him," said one of them critically. "He's an older man—you endangered his life! You know he isn't used to such things. How could you be so thoughtless?"

I apologized profusely.

The chief of protocol continued to improve and was soon able to sit up. A few minutes passed, and then an adjutant hurried downstairs with a message from the shah. "His Majesty is concerned about your health," he announced. "You have the honor to be present."

The chief of protocol needed help as he rose from the sofa, but it was obvious his strength was returning, since he climbed the stairs unassisted. Then, minutes later, he came bounding downstairs completely recovered. He sat down beside me again and told me that His Majesty had been very concerned about his health and assured me that none of what had happened was my fault. "Do not blame yourself, Mansur," he said kindly. He began to recount the symptoms of his disease, which symptoms had been initiated hearing the demonstrators railing against His Majesty.

I said to myself, *I've had enough. I'm not taking any of these people anywhere!*

About an hour later, Ambassador Zahedi arrived at Blair House and heard about the incident. "Come to the kitchen with me, Mansur," he said covertly. I followed him.

"Have you been associating with that second disgusting character?" he asked.

"Second? Who is the first?" I was puzzled.

"We'll talk about that later," Ambassador Zahedi responded. "Did you take him out to see the demonstrators?"

"Yes," I admitted, "I did. I had to—he insisted!"

"He used you." Ambassador Zahedi snorted. "You were his tool today."

"What do you mean?" I asked.

"You are obviously not familiar with these people from the royal court," he said. "On the flight to the United States, His Majesty was screaming at this character because of his conduct. His Majesty told him to get out of his sight—he never wanted to see him again. The chief of protocol put on this show to get back into His Majesty's good graces. He has proven his loyalty, and now His Majesty will see him. That's the whole story."

"I won't get taken in again," I said determinedly.

"What is done is done," Zahedi said. "But stay away from those people in the future."

After Ambassador Zahedi left, I had a chance to reflect on what a fool I had been to let myself be manipulated. I was angry and hurt, although I didn't then foresee the possibility of getting even.

When the shah's visit to Washington was over, he flew to Tarrytown, New York, with a few members of his party for a dinner reception at Vice-President Rockefeller's estate. Immediately following the dinner he was to fly to New York City to join the rest of his entourage for the trip back to Tehran. There were two planes waiting at Kennedy Airport: one for the shah, the empress, and high-ranking officials like the chief of protocol; the other for the entourage, who were already on board, awaiting the shah's arrival. The chief of protocol, for the time being on the second plane making arrangements, insisted that the door of the plane be opened so that everyone could descend onto the tarmac to greet the shah. However, airport regulations required that no passengers be allowed to leave a plane parked on the runway.

The pilot of the second plane said that the chief of protocol wanted to talk to me. "Fine," I said. "Open the door and I'll come up."

As I entered the plane, the chief of protocol accosted me. "I was invited to accompany His Majesty to Tarrytown, but because I was not feeling well, with His Majesty's permission, I declined. Before His

Majesty arrives, I would like to line everyone up to welcome the shah and pay their respects. Also, I and some others whom I have chosen will be flying back in the shah's plane, and we must be ready." I knew immediately that this man was trying to use me again. I had seen the guest list for the Tarrytown party, and the chief of protocol's name did not appear on it. This made me even more determined to serve him right.

I told him about the airport regulations requiring that passengers stay aboard while their plane was on the runway, but promised that when His Majesty arrived, we would open the plane door so that they could pay their respects. Those who were to fly back with the shah would then be able to transfer to his plane.

"Don't forget," he warned.

"I could not forget such an important thing, Your Excellency," I assured him.

"I must fly on His Majesty's plane," he pointed out. "I would be in trouble if I didn't."

I winked at the pilot, who was not especially fond of the chief of protocol either. After I left the plane, I spoke to him from the ground, telling him to keep the door closed and be ready to leave as soon as His Majesty's plane arrived. He laughed. "Whatever you say! I will be delighted to keep the door closed." Knowing that Ambassador Zahedi, a fellow foe of the chief of protocol, wanted to put his own man on the shah's plane, I was certain that my action would provoke no criticism.

Meanwhile, on the shah's plane, the director of Iran Air, an army general, was fussing meticulously in the cabin. Every few minutes he would scurry back and forth, fastidiously arranging the shah's slippers, his bottle of wine, his newspaper. He would hold the wine goblets up to the light and polish them vigorously with his handkerchief. There was not a thing out of place. Nervously he dashed out onto the steps of the plane. "Any news?" he asked breathlessly.

"Nothing yet," I told him calmly. "They are still eating dinner."

While the director was outside, a friend of Ambassador Zahedi's sneaked furtively into the cabin and hastily disturbed his careful arrangements. The poor general hurried back inside and, finding everything in disarray, began with shaking hands to put things back in their former positions. As he did so, he muttered to himself, "His Majesty's newspaper belongs here . . . the goblet should be a bit more to the left . . . the empress will sit here, and His Majesty here. . . ." He was in a dither and his constant fussing and muttering began to grate on my nerves. The more frantic he became, the more Zahedi's friend messed things up when he was out of the cabin.

Finally, the word came: "The shah's plane is approaching!" Everyone became tense. The director ran back and forth through the cabin, faster and faster.

As soon as I saw the shah's plane taxiing toward us, a childish impulse came over me. I rushed to the cabin, which was finally empty, and destroyed all of the director's painstaking efforts. I tossed the pillows all over the cabin, kicked the shah's slippers, crumpled the first page of the carefully folded newspaper, and flicked cigarette ashes into the spotless wine goblets. Pleased with myself, I regained my composure, left the plane, and solemnly took my place in the receiving line.

When the shah's party from Tarrytown deplaned, I hurried to ask Ambassador Zahedi if I would be in trouble for keeping the "second disgusting character" on the other plane so that he could not fly with the shah.

"Of course you won't be in trouble," he exclaimed. "Good for you! His Majesty will be very pleased."

The shah immediately noticed that the rest of his party was aboard the second plane. He stretched, straightened his clothes, and commented, "So only the people who came with me from Tarrytown will be flying home with me. Good!" He walked toward his plane while those in the second plane banged on their windows and screamed for us to open the door. The pilot of the second plane looked at me and laughed.

As soon as the shah and the director entered the cabin, the latter, seeing the havoc I had wrought, gasped, "What happened?" He began frantically to straighten things. The shah was unperturbed. "It's all right, it's all right," he assured the distraught man. "The plane must have moved and everything shifted. Don't worry about it."

Before the planes took off, Ambassador Zahedi, in my presence, praised my work to the shah and added an account of the trick I had played on the chief of protocol. "Since Rafizadeh was tricked by the chief, he has kept him on the other plane. Rafizadeh asked this obedient servant if Your Majesty would mind not giving the chief of protocol the honor of flying back with Your Majesty."

The shah turned to me and smiled. "No, we do not mind. You were right to keep him on the other plane." Obviously the shah knew that the chief of protocol had taken advantage of me in the Lafayette Park incident, and as he himself was less than eager to see the man, he told me, "You have done a good thing. We are pleased!"

Zahedi dismissed me so that he could talk privately with the shah, and I left the plane. I found the director standing by the door. "Mr. Rafizadeh," he said very seriously, "something very strange is going on here. There are either Communists or ghosts on this plane!"

I smiled. "Communists? No. But ghosts? Maybe. Have a safe trip and enjoy your flight. You will be practically alone with His Majesty —the rest will stay on the other plane."

"Thank you!" he exclaimed. "I need time to talk to His Majesty!"

Ambassador Zahedi joined me outside the plane and we watched the ceremonial flags being removed. As we stood watching, the people on the second plane continued to bang on the windows, yelling and screaming at us. We smiled and waved, watching the planes taxi down the runway.

CHAPTER TWENTY-ONE

Dark Secrets of the Shah's Sex Life

Still in conjunction with the 2,500th anniversary of the founding of the kingdom, though almost five years after the celebration and in celebration of the fiftieth anniversary of the Pahlavi dynasty, the shah decided to change the Iranian calendar so that it reflected the longevity of the monarchy, beginning with Cyrus the Great. Until 1976 the origin of the Iranian calendar had been the migration of Mohammad from Mecca to Medina on Friday, June 16, 622 A.D. Therefore, in 1976 when the shah suddenly ordered the calendar to be changed to reflect this new date, Iran was officially in the year 1355. With only fifteen minutes of deliberation, the Iranian Parliament gave its blessing to the shah's decree.

Imagine what would happen if the president of the United States were to announce at a press conference: "It has recently come to my attention that the word 'republic,' symbolic of my own political party, originated more than three thousand years ago in Greece. What is more, research into my ancestry has proven that I am also of Greek descent. From tomorrow on, we will change the date of our year from 1987 to 3000." On the very next day, every newspaper, document, timetable, and interoffice memo would be dated 3000. The speaker of the House would report gleefully on the gratitude of the American people to a president who, after so many years, had dug out the facts. Majority and minority leaders in Congress would voice wholehearted support for the president, pass his legislation within fifteen minutes, and announce receipt of more than a million telegrams from delighted citizens. Imagine that, at the same time, the FBI would arrest any reactionary who used old dates or opposed the new ones, sending the miscreants to torture chambers. Without exaggeration, this is precisely what happened when the shah thoughtlessly and single-handedly changed the religious date of origin of the Iranian calendar to his fictitious year of 2500, unaware of the consequences he would face.

Imagine that the president of the United States had added privately: "In our age of technology, what does the birth of Jesus in a stable have to do with the origins of the calendar?" Yet privately the shah said to a member of his inner circle: "What does the migration of Mohammad from one desert tent to another have to do with our calendar?"

The monarch incurred the relentless wrath of the religious people of Iran, for nothing will convince pious believers that a secular date is better than a sacred one that marks the progress of their divinity. Moreover, in a country rife with bureaucracy and corruption extending to every authority, high and low, the problems caused by the need to change dates on every record and document like deeds, filings, and birth and death certificates were unbelievable. The shah had gained nothing and caused himself untold grief.

In actuality, he had not planned his huge anniversary celebration and changed the Iranian date from a religious to a monarchical one without deep thought. His goal had been to destroy religion totally within the country and in the minds of its largely uneducated people, and supplant it with the absolute rule of his corrupt monarchy. He unleashed himself brutally now, not only attacking and killing the devoted but, in attempting to root out their beliefs, humiliating and offending them.

In May 1977 Dr. Baghai published and distributed a broadside challenging the shah's action. It read:

> We are of the firm belief that we can no longer campaign against dictatorship because of our lack of financial resources and man-power—with everyone in jail. The trickiest and most dangerous action of our government is its change of the origin of our calendar. Our calendar is a national pride as well as a religious one. Unfortunately, no deep thought was given to the change of dates, and, in fifteen minutes, the joint session of Parliament was able to effect it.
>
> I want to warn all those people that when they make a habit of setting precedents such as changing the calendar of a nation so easily, their habit will cause future trouble. By the same action in

the future, the Constitution can be easily changed. By such a precedent, the monarchy can as easily be changed to another form of government. Changing the calendar is a dangerous game. Do not play with the pride and faith of a nation. Don't throw matches into a tinder box. I am certain that there is a tomorrow, but that tomorrow will be too late.

Only in 1978, finding himself enmeshed in a trap of his own making, did the shah appear on national television to offer an abject apology, confessing his error and changing the date back to the original. He begged Iranians to forgive him. But it was too late.

Iranian society, like any other, has institutions; in Iran's case, two —the Iranian culture and religion. These institutions provide the monarch with his kingdom and the realm with a sort of stability.

The combination of Iranian culture and Islam brought about Islamic civilization. It is not true to say that Islamic civilization was brought about by the Iranian people, but the latter have made a great contribution to it. In fact, no other country can lay claim to Islamic civilization with a greater right. Almost all Islamic art is a mixture of Persian and Islamic culture. Virtually all the magnificent buildings and mosques in the Islamic world, including the Taj Mahal in India, were built by Persians. Still, the shah insisted on insulting both Iran and Islam.

On Kish Island in the Persian Gulf, the shah had built an enormous casino, one that ranked with Monte Carlo and other glittering play paradises. It was right out of the pages of *A Thousand and One Nights*. The magnificent palaces erected there for the shah and members of the royal family were of striking Eastern architecture, but were beautifully furnished in elegant Western fashion. Every conceivable luxury firm had a boutique on Kish Island, selling the latest, most fashionable, and expensive products.

All the expenses for construction on Kish Island—millions and millions of dollars—which should have been spent on the welfare of the Iranian poor, people who could not afford the basic necessities of life, came out of government funds. Yet the greatest irony was that the flight between Tehran and Kish was free, and nightly the wealthy, including the royal family, flocked to the plane for an evening's excursion of gambling and partying. Hundreds of the world's most beautiful prostitutes, and most handsome gigolos, keen for good business, came to Kish, too.

The shah deliberately timed the opening of the casino to coincide with an Iranian period of religious mourning in order to offend the pious deeply, to sully their faith. Nor did his affront end there.

In Shiraz, not a holy city like Qom, but an ancient center of deeply religious people all the same, hundreds of art and music festivals were held throughout the year, most with heavily antireligious themes. The shah, at the expense of the Iranians, invited actors and actresses from all over the world to attend these festivals. On several occasions, the shows were performed on the streets and offered, as a part of the play, performances that outraged the townspeople. In *The Pride and the Fall,* written by Sir Anthony Parsons, the last British ambassador to imperial Iran, one such incident is described:

> The theatre company had booked a shop in the main shopping street of Shiraz for the performance, which was played half inside the shop and half on the pavement outside. One scene, played on the pavement, involved a rape which was performed in full (no pretence) by a man (either naked or without any trousers, I forget which) on a woman who had had her dress ripped off her by her attacker. The denouement of the play, also acted on the pavement, included a scene where one of the characters dropped his trousers and inserted a stage pistol up his backside, presumably in order to add verisimilitude to his suicide. The effect of this bizarre and disgusting extravaganza on the good citizens of Shiraz, going about their evening shopping, can hardly be imagined. This grotesquerie aroused a storm of protest which reached the press and television. I remember mentioning it to the Shah, adding that, if the same play had been put on, say in the main street of Winchester (Shiraz is the Iranian equivalent of a cathedral city), the actors and sponsors would have found themselves in trouble. The Shah laughed indulgently.
>
> The political effect of such an incident would have been bad enough at any time. It was especially so when there were many indications of an upsurge of religious traditionalism throughout the country.

Perhaps some people will hold that this was an attempt by the shah to introduce a Western culture unknown to Iranians and especially to religious people, who balked at it. But this was not the case. He had forced on them a reign of lying, stealing, corruption, and terror that had nothing to do with Western culture, a reign that was wholly unacceptable to Iranians. They did not rise up against him because he was

modernizing their country, but because of the invidious material and
moral corruption he purveyed, particularly at the royal court.

Hundreds of wives had been forced to divorce their husbands and
to become mistresses to members of the court, including the shah's
family. Hundreds were killed outright or were addicted to drugs. The
shah's own elderly mother was well known for forcing the palace guard
of her choice to become her lover for a night. Princess Ashraf, his twin
sister, world worn, weary of all but sex and pornographic movies,
passed her time sleeping with any man who caught her eye, and perhaps
promoting him afterward.

The royal family's proclivity for lascivious behavior delighted the
gossipmongers in both the most fashionable salons and the humblest
bazaars. The people loved to speculate about the shah's latest lovers,
and whether or not the empress Farah and the princess Ashraf were
still fighting over who had the handsomest palace guards.

The shah's inner circle saw to it that he was provided with a
legendary collection of international pornography and erotica. He enjoyed watching porno films with both heterosexual and homosexual
themes. The shah also took a childish pleasure in all kinds of erotic
gadgets, but one of the most unusual bits of erotica was found in
Nivarana Palace. On the outside of the empress's bedroom chambers
were traditional ornate wooden doors, but on the inside of her bedroom
there was a second set of pocket doors. These doors were custom made
for the empress by a French craftsman. They were made of a delicate
flesh-toned leather and of a unique design. In order to slide closed this
second set of doors, one had to grasp both doors by finely wrought
leather handles. When the doors were closed, the viewer discovered that
each handle was a facsimile of one half of an anatomically correct,
perfectly crafted vagina. If you wanted to lock the doors, a penis-shaped
bolt did the job. After the shah left Iran, the revolutionary government
had a field day describing these doors on Iranian television. Their
discovery provided the new government with yet another concrete
symbol of the royal family's decadence and corruption.

Once, I was at General Oveissi's home in Connecticut with another
guest, Mr. Abolfath Ataba'i, who had served as a guardian and an
instructor in the skills of camping, horseback riding, shooting, and
hunting to Shah Mohammad Reza while he was the crown prince.
During the conversation, the name of General Hossein Fardoust came
up. He had been a longtime friend of the shah's, but had changed his
allegiance to the revolutionary government. In *Answer to History,* the
shah recalled Fardoust and his change of heart:

My father sent several other boys with us to make sure we would
not lose contact with our people. Among them was a boy named
Hossein Fardoust. I had known him at court since we were both
six years old; he was to become one of my closest friends and
advisors and ultimately betray me. He is now head of Savama,
Khomeini's Secret Service.

Princess Ashraf, in *Faces in a Mirror,* also recalled:

> . . . the Crown Prince's friend Hussein Fardust (a man who ironi-
> cally played a tragic role in our lives in recent years). . . . Fardust
> functioned as a kind of conduit for vital information on the highest
> level, which he delivered daily to my brother. Although my brother
> is always very reluctant to believe the worst of anyone, especially
> a man he treated like a brother, I am convinced that Fardust must
> have withheld vital information from the Shah and was, in fact, in
> active negotiation with Khomeini during the last years of the re-
> gime.

General Oveissi said he had been shocked by Fardoust's actions.
"How could a man's best friend betray him?"

Mr. Ataba'i stated that he had not been at all surprised and added,
"If I had been General Fardoust, I would have done the same thing."

Both General Oveissi and I were startled by Ataba'i's remark.
"Why weren't you surprised?" we asked.

Ataba'i then told us of an incident that had occurred during a
camping trip outside Tehran when the shah—then the crown prince—
and Fardoust were adolescents. Fardoust, on the orders of Reza Shah,
was always to accompany the crown prince, perhaps to influence him
to adopt his, Fardoust's, more studious ways. Their entourage included
guards, soldiers, and other hunters. The crown prince and Fardoust
each had his own tent, pitched side by side, and because Ataba'i was
serving as guardian, his tent was near the boys'. Ataba'i said that he
was awakened during the night by noises nearby. He heard labored
breathing and what sounded like the muffled sounds of someone in pain.
Because Ataba'i's first thought was that the crown prince was in trouble, he arose and tiptoed to the prince's tent and looked inside. Both
boys were there and he saw that the crown prince had grabbed Fardoust
from behind and was sodomizing him. Ataba'i quietly retreated and
said nothing.

He told us that this was not an isolated incident; it happened several

times later that he was aware of. He said he had felt sorry for Fardoust
—there was nothing Fardoust could do. In addition to being in a
vulnerable position himself, Ataba'i had to consider his family, especially his father, who was an army lieutenant. Ataba'i believed that
Fardoust had turned against the shah because of that abuse in his
childhood. "The shah raped him," Ataba'i stated. "If I had been Fardoust, I too would have turned against him."

This made me remember two earlier incidents. General Pakravan
had told me that no one was allowed to enter the shah's bedroom
without permission except Ernest Peron, another of the shah's boyhood
friends. Peron could simply walk in, without even knocking. Princess
Ashraf wrote of the long-standing friendship of the shah and his Swiss
friend, Peron:

> . . . and he also told me about two new friends he had made,
> diverse as they were. One of these was Richard Helms, who later
> became director of the Central Intelligence Agency and America's
> Ambassador to Iran. Another was Ernest Perron [sic], the son of
> the school handyman, a young man who came to live in Iran
> and remained my brother's close friend until the day he died in
> 1961.

General Pakravan had told me that Queen Soraya, the shah's second wife, was very annoyed with Peron. Several times he had barged
into their bedroom while she and the shah were in bed. The former
queen described their relationship in her autobiography, *Soraya: The
Autobiography of the Imperial Highness:*

> Another intriguer who complicated my life from the very begin-
> ning was a man from western Switzerland by the name of Ernest
> Peron, the most mysterious figure I have ever encountered at the
> Court of Teheran. Many people called him "the Persian Rasputin,"
> and although this was certainly an exaggeration he did nevertheless
> play a sinister role in the Shah's circle.
>
> So far as I could discover he had originally been a gardener, or
> perhaps a servant, at Rosay College. When Mohammed Riza [the
> shah] had finished his studies there, he had had this man brought
> to Teheran. The old Shah was very strict and did not tolerate any
> foreigners at his Court, but he made an exception for this Swiss.
>
> Peron never went home again. He had no official appointment
> but lived at Court as a personal friend of the Shah. Despite his

humble origins he was said to be Mohammed Riza's closest adviser. He visited him each morning in his bedroom for a discussion.

No one could say precisely what it was he did. Like many self-educated men he posed as a poet and philosopher. At the same time he acted as a sort of intermediary between the Shah and the British and American ambassadors. Shortly before my arrival in Teheran he had had a mysterious accident of some sort, and from then on he walked with a limp. Many people maintained he had been poisoned.

When I became Empress, Peron attempted to interfere in my private life as well. He frequently came to see me in my room, and would bring the conversation around to intimate matters which were no concern of his. One evening, when he began to question me in this way about my marriage, I lost my temper and said: "Please do not forget, Mr. Peron, to whom it is that you are speaking. It is unseemly that you should ask me such questions."

He was offended and withdrew. From that time on he never missed an opportunity of saying something disagreeable about me. I was, it was true, not his only victim. . . .

Peron died in 1961, and he took his secrets to the grave with him.

I heard, from several reliable men close to the shah, that Ernest Peron was the shah's sexual partner.

In 1964, after Peron's death, the shah visited the United States to see President Johnson. After their business was completed, the shah and his party went to the Waldorf-Astoria. His minister of court, Assadollah Alam, who had grown up with him and was considered his best friend, accompanied the shah.

That night there was a private party in the shah's suite at the Waldorf, and later in the evening I was ordered to go to Times Square to get the next day's *New York Times,* which was just coming out. The shah wanted to see what had been written about him and his visit. Around 11:00 P.M. I left to get the paper. Everyone was drunk. The papers were not at the newsstand and I had to wait until 11:30. I purchased several copies and returned to the hotel, arriving about midnight.

Because of my position with SAVAK, no one stopped me as I walked toward the shah's suite. When I entered, it seemed that everyone had gone; there was no one in sight, but the television was still on. To make my presence known to anyone who might still be up, I coughed and deliberately made some noise. There was no response. I walked into the living room and made some more noise. Again there was no response. Then I walked toward the shah's huge bedroom and saw His Majesty and Court Minister Alam, naked and lying in bed, fondling each other.

I was shocked and did not know what to do. I backed away, returned to the living room, and sat down. I began thinking about the many rumors that Peron had had a homosexual relationship with the shah.

Alam, naked, entered the living room to get some gin and saw me. "Oh, are you here?" he asked, startled.

"Yes, Your Excellency. I have the paper."

Alam excused himself, ran to the bathroom, and wrapped a towel around himself. He returned and addressed me again: "You can leave the paper." He paused and then asked, "How long have you been here?"

"A few minutes."

Suddenly I saw the shah, also naked, running from the bedroom toward the living room. Before the shah could say anything, Alam interceded. "Mr. Rafizadeh is here with the paper. You were taking a shower when he arrived."

The shah asked, "Is there anything about us in the paper?"

"One article," I answered.

"Thank you. Leave the paper."

While making a move to leave I politely asked that I be permitted to depart. With permission granted, I left the suite.

I had never seen two men making love before, so what I witnessed was startling, but to have seen the shah making love to Alam, his own prime minister, was more than I could grasp at that moment. I was so confused that I forgot where I had parked my car and wandered around the area until I found it.

Before the shah left the United States, Alam invited me to see His Majesty again, and highly praised me and my work. "Are you being promoted on time?" Alam asked.

"Yes," I answered.

"Do you need any financial help?"

"No, I have enough."

He then patted my shoulder and said that if I needed anything I should get in touch with him. He told me that if anyone in the government gave me any trouble I was to call him directly.

I did not disclose this information to anyone except Dr. Baghai, whom I confided in during my next trip to Tehran. He said that it was too bad Peron was dead—he would have been so jealous.

In addition to his homosexual liaisons, the shah led a very active and complicated heterosexual life. He had encounters with several internationally prominent actresses. He also dallied with extremely high-priced call girls who gave a new meaning to the term "high-priced." The shah was known to have paid up to $250,000 for special services.

Yet, in spite of the shah's vast wealth, power, and endless resources to satiate his sexual appetites, he still needed to fulfill another primitive hunger—his thirst for violence.

The newspapers in Tehran, desperate for any kind of nonpolitical material to fill their meager pages, ran a story about an alleged battle between a donkey and a tiger in which the donkey was victorious. This story captured the imagination of the public and whether or not it was possible for a donkey to kill a tiger was hotly debated for weeks.

Inspired by the news story, the head zookeeper of Tehran's Municipal Zoo thought of a new way to stimulate lagging attendance. One day, he put a live donkey into the lions' compound. The people were fascinated by the macabre spectacle of the helpless donkey being torn to shreds by the hungry lions. The zookeeper was delighted by the crowd's enthusiasm, and he made the "special feeding" a weekly event. The word spread, and soon throngs of adults and children packed the zoo on the scheduled days at inflated admission prices.

Iran has no animal-protection laws, but the press heard about the new goings-on at the zoo, and some journalists took very strong exception to this kind of barbarism. They incited the public to protest the exposure of young children to such sadistic acts. Under attack, the zookeeper acquiesced and reluctantly gave up his money-making star attraction.

All of the publicity about the donkey meanwhile had aroused the shah's curiosity, and he ordered that a donkey be brought to his private zoo. The shah and his inner circle watched with complete fascination as the animal was put in with the starving lions. The monarch's excitement mounted as the lions closed in on their prey, and the poor panic-stricken beast was torn to pieces.

Among the many activists who were virulently anti-shah was a teacher in Tabriz. He had a penchant for using extremely coarse and vulgar epithets while speaking about the shah in public, and so he was arrested by SAVAK. Even after being severely beaten, he did not relent. SAVAK transferred him to Evin Prison in Tehran, but, even under torture, he still continued his harangues against the shah.

When the shah was told about this man, and what SAVAK described as his consistently sick behavior, the shah flippantly commented, "Instead of a donkey he should be thrown to the lions."

About a week later the shah went to his private zoo with his cronies. General Nassiri, the chief of SAVAK, was also present. The shah, General Nassiri, and their entourage assembled by the lion compound. The imprisoned teacher, restrained by two guards, had been brought from Evin Prison. As soon as he saw the shah, he lunged toward him screaming, "Bloodsucker! Dictator! Butcher!"

The shocked onlookers covered their ears, not wanting to hear his curses, but the shah laughed and told the guards not to bother holding him back. Behind the curved fence, the curious lions watched the scene.

The minister of court, Assadollah Alam, currying the shah's favor, remarked, "His mouth should be filled with molten lead." The rest of the courtiers nodded in agreement.

As the raging man continued to scream profanities, the shah gestured to the guards, and in a single rapid motion they catapulted the helpless prisoner over the fence into the lion compound.

The hungry lions instantly pounced on their victim.

The shah shouted, "You dare call us names!"

Excited, his eyes ablaze, he moved closer to the fence and writhed with glee as he watched the teacher disemboweled and eaten by the ferocious beasts. When the shah had seen enough and was about to leave, he casually remarked to Nassiri, "Now you have one less headache."

When I returned to Tehran in 1976, I met with General Nassiri, and he confirmed that he had been with the shah at the royal zoo when the poor wretched man was killed.

"I didn't believe that they would really do it," he said. "When they suddenly tossed him over—I turned my head. I couldn't watch."

I didn't believe him.

General Nassiri met an equally horrible fate, being one of the first generals to be mercilessly tortured. Nassiri, transformed into a grotesque shambles of a man, was paraded before Iranian television cameras before being slaughtered by the firing squad.

The shah had attempted to destroy religion and to build his own kingdom on the corpse. Not only did he fall, but the specter turned on him. By his own actions, he gave the country into the hands of the religious.

CHAPTER TWENTY-TWO

SAVAK Out of Control

In 1976 the wife of the chief of internal security, the second most powerful man in SAVAK, was shopping at Charles Jourdan in Tehran, accompanied this day, as always, by several SAVAK guards. While browsing through displays of shoes, she realized that her purse was missing. It contained a lot of money and she assumed that it had been stolen. She immediately asked her guards for help, and one of them sought out the manager while others ordered the store's security men to lock the entrance, allowing no one to enter or leave. The SAVAK guards then stationed themselves in front of the door, and the manager, frightened by the heightening drama, placed an emergency call to the chief of internal security at SAVAK headquarters.

At the same time, a young engineer and his bride had finished their shopping and started to leave the store, only to find the exit blocked by SAVAK guards, who, when pressed, explained what had happened.

"But we're not thieves," the engineer protested. "And we're in a hurry. If you're suspicious, search us. But let us leave the store."

The guards ignored him.

"Don't say any more," his wife whispered. "We can wait like the others."

"But we haven't stolen anything. Why should we wait?" he replied.

"Please just be quiet. They're very serious."

"There's no reason for them to keep us here," he insisted. "They have no right."

"Keep your mouth shut," said one of the guards.

By this time, the operator had reached the security chief, who had telephoned home and learned from the maid that his wife's purse was on a hall table where she had forgotten it. He called the store manager with the information, and, greatly relieved, the manager hurried to the guards to tell them, requesting that the door be unlocked so that business could resume.

The engineer and his wife overheard.

"Wonderful," he commented, "all this fuss because a woman was absent-minded."

But the SAVAK guard refused the manager's request. "We need to hear it from the chief's wife," he said, pushing the manager aside as he went to find her.

"I don't believe it," the engineer said. "How far are you going to carry this?"

"Be quiet," implored his wife. "It's almost over; we can go soon."

"But the manager already spoke with the woman's husband; they won't even take *his* word."

"I'm frightened; please don't say any more."

"Listen to your wife," said the returning guard, as he unlocked the door.

"You had no right to lock this door in the first place," the engineer said.

His wife tugged at his arm. "No more! I'm begging you. Let's go now."

"That's right, shut up! I'm tired of listening to you," the guard barked.

But the engineer, even more angry, continued his protests, and their voices mingled heatedly.

"The fact that a woman . . ."

"Let's go; please, please, come with me," implored his wife.

". . . is absent-minded has nothing to do with us."

Customers were hurrying out the open door. The frightened woman pulled her husband toward it. "Come. It's over. Let's get out of here, please."

"Yes, it's over, but they had no right . . ."

"I'm warning you, don't insult us anymore," threatened the guard.

"It doesn't matter now. Hurry."

"But it does matter . . ."

"You stupid son of a bitch, I told you to shut up!" The guard pulled his gun and fired several shots into the man's head and chest. He died instantly. His wife screamed as she fell with him to the ground. The wife of the chief, without glancing down, picked her way around the two bodies and, followed by her guards, left Charles Jourdan.

Several weeks later I was in Tehran visiting the chief of SAVAK, General Nassiri. After our lunch at their home, Mrs. Nassiri brought up the incident.

"You know, Mansur, many people here believe it was me instead of the wife of the chief of internal security who was shopping that day. They heard only that it was the wife of the chief of SAVAK and assume it was me. They blame *me* for that man's death."

"I've told you," General Nassiri said, "there's nothing we can do about that."

"But I've lost all respect from these people," Mrs. Nassiri protested. "We have to do something, find some way to get it back."

"Nothing can be done."

"But I don't understand. If only you allowed the news media to report it, even if it's late, my name would be cleared." From the tension in their faces, I could see they had argued over this incident before.

The general stood up abruptly. "You see what kind of life they've made for me here, Mansur?" He motioned for me to follow him.

"General," I said as we walked in his rose garden, "I don't understand. Mrs. Nassiri is right about this. Even in New York I heard it was your wife. Why don't you do something about it? Surely you can find some way to put the story in the papers with an explanation for its lateness. Then Mrs. Nassiri's name will be cleared."

"It's not possible. You don't know all the details, Mansur. After that man was killed, I reported to His Majesty exactly what had happened. He had already been informed through other channels. His Majesty told me, 'It should not have happened. But now that it has, keep it quiet. Don't allow any papers to report it. Put the guard in prison for a short time, but no trial. To try him and punish him would only weaken the morale of the other SAVAK men. We don't need that now.' So, Mansur, given the orders I received from His Majesty, how can I report the incident to the papers just so people will know it was not my wife?"

"Then this killer will not be tried and punished for his crime?"

"Of course not! Are you kidding? His Majesty gave explicit orders."

Of course, in *Answer to History,* the shah took a different position:

Our Prime Minister was directly responsible for the day-to-day operations of SAVAK. As head of state, I could only intervene at the request of the Minister of Justice to exercise the Right of Pardon over condemned men.

I cannot defend SAVAK's every action and will not attempt to do so here. There were people arrested and abused. Unfortunately, this is not a perfect world. Worldwide police brutality exists. Inherent in police work is the potential for abuse and cruelty. My country, too, fell victim to such excesses. However, when I learned of abuse, I put an end to it.

Meanwhile, the conversations I had had with the CIA had convinced me by 1971 that its head office was unaware of the problems the shah's regime was facing. The shah was relying on SAVAK and the army, and, in my view, neither of these institutions was functioning as it was supposed to, and neither was likely to survive when the shah finally fell. The whole power structure in Iran would disintegrate. Because the United States supported the shah, it would then lose any influence it had had in Iran.

When I shared these views with the CIA officers, I could tell from their dubious expressions that they took my assessment with a grain of salt; nonetheless, they did agree to assign an officer to see me about once a week in New York, where I would brief him about the current trouble spots in the shah's regime.

The officer they assigned me was outstanding: He was familiar with the religion, culture, and history of the Middle East, and was aware of the current situation in Iran. He knew a little Farsi, and his Arabic was passable. During our first few meetings, he diligently took notes. Soon, however, he appeared with a tape recorder, indicating to me that this would save time, as the tapes could readily be transcribed. But the primary reason for the taping was so the CIA would have a record of the conversation in my own voice. I could see the logic in this, but I could also sense that the CIA suspected I might be a double agent for the shah or for SAVAK, and that I might be trying to elicit the CIA's true position in regard to the shah.

At another meeting I had with this officer, he said that he had instructions from his office that I should tape a message to the director of central intelligence (DCI) stating that what I had been saying was not said under duress, and that I believed my reports were for the benefit of both the United States and the Iranian people.

"I don't care. That's all right," I replied.

"I'm serious. The DCI would listen to that."

"Don't pull my leg. If you want that message, I'll send it."

As if this weren't ridiculous enough, he added that it could not be a simple statement. It must be in a question-answer format, with him asking the questions. I teased him, saying, "Why don't you make this very official? Before you ask your question, play the United States national anthem, and before my answer, play the Iranian national anthem.

"This is nonsense," I continued.

"Those are my instructions."

And so the tape was made. Because I was not trying to deceive them, I was unconcerned about their suspicion.

For almost two years the agent taped my explanations of every conceivable problem in Iran. There was nothing that we did not discuss. But after about a year, the agent would leave the room every thirty or forty minutes, saying, "You know the regulations of my office—I have to keep in contact with them via a public phone." Later I discovered to my chagrin that those trips to the phone were actually visits to a bar.

As the months went on, I noticed increasing lapses in his attention, to the point where he would actually drop off to sleep, lulled by the assurance that the tape recorder was doing his job for him. His growing problem with alcoholism finally forced me to report him to his senior officer for breaches of security.

In the first instance, he had invited me and my family, by then living in the United States, to dinner as a treat for them. I was to introduce him as the immigration officer who would help them obtain their visas. On the night of the dinner, when we arrived at the restaurant, he was not in the dining room. I found him at the bar, sound asleep, snoring loudly, his head resting on his arms. Appalled, I quickly awakened him. He gaped up at me. "Huh?" he mumbled.

"What are you doing?" I asked him. "My whole family is here!"

"Oh . . . oh . . . I'm sorry," he stammered. "I had a hard day today . . . had a few drinks before you came. I was depressed. You find a table . . . I'll wash my face and come over. Everything will be all right—you'll see."

Somehow I managed to introduce him and we had dinner. But he was back at the bar when we went home.

The second incident truly alarmed me. I knew that something had to be done. He had come to New York on one of his regular trips and we had taped four or five cassettes. The next morning, I went to the lobby of his hotel to pick him up to take him to the airport. He was sprawled on a sofa in the lobby, dead drunk. He had already checked out of the hotel and, lying next to him, accessible to anyone, were his luggage and a brown bag containing the tape recorder and cassettes.

On our way to the airport, I tried to impress upon the man the seriousness of the situation—the way he was jeopardizing my safety. "Look," I pleaded, "if someone picked up these tapes—God forbid!—and sent them to Iran to SAVAK, can you imagine what would happen to me and my family? I beg of you—do not drink anymore! Do you remember when your senior officer introduced us, how he stressed to us the importance of secrecy in our work together? He told you that because of the possibility of hijacking, you should never take any of the material on the plane with you. You're supposed to travel by train or let the office in New York send the material if you fly. How many of those security precautions are you following today? You don't need to worry—you are an American and nothing will happen to you. But if someone hears my voice on this tape, I cannot deny what I said. Then what? I would face the firing squad! I am trying to help the Iranian people, your country, your government, but you are completely irresponsible."

Contrite, he apologized and promised to be more careful in the future.

When I informed his senior officer about the agent's laxity, I learned that the CIA was already aware of the situation. The agent had given himself away. Often the head office had requested that I expand upon information given to them on a previous tape. My responses to these questions had often been fifteen or twenty minutes long, and while I was recording them, the agent had fallen into a drunken stupor, his snores coming through, loud and clear, in the background.

The CIA knew the situation had become untenable, and the agent was no longer assigned to me. The chief of the Iran desk in the CIA apologized for the man's indiscretions and said they were trying to retire him on disability, as they did not want to hurt his family by firing him for cause. I harbored no hostility toward the agent; of all the CIA men I had known, there were only three who were truly well versed in their fields, and this man was one of them. It was the stresses in the personal and professional aspects of his life that had played a large part in his alcoholism and subsequent negligence.

Within a year of his retirement, the agent died. Truly saddened by the death of a man I had respected despite his faults, I asked the chief of the Iran desk if I could pay my respects at the wake. He refused; instead, the CIA made special arrangements for me to fly to Washington, where I was picked up and taken to the funeral home before the

hour of the wake. The casket was opened, and I remember standing there looking down at his face. Poor man—I recalled his frustration over his assignment. He used to tell me, "You know, Mansur, the office doesn't want to listen to all these things you are telling them. All they want to believe is what Ambassador Helms is saying about the shah. Because he was the former director of the CIA, they put great faith in him. What they don't know is that Helms and the shah went to school together in Switzerland. They don't want to listen to us. We're wasting our time."

Helms had been appointed ambassador to Iran by President Nixon in 1973. In their youth, Helms and the shah attended Le Rosey School in Switzerland, where they had become fast friends. When Helms was appointed ambassador, General Nassiri remarked to me, "Mansur, be careful about what you tell the CIA in America. If you tell them something critical of the shah or Iran, they may pass it on to Helms. He in turn may tell it to the shah."

After that warning, I was sometimes cautious; but most of the time I was not.

Meanwhile, the shah had become more and more arrogant. Confident of Nixon's support, he believed he had carte blanche to say or do whatever he wished. He pronounced imperiously to the United States: "If you allow complete freedom of the press to continue, the United States will become Communist." He bragged that Iran would soon become the fifth most important world power, and proclaimed that the whole world should follow his leadership in forging an ideal democracy.

Realizing that the shah, instead of "forging an ideal democracy," was constructing the scaffold on which he himself would hang, I inquired of a CIA agent if I could ask him a very serious question.

"Sure. Go ahead," he said.

"You don't have to answer me," I began, "but has the CIA made any provision to have the army, SAVAK, or some politicians prepared to step in when the shah is gone? If you haven't, you'll be like a man alone drowning in the middle of the ocean, screaming for help. If you haven't already made plans, you had better start now. If you have no undercover people and no contingency plans, when the shah goes, you are dead."

He looked at me suspiciously. "We don't have any plans, and we don't need any. We have done nothing against the shah—why do we need a plan? We trust the shah, and he trusts us. Even our intelligence reports predict that the shah will be in power for a good many years to come."

"Okay," I said. "If you have these reports, and they convince you, fine. But what if he dies while skiing, if he is shot, if he dies in bed? Those circumstances wouldn't repudiate your report."

"Why did you ask me if we have an anti-shah group to take over?" he inquired warily.

"I didn't mean anti-shah people," I said patiently. "I just wanted to know if you have *anyone* to take over when the shah leaves."

"Having someone ready to take over is anti-shah!" he insisted.

"Interpret it as you like, but what I am concerned about is whether or not you have given any thought to this possibility. If you haven't, you should do so."

After this fruitless exchange, I walked down Fifth Avenue, brooding over what I had said to him. *God!* I thought. *I made trouble for myself tonight. Why did I say those things to him? I have made them suspicious of me. If they report this to Ambassador Helms and he tells the shah, what will happen to me?* I was very tense, contemplating the implications of what I had done. *But I told them what I truly believe,* I reasoned with myself. And I was comforted by the thought that Richard Helms was an honorable man who was unlikely to endanger me by passing this information on to the shah.

All too soon my fears resurfaced. A few days later I received a call from the same CIA man back in Washington. He and other CIA officers were coming to New York to see me. These officers interrogated me again about my suggestion that the CIA be prepared in case the shah fell. I gave them the same answers I had given earlier. When I was through, one of them sighed. "We've heard this before. For the past fifteen years we've been told that the shah is going to go. Mansur, believe me, he will be in power for many more years."

I shrugged. "If you want to believe it, okay. But the shah is on his way out," I repeated. "If you don't have anyone to take over after him, Iran will be in deep trouble and so will you. As I told you before, I don't want to know whom you have in mind or what your plans are, but only whether or not you are prepared for a crisis."

"We are puzzled by your question," one of the officers said warily. "You know we never act against the shah."

I could see we were back to square one. But my exasperation was beginning to mount.

"If the shah dies or is killed, in whom would you put your trust?" they then asked me. "Whom would you be able to contact immediately to put in touch with the CIA?"

"General Oveissi," I replied without hesitation.

"General Oveissi?" they questioned. "Do you believe he can do it?"

"Yes," I affirmed. "If something happened and the shah died unexpectedly, General Oveissi could control the country if the United States declared its support for him within twenty-four hours. But, of course, we shift from one dictator to another."

At dinner that night with the CIA officers, the one I most respected —an extremely capable, intelligent man who always wore a flower in his lapel—asked me to sit beside him. "Mansur," he began during dinner, "let me talk to you as I would talk to my son."

"Go ahead," I responded.

"We have been in touch with you for many years. You know practically everything that goes on in the office. You know the current officers, the retired officers, but you should know that from the first day you were in touch with us, some of our men felt that you could be a double agent of SAVAK or the shah. The question you asked seems very deceptive to my office. You asked us about a replacement for the shah. We are leery of this. The orders are that you must go under 'the box.'"

"The box?" I asked.

"The polygraph," he clarified. "If you come out 'clean,' then we will accept your veracity."

I paused. "Now you say you don't trust me. You insist that I take the polygraph."

"Otherwise, we won't see you again. Personally, I trust you, but the Agency itself has no heart—no feelings."

"I agree to go under the box," I said, "not because I want to see you people again, but because I want to put the record straight. Maybe this will convince you to act."

He turned to the other officer. "Mansur is going to do it," he said. "Let's have a drink!"

I took the polygraph a few days later. The operator concentrated on three major questions: Was I an agent of the Soviet Union or any other Communist bloc country? Was I an agent of the shah put in to deceive the CIA? Was I an agent of SAVAK put in to deceive the CIA?

I answered no to all three questions: Only one other person, through all these years, knew about my work with the CIA.

I came out clean.

CHAPTER TWENTY-THREE

Princess Ashraf at Kennedy Airport

Whenever Princess Ashraf and her entourage flew to New York, she was treated with great deference. An airline officer escorted her from the plane before the other passengers were allowed to debark, and then he ran ahead to have her passport stamped. A ceremonial welcome always awaited her: the Iranian ambassador to the United Nations, the New York consul general, and I, the chief of SAVAK, were always on hand to pay our respects. By the time she reached the immigration office, her passport would have been stamped at the diplomatic desk in customs, and she could proceed right through. Her passport was then returned to one of her aides. Because of her diplomatic immunity as head of the Iranian delegation to the United Nations, her twenty or more suitcases were never examined but would be taken directly to her home or hotel by her aides.

But this time, in 1977, as we approached the diplomatic desk, the airline officer called me over. "We have a problem," he whispered.

"What is it?" I asked.

"The immigration official won't grant her entry!"

The immigration official, a tall, imposing man dressed in a crisp gray uniform, observed us trying to get to the front of the line, pushing those already in line. "You people sit down and stop talking," he ordered sternly. "I'm taking care of someone else. Please be seated and we'll get to your case." There were three people in line ahead of us, including an Indian woman with several children who were squirming on the benches, but none of us paid any attention to the officer. We remained standing, talking to the princess, who was not about to sit on the spartan benches.

"Look, ladies and gentlemen," the officer said, becoming more and more irritated, "there are people ahead of you. Please sit down and stop the commotion. We'll be with you as soon as possible." He slammed the entourage's passports down on the counter. "You will just have to wait your turn. These people were here first!"

Grudgingly, the princess sat down, astounded at being treated like an ordinary human being. She beckoned to me. "What is the problem?" she demanded.

"I don't know, Your Highness," I said honestly. "There's some problem with your passport and we'll have to wait and see what it is."

"Have you told him who I am?" she asked indignantly.

"He already knows, Your Highness. He's seen your passport."

For approximately thirty minutes, cowed by the officer's authoritative manner, we sat in silence while he dealt with the people ahead of us. Finally, he gestured in our direction. "You! Who is in charge here? I want to speak to one of the officials."

We all looked at one another and gradually everyone turned toward me. "Rafizadeh," the princess said. "You go talk to him. He's nasty; be nice to him." I got up reluctantly and went over to him.

"Are you traveling with her?" he asked brusquely.

"No, sir," I answered.

"Who are you?" he barked.

"I am a diplomat stationed in the United States," I said meekly.

"Show me your identity card." I did so. "All right." He showed me her passport. "Look here. Her American visa has expired. The airline should never have allowed her to board. I cannot give her permission to enter the country. She will have to go back."

"Officer," I implored, "she's the sister of the shah and the head of the Iranian delegation to the United Nations."

He dismissed my protest with a wave of his hand. "I understand all that. That's beside the point. She has no visa; I cannot grant her entry. She must go back and the airline should be fined for not checking to make sure she had a valid American visa."

"What should we do?" I asked.

"About the only thing you can do is call the State Department and have them call my boss. I don't have the authority to do anything. Meanwhile, I'll check the other members of her party through. Explain the situation to her."

Having overheard part of the conversation, the princess was incensed before I had a chance to explain.

"Your Highness, your visa has expired. He cannot let you into the
country."

She was shocked. "What shall we do?" she asked.

"I don't know," I answered.

"Try talking to him again," she urged.

"I am afraid to—he'll yell at me! Let him finish checking the other
passports; then he'll call me."

When the remaining passports had been stamped, the officer called
me over. "Look," he said to me, "I understand the situation, but I must
do my job. These are the options—she can leave on the next plane, have
her visa renewed in another country, and return to the United States,
or, as I told you before, you could call the State Department and have
them call my boss with instructions. The only thing I can do myself is
call my boss and find out what he wants me to do. Which of these do
you prefer?"

"Talk to your boss," I said, relieved to be able to place the responsibility in someone else's hands.

"Fine," he said. "Now sit down and don't act as though this is a
party. We have business to conduct."

The princess began to curse the United States when I relayed the
information to her. "All they do is cause me trouble—they want everything to be legal!"

"Your Highness," I said patiently, "the officer has promised to
help. Let's wait and see what happens."

The princess became more and more nervous. "Where are my
suitcases?" she demanded suddenly.

"I don't know," I responded. "Perhaps the customs office is holding
them."

"You must make sure no one opens them!" she ordered.

"Yes, Your Highness," I answered, knowing full well that I could
do nothing.

She turned to Ambassador Hoveyda and began to curse him. "I
cannot do anything, Your Highness," he whimpered. "It's the law. You
have no visa."

After making some phone calls, the officer again called me over.
"I've talked to my boss. This is what we'll do. It is really the airline's
fault for not checking her visa; but then she had all her entourage with
her—why didn't one of them check it? I'll waive the requirement this
time, but as soon as she arrives in the city, she must send her passport
to the State Department to obtain a visa."

"Good." I sighed.

He showed me an application for the waiver and began to fill it out. "She has to sign this," he said.

The consul general, standing behind me, interrupted. "Can't we sign it for her?"

"No! Be seated, sir," the officer snapped. "I said she has to sign it."

"May I take it to her to sign?" I asked.

"No! Tell her to come over here—she has to sign it in front of me."

I went over to the princess. "Your Highness," I said hesitantly, "you must come up to the counter to sign the waiver yourself."

"I will not sign anything," she snarled. "God knows what the form says!"

"Please, Your Highness," I pleaded, "if you don't cooperate, you will be unable to gain entry to the United States."

"You're sure if I sign it I'll be able to enter?"

"Yes. I am positive."

The princess, having spent an hour in tension and frustration, was shaking noticeably. "Where are my suitcases?" she asked again. "Will I get them back unopened?"

"When Your Highness signs the waiver, your diplomatic immunity will prevent them from checking the luggage," I promised her.

"Rafizadeh, there is something fishy going on here today. I think what they really want is to open my suitcases," she confided to me.

Resentfully complying with the officer's order, she rose and stalked toward the counter. The officer turned the form toward her. "Sign here by the X," he said.

"What is this I am signing?" she asked me.

"It's a waiver," he interjected before I could answer. "I'm doing you a favor. I hope it doesn't get me into trouble."

She signed the form. "That will be five dollars, please," he said prosaically. Because she did not have a purse with her, I paid the fee. "Remember to check your passport next time," he said pleasantly. "Enjoy your trip. Next?"

By then the princess was seething and would speak to no one but me. The rest kept their distance, fearful of attracting her ire.

As soon as we left customs, her anger, so carefully controlled in front of the officer, exploded. "Who was supposed to be in charge of my visa?" she ranted. "Which of you idiots is supposed to be taking care of these things?"

No one dared admit that he had neglected to check her visa.

Meanwhile, the issue of the suitcases seemed to take precedence in the princess's mind over the difficulties encountered with her visa. Unlike the other trips, on which her aides had picked up her luggage and brought it to her home, this time the princess herself waited, counting each suitcase until she was sure all had been taken to the cars.

Her obvious preoccupation with her luggage aroused my suspicion. Driving back to New York, I wondered why the princess had been so concerned. Was there something in her bags that she did not want anyone to see?

When we arrived at her home, Princess Ashraf had regained her ladylike composure. "How are you, Rafizadeh? You must be very tired after such a long day." She paused and her eyes narrowed. "Be sure that you don't send a wire to SAVAK about what happened today," she told me. "If my brother, His Majesty, finds out, he will be very angry with me."

"I don't plan to," I reassured her.

I did not send a wire to SAVAK, but I called General Nassiri and recounted the incident. He laughed. "I wish they had thrown her out. Next time don't be so helpful, Mansur!"

I told him about her nervousness about the suitcases. "I think she had a huge amount of money in them," I said.

General Nassiri laughed again. He was completely skeptical. "Don't be a fool, Mansur," he said. "She doesn't have to carry money. Why would she carry money? That can be sent through the banks. Maybe she was bringing in some antiques for her son, Shahram. Or maybe she was bringing in drugs."

PART IV

CHAPTER TWENTY-FOUR

A Prize Soviet Mole

Many Americans believed that the shah was a steadfast friend of the United States. Had they not seen him themselves on American television declare his unqualified opposition to the Soviet Union? In a world of polarities, it seemed to Americans that so violent an opponent of the Soviets must surely be a friend of theirs. But such was not the case. The shah was charting a middle way and he played on American anti-communism to try to achieve his ends.

After the CIA helped establish SAVAK in 1957, the two organizations had sustained a good relationship until the late 1960s, when the shah decided that it was time to sever ties with the CIA and keep the truth about Iran from the Americans. He ordered the Iranian authorities to keep track of the actions of the CIA and the American advisers in Iran, and to politely inform the Americans that from now on, they would have access to information only through the top man in each organization.

By the early 1970s, SAVAK and other intelligence offices in Iran had made a complete about-face in their relations with the CIA. SAVAK had stopped informing the CIA about Iranian affairs and had begun surveillance on all CIA officers, tapping their phones and spying on them.

As part of its functions in Iran, the CIA was gathering intelligence about the country and investigating Soviet activities there. It was obvious to me that the Agency had failed miserably at the first function.

However, in its work against the Soviets, the CIA had an expert staff in Tehran. Their foremost objective was to determine how the Soviet KGB operated.

The shah and SAVAK were well aware of the CIA's interest in the KGB. Department 8 of SAVAK had been established to do the same type of work—counterespionage against foreign countries and especially the KGB. But although the shah had requested United States help in a mutual effort against communism, in reality he wanted SAVAK to work alone, so that Iran could take sole credit for any successes. In addition, by using surveillance on the American agents, SAVAK could pick up clues and then attempt to complete any operation the CIA had initiated. Besides seeking the credit for any accomplishments, the shah also wanted to have total control over Iran's relations with Russia, fearing Soviet retaliation for any misstep on the part of Iran.

While the CIA was often successful in obtaining information about the Soviets, it was SAVAK that deserved sole credit for a virtuoso performance against the KGB. To my knowledge, the Soviets have not to this day discovered what it was that exposed their spy. For security reasons the whole story cannot even now be told.

In 1975 General Oveissi disclosed to me that he suspected a very high-ranking army officer of spying for the Soviet Union. General Oveissi did not believe SAVAK and the Army Intelligence Office, then headed by General Moghadam, were capable of ferreting out the offender.

I was a bit skeptical. "You just don't like General Nassiri and General Moghadam," I told him.

"No, Mansur," he said seriously. "Listen to this. When we were involved in a border fight with Iraq, every time we planned an attack on the border, Iraq was waiting there to meet us. Someone in my office was definitely leaking information to the Soviet Union, which passed it on to the Iraqis. There is no question in my mind about this."

I discussed General Oveissi's suspicions with General Nassiri and General Moghadam, and both felt that there was little substance to his fears. They claimed that Oveissi was always looking for an opportunity to blame his military fiascos on them.

However, General Oveissi's suspicions were well founded. In 1977 SAVAK had grounds to believe that Major General Ahmad Mogharabi, chief of planning, was spying for the Soviet Union. The shah ordered that nothing about this be disclosed to General Moghadam's Army Intelligence Office and, of course, the CIA had to be kept in the dark. General Nassiri's failure to notify General Moghadam of the operation later created open enmity between the two men, as General Moghadam insisted that he should have been informed.

The spy, General Mogharabi, was a shy, unsociable man. He was divorced and lived alone except for his maid. According to his later testimony, he had been approached by the KGB while he attended military school in Tehran, and for almost thirty years he had spied for the Soviet Union. He was one of the KGB's most trusted agents. In his home in Tehran, as the CIA later revealed, he had been provided with ultrasophisticated electronic intelligence devices that had been given to no other KGB agent in the world.

The case was of such vital importance to the country that General Nassiri handled it personally with the help of a few select staff members. So that none of the other staff members would suspect anything was going on with this select group—as would have happened if these experts on Soviet activities had not kept up their daily routine while working with General Nassiri—the general arranged for his special cadre to participate in a series of small charades that resulted in their suspension from duty for several months' time. This cleared the way for them to work on the special project without arousing any suspicion within or without the office, and there was no way any information could be leaked to the Soviets, not even through idle conversation.

After a thorough investigation, it was discovered that a car registered to the Soviet embassy, though not with diplomatic plates, was routinely stopping in front of Mogharabi's house. The driver would get out and open the trunk, and after a few minutes he would close the trunk and drive away.

As it happened, General Mogharabi and the Soviets did not need to make any personal contact to transfer information. Mogharabi would feed the information into the devices inside his house and the Soviets, parked out front, would use the equipment in the car trunk to retrieve the data from the equipment in the house and transmit it directly to Moscow.

General Nassiri and the shah chose to put an end to the operation soon after General Mogharabi returned from a trip to the United States. He had been watched very closely and his phones had been tapped. When the KGB agents arrived at Mogharabi's home about midnight, a waiting SAVAK car approached from the opposite direction and rammed the KGB car head on. General Mogharabi dashed from his house to see what was going on but returned just as quickly. The drivers leaped from their cars, and a fight ensued.

All parties involved were taken to a local precinct where the police had been replaced by SAVAK employees for this operation. At first the Soviets, feigning ignorance of Farsi, tried to treat the situation as a minor one and offered to pay for the damage to the other car. They admitted that they were Russians, but not that they were diplomats. However, after the interrogation became more intense, they revealed that they were diplomats. The Russians demanded diplomatic immunity and insisted on the return of their car. They were told that because it had been involved in an accident, the police would temporarily keep custody of it.

SAVAK then called General Nassiri for further instructions. General Nassiri told them that if the men were diplomats, they could not be imprisoned, but instead should be taken to the Iranian State Department. They would wait there until the State Department received verification of their identities from the Soviet embassy.

On their arrival at the State Department, the Soviet diplomats, no longer concerned about being held liable for their conduct, began cursing the SAVAK officers in fluent Farsi, threatening them with retaliation. "We'll get you!" they shouted. "We know how to get even!"

In the meantime, General Mogharabi was imprisoned and his house was searched. All the electronic devices were removed from the house and the car—everything was in the hands of SAVAK.

As soon as the Soviet embassy was notified, it requested that the diplomats be turned over to it on grounds of diplomatic immunity. However, there still remained the matter of the electronic devices in the car. After the diplomats had been released and the car returned, the Russian embassy sent a memorandum to the Iranian State Department asking for the return of some "personal items" that had not been returned with the car. The State Department telephoned General Nassiri about the request, and the general replied, "Write back to them that if they will be kind enough to itemize the articles for us, we will be more than happy to try to locate everything for them." Needless to say, the State Department never received the itemized list.

The CIA was delighted that a KGB agent had been caught, even though it had not received notification of the existence of such an agent prior to his arrest. The agents made two requests of SAVAK. Fearing that the KGB agent would be executed without divulging his valuable information, the CIA asked to interview the man. It also wanted permission to examine the sophisticated electronic devices that had been confiscated.

General Moghadam, upset at being bypassed, requested that the shah not give in to the CIA's requests. The general also expressed concern about settling the matter without unnecessarily antagonizing the Soviets.

Shortly thereafter, Admiral Stansfield Turner, director of central intelligence, invited General Nassiri to lunch at CIA headquarters when Nassiri visited Washington. I also was invited to the luncheon. The CIA explained that the Iranian ambassador, who would normally have accompanied us, didn't have security clearance, and apologized for not being able to invite him, too. This was a great privilege for us, as very few foreign citizens were allowed to enter CIA headquarters.

In the top-floor dining room overlooking a beautiful pastoral scene in northern Virginia, Admiral Turner began questioning General Nassiri privately about the clue that had alerted SAVAK to General Mogharabi's activities. General Nassiri explained the whole operation, neglecting to eat his lunch. The admiral was delighted with the story and could readily understand how the head of the KGB must have felt when he learned the news about his spy. Admiral Turner thought the idea of making the KGB list the missing items was ingenious, and said he could imagine himself in their place if asked to itemize such sophisticated devices.

As we left headquarters, General Nassiri confided in me. "I don't know what it is about that man, but I like him. He's very charming. I felt so at ease talking with him that I probably said more than I should have. Mansur, if the shah ever finds out . . ."

"Who is going to tell the shah?" I questioned. "The shah will never find out."

"The admiral was very diplomatic," General Nassiri continued. "He didn't ask anything of me, but I know the CIA wants those devices and they also want to talk to General Mogharabi. We cannot agree to that."

Shortly thereafter, another luncheon was given in Washington in honor of General Nassiri by the chief of the CIA in Tehran and a Washington-based senior CIA official, the one who always wore a flower in his lapel. We lunched at a lovely restaurant on the outskirts of the capital, and the man with the boutonnière slipped into the seat next to mine. He cleared his throat and in an unobtrusive manner said to me, "Look at me, Mansur."

I turned to him. "What?" I asked.

"We want those devices?" he whispered.

"Leave me alone," I said. "Talk to General Nassiri."

"No," he insisted. "I want you to do something about it."

"I am not going to do anything!" I retorted. "It would get me into trouble. How could the general justify giving you those devices? You are asking too much."

"Remind the general that we already have one of those devices, which we salvaged from a river about ten years ago. We have shown it to him already. But ours is covered with rust—these are brand-new. We want to see those devices. Come on, Mansur," he wheedled. "Talk to him."

General Nassiri began to tease us about our private conversation. "Tell me what's going on."

"All right," I said. "He won't leave me alone about those devices. The CIA wants to see what they're like. They're useless to us because we don't understand them, but they would be very useful for them."

"Okay," General Nassiri responded, "I'll think about it."

At this point, the chief of the CIA in Tehran, feeling that he was being totally ignored in this transaction, began to rub his hands together. "Okay, let's do it this way. When the general and I get back to Tehran, we will talk the matter over and resolve it to everyone's satisfaction."

"Fine," General Nassiri agreed.

"No!" the officer with the flower hissed to me. "Talk to the general again. I want his promise right now! Do you hear me? I want it now!"

General Nassiri, noting our squabble, asked what the argument was about.

"Mansur will tell you," the senior officer said.

I shrugged. "You know him. He refuses to give up. He wants your word on the matter right now."

The chief of the CIA in Tehran sat back and crossed his legs, then clasped and unclasped his hands. "All right," he said. "When we go back to Tehran, we'll discuss it. We won't discuss it anymore here. Everything will be taken care of when we get back to Tehran."

The CIA officer shook his head decidedly. "No! I want his decision right now!"

"General," I said, "he will not give up until he is positive he will get those devices."

The general gave in. "All right. Tell me the way you want them sent."

"You can give a command to the appropriate officer in Tehran through Mansur, right now," the senior CIA officer said matter-of-factly. "I will notify my team of experts in London to pick them up. This is the only way to do it."

"Are you going to inform the British about this situation, as well?" General Nassiri asked.

"That is not our intention. We want those devices out of Iran immediately," the senior officer responded, "and this is the fastest way."

"Then I'll have Mansur send the wire today," General Nassiri agreed. "I'll instruct my officer to give the devices to your agent, but after you're through with them, you must return them to us."

Knowing that he had been bypassed in this deal, the chief of CIA in Tehran gave me a withering look.

I never learned whether or not the devices were returned to Iran, but I did find out that they were examined carefully and proved to be a wellspring of information for the United States.

One demand having been met, the CIA was then eager to have a team of experts interview General Mogharabi. I called General Nassiri repeatedly about this, but he said, "It is very difficult to get permission for such a thing." General Moghadam opposed it because he felt he had been slighted in the whole matter, and the shah was unwilling to share any information with the Americans that would further antagonize the Russians.

I pleaded with General Nassiri to keep General Mogharabi alive, even if the interview was not granted, as he was a valuable source of information. General Nassiri said he would do his utmost, but there was only a remote chance of saving the man's life.

I also appealed to General Moghadam. "Imprison him for life if you must," I told him, "but please do not kill the man."

"That is a reasonable way to handle this matter," General Moghadam agreed, "but the shah wants to execute him. He's afraid of the Soviet Union."

My pleas were in vain. Eventually General Nassiri called, saying, "The Mogharabi case is over, Mansur. The shah has given the order to execute him, but there is a very slim chance for his life, as he has decided to plead guilty to a lesser charge, hoping he will be sentenced to life imprisonment instead of death. General Moghadam is being totally uncooperative, but you might make one more attempt to convince him."

I called General Moghadam again. He blamed the decision wholly on the shah. "I have done my best," he insisted, "but it is to no avail." When I called General Nassiri to tell him this, he said scornfully,

"General Moghadam is lying. He put pressure on the shah to have General Mogharabi killed."

General Mogharabi had appealed to the monarch for clemency and asked that his sentence be commuted to life imprisonment. I do not know who was truly responsible—General Moghadam or the shah— but on December 26, 1977, I read the following in *The New York Times:*

> TEHERAN, Iran, Dec. 25 (Reuters)—An Iranian general convicted of spying for an unnamed foreign country was executed today, the official radio reported.
>
> The radio gave no further details on the death of Maj. Gen. Ahmed Moqarrebi [sic].
>
> The 56-year-old general was sentenced on Dec. 4 after a secret two-day trial by a military court. His appeal against the death sentence was dismissed by a special appeals court at an open hearing on Dec. 18.

(When the SAVAK employees were put on trial after the shah had left Iran, the Revolutionary Guards, a mixture of Communists and religious people, continually asked them if they knew where General Mogharabi's file was. There was no file found in SAVAK. [The Soviets were still trying to determine why their agent was caught.])

I was also involved in a similar case, when a lone Russian hijacked a small plane and flew it to an airport in northern Iran. There he demanded to be sent to the American embassy in Tehran. Some military intelligence officers picked him up and brought him to Tehran, where he was held in custody. The Americans demanded that he be turned over to the embassy.

Again I became an intermediary, asking General Nassiri to turn the man over to the embassy. His reply was "The man is not in my custody. You will have to talk to General Moghadam." I went to General Moghadam, who told me that General Nassiri was wrong; it was Nassiri himself who was in charge of the man, but Nassiri didn't want to turn him over to the American embassy. Both generals pointed out that the shah planned to return the hijacker to the Soviet Union. The Americans knew that if the man was returned to the Soviet Union, he would probably be killed, and this precedent would discourage future escapes. "Use your influence," the CIA appealed to me, "and have the man sent to the embassy. If you cannot get him to the embassy, try to have him kept in jail, but don't let them send him back to Russia."

After a long series of appeals for the man's release, one night after midnight I received a call from General Moghadam in Tehran. He told me that the Soviet ambassador had met with the shah that day, and that the shah had called him. "I have to turn the man over tomorrow morning to the Soviet embassy," Moghadam said.

"Isn't there any way to avoid this?" I inquired urgently.

"No," he answered flatly. "The decision has been made."

I immediately notified the senior CIA officer in Washington and suggested that the CIA chief in Tehran make one final appeal to the shah. "If the man in Tehran could do it," the officer said resignedly, "I wouldn't bother with you, Mansur."

In a few hours the man was turned over to the Soviet authorities and sent back to Russia the same day. I never learned what happened to him.

In America the phrase most often used to characterize the American-Iranian relationship was "The shah is America's best friend and ally." Unfortunately, it couldn't have been further from the truth. The reality was that the shah feared the Soviet Union more than he did the United States, because of its proximity to Iran and his inability to penetrate its hierarchy.

Besides, the shah was incapable of having a genuine friendship or trusting anyone other than himself.

CHAPTER TWENTY-FIVE

Weary of Killing

After Nixon's resignation and Gerald Ford's inauguration, the shah had been uneasy. It was, as a *New York Times* article of April 26, 1975, put it, ". . . a time of some uncertainty in the generally friendly relations between the two countries. . . ."

The shah was fearful of American newsmen and the unfavorable press he was receiving. After Watergate in particular, he was disturbed by the immense power of the press in the United States, as witnessed by the enormous demonstrations that met him on every visit, as well as the crowds of reporters.

The relentless pressure from these two groups had an effect, causing him to reflect on the one question they always pounded at him, the number of political prisoners in Iranian jails.

The shah made his decision. No more prisoners.

He instructed General Nassiri to kill instead.

In addition, the shah instructed General Nassiri to have SAVAK issue publications to prove that all the disorder and lawlessness were being caused by guerrillas, Communists, and religious fanatics. And here, with the initiation of the shah's new policy, the real problem began.

From 1960 on, whenever the shah had visited the United States, I had always been on the scene, coordinating security. Each time, I had had the opportunity to watch him closely, to observe his behavior with each successive president and with the press. Never had I seen him so weak as when he met Kennedy, and never so mighty and arrogant as when with Nixon.

Now, on May 15, 1975, I watched as President Ford greeted him. The shah glanced nervously at the waiting crowd of reporters. Gone was the proud stance—head back, chin out, arms akimbo. His eyes were glassy, unfocused. One hand clutched the other wrist behind his back, both hands trembling as if palsied. His shoulders sagged. His face was haggard.

Intelligence from his inner circle had told me of how deeply disturbed the shah had been by the debacle of Watergate, of his fear of the men who had exposed it by chipping away relentlessly, the same men who now faced him on the White House lawn. At his press conference, completely out of character, he smiled widely and called various reporters by their first names, answering them unctuously in friendly tones. This was an anxious and worried man.

Not only had the shah lost self-confidence, but his key men had begun to tire of his contradictory orders, to lose faith in him. All were one another's enemies, but in every individual conversation I had with them, they indicated their mutual disgust with the shah. His fostering of innumerable factions had had its final divisive effect: Though each was against the others, privately they were now all against him. Not a single person had faith in the future, the shah or any part of his entire system.

By the time Jimmy Carter became a serious candidate for the presidency of the United States, the shah was aware of Carter's stance and background as a man greatly concerned with human rights, one caring little for protocol; the shah was deeply troubled. Carter was a political weed, seemingly springing up from nowhere, with no apparent political alignment, a man with a reputation both for devotion to his ideals and religious zeal. The shah was also aware that America, after Watergate, would be bent on housecleaning, and that the resultant sweep would probably oust Ford.

In 1975–1976, at my home in New Jersey, General Nassiri and I watched the debates between Ford and Carter, who was referred to in the shah's inner circle as the "Boar" because of his prominent teeth.

General Nassiri commented, "Looks to me as if the Boar will win. That's the end of the road."

He then said, with great fervor, that his only hope was that the shah would dismiss him before the real trouble started. "None of the security forces are going to agree to his new plan. They're not going to take part in wholesale killing. I know it. They're fed up."

"General," I asked, relieved, "I want to ask a favor."

"Of course," he said, "Anything for you. What is it?"

"I know how hard it is to get out of SAVAK, but I want out. When you know he's going to dismiss you—if that day comes, will you accept my resignation?"

General Nassiri was quiet for a moment. Then he said slowly, "Okay. Write your resignation but don't date it. Give it to me and as soon as I get a whiff of anything that tells me I'll be out of office, I'll sign it." He paused. "Don't come back to Iran. I'll do it."

The next day I handed him my resignation. He read it. "Very good. I'll take care of it."

Before his departure for Tehran, we chatted at the airport.

"Mansur," he said, "if the Boar is elected, the shah is sure to collapse. No one will be able to make him believe he'll have support in the United States anymore."

When General Nassiri's flight was called, and as I bade him good-bye, I asked once more, "You won't forget?"

"I won't forget," he said, and walked to the gate.

In 1977 I visited Tehran and went to see General Nassiri in his office. He asked me what my plans were for lunch. When I said I had none and planned to go home, he said, "No, don't. I must see His Majesty now, but please—I want you to join me at my house for lunch. Come at two o'clock."

The summer day was blisteringly hot and I was tired, but because General Nassiri had seemed preoccupied and strangely insistent, I went to his home at two o'clock, as requested. General Nassiri had not yet arrived. I talked with his wife for a while. She then lunched by herself and, leaving me in the living room, went to take a nap. Two-thirty. Three. I paced back and forth in the Nassiris' living room, occasionally sitting down for a brief moment on one of the two long sofas, immediately jumping up again to look outside. At three-thirty, I heard a car door slam. Glancing outside, I watched the guard hand General Nassiri a stack of large blue folders. General Nassiri, looking weary, came up the walk and entered the living room, sliding the pile of folders onto the nearest couch. Without a word to me, he scuffed his feet out of his shoes, kicked them off into a corner, and slumped onto the other couch. He put his crossed legs on the coffee table and sighed deeply. Finally, he spoke.

"God, I'm tired. Did you have lunch?"

"No, General, not yet. I wanted to wait and eat with you."

"I'm not hungry. You go ahead."

"Did you have lunch already?"

"Lunch? No. What kind of lunch? Poison, that's what I had."

"What's wrong, General? What are you talking about?"

"The shah is sick, that's what."

"What happened?"

"I'm tired, tired, tired! Tired of killing. Sick of it. Goddamn! I have children! I can't do it anymore."

General Nassiri covered his eyes with one hand. He slumped down further, dropping his head. His voice was so low that I bent toward him to hear.

"You know how many cars—Mercedes-Benzes—we destroyed last week?" he asked. "Brand-new. In the business district. How many fires? How many people killed on the spot?" General Nassiri's voice grew louder now. "And it's not enough! He's telling me today it's not enough. Do more! Do more! I can't. I can't anymore. I have a conscience. I have children."

"For God's sake, what is the reason for it? Why?"

"For proof. To prove that it's terrorist work. To make the people believe that enemies exist. And that the enemies are Communists." General Nassiri flung himself back against the cushions and twiddled his thumbs furiously. "Sick! I'm sick and tired of this. But what can I do? Remember, I told you in New Jersey that I'd never live to see my child's graduation? I won't. I won't see the day. This game has no end."

"Surely you can get out," I said. "Make excuses. Tell him anything. Tell him you did it, but don't do it. That's all."

"Impossible. How could I do that? He gets reports through a lot of channels. He'd find out."

"Resign, then."

"I can't. He'll never let me go. He'd get me somehow. Cause me trouble. I'm up to here in blood!" General Nassiri grabbed at his left shoulder with his right hand. "Up to here! How can I get out? You can't wash off blood with water."

"General, you have to calm down. Come on. You must eat something. May I ask the chef to bring the food in?"

"You eat. I'm not in the mood."

"Eat just a little, General, please. Have a drink at least."

We moved to the table, but General Nassiri only played with the food on his plate. Suddenly he said, "The shah lost his temper. He was furious. He kept saying, 'You must do more!' Goddamn America—that president they have!"

"What's he got to do with it?"

"If Carter wouldn't put so much pressure on him about human rights, this wouldn't happen." General Nassiri calmed down a little. He took a few bites of food.

I didn't feel very hungry either. "Why don't you tell him you're sick? Exhausted. That you need a rest."

"That wouldn't do any good either," General Nassiri answered. "The only hope I have is maybe that he'll come to some understanding, that he'll release me."

At that moment, the maid walked in and handed General Nassiri the newspaper. He glanced at it for a moment and then waved it in the air. "Look at that! The whole front page! Fire, robbing, killing. But that's not enough for him!" He threw the paper to the floor.

"General, you said you were expecting guests at six o'clock. It's almost five now. Why don't you lie down awhile. Rest."

"Mansur, I can't rest. Tell me, my friend. What should I do?"

"Just don't do it."

"Impossible," he said. "Impossible. How can I get out of it? You ever see a long hair in a piece of dough? How do you get it out? You can't. Once the dough is baked, that's it. I can't get out."

General Nassiri looked beaten. His eyes were red-rimmed. We left the table and went to sit by his pool, the sun no longer fierce. The water glinted, barely rippling.

"A drink, Mansur?"

"Cold beer, I think."

"Me, too. Ah, beer and a hamburger—purely American," he ruminated. "Oh, I wish I could see that day. The United States. But it's not going to come."

When several other guests arrived to see General Nassiri, I made excuses and left. General Nassiri shook my hand and asked me to come to his office the next day. I went home, dismissed the chauffeur, and went out to a pay phone to call Dr. Baghai. "I'm coming to see you," I said.

"Come," he answered.

It took an hour to relate General Nassiri's and my conversation. Dr. Baghai smoked his pipe and nodded occasionally. When I had finished, he said, "He's absolutely right. He's finished. There's no way out. All dictators end the same way. He's right. The shah wants more blood. Jesus! I can see exactly what will happen."

"He asked me for suggestions."

"Too late, Mansur. He should have said no long before this. He'll never get out. The shah will never leave him alone."

A few months later I visited General Nassiri at his home again, and found him sitting and watching American cartoons on television. Because he had young children who enjoyed American cartoons, he had asked me to send some videotapes of them. The children had enjoyed them so much that he asked me to send more, which I did. On this particular day, I discovered that the general himself would often come home from the office and all he would do was watch the cartoons. I asked him if he enjoyed them. His reply was very serious. "Sure, they keep you busy and away from thinking." After what he had told me that summer, I knew what it was that he didn't want to think about.

CHAPTER TWENTY-SIX

Coup Against the Shah

In 1977 on a visit to the United States, General Moghadam, then chief of army intelligence, stayed with me at my home in northern New Jersey. By then, his disagreement with General Nassiri had become extreme. General Nassiri was furious with General Moghadam. General Moghadam hated General Nassiri.

As we sat together in my family room, General Moghadam's murderous tones and his vehement words surprised me.

"As soon as I get the chance, I'll put Nassiri in front of a firing squad," the general said.

"Why, General?" I asked. "What has he done that would make you say such a thing?"

"What right has he to arm people, get them involved in arson and bank robbery, simply in order to kill them? An agent who penetrates a target doesn't have the right to arm the target. He has no right to induce people to commit crimes like that. Who else is responsible?"

General Moghadam's argument was provocative. I could not contradict what he was saying, so I bluffed.

"General, I've been told that in your time such things were common." No one had told me any such thing.

"That's not so. They told you lies," General Moghadam said indignantly. "In my time in SAVAK, it's true sometimes it happened by accident. They'd ask an agent to provide a pistol. Maybe to help them in a bank robbery. If we didn't give them arms, they'd kick the agent out. Therefore, I gave orders to give them arms. But we were always careful. We knew who had them and what they planned. That's the difference between my time and General Nassiri's. A vast difference."

"Well, it's all news to me. But you agree that what they're doing now they were doing then?"

"Yes," he said with reluctance. "But we did it carefully. So our agents wouldn't lose their jobs."

For an hour, General Moghadam detailed the whole process by which SAVAK under General Nassiri had armed people and encouraged and entrapped them in crimes that would lead to their destruction. I asked him how many people he thought were involved.

"Several hundred at least," he answered.

"That's all?"

"Yes."

"And His Majesty? Does he know about it?"

"Of course."

"Then why punish General Nassiri?"

"First of all, he should say no to him. General Pakravan said no to the shah. General Nassiri shouldn't induce people to do these things. Nassiri's a good dancer. He dances beautifully to the music."

General Moghadam was referring to an old joke about a woman and her husband who were captured by bandits. The woman, forced to dance naked by her captors and watched by her bound and gagged, helpless husband, is later reproached by him after their release. "What could I do?" she asks. "You couldn't help me. They forced me. You couldn't stop them."

"Yes," answers the husband. "But you danced with so much pleasure. You used all your talents! You danced beautifully!"

"You know and I know that General Nassiri is old," I said. "He's not ambitious. He's anxious to retire, not to keep the job. You'll probably get it. When you're the boss, what will you do?"

"I'll certainly put an end to this shameful business. I can't stand what they're doing—giving potassium cyanide to people."

"I understand that terrorists take cyanide capsules rather than reveal anything under torture or face the firing squad."

"Bullshit. No. Who knows if they took them themselves or whether SAVAK shoved the capsules in their mouths?"

"If I'm wrong, say so. What you're telling me is that SAVAK does this kind of thing?"

"All I say is, I don't buy it. You ask General Nassiri yourself. He knows better. If I get the chance to be boss, every one of them, General Nassiri too, will go on trial. And they'll face the firing squad."

"You'll do that?"

"I certainly will!"

"I can't believe it. I just can't see you doing it. He was your boss. He still is. How could you do it?"

General Moghadam got up from the cushion he had been reclining on in the corner of my family room. His face was taut, a white line edged his mouth. "Look, you're not inside SAVAK. You have no idea what's going on. Killing several hundred people seems pretty monstrous to you. What about all those young men and women who were armed by SAVAK and then murdered by them? What about that?" He glared at me, banged his fist on the mantelpiece. "I tell you, I'll kill them all! Every single one. I won't let one of them get away!"

"General, be calm," I cautioned. I hesitated. "But I still don't understand how you can do anything about it if the shah is involved, if he knows all about it."

"Mansur, you know me and my family. So many years. Do I have any bank accounts around the world? You know my house in Tehran. Is it a rich man's house? Why shouldn't I fight with the people? For the people, not against them. I worked hard in my life. For what? And I know how to get even with the shah!"

"How?"

"C'mon," he said in disgust, "I'm not a fool. You think I don't know that he told General Nassiri he's the boss? That he should check on me? And then he told me the exact same thing about Nassiri. I'm no fool! Give me a Scotch. Sure, I know all about it. He's going to take his beating. He's like the old man who made the kids leave off tormenting him by saying the neighbor down the street was giving out free candy. He fooled several bunches of them and then he started to believe it himself and went there, too. They tore him to pieces for his lies, even the neighbor. His Majesty will get his, too. Don't worry."

General Moghadam then tried to persuade me to resign from my job in the United States when and if he became chief of SAVAK. "Come back to Tehran and work for our cause," he said.

"Our cause? Are you sure we have the same cause?"

"Yes, I'm sure. I know you well enough. I know your connections. We can work together. Slowly we'll get rid of the shah."

"All right, General. I agree with you one hundred percent. I'll resign as soon as General Nassiri leaves his job. But I'm not coming back to Tehran to work with you, because there's going to be a bloodbath. What you told me tonight is unbelievable. That is, I believe you, I'd heard rumors and tales, but not ever from the lips of a man like you. I don't think you'll be able to carry the burden. It's too heavy—much too heavy."

"No. I'll manage. I'm with the people, the masses. I go along with them. If they get rid of General Nassiri, we'll keep the shah confused and get rid of General Oveissi. Then we'll unleash the people. Then here we go."

"I don't doubt it, General. We can do all of that. I'm sure of it. No problem. General Oveissi, too. But what about you? How will you survive it?"

CHAPTER TWENTY-SEVEN

Conversations with Three SAVAK Chiefs

On May 21, 1978, General Nassiri called me from Tehran.

"I've just been with His Majesty for almost four hours," he said. "We had a huge disagreement. Two weeks. That's it. I'll be out. I can't find your letter. I'm behind my desk right now but I can't find your resignation, Mansur. I'm sorry. Send me another one immediately. Use the diplomatic pouch. Right away."

"Well, are you happy about it?"

"No, I'm not happy. I'm seventy-one years old and he's got still another job for me. No release for me. Thirteen years. Thirteen years with SAVAK. I'm superstitious, you know." He sighed. "No one knows yet. Don't tell anyone except the CIA"

"What about Ambassador Zahedi?"

"Don't tell him. Wait. Just the CIA."

"May I ask who's next?"

General Nassiri's tone was sarcastic. "My best friend, Moghadam."

"Does he know?"

"No. He doesn't. Don't tell him."

As soon as our conversation ended, I sent another letter of resignation to General Nassiri's personal attention and called the liaison officer at the CIA to inform him.

"We don't know anything about it," he said. "Are you sure?"

"Yes."

"Why?"

"It's a long story."

"Who's next?"

"Moghadam, his 'friend.' "

"No kidding! Does he know?"

"No. He knows nothing yet, so don't tell him. The general told me just to tell you."

I was sure that the CIA would immediately inform its chief in Tehran. He would not be pleased at receiving the information second-hand, Washington informing him instead of the other way around.

I called General Nassiri a few days after I had received his reply accepting my resignation and advising me that the proper office would contact me to effect a transition and process the legal details. This meant appearing before a board of SAVAK officials and swearing an oath to reveal nothing of my affiliation or activities with SAVAK. General Nassiri couldn't talk and returned my call that night.

"Five days," he said. "On June seventh, the new boss will be behind my desk. My new assignment is ambassador to Pakistan. Tell Ambassador Zahedi right now. As soon as Moghadam is in office, call him. Congratulate him. Send him flowers. Tell him not to be hostile to me. After all, I gave him a good recommendation for the job."

"General, it won't look good if I call after the news is announced officially. What if I call a few days before?"

"No. Nobody knows. One day before, okay. But not a few days. The day before, I'll be going to the royal court with him to see His Majesty. You want to break the news before that? No good."

"General, please. Let me do some hammering [bragging] for you."

"Well, okay. But be careful, huh? Tell him I told you."

I couldn't wait until the last day. I had known General Moghadam so many years. I could still picture him in his office as chief of military intelligence, sitting alone with little to do, drinking hot chocolate. So I called him four days early. He was glad to receive my call and very talkative. He mentioned a few mutual acquaintances and inquired after his family, all in the United States.

I interrupted him. "Who is with you?"

"No one. Why?"

General Moghadam evidently still knew nothing. "General, I have some good news for you."

"News? What news?"

"You're the boss."

"Who said so? The CIA?"

"No. General Nassiri."

"Hmm. I'll be damned."

"Listen, General. He gave you an excellent recommendation to His Majesty. Please be good to him."

"First, I'll put him in handcuffs! Then I'll get rid of the shah! When will I be in?"

"In a few days. Don't tell anyone."

"I won't. I won't. Nassiri said he recommended me?"

"Yes."

"Don't believe it. He had no choice. Who else do they have besides me? Does anybody know?"

"The CIA."

"When did they find out?"

"I'll tell you later on."

"That's the reason, then. No one from the CIA has been here for several months, but in the past few days many of them came to see me."

"We'll talk about it when I see you."

"How long have they known? A friend in need is a friend indeed, all right."

"Don't tell anyone, General."

"I'm not a child. You don't have to warn me. But you can bet things are going to change!"

On June 7 a *New York Times* article announced General Moghadam's appointment as chief of SAVAK.

Within a few days I flew to Tehran and went straight to General Moghadam's office. No sooner had I been announced than the general himself came out to greet me and took me back to his office, the same room in which I used to meet General Nassiri, but it was altogether changed now. General Nassiri's huge leather chair was pushed against a wall. In its place behind the large desk was a small, straight-backed wooden chair. The floor was bare. General Nassiri's beautiful Persian rug was gone. The room was simple, utilitarian.

We sat down, and he told me about his dreams for Iran's future. He hoped for the shah's downfall and the destruction of the monarchy.

Later that day the chauffeur drove me to General Nassiri's house in the moutains. He had aged terribly. I knew he had injured his back, but now his whole frame shook, palsied. His eyes were ringed and sunken, his face deeply lined and drawn. I glanced around to recover my composure. The whole of Tehran was visible from the terrace of his house. We discussed my meeting with General Moghadam, and I tried to assure him that it was all a misunderstanding and that he shouldn't worry about General Moghadam's threats. However, his face was full of fear. He shook even harder, the tip of his cane stuttering on the terrace pavement.

I left General Nassiri feeling very depressed. I wanted to help him, but I knew Moghadam was determined to destroy him.

I made an appointment with General Pakravan, and the chauffeur picked me up at the appointed time.

"Him, too?" asked the chauffeur. "He's a good man. You have to pay him a visit."

I found General Pakravan in his library, relaxed, casually dressed in old corduroys. We embraced. Talked. When I told him about the furious quarrel between General Moghadam and General Nassiri, he took General Moghadam's side.

"Moghadam's right. Nassiri's wrong. He ruined the name of SAVAK. He's killed so many people. Now he has to pay the price."

"What do you think will happen to this country—all these riots, killings, demonstrations?"

"I see nothing but destruction for us. Good and bad. Down we go together."

"Any solution?"

"None."

"You're probably right, General, but isn't there any way to persuade His Majesty to stop this slaughter?"

"Did you talk to Moghadam about it?"

"Not really. He said he wasn't going to kill anyone. He cursed Nassiri for doing it."

General Pakravan muttered something. Then he said, "His Majesty doesn't—won't—understand."

"I have a suggestion. Maybe you could make an appointment with him. He always listens to you. Talk to him, General. Tell him things are falling apart."

"Me?" General Pakravan laughed, pointing at his chest. "Me?"

"Yes, you."

General Pakravan got up and motioned for me to follow him to the other side of his library. He pointed at a picture of himself and the shah walking on a runway at Tehran Airport.

"What do you make of that?" he asked.

"I don't know. Looks like he's talking over his shoulder at you. Your neckties are flying. It must have been very windy. Why?"

"Talking . . . a lot of people made the same mistake. That was before he exiled Khomeini. He's furious! Spitting mad. Cursing me. For disagreeing with him about killing Khomeini. He called me a fool."

We sat down again. General Pakravan shook his finger at me.

"Listen. I haven't seen the shah in almost a year. Now you're asking me to get an appointment with him? He'd never listen to me because he's too arrogant."

"No chance at all?"

"None. He doesn't want to see me and I have no desire to see him. What could I tell him that I haven't said before? There's no hope. They're all crazy. Maniacs. I don't feel sorry for myself. I've had my life. But the people . . . They'll be killed, killed, killed, before it's over." He passed both hands over his face and held them to his temples. "Did you talk to Dr. Baghai about it?"

"Yes. I told him I was coming to see you."

"What does he think about it?"

"Same as you."

"Yes. That's it. The end. Finished. There's not a thing we can do."

We talked late into the night. It was the last time I ever saw General Pakravan.

Later, Dr. Baghai told me about *his* last meeting with Pakravan.

"General Pakravan said, 'I have always been against dictatorship and for democracy, but fate didn't allow me to live in a democracy. I suffered under a military dictatorship and could tolerate it but now I foresee a mixture of a military and a religious dictatorship in Iran's immediate future. I don't think that I can live with that and I have begun to look for a gentle poison. Yes—I am even contemplating suicide.' "

In 1979 General Pakravan would face the firing squad of Revolutionary Guards. Rumor held that he sent a message to Khomeini saying that he had opposed the shah's plan to kill Khomeini and had lost his job because of it. "Now you want to kill me." Rumor added that Khomeini's reply was "You should have killed me when you had the chance. I'm not a fool like you."

While in Tehran I also went to see General Oveissi, my friend for many years, then commander of the ground forces. A few of his friends and I were having drinks in his den. General Oveissi, a good Muslim, was abstaining. I had explained to him in brief the fierce quarrel between General Nassiri and General Moghadam.

"Hah!" he exclaimed. "Both of them are wrong and they both belong in jail. When we hold our security meetings, they never stick to the issue. All they do is chant the shah's praises and make propaganda statements."

I laughed. "That's what General Nassiri and General Moghadam say about you."

"No. Not me. Maybe once in a while I say a little something so that the shah will hear about it and I don't make an enemy."

"No matter who sings the shah's praises," I replied, "the day will come when your whole army won't be able to solve our problems."

The discussion was getting hot. General Oveissi was furious at my remark.

"You mean to tell me that a bunch of jackasses can stand up against the shah's army? Impossible!" he exploded.

We were interrupted by the announcement that dinner was served. Unsure of exactly how angry General Oveissi was with me, I headed for a seat at some distance from him.

"No, no, Mansur, over here," he said. "Sit next to me." He hesitated, then in a lower tone he said, "You have no experience with the people here tonight. Don't talk like that in front of them anymore. But you are right. And I agree with you."

"Then what are you going to do?"

"I'm not stupid like Nassiri and Moghadam."

"Well then, what?"

"Before the real trouble starts, I'll get out. I'm not going to be trapped."

CHAPTER TWENTY-EIGHT

A Broken Shah in Niavaran Palace

I agreed to go back to New York and keep my job as chief of SAVAK in the United States. Because of the huge unrest in Iran, General Moghadam proposed to take me with him to his next meeting with the shah.

"Let him think it's his plan," Moghadam said.

I had last been received in the royal palace after Carter's trip to Iran in December 1977. Since then the shah had changed utterly. He was gaunt, his eyes huge, protruding, and unfocused, heavy rales produced by his breathing shaking his chest and shoulders. He did not move or smile as we greeted him. General Moghadam spoke first. "Mr. Rafi-zadeh, as you know, resigned under General Nassiri, but because of the marvelous work he is doing in the United States, with your blessed permission, I want to rehire him, to have him continue in his office."

Now the shah looked fixedly at me, still with that glassy stare. His voice was without force. "You are getting tired of the United States? Of SAVAK?"

I didn't know how to answer.

He spoke again. "How is your relationship with Ambassador Zahedi?"

"Good, Your Majesty. Very good."

The shah glanced at Moghadam. "We don't want to annoy Zahedi. Does he know you resigned?"

"Yes, Your Majesty."

Now the shah held up both arms. "We wouldn't want Zahedi to feel bad. Give him some credit in it." To Moghadam, he said, "Since Rafizadeh resigned, ask Zahedi how he feels about it." He smiled and nodded at me. "He will approve of the reappointment, no question. Just give him credit. Now, Mr. Rafizadeh, isn't there any way we can put a halt to this bad press we're getting in the United States? What are we going to do about these newsmen?"

I shrugged. "Your Majesty, I just don't know."

"Tell me, Zahedi always claims he knows everyone—Republicans and Democrats both. Is that true? Does he really know them?"

"Yes, Your Majesty. It is true."

The shah pulled nervously at the hair on his left temple. "It doesn't make sense. No sense at all. We hope you're right. But one way or another, this bad publicity must cease! Why do they pick on me? What do they want from me?" His fingers kept twisting a lock of hair. "Why can't they leave me alone? We'd be all right. We'd . . ." He stopped pacing and faced me. "Tell me, is this true? Zahedi said that at a Cabinet meeting when the waiters served coffee and all the members stopped talking, President Carter told them to go right on with their conversation? That the waiters weren't strangers? Is that right? Is that possible?"

"I don't know, Your Majesty. If Zahedi said it, it must be true."

"He told me that a lady who was in charge of the Arms Sales Committee under Carter rode her bike every day to her office. For such a position, there's millions of dollars involved. A bicycle! I can't believe it. Could it be so?"

"Again, I don't know, Your Majesty. I'm sorry, I don't know the story or the woman, but if Zahedi says so, it must be true."

"I can't believe these things," he said, baffled. "They don't seem possible. No matter! Tell me, to your knowledge would it be better if we called back our press attaché in Washington and sent in a new man? Would that stop all this bad press about me?"

"With your blessed permission, Your Majesty, to the best of my knowledge, if you will permit me to say so, there is nothing we can do to control it. Look what happened to Nixon."

"Yes, that's true." He sighed. "He should not have lied."

Moghadam's brow rose in astonishment. The shah didn't notice. "At any rate," he continued, "your job is to persuade them in the United States that if anything happens to us, that's the end of the Middle East. There will be Communists everywhere. That's all there is to it. I'm looking to the United States and the Middle East is looking to me." The shah made several comments about the bad press he was receiving and about the influence American newsmen had. He suggested again that I attempt to buy them off.

On the strength of the look Moghadam gave me, I answered, "Your Majesty, that's their virtue. It would be the worst thing to do."

General Moghadam then asked the shah's permission for me to leave.

"Do your best," said the shah in parting.

Before I left Tehran, I visited Dr. Baghai. He was particularly interested in my appraisal of the shah's appearance and behavior.

"I think he's done," Baghai said. "Completely. There's nothing left functioning."

I told him of my plans to return to the United States, and that I intended to get passports for myself and every remaining member of my family.

"You have a diplomatic passport already."

"It won't be long before I have to relinquish it," I replied.

"I see," he answered.

"There is only one great sorrow for me in going. Perhaps, Doctor, we will never see each other again."

After that I went to SAVAK to see the man in charge of passports. I asked to speak to him privately. When he consented, I opened my briefcase and spread my bundle of applications on his desk. "I want passports for each of these," I said.

"So many?" He leafed through them.

"Yes."

"You, too? You already have a diplomatic passport. The office can't issue two passports for you."

"That's why I'm here."

"Does the chief know about it?"

"That's why I'm with you."

"You smell something?"

"That's why I'm here."

"Promise to tell me what it is you smell?"

"Yes. Promise."

"I can't do them all at the same time. Four a day. Husbands and wives—it'll take two days."

"Fine."

"Can you tell me anything?"

"The day will come when they'll ask for my diplomatic passport. I'll be left with no identity."

"Same with me!" he exclaimed.

"You got the message."

He rose from his chair and kissed me, once, twice, three times. "Thank you! Thank you!"

"You didn't hear a thing," I warned.

"Not a word."

In three days he called me back to his office. On his desk was an enormous bundle—each passport stamped and valid. I tried to give him the fee required for each passport.

"No. No money," he said.

"Take it. It's what's due."

"Nothing. I owe you."

I stuffed the passports in my briefcase.

After I arrived at my family's house in Tehran, I called an American friend at the American consulate, a beautiful person, compassionate and understanding, and invited her to our home that afternoon. As she sat down, I spread the passports in front of her and told her that I needed four-year multiple visas for each.

She stared at me in amazement. "Mansur! What on earth? So many! I can't get visas for all of these. Especially you. You have a diplomatic passport. I can't get you another visa."

"If you can't, don't. But get them for the rest of my family."

"Not all at once. As soon as I can."

"Do your best."

"I can't get one for you. The American consul will want to know why."

"I'll leave it to you."

"You see trouble?"

"Yes. And soon. I'll have to surrender my diplomatic passport to the next regime. That's the reason."

"You believe that's going to happen?"

"No question about it."

"May I tell my husband in the embassy? It's such a blow to me! A SAVAK man feels such a thing. As Americans we don't realize the situation and see only what the shah wants us to see."

"It's true, though. Your ambassador just doesn't understand."

She thought for a moment, head bent. Her hand to her eyes, she fiddled with the passports. "You, too?"

"Yes. Soon, it will all be history."

She left carrying them all. Within a few days, she returned. Visas granted. Immediately I called all the adult members of my family to a meeting. I spoke briefly, telling them my concern was with their safety. "We have all worked for freedom and with good intentions, but our father warned us that the day would come when the dry and the green wood would burn together. Now I hear the drum." I stood up, handed each member of my family his or her passport and those of their children.

"I wondered why you wanted all our pictures," one of my brothers said.

CHAPTER TWENTY-NINE

Conspiracy Tales

The American news media and the British Broadcasting Company unwittingly shared in the responsibility for the final phase of the shah's downfall. In Iran there were two major reasons given for this: the belief that the superpowers determined Iran's fate and a lack of understanding of the American government.

The majority of the Iranian people, including the shah, firmly believed that everything that happened in Iran politically was somehow the result of the involvement of Washington, London or Moscow. They so firmly believed in this master-plan-carried-out-by-external-forces theory that they could not conceive of taking any action or responsibility for their own destiny, because no matter what they did, it was part of the master plan. Gary Sick recognized this problem in *All Fall Down* (page 33):

The . . . most important factor in the communications short circuit between Iran and Washington was the Iranian penchant for conspiracy theories. . . . To this is added the conviction that any significant political, economic or social upheaval in Iran must be traceable to the manipulation of external powers. And finally, events are perceived as neither random nor aimless; rather, they must be understood as purposeful and integral to some grand scheme or strategy, however difficult it may be to fathom.

Numerous cases of this type of rationalization could be cited. For example, if someone like Dr. Baghai was jailed or if someone like Khomeini exiled, these Iranians would say that the sentence was really an act of purification for that person and that in the future he would be "taken off the back burner" and placed in a leadership position when it was time, according to the plan. This "punishment" was a way to cleanse the person, to make him famous, to make a saint of him, because he would apparently have suffered for the cause.

If the shah had remained in power, they would have said that it was logical. The British had put Reza Shah into power; the Allies had exiled him to Johannesburg and placed his son on the throne at the age of twenty-one; and if the shah remained in power for another twenty years, again it was because the superpowers had decided. If, on the other hand, the shah fell, it was because these same external forces had decided that also.

If Khomeini, who ostensibly had been exiled by these same external forces, took over, it was because it was part of the overall plan. It was believed that this had been decided twenty years earlier. After all, who but these forces could bring a mere clergyman into power?

This aberrant thinking also appeared at the highest level of government—no matter who was in the leadership. Whether it was the shah or the revolutionary government, no one could ever imagine that any opposition existed without the consent of Washington or London. No one believed that there might be some Iranians, unaffiliated with any outside power, who truly did not approve of the regime.

The revolutionary government complains that the United States is "Satan," and it blames the war between Iran and Iraq on the United States. It believes that any change in the government will come about because of Washington's or London's intervention, and not because of Iranians.

Whether under the shah's regime or Khomeini's, the opposition were always seen as puppets of external powers; accordingly, some were jailed, others executed. The shah believed that his fate was decided at a meeting in Guadeloupe in January 1979, a meeting attended by President Carter, President Giscard d'Estaing of France, Chancellor Schmidt of West Germany, and Prime Minister Callaghan of Great Britain. The shah wrote in *Answer to History:*

I believe that during those meetings the French and the West Germans agreed with the British and the American proposals for my ouster.

The crown prince Reza was of the same opinion. After the revolution, we met on a flight from New York to Washington, and he told me that his father had lost his throne because of the decision at Guadeloupe. He went on to say that God had punished all participants at that meeting. All four had lost their bids for reelection.

Even the most educated Iranian technocrats believed, and continue to believe, that Iran's problems could be solved at a summit conference. If there were such a conference between Reagan and Gorbachev, the two could decide what would happen to Iran. Their calm self-assurance would be unassailable; they would simply say that Iran was on the agenda for the meeting. The only question would be which nation would end up with Iran. Would Reagan trade Iran to Gorbachev for some other country, such as Cuba or Afghanistan? These Iranian technocrats believe that the superpowers trade countries, much as children trade baseball cards. As the shah once asked Nelson Rockefeller, "Is it conceivable that the Americans and the Russians have divided the world between them?"

Under the shah and later, most Iranians did not understand the setup of the American government. They could not grasp the idea that the government did not control every aspect of American life. They could not believe that a demonstration could occur in front of the White House in which people honestly spoke out against the government's policies. They believed that if the U.S. government had not wanted the demonstration it would simply have sent in police to chase away the demonstrators.

Using this same faulty logic, many Iranians could not believe in the free press of the United States, or of Britain. They believed that whatever the newspapers printed or the television stations broadcast was done with government backing. This is difficult to prove, but I saw the effects the media had on Iranians who thought this way.

The role of the U.S. media in the downfall of the shah began in November of 1977. When he went to the United States to see President Carter for the first time, there was talk within Iranian circles that because President Carter was pro-human rights, he would not support the shah's regime because of its poor record on such rights. These people were waiting for some evidence to support their prediction, and they believed it came during a reception for the shah on the White House lawn. A fight broke out between two groups demonstrating nearby, and the National Park police eventually used tear gas to break up the fray. The gas drifted toward the White House and got into the eyes of the president, the shah, and other dignitaries. Many Iranians,

believing that nothing like this could have happened without government support, saw this as a sign that the president was against the shah,
the more so as American television and newspapers reported the event.

Thereafter, a film was made of the shah's visit to the United States,
including the incident on the White House lawn. There were no more
than five copies of the film because it was for official use only, not for
general distribution. I had one copy and I gave one to the CIA. This
film was later shown in Tehran to a group of Iranian government
officials; it had the same effect on these people as the television broadcasts had had on the dissidents described earlier by Gary Sick.

I witnessed the effect the film had on government officials during
President Carter's trip to Tehran at the beginning of 1978. Ambassador
Zahedi, although he was not on good terms with the government and
had not been in Iran since the early 1970s because of his strained
relationship with former Prime Minister Amir Abbas Hoveyda, was
required by protocol to be in Tehran during Carter's visit. As it happened, he was going to be in that city only for the few days of Carter's
visit. I, too, was in Tehran—as liaison officer for President Carter's
security team.

Houshang Ansari, the head of the National Iranian Oil Company,
arranged a magnificent party in Zahedi's honor and invited about
eighty people—practically every influential man in the government of
Iran. Because there had been so much talk within the Iranian government about the shah's visit to the United States, I was asked to bring
the film along.

General Nassiri, who was still chief of SAVAK at the time, declined to attend the party because General Moghadam, the military
intelligence chief, was going to be present. General Nassiri made his
excuses to Ansari, saying that he had already seen Zahedi, and that he
was sending me in his stead. Prior to the party, however, General
Nassiri asked to view the film, which was shown in the screening room
at his home. After seeing the film, he said that he did not believe the
shah was going to survive. In spite of my attempts to reason with him
and tell him that this was a spontaneous demonstration, something that
is the legal right of the people in America, he steadfastly held to the
view that it was set up by the government and that the film was proof
that Washington was not behind the shah.

As the shah leaves for Egypt from Tehran Airport on January 16,
1979, an Iranian Army officer kisses his hand in farewell.

Mansur with Princess Ashraf
(center) in Jacksonville, Florida

ELI AARON

Mansur and
the shah at the
Waldorf-Astoria
in April 1962

Mozafar Rafizadeh,
former Ambassador to Washington
Ardeshir Zahedi,
and Mansur

Mansur and
Mozafar Rafizadeh

Mansur with Dr. Baghai in Tehran in 1972

President John F. Kennedy, the shah, Mrs. Kennedy, and the
empress Farah Diba at the Iranian embassy in Washington, D.C.,
on April 12, 1962

From left to right: the shah's son, Prince Ali Reza, Empress Farah
Diba, President Richard M. Nixon, Crown Prince Reza, and
President Anwar Sadat at the shah's funeral in Cairo on July 29, 1980

Prince Ali Reza,
the only full brother of
the shah

Asadollah Alam,
prime minister of Iran
from July 1962 until
March 1964

General Gholam Ali Oveissi,
commander of the
armed forces

Mansur with
Vice-President George Bush
in New York in 1983

Dr. Mozafar Baghai in the United States in 1986

CHAPTER THIRTY

Dr. Baghai

In mid-October 1978, Ambassador Zahedi stopped in New York on his way to Tehran, which was as usual in a state of turmoil. All the Iranian diplomats in New York wanted to see the ambassador to ask his opinion of the crisis in Iran.

The ambassador had asked me to pick him up at the airport so that we could have a private conversation on the way into the city. He asked me to let Dr. Baghai know that he would be calling him. "I want to take Dr. Baghai to the shah. We hope he can help resolve the current crisis," he said.

Just two and a half months before the shah left Iran, Ambassador Zahedi called Dr. Baghai and asked under what conditions the doctor would assume power as prime minister. Also the ambassador asked him what chance he saw for the shah.

Dr. Baghai replied, "Let me answer your last question first. The chances I see for His Majesty, the shah, are ten percent, and I see a twenty percent chance for the crown prince at this time."

Zahedi, surprised by the doctor's answer, asked, "Who gets the seventy percent chance?"

"Seventy percent is for Khomeini."

The ambassador was shocked. "You will see His Majesty, Doctor?"

"You arrange it."

After twenty-four years Dr. Baghai and the shah were about to meet. The last time the monarch had received Dr. Baghai was in 1954, when the doctor had warned him, "One day the people will besiege this very royal palace." The shah had responded, "And when they get here, we will meet them with machine guns."

Dr. Baghai had raised his cane and pointed it at the shah, saying, "And those same guns can be turned toward the royal palace. God bless you. May God grant you a pleasant ending, Your Majesty. Good-bye."

Dr. Baghai is one of those rare human beings who believe in obeying the law of the land. He is a strict adherent of nonviolence and always respected the Iranian Constitution and the shah as its monarch. The shah knew he was honest, true in his beliefs, and also knew that Dr. Baghai had turned down several opportunities to lead the Iranian people against him.

In January 1979 at the royal palace, after his visit with the shah, Dr. Baghai described the monarch as being very groggy, having a light-brown cast to his skin, and wearing a lot of heavy skin cream and makeup on his face. The cream was so heavy and of such a consistency that it threatened to drop off his face onto his collar at any moment. The doctor also reported that the shah seemed dazed, almost as if he could not believe this had all happened and that his regime was on the brink of collapse.

The shah asked the doctor what suggestion he had as to the best way to control the situation.

Dr. Baghai responded, "I have no suggestion."

"Doctor, what can you do to bring peace back to my country?"

"I have no suggestion and I don't see any way that I can do it myself," he replied.

In the same weary manner in which he had been questioning Dr. Baghai, the shah asked, "Who do you recommend?"

"A man like Ahmad Ghavam." (Ghavam had been prime minister when forty-five demonstrators were slaughtered in front of Parliament in 1951.)

At the mention of Ghavam's name, the shah's eyes suddenly opened wide and he said, "He's dead."

"I know he's dead, Your Majesty, but you asked who could do the job and he's the one who could have."

Again the shah asked the doctor if there was anyone who could do the job, but without waiting for an answer, with a distracted manner and groggy voice, the shah began to ramble on about the kinds of mistakes the government had made that pushed the country to this point.

Dr. Baghai later told me that, recognizing the shah's extremely poor health, he did not believe it ethical or fair to remind him of how much advice he had been given that, if heeded, could have prevented the current unrest.

The shah then asked the doctor, "What chances do you see for me?"

"I said to Zahedi three days ago that Your Majesty's chances were about ten percent, but today they seem less."

For the second time the shah was startled out of his lethargy and sat forward in his chair. Soon he sank back into the chair. The two men just sat and looked at each other. After a few minutes the shah's lips began to quiver and, in that weak, dazed voice, he asked, "So, you cannot help us in any way?"

"I'm sorry. It's too late."

The shah, whose breathing was labored and rapid, simply stared at him.

Finally, the doctor rose and said, "Your Majesty should rest. Please permit me to leave."

A few days later Dr. Baghai was invited by the empress to meet with her in her office. Unlike the shah, the empress was alert. However, she was distraught and from the beginning of the meeting she was in tears. She related to the doctor how upset His Majesty had been by their recent meeting.

"I couldn't help it," the doctor told Her Highness. "I had to tell him the truth."

The meeting lasted for more than an hour, during which time the doctor told the empress that the shah had been warned of what would happen.

"Several times we tried to talk to the shah and convince him," she told the doctor, "but it had no effect. It's too bad." As Ambassador Zahedi and the shah had done earlier, the empress asked Dr. Baghai what future, what chance he saw for the monarchy in Iran.

"It's minimal—there is practically no chance."

While she continued to weep, the empress asked, "Do you have any recommendations? Are there any conditions under which you would assume power?"

"Forgive me, Your Highness, but as I replied to His Majesty, 'It's too late.' I cannot help."

"Is there anyone else you would recommend?"

"At this point I have no one."

"What do you foresee if Bakhtiar comes to power?"

The doctor shrugged and replied, "Nothing. I don't see that there is anything he can do."

The empress pressed the issue: "So, if Bakhtiar comes to power, what can you see at the end of that road?"

"To benefit the monarchy? Nothing. It would be even worse."

The empress continued to be very emotional and was still crying. The doctor, wanting to spare her more distress, quietly left.

CHAPTER THIRTY-ONE

The United States Proposes Military Coup

In November 1978 I learned that Carter's national security adviser, Zbigniew Brzezinski, and Ambassador Zahedi favored a military coup in Iran. I still do not know which of the two men first advocated the plan and then persuaded the other, but I am certain that both endorsed it. Henry Kissinger, Nixon's national security adviser, also agreed to sanction it, but with the following stipulations: (1) All political prisoners who had been released by the shah must be reincarcerated and (2) certain others still in custody, such as General Nassiri and Prime Minister Hoveyda, must be released. There was only one man they thought capable of carrying out such a coup—General Oveissi, the martial-law commander.

With this powerful American backing, Ambassador Zahedi contacted a few prominent Iranian army generals, who proceeded to implement the plan in the following manner. While General Oveissi was at work in his office, the generals entered and attempted to convince him of the urgency of bringing the chaos in Iran to an end. If something was not done, they warned him, even they and their families might be killed. "We'll be killed behind our desks," one general exclaimed. "Let's do something!" They did not oppose the shah, they emphasized; they wanted to protect him and save the country. To do this, the shah must be sent to Kish Island or Kerman, where he would be temporarily isolated; the political prisoners must be reincarcerated; and others, such as General Nassiri, must be set free. When the military had succeeded in reinstituting order in the country, the shah would be allowed to return. "We are in grave danger, and you are the only one who can lead us out of this trouble," they concluded.

General Oveissi was adamant. "I swear that I will protect the monarchy," he insisted. "I will not do anything against the shah—I will take orders only from him. Get out—I do not want to hear any more about this matter." The generals left. (Two of them were killed during the revolution, one behind his own desk, as he had predicted.)

Shortly after the generals' visit, General Oveissi telephoned me, vaguely outlining the attempt made to enlist his participation in a coup. He was quite nervous about the whole affair, unsure of whether the request was authentic. The whole plan might have been a ruse, he realized; the generals might have been sent by the shah to test him, because General Oveissi knew that the shah was afraid of him. The general had told me earlier he had learned this when he heard about a conversation between the shah and General Gholam Reza Azhari, the chairman of the Joint Chiefs of Staff.

At that time, the shah had called Azhari to the palace to appoint him prime minister. "Your Majesty, your obedient servant is an army man, not suitable for the job," General Azhari had protested politely. "Your Majesty needs a strong man who is feared by the people. The health of your servant is poor—he has a heart condition, which may impair his ability to serve Your Majesty. With your blessed permission, may your servant recommend General Oveissi for this position."

"You know that we have complete trust in you," the shah had responded. "We do not have that kind of trust in General Oveissi."

I became involved in the proposed coup three days after the generals' meeting with Oveissi, when the CIA asked me to be its intermediary with General Oveissi. The Agency's objective was the same as that of Ambassador Zahedi and Brzezinski: The shah was to be sent to an island, General Oveissi was to lead the coup, and when order was restored in Iran, the shah was to be brought back.

"Whose idea is this? Yours?" I asked the CIA men.

They shook their heads. "No."

"Who shall I tell the general is behind this plan?" I inquired.

"The American government," they responded.

I told them I was aware that Oveissi had already been approached by several Iranian army officers and that he had flatly refused their proposal. The CIA agents claimed complete ignorance of that meeting and said that if it had occurred, the *modus operandi* was completely ineffective. Their strategy was to have me, in a circumspect manner, present the same proposal to the general. "Tell him that this message comes directly from the government of the United States," they stressed. "Warn him that he must not disclose it to anyone—not even to Ambassador Sullivan."

"Will you do this, Mansur?" they pressed.

"It won't hurt to talk to him," I reasoned. "Discussion is always beneficial."

I agreed to convey their message to General Oveissi; however, I emphasized that the conversation had to be secure from interception by satellite. To assure this, CIA agents came to my house the next day, after I had managed to get my family out of the house without their suspecting anything, and installed a device to garble the telephone conversation. The agents told me that they would leave the device with me throughout the crisis. Then they left me alone to make the call to General Oveissi.

"Are you alone in your office?" I asked when I reached him.

"No," he replied. "Is there something important you wish to discuss with me?"

"Yes."

"Call back in thirty minutes," he instructed.

When I called back, I succeeded in giving him the full details of the plan, assuring him that the phone was secure. He laughed. "Secure? It makes no difference if it is secure or not. I have nothing to hide."

Without hesitation, he again rejected the plan outright. Just as he had told the generals, he said he had sworn to God never to go against the shah. I told General Oveissi that the United States was trying to help the shah, but the general refused to act without the shah's knowledge. He was also concerned, he informed me, about bearing the responsibility for all the blood that would be shed. He knew that if he was caught by the shah and his people, he would face the firing squad. He was also wary because of the lack of cohesion within the various elements of the American political system. "It seems to me," he observed, "that there are governments within the government in the United States. No one knows who is boss—who should be making decisions." He laughed again. "All the factions have to sit down together and work out their differences; they have to determine what they want to do. Tell them I don't want any part of this."

I asked if he could suggest any alternative. "No," he answered. "I know of none. Tell them that a coup is not a viable solution to the problem in Iran. What we have to do is avoid more chaos; this will do nothing to restore order. Does the American ambassador, Sullivan, know about this plan?"

"No," I responded. "It's top secret."

He scoffed, "Very good! They don't even consult their own ambassador, and they want me to go along with them! When you lower a person into a deep well with a rotten rope, the rope will break and the man will never get out of the well. I refuse to go into this deep well with rotten American rope!" It was apparent that he saw no solution to the crisis. "Just between you and me, Mansur," he confided, "I myself am trying to find a way out of the country. Tell my wife and family not to come back—I will join them."

After I completed the call to General Oveissi, the CIA agents informed me that the garbling device was damaged, possibly not functioning correctly, and they removed it, promising to return with a new one. The replacement device never came.

Meanwhile, although General Oveissi had categorically rejected any connection with the coup, a rumor began to circulate that he planned to lead one. In *The Pride and the Fall,* Sir Anthony Parsons demonstrated how pervasive the rumor became:

> In mid-October, [Ambassador] Sullivan and I called on General Oveissi, the Martial Law Commander, with the approval and support of the Prime Minister. We told him that rumours were circulating in the officer corps that Britain and America would favour a military takeover of the government. We wanted him to know that these rumours were baseless. Both our governments favoured progressive democratisation as the only way to solve the crisis.
>
> A reversal of this process would face us with severe problems of domestic opinion in our own countries.
>
> The effect of a military coup on Iran's Western friends and allies would be disastrous. Other rumours of diminution of British and American support for the Shah were untrue. General Oveissi took our points without enthusiasm.

General Oveissi, however, knew more than both the American and British ambassadors. He knew that the proposed coup was not just a rumor but an actual stratagem, and his "lack of enthusiasm" undoubtedly stemmed from the fact that he knew their points were inaccurate. Either Sullivan and Parsons were lying, or they were grossly ignorant of the facts. The general knew, too, that the men who had first come to see him were emissaries from Ambassador Zahedi.

CHAPTER THIRTY-TWO

General Oveissi

The BBC regularly broadcast news of the outside world to Iran and, because of a mentality nurtured from long years of lies and deceptions fostered by their own government-controlled Radio Iran and the ultraconservative Voice of America, which was anxious to stay in the shah's good graces, Iranians faithfully and utterly credulously listened to BBC broadcasts, learning from them of the daily riots and demonstrations in Iran, news they could hear nowhere else. (This readiness to believe what foreigners said, particularly the British, was fully demonstrated later when Iranians refused to credit Radio Iran's reports of the shah's death until the BBC had confirmed them.)

The shah was well aware of the potency of the BBC broadcasts and was deeply angered by them. His SAVAK commandos set fire to the British embassy to frighten the BBC. Ambassador Sullivan, in *Mission to Iran,* described meeting with the shah. He recalled the Shah's comments on the BBC after he had flown in a helicopter over the burning capital, a wasteland with hundreds of buildings ablaze:

> He seemed surprised when I told him the British Chancery had been burned. . . . He then began a rambling discourse about the activities of the British Broadcasting Company and the reports they had broadcast concerning Iran. He felt, he said, that any attack on the British compound had probably been inspired by those broadcasts, which he considered sympathetic to his opponents and overly critical of his regime.

All day long I had heard rumors that the burnings were an action by professional arson squads of SAVAK, who were using this means to provoke the Shah into a drastic reaction that would install a military government . . . and asked him whether he felt they were true. [He] shrugged his shoulders, and said, "Who knows? These days I am prepared to believe anything."

In actuality, the shah not only tried to silence the BBC, but also fervently sought permission from the United States, particularly from the president, to establish a military government in Iran. Chaos prevailed everywhere, fomented by the shah's forces. Riots and demonstrations were the order of the day throughout the nation. The shah had succeeded in elevating the machine gun to power, but could no longer control it. Now Sullivan placed the weapon again in his hands even before he asked for it. In that same meeting, after describing his helicopter tour, the shah told Sullivan his plans:

> . . . He said he felt he had no choice but to establish a military government. He asked me whether . . . Washington would support him in this move. I told him that I had already anticipated this request and had received Washington's assurance that he would be supported in this action by the president and the United States government. He seemed enormously relieved and ordered a whiskey for me.

The shah had achieved his goal and drank to it. Later General Oveissi told me that the shah received him privately and told him to do something to prevent his soldiers from stopping the fires set by SAVAK incendiaries.

"All they're doing is burning tires—for the most part," said the shah, smiling. "Tires make a lot of smoke. People get scared. That will help you when you want to fire on them."

Oveissi raised his hands in resignation. "I will obey Your Majesty's orders, but let me bring to Your Majesty's attention that if tomorrow we find it necessary to reverse those orders, it will be impossible. The people . . . the situation is out of control already."

The shah was annoyed. "Our machine guns will keep everyone quiet."

Oveissi said he left the palace with firm orders not to interfere with the fires and destruction. A few weeks later, at his regular daily meeting with the shah, His Majesty, obviously anxious and disturbed, said, "It's time to quell this disorder. It must be controlled!"

"Your Majesty," answered Oveissi, himself deeply troubled, "my soldiers are stationed in the streets in armored cars. People walk right up to them and shake their hands and give them red carnations. 'Brother,' they call them, or 'cousin'! My soldiers refuse to fire on them anymore."

"Then you had better call your soldiers back to the base for a time. Lecture them. Build up their morale."

"With your blessed permission, Your Majesty, it's impossible."

"If that is true, you must order an all-out attack on a large area—several blocks. You'll scare the people so thoroughly that they'll run off and never come back."

Oveissi did not dare tell the shah that he wouldn't give such an order. He only replied, "Your Majesty, the soldiers will not obey. They will not fire."

The shah fixed him with a glassy stare. "No way to control it?"

"I don't see any."

The shah pondered for a while. At last, he said, "What if we set up a plan to have some of your soldiers attacked in the street by the commandos—kill a few of the soldiers? That way the rest will get excited and fire on the crowd. How about that?"

Oveissi told me he felt like a mouse in a trap. He answered slowly, "There is only one way I would do it—fire indiscriminately. Every single person, no matter who it is. The people, SAVAK, everyone. A bloodbath. But if the people do not give up, they will come to the palace. I won't be responsible. My second suggestion is that I resign."

The shah gave him an angry look. "You go to extremes. You see everything in black and white."

"Your Majesty, there is no other way."

"Why do you refuse to go along with my suggestion to trick them into firing?"

Oveissi knew he was on treacherous ground; he hesitated, then said, "Your Majesty, I am a soldier. I don't believe in tricks. You either do something or you don't. Tricks are what brought us to this point."

The shah answered him mildly enough. "Think it over again."

Oveissi stood up. Emboldened, he pressed further: "Your Majesty, I kiss your feet. But I cannot bear to see my soldiers—all uniformed, in tanks and armored cars—all wearing red carnations. I'm not commander anymore. And it's not for me to sit behind a desk and command. I see only two solutions. Call all my soldiers back to the base and let the people do what they will—or kill everybody. The biggest risk is that the soldiers won't obey, and that the people won't give up and will find their way to the royal palace."

The shah spoke in a haughty tone. "Then we agree to your dismissal from your command."

Oveissi moved forward and bent to kiss the shah's hand. "Thank you, Your Majesty. With your blessed permission, I can no longer stay in Iran. I will obtain my passport and leave for the United States."

The shah gave him a dubious look. Oveissi spoke quickly: "Of course, if at any time Your Majesty needs me or my services, he only need call me. I will be here within hours."

The shah seemed reassured.

Oveissi lost no time in applying for his passport.

It was refused. The shah had not been deceived after all.

CHAPTER THIRTY-THREE

The United States Abandons the Shah

"I'm in no mood for a political discussion," the CIA senior officer (who always wore a flower in his lapel) said abruptly as he got into my car at La Guardia Airport. It was early in December 1978. "Do me a favor and don't talk," he continued. "Just take me to the restaurant."

Respecting his wishes, I drove in silence. Even after we had arrived at the restaurant and ordered our drinks at the bar, I did not try to draw him into conversation. Finally, he broke the silence. "Mansur, I came here especially to talk to you tonight," he said. "Just listen. Don't give me any arguments. What I'm going to tell you is just between the two of us—don't tell anyone about it. The United States government has finally come to a decision: We're no longer going to support the shah. We're going to sit back and observe. I'm sorry that during all these years our office did not understand the situation."

There was nothing I could say. I could only stare at him.

"I know what you're thinking," he said, holding up his hand. "You warned us about this and we didn't listen. Now it's too late for us to do anything about it. I won't argue with you about that."

"You know, if your office had listened ten years ago, the situation would be very different today for both the Iranian people and for the American people," I said.

"Look," he protested, "I ask you for a favor—don't rub salt in our wounds. Take my advice: If you have any close family in Iran, get them out; the storm is coming. All you can do is go home and relax—watch the news. Nothing can be done. We'll let matters take their course. Remember," he stressed, "we're not telling anyone about our decision to withdraw support from the shah."

"Does Ambassador Sullivan in Tehran know?" I asked.

"It's not my job to inform him," the CIA man said. "I don't know if the State Department notified him."

After we had finished dinner, he asked me a question. "Try to be objective and give me your opinion. When the crisis comes—and it is apparent that the shah is going to leave the country—do you think SAVAK or any other security force will continue to function?"

"No," I replied with certainty. "Everything will fall; there's no unity among these organizations. The shah designed it that way. When he goes, everything goes."

"Brzezinski has been telling us the opposite. He thinks that these organizations will continue to exist and function, and Ambassador Zahedi agrees with him," the senior officer stated.

"They may think what they like," I responded, "but I disagree with them."

"We have another report from Tehran saying that when the shah offered the position of prime minister to Dr. Baghai, the doctor refused. Why? Would you ask him for us?"

"I don't have to ask," I told him. "I know that the doctor is not interested in power. He feels that at this point there is nothing he can do to help the shah."

"The shah is just about at the end of the line," the senior officer reiterated. "All we can do now is wait and watch."

On December 27 General Moghadam called from Tehran to tell me that, of all the prospective candidates who had been considered for the post of prime minister, Shahpur Bakhtiar impressed him the most. Unlike the rest, who either refused to accept the position or else proposed conditions for doing so, Bakhtiar was willing to assume the post unconditionally. "Tomorrow night," General Moghdam said, "I will be taking Dr. Bakhtiar to the royal court to see the shah. I want you to talk to the CIA about it, and please ask them to support him."

"I'll deliver your message to the CIA," I told him, "but first I would like to tell you something. Bakhtiar is not capable of accomplishing anything. He has no followers, no charisma, no background—nothing. He's not even intelligent and he worked for the British oil interest. I don't think the plan is going to succeed. But, nonetheless, I will convey your message to the CIA."

"No! That is not enough!" he exclaimed. "I want you to give a good recommendation. Do not discourage their support."

"Be reasonable," I told him. "How can I give a good recommendation for something I do not believe in?"

General Moghadam was adamant. "If His Majesty is right in choosing Bakhtiar as prime minister, he'll gain support from the British and consequently from the Americans as well."

"All right," I responded. "Let's hope so. But you are overlooking the real problem, and that is that no one—whether Washington or the British or anyone else—can help. The situation is out of control. Why can't you see that?"

I did convey General Moghadam's message to the CIA, which said that there was little chance of American support for Bakhtiar, but that the message would be passed on.

Bakhtiar was presented to the shah, who, according to his own account in *Answer to History,* ". . . finally decided to name Bakhtiar Prime Minister after [his] meeting with Lord George Brown, once Foreign Secretary in Britain's Labour Government . . . [who] strongly endorsed Bakhtiar. On December 29, Shahpur Bakhtiar was asked to form a civilian government." Apparently General Moghadam had been right. Lord George's endorsement of Bakhtiar—a man whom the shah had "always considered . . . an anglophile and an agent of British Petroleum"—convinced the shah that Bakhtiar's appointment would guarantee British support.

At midnight a few weeks later, I received a telephone call from General Moghadam. He spoke very politely and very formally. When he informed me that he was with Dr. Bakhtiar, I understood his reticence. "The situation has become very grave in Iran," he told me. "We have heard that Khomeini will be arriving on February 1 [1979]. The prime minister and I would like you to ask the CIA to make every effort through the international community—especially the French government—to delay Khomeini's arrival for two or three weeks.

"Make sure they know the religious people are supporting us," he urged. In the background I could hear someone telling him, "In two or three weeks we can gain control of the country!" Our conversation was over.

At 4:00 A.M. in New Jersey my mother's telephone rang. Knowing that I am a heavy sleeper, General Moghadam had called my mother, who awakened me. This time General Moghadam was able to be frank because he was alone. He told me that it was Bakhtiar who had requested that he make the earlier call. But he urged me to make the strongest case possible to the CIA that the United States attempt to prevent Khomeini's coming to Tehran. "As a personal favor to me, ask our CIA friend to press this issue," he pleaded.

"Certainly, I'll convey your message," I assured him. "But I'm telling you right now that they cannot do anything about it. Why don't you do yourself a favor?"

"What?" he inquired.

"Leave the country," I said firmly. "You don't realize the danger you're in."

When I reached my CIA contact and conveyed the message, he laughed. "They must think we're supermen! There's nothing we can do."

A week or ten days before Khomeini's arrival in Iran, General Moghadam called me from Tehran again and told me that General Nassiri's best friend, General Khowsrodad, had talked with some of his colleagues and they had a plan to kill Khomeini. As soon as Khomeini's plane entered Iranian air space, General Khowsrodad and his colleagues would shoot it down—no matter what airline it was or how many lives were involved. General Moghadam added that he had ordered his forces to keep an eye on General Khowsrodad and to keep him under control, but he was vague about whether he had spoken to General Khowsrodad and about how the general would be controlled. He asked me to relay this intelligence to the CIA.

Before I had a chance to call the CIA, the Agency called me from Washington to say that it had learned that General Khowsrodad planned to destroy Khomeini's plane while it was in the air. There were three points that the CIA stressed concerning the situation. First, I should speak with General Moghadam and get his cooperation in making sure this didn't happen. Second, it would only cause bloodshed. Third, the CIA wanted no part of it—it would not solve the problem.

When I told the CIA contacts that General Moghadam had already informed me about the plan, they asked me to call the general back and get him to make sure that General Khowsrodad was under control and could not carry out the plan.

I called General Moghadam and delivered the message. He assured me, and told me to assure the CIA that General Khowsrodad and his co-conspirators would be controlled and Khomeini's plane would land safely. Then he reiterated his assurances. "Remember, I prevented that bloodshed."

"I'm aware of that, General," I said. "It is to your credit that you stopped them. But that has absolutely nothing to do with the matter.

The CIA has refused to act. There's nothing more that can be done."

General Moghadam was insistent. "I'm going to stay. I'm going to fight! And I want my wife and children with me. I want you to see to it that they are sent back to Tehran right away. Inform the CIA that you're sending my family back to me. I'm not a general like Oveissi who flees for his life."

I tried to reason with him. "General," I said, "you're a patriot. You're going to fight for your country. I understand that. But what can your family do? Let them stay in the United States until the crisis is over."

"No," he said firmly. "Put my family on the next Iranian Air Force flight to Tehran."

"All right," I said resignedly. "It's your family. I'll do as you say."

"They'll be leaving from McGuire Air Force Base," he told me. "I want you to put them on the flight yourself." He was too obstinate to listen to reason, and I knew nothing I said would convince him. Because he trusted the leaders of the National Front—Bazargan and Bakhtiar —General Moghadam was certain that they would be able to bring peace to Iran.

His family arrived at McGuire Air Force Base, scheduled to fly home on the same day that Khomeini was supposed to arrive in Tehran from Paris. I arranged a conference call between General Moghadam's family, the general, and myself. I didn't listen in on the conversation between the general and his family, but when they were through, I picked up the phone and appealed to General Moghadam one last time to leave his family in America. "It's after midnight and very cold here," I told him. "Do you still want me to put your family on the plane tomorrow?"

"Certainly," he insisted. "You must."

"You do know that Khomeini's flight is arriving from Paris tomorrow as well?" I pointed out. "Aren't you concerned that this might be dangerous for your family?"

"I'm aware of the scheduled arrival of Khomeini's flight, but there's no danger. When Khomeini arrives, he'll go directly to the holy city of Qom. If Bakhtiar does not succeed as prime minister, then Bazargan will take his place. His right-hand man, Dr. Yazdi, will negotiate between us and the United States. He's worked with the CIA, you know."

"Fine," I said. "Then at five tomorrow morning I'll be at McGuire to see your family off."

Although I had a few hours to sleep, I could not. I thought to myself how wrong General Moghadam was. I was certain that none of these National Front people would ever succeed in establishing a government, and General Moghadam himself might well lose his life.

After a two-hour drive to McGuire, I saw to it that General Moghadam's wife and children boarded the Royal Iranian Air Force plane on that very cold, snowy morning. It was the last time I saw an Iranian Air Force plane bearing the royal insignia, for the shah had already fled Iran, even before Khomeini's return, and it was also the last time I saw the general's wife. Although she later returned to the United States after her husband had been killed, I could never bring myself to call on her.

PART V

CHAPTER THIRTY-FOUR

Three Former SAVAK Chiefs Executed

When General Nassiri returned to Tehran from Pakistan, first he was held under house arrest, then jailed before he was killed. The arrest of Prime Minister Hoveyda and numerous officials followed immediately, just as General Moghadam had predicted. Later, in a jailbreak, a number of them escaped. Not General Nassiri. He stayed. When Khomeini returned in triumph after the shah had fled, General Nassiri was still in prison.

I made a last attempt with General Moghadam after the shah's departure. "You're still chief. Why don't you let him go?"

"Never," he answered. "I told you. He has to stand trial."

"Why?"

"The big one is gone now."

"And good for him, too! That's his best punishment—to leave his country and his throne in fear and disgrace."

But on February 13, 1979, General Moghadam called me. He sounded despairing. "Mansur, I can't believe it. General Nassiri's in terrible shape. They beat him so badly that he can't even talk. When they exhibited him on television, he had to use his fingers to answer their questions about his budget. Please! Please get in touch with the CIA and see if they can't do something!"

"What should they do?" I asked. "You tell me!"

"They have men in the Revolutionary Council."

"What! Like who? CIA agents in the Revolutionary Council?"

"Yes. Two of them. Dr. Ibrahim Yazdi and Sadegh Ghotbzadeh."[12]

"I don't think the CIA is capable of doing anything," I said. "But I'll talk to them."

"You don't know how much guilt I feel," said Moghadam. "Can't you do something there?"

"I don't think so. I wanted to save him, to be a witness against the shah in the future. But I'm afraid it's not going to happen. I'm sure no one can help now. The shah has a free hand now. One of the most important witnesses is a dead man already."

"Call the CIA, Mansur. Right away."

"Of course. I'll do it now."

The man I contacted at the CIA had long been an acquaintance of mine and of General Nassiri. He was appalled, but could not help. He listened quietly, then said, "You were right in what you told him. There's absolutely nothing we can do. Who does he think we are? Anyway, my son, you have ruined my day. Good-bye." He hung up.

A few days later, on February 16, I was listening to the news on my car radio as I drove. The commentator said that General Nematollah Nassiri, former chief of SAVAK under the shah of Iran, had been executed by firing squad.

On April 11, 1979, it was announced that General Pakravan had been executed.

Two witnesses gone. Only General Moghadam was still alive. When I had last spoken with him, he said his plan had not worked out because he had pinned his hopes on people who were naïve and incapable.

"Who?" I had asked.

"Both prime ministers—Shahpur Bakhtiar and Mehdi Bazargan."[13]

"I remember when you told me that Bakhtiar was a capable man, that Bazargan was strong and knew what he was doing."

"I'm not God. Don't rub salt in my wounds. Tell me, Mansur, do you think I'd be better off if I didn't rely so much on the CIA? Maybe Mossad could help."

"You see trouble coming?"

"A lot." General Moghadam laughed harshly. "You know what Bazargan and the rest of these characters called me? Angel! Damn. I think I'll be an angel in heaven soon!"

"Don't talk like that. Keep your head on."

But it was the last time I spoke to him. Later Moghadam was jailed by the revolutionary government. During the time he was in jail, his son was middleman between us. Moghadam's every message pleaded that I do something to aid him. Again I approached the CIA, but I knew the answer: zero.

One day when I knew his son would be visiting him, I sent a message urging the general to try to get help from Bazargan and others he had helped in the past.

"Tell him to ask again," I instructed his son. "Those men still have a lot of power." But Moghadam's son called to tell me that his father had refused to see him. I was puzzled, for I knew how deeply General Moghadam loved his children. The only possible reason for his refusal was that he had been so beaten and brutalized that he didn't want his son to see his condition. Only a few days later, I heard that he had been executed—not by a firing squad but in his cell, with a bullet in the back of his head.

All four chiefs of SAVAK were dead: one, Teymour Bakhtiar, executed by the shah's own orders and the other three killed after the revolution. The shah would appear before the bar of history with no one to contradict him. Of General Pakravan, a highly educated man, who accepted full responsibility; of General Nassiri, a brave soldier; of General Moghadam, whom the shah considered "more a philosopher than a soldier," the shah would claim they had acted of their own accord and had in their own testimony absolved him of any guilt with regard to SAVAK and its deeds. In *Answer to History* the shah wrote:

> I was deeply moved when I heard that before being tortured and assassinated, Mr. Hoveyda, the former Prime Minister, and the former heads of SAVAK, Generals Pakravan, Nassiri, and Moghadam, had insisted that they had never received any order whatsoever from me with regard to a suspect, an accused man, or a condemned one.

While General Moghadam set about destroying selected documents in Iran, the CIA, aware of this, suggested that *all* documents should be destroyed. General Moghadam's reply was "I am doing housecleaning. I will eventually destroy those which could be detrimental to the United States as well." But for some reason, whether for lack of time or opportunity, those documents were not destroyed.

The CIA had reason to worry about some of them: The United States had sold much military hardware to Iran; some of the items—top-secret weapons—were accompanied by highly classified manuals. At the time of the sale, some congressmen and senators argued that Iran did not have proper security precautions for such sophisticated equipment, but the Nixon administration successfully pushed approval of the sales.

The Phantom jets had a training manual and a special device (electronic countermeasure pod) that could be removed to make the planes' weapons inoperable. Because the shah did not trust the air force officers, the directions for making the weapons inoperable and the manuals had been entrusted to General Oveissi a year before the revolution. At that time, General Oveissi told me that he also had in his possession a top-secret contingency plan that had been drawn up by the United States and Iran in case of Soviet attack. However, after SAVAK had caught General Mogharabi spying for the Soviet Union, General Oveissi, perhaps because of the lack of security, told me that he felt these classified materials should be turned over to SAVAK. When I discussed this with General Moghadam, he was unreceptive. "Let them keep their own equipment secure," he told me. Later I learned from General Oveissi that these items had been sent to SAVAK, although General Moghadam would not confirm this. "Wherever they are, they are safe," he said confidently.

Because General Moghadam was killed and there were no survivors to reveal the status of the American documents, the CIA contacted General Oveissi repeatedly after he moved to the United States to try to discover what had happened to them. General Oveissi told the Agency that the documents had been in his office and he had transferred them to SAVAK, but he did not know what had happened to them after he left Iran. He still had contact with the army generals, and when he questioned them, they told him the papers were no longer there. I don't believe that the CIA determined where those documents were until the truth was revealed in the Iranian newspapers.

When SAVAK was taken over by the revolutionaries, it was learned that these materials and the electronic countermeasure pods had all been stolen by the Communists and sent to the Soviet Union —a devastating blow to the United States. The Iranian newspapers reported that the Communists who later confessed to the theft had been killed by a firing squad.

No one can blame General Moghadam for what happened. He had destroyed the papers that incriminated him. Those that affected the United States were not his chief concern.

Later I learned that some documents in the Iranian embassy in Washington had been destroyed. Had they not been, I was told, they would have caused a scandal. These papers had been kept in a safe at the embassy by Major General Mokhateb Rafii. They had nothing to do with political or diplomatic activities, but related to matters of a sensitive nature, mostly bribery—to American politicians and media stars.

For instance, Ambassador Zahedi sent a letter to the shah through a diplomatic pouch stating, in effect, that Congressman John Murphy (who was later indicted and tried in the so-called Abscam scandal) was doing a good lobbying job for Iran in Washington, and that the ambassador suggested Murphy be given $50,000 or a free hand in a business venture in Iran. Generally, when the shah received this type of letter, he would, in his own hand, write his reply or his orders on the letter. In this case, he had written, "Do not give Murphy cash, but give him a contract with our bank in New York." The Special Office of the royal court did not wire or phone the replies to these letters. Instead, they photocopied the letters with the shah's written directions and sent the copies to Zahedi.

All of Rafii's documents were of this nature. There are other examples. The ambassador wrote to the shah asking him to suggest an appropriate birthday gift for a United States senator. The shah sent a magnificent carpet. When the ambassador inquired about a birthday gift for a diplomat's wife, the shah sent beautiful jewelry. Sometimes Henry Kissinger would ask Zahedi to send a message to the shah. He might suggest, for example, that the best thing the shah could do was to recapture all the political prisoners and put them back in jail. Kissinger felt that this would calm the situation in Iran.

On at least one occasion the ambassador wrote to the shah telling him of the good publicity that Barbara Walters was generating for the monarch. The shah responded by sending her exquisite jewelry. In another case, Marion Javits, the wife of Senator Jacob Javits, was doing public relations work for Iran Air and some other PR for the shah. When this became known, she had then contacted the U.S. Justice Department and registered as a foreign agent. When Zahedi wrote the shah that she had had no choice but to register, he replied that she had been very smart and that it was the best thing she could have done. Then the shah asked who had put her on the official payroll in the first place. He said that she should have been paid discreetly—under the table.

There were lots of papers of this type. All were burned by General Rafii and a low-ranking officer at the embassy in Washington. When revolutionary government representatives came to Washington, they stated that they wanted to start an "Irangate" (similar to Watergate) and they expected to be able to do this with documents found at the embassy. General Rafii told me that when they opened the safe at the embassy, all they found was a holy book.

In 1985 General Rafii, by then impoverished, complained to me that after he had saved the reputations of various American politicians, of Ambassador Zahedi, and, by the same token, of the shah and his son, no one had had the courtesy even to thank him. "Can you imagine what would have happened if those papers had fallen into the hands of the revolutionaries?" he said. "There were hundreds of letters with the shah's handwriting on them that fully documented acts of bribery."

I asked the general, "Did you approach the royal family about your financial problems?"

"No," he said. "I've heard that they claim they don't have any money. They say that they're broke."

I laughed to myself at the very idea that the royal family was broke. Yes, the empress had stated several times that they left most of the family fortune and jewelry in Iran when they fled. But she shouldn't have any complaints. Even though she had not been a princess before her marriage—she was a commoner whose father was a military man and not wealthy—she was not poor. And the jewelry she was talking about did not belong to her—it belonged to the state. In spite of what she said, she had brought out so much jewelry that when the lesser pieces were sold, they brought $30 million. Also, I'm aware of one numbered bank account in Switzerland that contains $2 billion in her name only. Now they were saying they did not have any money. Maybe they thought we should start a charitable organization for them. I thought about how much money I estimated the entire royal family to have: at least $16 billion.

In 1983 General Oveissi asked the United States government for $800 million to overthrow Khomeini. At that time I spoke privately to a high-ranking officer in Washington about this. He asked, "Oveissi wants eight hundred million dollars?"

"Yes," I replied.

"That's impossible. We could never do that." After a short pause, he continued. "So the shah's family and the rich Iranians in exile want to return and get back into power?"

"Yes, that's right."

He got up from his desk, went to the files, took out a folder, and did some mathematical calculations. "Look, I'm just talking about the shah's family, not the rich Iranians. If they gave just five percent of their own money toward this cause, it would come to eight hundred million dollars. Why don't they pay it if they want to get back into power? Why should the American taxpayer foot the bill? Besides, there's no way we can do it."

I reminded him that General Oveissi had promised to repay the money when he got into power.

"Fine, Mansur. I heard that remark also. Why doesn't the shah's family give Oveissi the money and they can be reimbursed afterward?"

I left the office, disgusted. I had never dreamed that the shah could possibly have *that* much money. It was overwhelming. Then I remembered that the shah's father had done the same thing. Although the shah's father always maintained he was a poor soldier when he had been exiled to Johannesburg in 1941, word had leaked out that he had squirreled away fifty-six million pounds in British banks. In the late 1940s the shah demanded that the British government return the money. The British agreed to return five million pounds in cash and the balance in trade payments, which would be funneled into the shah's coffers. So, in reality, the shah had begun his reign with quite a substantial nest egg.

The shah was truly his father's son.

History was repeating itself.

The issue was the same—money—the only difference was the players.

CHAPTER THIRTY-FIVE

The Shah Battles Death

In the months immediately preceding the shah's downfall, he consulted with a variety of advisers. He met with a continuous stream of close friends, relatives, and, leaving no stone unturned, even an occasional foe. Finally, in desperation, he had his future predicted by a series of internationally acclaimed fortune-tellers. His fears were assuaged when the consensus was that his future looked secure and merely included a long, pleasant trip.

Even though I am sure he took comfort in the knowledge that his future was secure, a point was reached when the shah realized that the situation in Iran could become life-threatening at any moment. He feared for his personal safety and let it be known to both the American and British ambassadors that if it were up to him, he would leave the country in fifteen minutes.

When the inevitable happened, the shah and his family's hasty departure still managed to include all of the theatrics that marked any of the other official public appearances the shah's image makers had orchestrated. He wore a conservative business suit and the empress Farah, a somber dress with no visible jewelry. They made sure that the cameramen managed to capture several shots of a humble soldier breaking from the ranks, prostrating himself before the shah, and trying to kiss his feet. The shah, with tears welling up in his eyes, stopped him and helped him up.[14]

His loyal followers even spread rumors that the shah had taken a

little Iranian soil with him and looked at it constantly. He cried as they
flew over the Iranian border to Turkey, kissed the soil sample, and put
it in his pocket.

The shah knew that this time his troubles were far greater than
during the 1953 coup d'état which had forced him to take a brief
"vacation." He still hoped that his powerful allies would soon restore
him to power for their own selfish interests. And he vowed that when
he returned he would squelch the Muslim fanatics once and for all.

During the last tumultuous weeks in Iran, he had weighed his
invitations carefully and decided that Egypt would be the most politically expedient choice. Egypt, a Muslim country, would be good for his
image, and Sadat was a personal friend. The shah felt confident that he
would be treated well there because of all the financial aid his regime
had showered on Egypt during the Sadat administration. The United
States had also extended an invitation, but he decided to punish the
United States for previous slights and chose to embarrass President
Carter by not going there.

The shah, his family, and their entourage arrived in Egypt on
January 16, 1979. They began what would turn out to be a doomed
odyssey. At first they were greeted warmly by the Sadats and spent time
in their company. The shah, who had never been a religious man, was
repeatedly photographed at Sadat's side praying in various mosques.
After a short stay, veiled in secrecy, the shah and his party moved on
to another Muslim country, Morocco.

Soon King Hassan II made it clear that the shah was a political
embarrassment and should make plans to leave. While he was in Morocco, the shah began to get cautious messages from the United States.
It seemed that he was no longer welcome there either, as he had been
earlier. He had to seek other alternatives.

New advisers, provided by Nelson Rockefeller, made arrangements
for the shah's party to go to the Bahamas. King Hassan provided the
plane and the shah and his entourage flew to Nassau. The family was
ensconced in the Paradise Island villa of the owner of Resorts International. It was not very large but had a beautiful view of the ocean, and
their stay took on the character of a real vacation. The shah mingled
with the tourists and even gave out autographs. But the English were
not very comfortable with the shah living on a British island and
decided not to extend his tourist visa. They gave him ten days to find
another haven.

Two days before his visa expired, and as a result of Henry Kissinger's intervention, the shah received an invitation from President

Lopez-Portillo of Mexico. He and his family were welcome to come to Mexico.

On June 10, 1979, they all arrived in Mexico and moved into a luxurious villa in Cuernavaca, a resort area about an hour and a half away from Mexico City. In Cuernavaca the shah and his family had privacy and numerous servants. They entertained former President Nixon, Henry Kissinger, and other friends. This relatively tranquil period ended when the monarch's health began to fail and he was forced to acknowledge publicly his six-year battle with lymphoma. He needed the sophisticated medical treatment that he felt was available only in the United States.

The Mexican government left the door open and said that he was welcome back whenever he felt he was well enough to return.

Finally, President Carter permitted the shah to come to the United States for "humanitarian reasons." His Majesty was admitted to Cornell Medical Center at New York Hospital on October 22, 1979, where, in addition to being treated for his malignant lymphoma, he had surgery for an obstruction and removal of gallstones on October 24.

While the shah was in exile, the press, responding to allegations raised by the revolutionaries, questioned him about his role in the government. According to the Constitution, the shah was a constitutional monarch, a mere figurehead. He maintained that he had not exceeded the limits of the power given to him by the Constitution and that he had done nothing illegal.

In order to support this contention, the shah utilized the statement General Pakravan had made before he was executed. General Pakravan, a dignified, honorable man, had said, "I assume full responsibility for every action taken by my office," thus clearing his subordinates of any blame. But the shah twisted General Pakravan's meaning to exonerate himself.

The shah's sister, Princess Ashraf—a true Jezebel—also tried to exculpate her brother from any responsibility for the evils he had committed in Iran. Knowing that several generals (including General Oveissi) were living in the United States in financial distress, she tried to take advantage of their vulnerability by attempting to bribe them.

I was told by General Oveissi that Princess Ashraf called him to her home in New York for a clandestine meeting. "You know," she said confidentially, "that my brother, the shah, is in a very precarious situation. I have a plan to benefit both him and you. I would like you, with two or three more of the best-known Iranian generals, to tell the press that throughout the time you served as commander of the royal guard, as commander of the gendarmerie, as commander of the ground forces, and as chief of martial law, the shah never gave you any orders. I'll talk to Barbara Walters, and she'll interview you on TV. Everything you did, you will say you did on your own. I leave it up to you to find other generals to corroborate your testimony. In this way we'll exonerate the shah from any blame. If you'll do us this favor, I'll talk to the shah, and he'll make it well worth your while."

I asked General Oveissi what he planned to do.

"To be honest, Mansur," he said, "I don't want to do it. I've already been given the title 'Butcher'; if it comes from my own lips, it will go down in history that way! But you know," he continued, "I have two small children, and no money. And these people have money. I don't know what to do."

"What did you tell her?" I asked.

"I didn't promise anything," he said. "I told her I would sleep on it."

"Why don't you wait until you find out exactly what they plan to do for you?" I suggested.

Princess Ashraf also tried to test General Oveissi to see if he would clear the shah's name in public. She would arrange for someone to approach General Oveissi and question him about the shah's involvement in the killings in Iran. To make the princess happy, General Oveissi would lie blatantly. At one dinner party, a guest, instigated by the princess, asked, "General Oveissi, if His Majesty had permitted you to kill, would the country have fallen into this situation?"

Before answering, General Oveissi pressed my foot with his under the table, indicating that whatever he said was meant to be tongue in cheek. "Never in my twenty years in office," he began in a stentorian voice, "did the shah order me to kill. He is a peaceful man. It was I who wanted to kill. That is the reason I had to leave the country. The shah said, 'I don't want you to kill anymore.' Ahhh, I never before appreciated the wonderful man he is."

After dinner was over, General Oveissi chortled, "Now, Mansur, for three days they'll be off my back!"

General Oveissi could ill afford to alienate the princess; he truly loved his wife and children, and without the princess's assistance, he could be left with nothing.

I was aware that even more force was brought to bear on General Oveissi when the shah himself later attempted to convince him to cooperate with the princess's scheme to clear his name. "You were always a patriot," he said, flattering him. "You have done much for the

country, and because of the stellar reputation you have earned in Iran
during the last twenty years, your statement will be invaluable to us.
Have you talked to any of the other generals to determine whether or
not they will also give such an interview to Barbara Walters?"

General Oveissi was quick to ingratiate himself. "Your Majesty,"
he said effusively, "your obedient servant will be at Your Majesty's
disposal; your servant will do whatever he can. Several other generals
have already been contacted, and they will also be delighted to assist
Your Majesty."

The shah's eyes sparkled with happiness. "Princess Ashraf will
make all of the arrangements for the interview." He paused. "I am
aware of your bad financial situation. I have ordered that you are to be
well taken care of."

General Oveissi told me later that he knew the shah had not done
anything to aid him before, but he was certain he had given the order
the minute Oveissi had stepped out of the room after the interview. I
never asked General Oveissi how the shah rewarded him; all I know
is that he became a homeowner and had a bank account, too.

Nonetheless, the general was very evasive about setting a date for
the interview. Politely, he sidestepped the issue and always managed to
have an excuse. But one night when I went to Kennedy Airport to pick
him up after his return from a trip to Paris, I saw Princess Ashraf's
Rolls-Royce, with her chauffeur and some aides, waiting to take General Oveissi to her home that night. I reached him just as he left customs
and warned him.

"Oh, God! No, Mansur!" He groaned. "Play a game with them. Say
your mother is sick and I have to go see her, or tell them I am airsick
and can't see them tonight. I don't want to see her—I don't want to
make any statements to the press. They want me to say I was responsible—responsible for what?"

When we left the terminal, the princess's aides accosted us and tried
to force General Oveissi toward her car. He pleaded illness and said he
would be sure to present himself the next day if they would only let me
take him home. Reluctantly, they acceded.

On the way home, General Oveissi told me he was in a quandary.
While he was in Paris, the princess had called him several times, insisting that he fulfill his promise to His Majesty the Shah, and demanding
that he set a date to go on TV and state that he had acted on his own
and not on the orders of the shah. "What shall I do, Mansur?" General
Oveissi asked desperately.

"There are two ways of handling this situation," I advised him.

"You could go to see her tomorrow, and be frank with her. Tell her that this is not a good time to give the interview, either for you or for the shah. Or you could set a date for the interview with Barbara Walters, and while on the air, you could tell her that everything you did was by the shah's orders. And because Black Friday bothers you so much, you could set the record straight and say that Black Friday happened before you were appointed commander of martial law."

General Oveissi laughed. "No, I cannot do that. I'll take the first option. I'll tell the princess that this is not a good time."

His tactics worked; Princess Ashraf finally gave up.

Meanwhile, the shah had received visits at New York Hospital from Iranian ex-diplomats and other dignitaries. After some time, members of the shah's inner circle approached me and inquired why I had not gone to see him. "I don't want to see him suffering," I told them truthfully. "Besides, I wouldn't know what to say."

But after General Oveissi visited the shah and had informed me that His Majesty wanted to know why I had not called on him, I could no longer postpone a visit.

The very next day I gathered my courage and went to the hospital. I walked slowly up York Avenue, hoping that the brisk air would help prepare me for the ordeal that was to come. I used the emergency entrance, avoiding the ever-present anti-shah demonstrators who surrounded the front entrance of the hospital. At the shah's floor, the guards stopped me. One looked up, recognized me, and said, "Oh, it's Mansur. Let him through."

When I was announced, the shah told the guards to admit me. I entered the room hesitantly, bowing in obeisance, and stood waiting politely. The shah, propped up in a half-sitting position, beckoned to me. I approached and stood beside his bed. I looked at him, and he returned my gaze. I hardly recognized him. His features were the only thing that preserved his identity; he had wasted away to a gaunt shell.

In spite of myself, I began to weep, and seeing my tears, the shah wept, too. After a moment he reached for a tissue and wiped his eyes. When we both regained our composure, he offered me a seat.

I demurred. "Your Majesty, thank you. But I prefer to stand."

"You know the demonstrators are here twenty-four hours a day," he said morosely. "They won't leave us alone."

I nodded, still overcome with emotion, and barely able to speak.

"They don't believe that I'm really sick," he went on.

I shook my head. "No, Your Majesty, they do not."

"Do you have any recent news from Iran?" he asked.

"Nothing, Your Majesty. I know only what's in the papers."

"They've killed many people," he stated flatly.

"Yes, Your Majesty, they have."

"I feel sorry for our three generals—our chiefs of SAVAK, they were killed so brutally."

"Yes, Your Majesty."

"How is Dr. Baghai?" he inquired, changing the subject.

"He's fine, Your Majesty. He remains true to his principles, as he always has," I responded.

"Have you spoken to him recently?"

"Yes, Your Majesty. I speak to him frequently."

"What is his prediction for the future? Is there any hope that our crown prince will be able to assume the throne?" the shah asked.

"With your permission, Your Majesty, he doesn't see any chance."

The shah raised his eyebrows in surprise. "Why not? The people in the country are fed up with Khomeini, and some of the generals in exile may well succeed in seizing control. Then they will enforce the Constitution and bring the crown prince to power."

"With your blessed permission, Your Majesty, I've already spoken to Dr. Baghai about this possibility, but it's his belief that those generals cannot topple Khomeini, and even if one of them did, he would not turn the power over to the crown prince; he would take the title of shah himself."

"So he sees no future for us?" The shah asked wistfully.

"Your Majesty, let me clarify the doctor's statement. He sees no possibility that those generals can topple Khomeini—they will never attain the power to give to the crown prince."

"Now I see his point," the shah said slowly. "For thirty years the doctor gave me good counsel, and I never listened. My advisers disliked the doctor and misrepresented him to me. Now I know that it is too late for me to heed his advice."

"If Your Majesty will permit me, many times the doctor wrote open letters to the royal court predicting this crisis."

"Yes," the shah said, "I do not deny that. Almost a year ago I called on the doctor for help. He reminded me of his warning about the consequences of my government actions; I could not answer him. I could not look him in the eye. I am suffering from the ill advice I was given. Some of those advisers now work for Khomeini; and some of them"—he spread his arms helplessly—"have disappeared from the face of the earth."

I had no reply. I could only look at him.

"Who is this Dr. Yazdi who wants to examine the files to see whether or not I have cancer?" the shah asked. "Is he a CIA agent?"

"It is a strong rumor, Your Majesty," I responded.

"He's been in close touch with the American government; he's traveled with an American passport: Is he an American citizen?"

"Yes, Your Majesty. Our records say so."

"It's very hard to understand this country," the shah stated. "While I've been in the hospital, I've had more time to read the newspapers and watch television. It's amazing how much freedom the press has here! It's unbelievable that they're allowed to question and criticize the government as they do. If I give a message to the American government, or if they send some message to me, it will be on the news that same evening! Zahedi told me many times how free the press is in the United States, but I didn't believe him. I couldn't understand it . . ."

There was a lengthy pause. Finally, I said, "Your Majesty, you are tired. I just came to pay my respects. Now, with your blessed permission, I ask to be dismissed."

"You may go," he said quietly, "but please come again. And when you call Dr. Baghai, give him my regards."

I bowed and backed slowly from the room.

A Persian proverb came to my mind: "A live elephant and a dead elephant are each worth a hundred dollars." The shah had lost his power, his health, and his country, but he was still the shah, and I treated him with deference as befitted his position, even though it was apparent that he would never admit that it was he who was responsible for Iran's sorry condition.

On my way out of the hospital, I used the front entrance, passing through the demonstrators, who were waving placards. One read DR. YAZDI, NOT THIS CAPITALIST HOSPITAL, SHOULD CONFIRM THAT THE SHAH IS SICK!

Back on York Avenue, I pondered the shah's realization of the virtue of freedom of the press. "Oh, God. Now he understands," I thought sadly, "but it's too late."

On November 4 the American embassy in Tehran was seized and American hostages taken.

CHAPTER THIRTY-SIX

U.S. Embassy Hijacked in Tehran

In World War II the allied forces believed the accusation that Reza Shah was a Nazi sympathizer and in 1941 forced him into exile in Johannesburg, South Africa. He died in exile three years later. His body was temporarily interred in Al Rifai Mosque in Cairo, through the remainder of the war. When his bones were returned to Iran in 1950, a national holiday was proclaimed. A magnificent white marble tomb was constructed for him south of Tehran, and he was honored with the title "Great," thereafter being known as Reza Shah the Great. A military guard was positioned at the tomb and the grounds were kept immaculate.

His son, Mohammad Reza Shah, hoped the tomb would become a shrine to which the people would make pilgrimages. Disappointingly, the people did not respond. Still, it became protocol for visiting dignitaries to make a pilgrimage to the tomb and to lay flowers at the gravesite. Visitors from smaller, less powerful nations would be required to visit the tomb prior to being received at the royal palace. If the dignitary had a high position in a powerful nation, such as President Nixon, he would see the shah first, but the next day would visit the tomb of Reza Shah the Great.

Years later, in November 1978, an Iranian diplomat, Mohammad Nasser Ghoshbegi, stationed in Washington, departed for Tehran on a mission. He stopped over in New York City on his return to Washington. Eager to find out the latest developments in the growing unrest in

Iran, I met the diplomat for dinner. He complained how exhausted he was and told me that he had not come directly from Tehran, but from Cairo. When I questioned him about what he had been doing in Egypt, he told me that he had taken a crate of books there from Tehran. I was puzzled why a diplomat, especially in these tense times, was delivering a crate of books. I joked about the necessity of a diplomatic escort. He leaned toward me and whispered, "Top secret." He said the shah had decided to move his father's bones out of its magnificent white marble tomb because he was afraid of what the future might hold. They had opened the grave, removed the bones, replacing them with a bouquet of roses, and closed the tomb again. The bones were placed in a crate, which was then marked BOOKS.

I said, "This is shocking news. Why did the shah do this?"

"He's afraid of his own shadow. He doesn't see any future for himself or his family."

When I asked, "Who else knows about this?" he replied again that this was "top secret" and that no one else knew, not even the head of SAVAK.

At this time we were both aware that Ambassador Zahedi was doing his own "spring cleaning" in the embassy, making copies of all the documents accumulated during his ambassadorship. He was sending these, along with his personal possessions, via this same diplomat to Montreux, Switzerland. Cynically, I joked, "You're going to be making frequent trips to Switzerland. If the shah isn't leaving his father's bones in Iran, we certainly can't expect the ambassador to leave his things at the embassy. Who knows what's next?"

The shah truly knew his people. After Khomeini took over in 1979, a huge angry mob raced to the tomb of Reza Shah. Those in the forefront opened the tomb and found only dead roses. Disappointed, they proceeded to desecrate the tomb in the vilest possible ways, even using the sarcophagus as a urinal. A few weeks later the entire magnificent white marble building was razed to the ground. Today only the barren land remains.

Because there had been a seemingly excellent relationship between the United States and Iran during the shah's regime, the CIA had never felt it necessary to gather any more than superficial information about the country.

What caused this complacency? An agreement in 1962 between the shah and the CIA resulted in the Agency's negligence in gathering intelligence in Iran. According to General Pakravan, after Prime Minister Amini had been dismissed by the shah, the shah had made a pro-

posal to the CIA. If the CIA wanted to know anything about Iran, it
had only to ask him for the desired information. In return, the CIA was
to agree not to spy on Iranians or to be in contact with any opposition
groups. Unfortunately, the CIA honored its side of the agreement. It
was a grave mistake not to be in contact with the Iranian people; the
CIA would remain in the dark as to what was really happening in the
country.

Gary Sick was aware of some of the elements to this problem as
mentioned in an endnote in *All Fall Down:*

> . . . U.S. intelligence in Iran was focused almost exclusively on the
> USSR, and to operate effectively it needed the cooperation of the
> shah and his government. Moreover, it had been many years since
> the CIA had had the kind of contacts within the opposition that
> would have permitted it to influence the course of events. . . .

This was one factor that had motivated me to give intelligence to
the CIA. I knew that the Agency was not informed of what was really
happening in Iran. However, I was aware that the CIA might not be
receptive to the information I gave it. It might take everything I told
it with a grain of salt. It would suspect deception on my part. These
suspicions prevailed into the 1970s and in order to allay the Agency's
fears, I submitted to the polygraph test.

There were many questions and conjectures regarding my position
as chief of SAVAK in the United States. In any foreign service an officer
is usually stationed in a country for a term of four years. In exceptional
cases the term can be extended to five or six years. I had been in my
position for about fifteen years prior to taking the polygraph. The CIA
and many Iranians were puzzled by this. The CIA thought I might be
a triple agent. Why else would the shah keep me in the United States
for so long? Some SAVAK employees and some Iranian government
officials, believing that I was a CIA man, thought that was why I had
held my position for so long. It was almost impossible for an Iranian
government employee to stay in one country for such a long time and
never be reassigned. During the period of my service, I saw three chiefs
of SAVAK and eight ambassadors to the United States come and go.

They all tried to find out my secret. Each side made its own interpretation, but I knew the facts. I had had a good relationship with three
chiefs of SAVAK—Generals Pakravan, Nassiri, and Moghadam—and
they were responsible for keeping me on the job in the United States
for almost twenty years. Because of the way I had played the game—

often advising them, knowing so much about their personal lives, having done many personal favors for them over the years, having so many valuable connections as to be indispensable—none removed me from my position.

Not until six months before the fall of the shah did the CIA realize I was painting a true picture of Iran, but by then it was really too late. The Agency attempted to discover how Iran had gotten into its crisis, but again its findings barely scratched the surface, revealing nothing of significance. Because neither the CIA nor the embassy had any connection with the opposition over the years, they had not established any contact or built any bridges to dissident groups, a major function of the agency in other countries. Sick also pointed out:

> For at least a decade the United States had viewed its relations with Iran almost exclusively as relations with the person of the shah. There probably was never a formal order to avoid contacts with Iranian opposition groups, but there was a clear awareness that the shah was annoyed and suspicious about such contacts and they gradually dried up. The State Department report of August 1976 put it succinctly: "The Embassy . . . has difficulty in developing information about dissidence . . . because of Iranian sensitivities and the Government of Iran's disapproval of foreign contacts with these groups." Thus, primary attention was devoted to contacts with officials in and around the court, rather than invite the shah's wrath.

No Iranians stepped forward soon enough to help, because if the shah or SAVAK had found out that they informed the CIA, they would have been in serious trouble. Consequently, neither the CIA nor the shah's regime did anything that might have averted revolution.

But when the revolution began to brew, people sprang into action. During the six months before the fall of the shah, when I was in daily contact with the CIA, I was amazed to find that, of all the Iranian politicians and high officials in the government, only about a dozen failed to volunteer intelligence to the CIA. None of them would have thought of doing so earlier, but once the shah was in trouble they flocked to the CIA to cooperate.

After the fall of the shah, President Carter issued an executive order for the United States to refuse contact with any officials from the shah's regime. The Iranians, however, would not give up. They wanted to give information about SAVAK and the army even though it was useless to do so. It was like listing the contents of an uninsured house after the house had burned down. The United States simply was not interested. But after November 4, 1979, when the embassy was seized and the Americans were taken hostage, the White House was devastated and had no choice but to rescind the executive order and to get in touch with the shah's supporters; the numbers willing to give information had tripled by that time. "Find out everything you can about the hostages" was the new order of the day.

Because the CIA had no valuable contacts within Iran, it was forced to rely on the help of these volunteers. For about a year the CIA received intelligence through all available channels. But of thousands of pieces of intelligence obtained regarding the hostages, practically all were fabricated. There were reports that the hostages had been beaten, killed, sent to live with Iranian families. Others stated that the diplomats had been handcuffed, that the hostages had been forced to play Russian roulette, that hundreds of students had been beating the prisoners. I felt sorry for President Carter, who must have been terribly confused.

Meanwhile, because of the strong possibility that the Iranians would take American hostages if the United States granted the shah entry, I redoubled my communications with the CIA. I implored the Agency to remove all personnel and sensitive documents from the embassy in Tehran. I said that it would be very risky for the Agency and the embassy personnel to stay because the concept of taking hostages was deeply ingrained in the Iranian culture. Far from being an unusual occurrence, hostage taking had long been an acceptable *modus operandi*, backed up by ample historical precedent. But I was talking to deaf ears.

Trying to make the CIA comprehend the seriousness of the situation, I cited a famous sixth-century Iranian folktale, magnificently written in Persian literature.

"A man stored a few hundred tons of iron with an old friend. A few years later he went back to get it and it was gone. When the owner asked where it was the friend said, 'We've been checking it all along but the last time I checked I noticed that the mice had begun to eat it.'

"The man didn't register any reaction but merely shrugged and said, 'Oh! The mice? I guess I just had bad luck,' and he left. "A week later the man who had swiped the iron was frantic. His son was missing. Desperately, he confronted the man he had swindled. 'My son is missing! Have you seen him?'

" 'I saw an owl flying off with him.'

" 'What do you mean you saw an owl flying off with him? An owl doesn't carry off boys!'

" 'In a town where mice can eat iron—owls can carry off boys.' They looked at each other and smiled. 'Give me back the iron and you'll get back your son.' "

I went on, "Hostage taking is repeated over and over in our history books and our literature. What makes you think your people are so special that they are immune from this? Even Genghis Khan's ambassadors were taken hostage in Iran, and killed. History will repeat itself!"

The CIA officers looked at me in utter disbelief. "What does Genghis Khan have to do with this?"

So I told them another story.

"In 1218 Genghis Khan sent tradesmen and ambassadors to Persia. They were captured in Khorezm, tortured, held hostage, and ultimately killed by the governor of Otra in the presence of Khorezm Shah. Genghis Khan was so outraged when he heard about the murder of his men that he dispatched his army to Khorezm. It took them six years to reach Persia, but in 1225 he wreaked his revenge. His hordes massacred the entire province. They came, they killed, set fire, took, devastated all living things, and left.

"Look! This is the Iranian way of doing things. Even if they know evil might come out of it," I said.

They laughed. "We don't care how Genghis Khan made his reputation."

I tried to tell them that even I had been involved in a hostage-taking scheme. In 1951 I and some of my fellow party members raided the office of Norman Richard Seddon—the head of the Anglo-Iranian Oil Company. We had planned to take hostages but at the last minute changed our minds. Instead, we just scared the hell out of them and let them escape, but we took every document that looked important and we did get some very serious stuff. The papers we took were used as the incriminating evidence against the English in their trial at the International Court in The Hague. "Don't be fools!" I repeated. "Close the embassy! Get everything out! The shah doesn't even trust leaving his father's bones in the hands of his very own people—and you trust your personnel and classified documents?"

The CIA men continued to disbelieve me. I had the sinking feeling they were doomed to learn the hard way.

Then on February 15, 1979, I talked to the CIA men again and told them I had just seen Ambassador Sullivan on TV profusely thanking Dr. Yazdi and the Revolutionary Guards for rescuing him and his staff when the United States embassy was attacked by terrorists. When they asked my opinion of what had happened, I answered that I did not know who the culprits were, but I felt that Ambassador Sullivan had made a serious mistake in thanking Dr. Yazdi and the guards.

"Why shouldn't he have thanked them?" they asked.

"The embassy," I said, "is the property of the United States. It is technically American soil. When he spoke with the press, instead of thanking them Ambassador Sullivan should have stated that he was going to protest to the Iranian State Department, demanding the punishment of those responsible for the assault. He should also have told them that if the American embassy was not safe, he would ask the president to call the Americans back home."

The CIA men agreed with me, but they said, "We cannot tell the ambassador what to do."

"I realize that," I said resignedly. "But this mistake will cause more problems in the future. Someone has to draw a line somewhere. Today or tomorrow, they are going to take your diplomats hostage. You should call them back immediately."

"But the embassy is safe," they told me.

Later that year, on November 4, the American embassy was seized.

I was relieved when I was told later that the American ambassador had sent all the documents out of Iran. But distressingly the matter did not end there. Three weeks after the takeover of the embassy and the seizure of the hostages, I met with a CIA man who, barely containing his anger, told me that there were documents still left in the embassy.

"What?"

"There are documents left in the embassy," he repeated.

"You told me those papers were taken out. What's left?"

"We don't know."

"What do you mean you don't know?"

"All we know is that some documents are there."

"First you tell me they're out, then you say they're in."

"All reports indicate that all the documents are back and in the embassy."

I couldn't believe it! "How can there be documents left?" I exclaimed. "Who did it?"

"Forget who did it," he said. "There are papers there from the files and desks, but indications are that the important papers were shredded at the last minute and put in the garbage. What will happen?"

"It will be as if a heavy stone were tied around your American foot and you were thrown into the water. You will drown."

The documents were never removed and the damage was done. The blemish on the integrity of the United States' operations will fester for generations to come and impede the country's efforts to gather intelligence. Who will trust the United States? Will the United States be able to develop an accurate picture of what is happening in the Middle East?

CHAPTER THIRTY-SEVEN

The Shah Dies in Egypt

As the hostage situation rapidly developed into a major crisis, the shah's presence in the United States suddenly became politically untenable. On November 8, 1979, he expressed a willingness to leave the United States as soon as his treatment was completed. On November 29 the Mexicans did an about-face and rescinded their invitation, claiming that his return would be contrary to Mexico's vital interests.

The American government developed a temporary plan. On December 2 the shah and his family were to be flown to Lackland Air Force Base near San Antonio, Texas.

When the shah was about to be discharged from New York Hospital on December 2, 1979, one of his security men, a friend of mine, called me to ask if I would like to be present when the shah left. Curious, and wanting to see the shah once more, I quickly agreed.

For the shah, leaving the hospital was a major undertaking. There were still twenty-four-hour demonstrations going on; the press was also keeping vigil outside, hoping for a chance to interview him as he left. His plane was scheduled to leave from La Guardia Airport, where a news crew was waiting to take photographs and interview him. Since the shah had no desire to face either the demonstrators or the newsmen, a clandestine departure had been devised.

After midnight the shah would be taken in a wheelchair down the elevator to the tunnel connecting the medical center to Memorial Sloan-Kettering Hospital, to the East Sixty-eighth Street exit of that hospital, and finally onto First Avenue. No cars would be waiting at the exit. They would be parked a short distance away, and the security men would radio for them to come immediately to take the shah to the airport. The shah was very pleased with this plan, as it meant he would avoid both the hostility of the demonstrations and the inquisition of the reporters.

I arrived at the hospital around midnight. Later, standing among the security people, I had ample opportunity to observe the shah without his noticing me. He was distraught; I could see the fear in his eyes. When we entered the tunnel, the security was very tight. The FBI men were loaded down with equipment, their pockets bulged with pistols. The air was filled with the squawking of their radios as they kept in touch with each other along the route. The whole commotion unnerved the shah. As he glanced around furtively, he recognized me and I bowed to him. His eyes widened at the unexpected display of respect amid the callous indifference of the security men, many of whom had their backs to him, perhaps unaware of the disrespect this action showed. The shah called my name and I walked over to him. "This is a good plan, don't you think?" he asked weakly. "I didn't want to see those people."

"Yes, Your Majesty," I said.

I moved deliberately to the side, where I was out of his line of vision, and where he could not see how touched I was by his frailty.

At the East Sixty-eighth Street exit and on First Avenue, there was no indication that anything out of the ordinary was happening; passersby were going about their usual nighttime business.

The vehicles appeared as if out of nowhere. As the shah was being helped into a van (they didn't use an ambulance as it would have been too conspicuous), he spotted me again. "That was good planning," he said. "There is no one here."

"Yes, Your Majesty," I nodded again. "No one knows."

Standing next to the door, I bowed to him once more as the van doors closed. "I wish a safe trip for Your Majesty," I said. I had been the only one to show any respect or even pay attention to him. The shah smiled and said, "Good-bye" as the vehicles moved away.

I learned later that at La Guardia, the plane's engines were running, and as soon as the shah arrived and was taken aboard, the plane took off for Texas. The reporters in the terminal had been waiting for news from their colleagues that the shah had left Cornell Medical Center, but no message ever came. They watched in complete surprise as the shah's plane ascended. All their carefully laid plans had been in vain.

In the next few days the U.S. State Department desperately tried to find a country that would grant the shah asylum. I learned through the CIA that Hamilton Jordan, Carter's Chief of Staff, had been sent to Texas to inform the shah that it would be in the United States' best interests if he left the country. The shah, annoyed, asked what place the United States had selected for him to go to. He was told that after the State Department had checked with practically all the nations of the world, none would have him. In his book *Crisis,* Jordan recorded the following conversation between himself, Lloyd Cutler, and the shah:

> "But what about Austria and Switzerland?" [the shah]
> "Neither is willing to receive you at this time." [Cutler]
> "Are you sure?" the Shah asked, disbelieving.
> "Yes, Your Majesty. Our ambassadors have seen the foreign ministers of both countries in the last forty-eight hours."
> "I must admit that I am surprised and disappointed," he said in a low voice, loaded with grief. "It seems that no one wants me."

Jordan said that Panama was willing to welcome him. The shah hesitated and said he would prefer a European nation. Jordan, apologizing for being blunt, said that although Egypt had offered asylum, it might be difficult for President Sadat if the shah went to Egypt, and that Panama was the only alternative.

Dr. Baghai, in a letter to Prime Minister Alam in 1962, had predicted this outcome:

> . . . In my previous letter to you, I predicted that you and His Majesty "will spend the rest of your lives in Europe walking hand in hand through the avenues of Paris."
> I regret, because of our present situation, that I must take back what I said. No longer do I see that day. On the contrary, no country anywhere can be expected to grant you asylum.

While the shah recovered, his aides desperately shopped around for a country that would accept him. Finally, Hamilton Jordan presented the monarch with an invitation from Panama's General Torrijos. They were welcome to stay on Contadora Island. An oral agreement was reached guaranteeing the United States' full support in the event the shah needed medical or security aid. He would have access to Gorgas Hospital in the former Canal Zone. It was an up-to-date medical facility, and if he needed more care than the hospital could provide, he would be able to return to the United States. Soon after the shah accepted Torrijos's offer to come to Contadora Island, President Carter called His Majesty for the first time since New Year's Day, 1979.

On December 15 the shah and his entourage moved on to Panama. Once there, President Royos and General Torrijos visited often and invited the shah to their homes. His cancer was in remission and he even felt good enough to give David Frost, the English television personality, an interview.

Unfortunately for the shah, the political climate in Panama deteriorated rapidly after January 12, 1980, when Iran's new rulers demanded that Panama arrest him. He was not surprised by the Iranian government's demands, but by Panama's hesitation. Instead of treating the demand with contempt, the Panamanians had hesitated, and rumors began to circulate that they were negotiating an extradition agreement with Tehran.

The shah's position as a privileged guest quickly changed to that of a not quite pampered prisoner. The quality of life crumbled. His phone was tapped. His security became lax and his staff was cut. At the same time, the shah's health began to fail again and his American physicians were flown to Panama. They decided that more surgery was immediately needed, and they operated. During that time, word leaked out that the Panamanians had struck a deal with Tehran and that the shah was going to be extradited at any moment.

David Rockefeller and Henry Kissinger worked frantically around the clock to get the shah out of Panama before it was too late. They claimed that they didn't want him returned to Iran for humanitarian reasons.

They had to find a country willing to take this dying political pariah. On March 24 the Shah and his family were spirited out of Panama and returned to Egypt, just twenty-four hours before the revolutionary government was due to present Panamanian authorities with a formal request for his extradition. Tehran had been cheated of its prey. But his odyssey had come full circle. On July 27, 1980, four months after he arrived in Egypt, Shah Mohammad Reza Pahlavi died.

PART VI

CHAPTER THIRTY-EIGHT

Empress Farah

While I was in Cairo a few months after the shah's death, I went to pay my respects to the empress Farah. Over the past several years I had had ample occasion to observe her during her official visits to the United States. Her imperious ways and her lack of concern for others had been tolerated when she was the wife of the shah, but now circumstances were drastically altered. I was interested to see if her attitude had changed now that she was no longer free to do as she pleased and was entirely dependent on the goodwill of President Anwar Sadat and the Egyptian people.

President Sadat had kindly tried to provide the empress with a residence suitable to her former station. When I was ushered into the ancient Egyptian palace where she lived, I noticed a strong, musty odor pervading the air. Posing like the widowed empress she was, dressed completely in black, her hair pulled severely back from her face, she held out her hand for me to kiss and asked that I be seated. "You see the way we've ended up?" she said disgustedly. "This whole place is deteriorating—rotting! The bathrooms don't even have modern facilities." Abruptly she changed the subject. "Have you heard any news about Iran?"

"Nothing but what's in the papers," I responded.

"What are the Americans going to do—will they help the generals in exile overthrow Khomeini?" she asked eagerly.

"It is unlikely," I responded. "Right now they're concerned about

the hostages and they won't do anything that might cause them harm.
I don't know how much support the generals have, but I doubt that
they'll be able to do anything."

"Do you know what President Sadat told me about the Americans?" she asked scornfully. "He told me that the American administration is like a baby that has to be forced to eat what it doesn't like.
Someone must tell them that they were wrong in not backing the shah."

"The Americans did their best to save the shah," I responded. "It
was an impossible task."

"No," she insisted, "you are wrong. Someday, when I have the
opportunity, I will explain why. Not only did the United States not help
the shah, but they pulled the rug out from under his feet." She paused.
"What are your feelings about the future of the crown prince?"

I explained the importance of an education for her son, emphasiz-
ing that he should stay out of politics. "Getting an education is the best
way for him to prepare for whatever the future has in store for him,
Your Highness," I told her.

"It's unfortunate that he's not at home to hear your advice," she
replied. "I didn't expect you, and I allowed him to go with President
Sadat's children to see a movie."

She expressed gratitude for all the help that President and Mrs.
Sadat had given her family, but she had nothing good to say about
President Carter. "President Carter tried his best to have His Majesty
sent from Panama to Tehran to be killed by Khomeini. We had to pack
and run away like gypsies. If it hadn't been for the help of a few good
friends, His Majesty would have been murdered."

"I can't believe that President Carter would do such a monstrous
thing," I protested. "He's a decent man—a man of integrity."

"You don't know," she snapped, cutting me off. "You don't know
the heartless man that lies behind those glassy eyes."

"Your Highness," I said politely, "you have more information than
I do, but I still cannot believe that President Carter would have sent
the shah back to Tehran."

Next she criticized Ambassador Zahedi, claiming that he had been
mostly to blame for the shah's problems because of his habitual lying.
She wanted to inform Washington that Zahedi was not a representative
of the royal family and that whatever he said was merely his own
opinion. I told her that the American authorities already knew that
Zahedi spoke only for himself, but I assured her I would convey the
message to them again.

I could see that it was futile to try to convince her that her family's involvement in the government had contributed to the shah's downfall. I forced myself to remain silent, since there was no point in making her feel worse about her current situation. *She is never going to accept her part of the responsibility,* I thought to myself. *Blaming others is a way of life for her. Nothing has changed.* I requested permission to leave; she extended her hand and I kissed it.

As I walked through the towering pine trees toward my car, reflecting on my visit, I knew that it was not only the empress who displayed such reprehensible behavior. Nearly all the upper strata of Iranian society shared her desire to promote themselves at the cost of others.

CHAPTER THIRTY-NINE

Crown Prince Reza

In May 1982 I was invited by the crown prince, the shah's son, to visit him at his villa in Rabat, Morocco. The afternoon I arrived we went for a walk on the beach, and as we sat down, he said confidentially, "Mansur, I have some top-secret intelligence to disclose to you."

"Please tell me," I said, intrigued.

"Did you know," he began, "that my father, his minister of court, Asadollah Alam, and his physician all died of the same disease—malignant lymphoma?"

I had known that all three had died of cancer, but I had not known that it was the same type of cancer. The fact did not seem significant to me.

"Aren't you going to ask me why?" he rushed on eagerly. "In the early seventies, the three of them vacationed at a European resort. While the three were together, the CIA managed to bombard them with radiation, and that caused their disease. The CIA—they were the ones who killed my father!"

I was amazed, not at the news, but at the crown prince's belief in the story. But he was a young man; I did not argue with him. All I said was "You have access to such information—I don't."

I was also aware that the CIA was actively assisting the movement to bring the shah's son to power.

I thought about the CIA, which I knew all too well—certainly a strong foe but with definite cracks in its armor. And I thought about the Iranian people, who feared the CIA so much, believing that it was the cause of all their suffering. If an uneducated man had related the crown prince's story, I would have thought nothing of it. But the son of a shah who presented a fantastic tale as "top-secret news" boded ill for the future of Iran.

In October 1982 the crown prince invited me to Egypt and took me to the radio station from which he was clandestinely broadcasting to Iran. A car sent by the Egyptian intelligence office picked me up at my hotel to take me to the palace where the prince was residing. From the palace we were to go to the outskirts of Cairo to see the radio station. As we drove, the palace radioed the chauffeur that he should park the car out of sight behind the building and that I was not to get out. After a while I asked the chauffeur if I could leave the car to smoke. He answered, "Don't go far from the car. The instructions were that you were to stay in the car."

"Thank you," I said as I stepped out.

After we had waited for approximately thirty minutes, the general who had sent the car to get me approached and said, "Follow me." As I did so, his pace quickened. We kept going faster and faster as we approached the palace. By the time we reached the stairway at the palace, we were running and I ran behind the general all the way up the winding staircase and into a large room. I was out of breath by the time we entered the room.

The crown prince was standing with one foot up on a chair and he shook hands with me as he said, "Sorry for the delay. I couldn't let you in. Do you know why?"

"No."

"I don't want my mother to know you are here and that we're going to the station. Because she believes her family to be experts in radio and television, she would want them to be my advisers. [Relatives of the empress had been prominent in the radio and TV media in Iran.] Besides that, she hates you!"

The crown prince offered me a drink. "I'm going back to see my mother and tell her I'm going out for the evening. I'll be back," he said.

After the prince had left the room, the Egyptian general began to talk to me. "Whatever the crown prince wants, we have to please the crown prince, not the empress. Did you ever read Machiavelli's *The Prince*?"

"Yes, a long time ago."

"Then you understand me and you know why we have to hide you from the empress."

The general began to discuss the trip to the radio station. "I want to warn you about something. The Iranian employees of the station are sometimes lazy and don't give us a new tape to broadcast. Sometimes for the evening broadcast they give us a copy of the tape that we used in the morning. If they complain about me tonight to the crown prince, I'll bring up the subject of those tapes. You warn them in Farsi, so they'll be sure to understand. Okay?"

I had heard that the radio station staff had complained that they were not being properly paid. Now it became clear to me what the general had been doing: He was paying the Iranians only part of the money the crown prince was providing and putting the rest of the money in his own pocket. This practice, common enough in Iran, apparently flourished in Egypt, too.

Changing topics, the general said, "Between you and me, the crown prince is jealous of his brother and the mother is backing the younger brother to be the next shah."

The crown prince returned, and we had to leave the palace just as furtively and hurriedly as we had entered, running all the way to the car so that his mother would not see us. He sat in the front with the chauffeur and I sat in the back. The general followed in one of the escort vehicles.

During the drive to the station, which took approximately an hour, the crown prince told me that when he came to power, most of the people around him who were helping him were not going to have jobs. He was going to put them in jail. As he began to talk about Ambassador Zahedi, and how to eliminate the ambassador from his team, I became lost in my own thoughts. The whole trip had suddenly become amusing. All I could think was *Here we go again!* Here again were the corruption, the contradictions, the shifting of sides or positions, the jealousy. How could one trust this young man?

I recalled the advice General Nassiri had given me years earlier concerning the shah's jealousy of his sisters, his brothers, even his wife. I had reported that a speech made in the UN by one of the shah's brothers had been good; the delegates had liked it and had clapped in approval. The general had told me never again to send a wire that too highly praised a speech made by any member of the shah's family. If a speech was well received, I should minimize its effect in my report.

I also remembered a comment that General Pakravan had made about certain kinds of articles that had appeared in the press, especially in *The New York Times,* which had praised the general. "They're poison for me," he said.

"Why?" I had asked.

"His Majesty gets mad. He's like the eagle—he doesn't want any-one to fly above him."

After returning to my hotel in Cairo, I thought about the crown prince's statement that his mother hated me, and remembered an incident that had occurred a few years earlier.

General Nassiri had phoned me and told me that he had wired me $47,000. This money was to be taken in cash to a bar in Greenwich Village, and General Nassiri had instructed me, "Be there precisely at seven in the evening. Don't be late." I was to meet a man at the bar, and I would recognize him as follows: He would be carrying a recent issue of *Time* magazine (the general described the cover for me), and after he sat down at the bar and ordered a drink, he would set the drink on top of the magazine. The general stressed: "Do not ask for a receipt!"

The traffic in downtown Manhattan was heavy and by the time I parked the car and entered the bar, it was 7:45 P.M. I wondered if there was any use going in. Had the man waited? As I looked around the bar, I saw a man whose drink was sitting on top of a copy of *Time.* It was as Nassiri had described, so I approached the man, who was about my height but very skinny, with long hair and a beard, both dirty. He was dressed in tight jeans and a leather jacket, which were also dirty. There was a strange look in his eyes; I suspected that he was on drugs. He recognized me and abruptly asked if I knew what time it was. I said that it was 7:45, explained that I had been caught in traffic, and apologized for being late. In an insolent tone of voice he said, "You were supposed to be here at seven. Do you have the package?"

"Yes, it's in my case."

"Let's have it."

"Can't we go to the men's room for the transfer?"

"No! Give it to me here."

I couldn't believe that a chief of SAVAK was being asked to do this. Why was I meeting with this man, so slovenly and so arrogant? His attitude annoyed me so much that I asked for a receipt.

Angrily, he asked, "Weren't you told not to ask for a receipt?"

"Yes."

With that, he shoved some change across the bar to the bartender, picked up the package, and left.

The next day General Nassiri called me and he also asked me angrily, "Weren't you told not to ask for a receipt?"

"Yes."

"Now the empress is furious."

"General, who was that man and why was he getting forty-seven thousand dollars?"

"He's a musician. You know the empress has many friends like that."

Now, years later, I wondered if that was the reason for the empress's intense dislike of me.

Before my departure from Cairo, I made a journey to the shah's tomb in Al Rifai Mosque. I did not fully understand why, perhaps partly because of a very strange nostalgia. While standing by his grave, I found myself unexpectedly affected. This king of kings and mighty sultan had enjoyed the support, and to some extent the adulation, of eight U.S. presidents. The shah had had his own strong assessments of each of these men: He felt that Roosevelt and Truman had ignored him; he saw Eisenhower as a father figure; Kennedy was an enemy; Johnson was viewed as the shah's own propagandist; Ford was a joke; Carter, the Boar, was considered another enemy; and Nixon was loved as a friend. I wondered what the shah had been trying to prove when he contributed millions of dollars to Nixon's campaign and also deposited several million in a Swiss bank account. Nixon had given the shah almost carte blanche in obtaining weapons from the United States. He visited the shah while he was in exile, and he had flown to Cairo and attended the shah's funeral in the very room where I was now standing.

I tried to think about what the shah had done for his country. There had been progress—he had built roads and buildings, developed a modern army, even introduced Western technology. Yes, there had been some prosperity—the average Iranian's income rose and the country experienced a period of economic development. But while accomplishing these things, the shah took away the rights of the people. Iran forfeited freedom under his rule.

I recalled how the shah had sent his father's remains to Cairo. I began to make some comparisons between father and son. From the 1930s through 1953, the Iranian people had had virtually no prosperity or economic gains compared with what they had attained after 1953, but the measure of freedom they had had under Reza Shah was far greater.

Now Shah Mohammad Reza Pahlavi was dead and in the tomb that lay before me. There is an old saying, "As with all dictators, he had taken the good things he had done with him." It was too high a price to pay for the little progress he had accomplished. His legacy to his country was another dictatorship—a religious tyranny.

My thoughts were finally distracted by a religious man, who walked over and offered his services. "Would you like me to say a prayer for the shah?" he asked.

"Please," I said.

As he was chanting in Arabic, I gave him money and asked him to continue his prayers.

Then I turned and walked out of Al Rifai Mosque.

CHAPTER FORTY

Visit to the Shah's Grave

In Cairo the following October 6, twenty-six months after the shah's death, I made yet another trip to his grave.

The cab took me to Salah al Din Square, an ancient square lined with dust-laden trees whose leaves looked sere and dead. Hundreds of people milled about, waiting for a bus. We stopped in front of an old building. It was suffocatingly hot. Dust was everywhere.

"Would you like me to wait for you?" the cab driver asked.

"All right," I agreed.

He pointed toward Al Rifai Mosque, then accompanied me as I walked toward it. One of the men in charge of the building approached us. The cab driver said to him in Arabic, "He's an Iranian. He wants to see the shah's grave."

The man nodded. "Come in." He motioned to me. "Take off your shoes." The floor was so dirty that I hesitated to comply. The guide brought me a pair of paper slippers. He took me to Sheikh Ali Rifai's tomb, where we stood and paid our respects. He guided me to another room. "Your shah's brother-in-law, King Farouk, is buried here." The guide pointed to another room. "And your shah is in the adjacent hallway."

In the hallway there was a single bouquet of wilted white flowers. The guide told me that the empress Farah had sent them a few days earlier. A Persian carpet, its pattern obscured by dust, covered the tomb. Pulling aside the carpet, the guide revealed a wooden cover.

"Your homeless shah is deposited here," he told me, implying that this would not be the shah's permanent resting place. "If you'll pay me fifty cents," he said, "I'll sweep the carpet for you."

I nodded. "Go ahead." I was sorry I had agreed, for he scurried off and returned with a large broom and began to sweep wildly. Soon I was choking from the dust-filled air. "That's enough! Please stop!" I begged, handing him two dollars. He told me that he had two children, and really needed more. I quickly gave him another fifty cents. He grinned and stopped his frantic sweeping. "Please leave me alone now," I told him. "I'll be out in a few minutes."

I contemplated the scene before me. Could the shah ever have dreamed that he would be buried in such a place—that all the sumptuous palaces, the exquisite roses, the priceless jewels, would be replaced by some dead white flowers and a filthy Persian rug?

But then could I ever have dreamed that the day would come when I would visit the shah's grave and pay three dollars to have it cleaned? I reflected on the inscrutable ways life treats us: Even power and riches cannot prevent a man from coming to an ignoble end if that is his fate.

As we drove back to the hotel, we passed the imposing white building where President Nasser rested. He and the shah had been bitter enemies. What an irony it was that the two men were buried in the same city; the shah would not even visit Egypt while Nasser was president.

Back at the hotel, I could not shake off my melancholic thoughts. The words of a favorite poem by Omar Khayyam came to mind:

> But if in vain, down on the stubborn floor
> Of Earth, and up to Heav'n's Unopening Door,
> You gaze To-day, while You are You—how then
> To-morrow, when You shall be You no more?

PART VII

CHAPTER FORTY-ONE

Death Threat

In March 1986, after the CIA had received some intelligence about this book, a senior officer, whom I had not seen since severing my ties with the Agency in 1983, set up a meeting in New York City.

Justifiably, I was very apprehensive about this meeting. My intuitive juices started flowing, and I realized that I had to protect myself. I considered my options and called the FBI beforehand. I told them that a senior CIA official was coming to see me regarding a book I was writing about my political experiences, and that I would let them know when and where the meeting would be taking place.

I met with the CIA officer on Wednesday morning, March 26, 1986, in a nondescript hotel suite. He was seated behind a large desk, and we began talking about the "old times" when I was associated with his office, but the conversation's direction quickly changed. He was anxious to tell me about the developments at the CIA and how "Old Bill" Casey had gotten rid of the "assholes" and had changed the operation tremendously.

Finally, he got to the real purpose of our meeting. His office was very concerned about my book, and, because he was an old friend, he had volunteered to serve as a go-between to prevent me from making some serious mistakes.

Ultimately, we began to talk about the contents of my manuscript. He listened calmly as I told him about the early biographical chapters, but when I got to my experiences with the CIA, he became very angry and defensive. He accused me of being hostile toward his office and of placing the CIA's "new reputation" in jeopardy. He implored me not to include material he felt would be damaging. "The office made mistakes in the past," he admitted, "but the office Old Bill operates today is different. By publishing this information you would give the office an even more terrible reputation—not only here but abroad." Above all, he explained that it was out of the question for his office to allow the book to be published. He had a better way to handle it. He suggested that I come to Washington, where we could review the manuscript in a civilized way and take out those parts that the Agency was not comfortable with. Then they would assign a writer to me, who would help me to replace the stricken sections with some more acceptable material.

The CIA was demanding carte blanche to rewrite my book—to rewrite history!

I emphasized that I wasn't interested in harming the CIA, but merely in informing the American people of the truth, in clarifying a very important part of history that I had witnessed. I would never willingly compromise agents or their current intelligence-gathering methods. And as for the CIA's "new reputation," I said, William Casey could not be held accountable for things his predecessors had done.

Failing to overcome my resistance, the official tried a different tactic. "Give us the manuscript and we'll give your cost plus whatever you think three years of your own time is worth. No receipts necessary. Just give us the total."

I knew that I could walk out of that room with a promise of a tax-free $1 million or more. I turned him down flat. The CIA man banged on the desk. "Asshole!" he yelled.

Finally, he calmed down after a visible effort to get himself under control. "Give me the manuscript, Mansur," he cajoled.

Again I refused. "I wrote this because of my beliefs, not because I am hostile toward your office," I said.

He demanded to know who had the manuscript and if any of them were known to be anti-CIA. He wanted to collect all of the copies before "this thing gets out of hand."

I didn't reveal any names but made sure that he knew there were several copies around.

The rest of the evening was spent rehashing old topics, but he never stopped urging me to bring him the manuscript. When he finally decided to call it a night, his parting words were "Bring it tomorrow!" I was emotionally drained. It was after midnight.

When I saw him the next day, first he mocked me. "You always used to come with a briefcase. Now you have no job and no briefcase." Then he got right to the point. "Where is the manuscript?" I told him that when I'd said no the previous night I'd meant it. Then he said, "Mansur, I have to have it! I promised the office I would bring it back with me."

He began to threaten me. "If you think that you'll ever get to publish this book, you're mistaken. You know Old Bill. He's a tough man. He doesn't tolerate this kind of bullshit. In the nineteen sixties the CIA went down because of the Vietnam War, because of activists, and a lot of assholes: people at *The Washington Post, The New York Times,* Frank Church, and that kind of garbage. We're still trying to build up the image of the Agency, and we've been successful, but we still have a problem with the young people. They don't want to work for the CIA because of the prevailing negative attitude. The belief that we're incompetent, or we're killers. This book certainly wouldn't help. So old Casey's not going to take it."

His blue eyes glaring, he pulled out all the stops and put it to me. "The Bureau [FBI] will get rid of you. Picture this. You are being interviewed or giving a lecture somewhere. A man in the crowd shoots you. Who could figure out who shot you? One of the shah's people? One of Khomeini's people? After all, you were SAVAK!"

I was angry and scared. I had been a professional in this business long enough to know that one didn't drop the boss's name in a death threat casually. Obviously, he had been mandated by headquarters to use whatever means necessary, even murder or its threat, to silence me.

I tried to act calmly even though my insides were shaking. "I've enjoyed my life," I said. "I've worked with famous people, traveled— it's been interesting. If the FBI is going to do it, I can't stop them."

He quickly interjected, "They will, you know!" He warned me, "You wouldn't have one friend left in the American government. They'll be the ones to carry out the order. Mozafar [my brother] will find you in a pool of blood."

He was depressing me as much as he was scaring me. How naïve I had been to think that if the likes of him knew what was going on in Iran, they would stop the shah. I felt desolate. I had put my faith in the wrong people for twenty-five years. I broke down and cried. He seemed pleased, probably thinking that I was finally going to surrender.

Gently, he said, "Bring in the manuscript. Let's negotiate. Don't allow yourself to be manipulated by people who just want to make money for themselves."

Again I repeated, "It's the principle. The American people have a right to know what went wrong in Iran. How do you know this book is so damaging?"

"Because I know you and how much you know," he quietly responded, "and how critical you always were. That's enough." Then, matter-of-factly, he said, "You still have time to think about it, but a few things just might happen to you before this book ever gets published." In a very businesslike way, he recited the possibilities:

"One, William Casey's office will get in touch with you and ask you to come and speak with him.

"Two, we will get in touch with the vice-president's office. Since he is your friend and might have influence on you, he may call to discuss this with you.

"Three, I will go to them [Casey] and tell them how much time and money you have spent, and I'll get back to you.

"Four, I won't see you again but the legal department will come to see you."

Then his voice turned menacing. "Where do you want the flowers sent?"

(The CIA officer who was threatening me was ironically the very same one who had warned me three and a half years earlier that I was on Khomeini's hit list.)

That night I informed an FBI official I had known for years what had transpired. He was shocked and furious that FBI personnel were being characterized as front men to kill for the CIA. He insisted that I make a log of what had been said to me while it was still fresh in my mind.

I couldn't sleep a wink that night. I was living a nightmare. I kept imagining how the CIA would carry out its threats against me. Would a mugger attack me? a car malfunction? a gas tank explode? maybe a drug overdose?

However, my greatest fear was the suppression of my manuscript. I wanted to make sure it got published no matter what happened to me.

I met with my lawyer Melvin Gittleman. I told him about my meetings with the CIA and its attempts to persuade me, bribe me, its threats to kill me. The CIA's behavior shocked and angered him. He had expected an attempt to censor the work but not a threat on my life. He encouraged me to fight back, saying, "Don't worry about the manuscript. I'm making some more copies and I won't even tell you who has them. That will be your best protection. Nobody knows where the copies are."

Next, I called Dr. Baghai, my mentor, who fortunately was visiting in the United States at the time, and invited him to my home. I desperately wanted to talk to him. He had already read and corrected the manuscript, and I needed his wisdom and guidance.

"My choices are clear," I explained to him. "I either take a huge amount of money and let them censor my book to their heart's content, or I run the risk of assassination at the hands of the CIA." Dr. Baghai remained calm. "Resist the intimidation. Publish the book," he said. He took my silence as a sign of fear. It was completely out of character for him to advocate a course that might lead to violence. When I was a youthful activist, he always counseled firm but peaceful resistance. "Courting an assassination is not a policy I would usually recommend," he continued. "But there are times when you have to pay for the truth, even if it's with your life. It's time to take the risk, son. You owe it to Americans and to Iranians, especially the younger generations. You have an obligation to tell and they have the right to know."

With a lump in my throat, I responded, "Yes, sir."

The CIA escalated its harassment. It had the Justice Department contact my attorneys, threaten to alter my immigration status, and subpoena me if I didn't cooperate fully. The Agency continued to demand that I turn over my manuscript for censorship, and give it the names of everyone who had read or worked on the manuscript.

After several tense meetings between the Justice Department attorneys, my attorneys, and myself, nothing was resolved. At our last meeting, held on September 8, 1986, at my lawyer's office in New Jersey, I was extremely indignant at the behavior of the Justice Department and couldn't contain my feelings. "You, as the representatives of the very Justice Department who threw President Nixon out of office because he broke the law, should enforce and respect the law! It was one of the greatest things that ever happened in this country. With that one incident, Americans proved that no man is above the law." I told them that the people look to the Justice Department to ensure that there will be a democracy in the future, but if the department tried to prevent the public from knowing the truth now, twenty years from now we would not have the kind of democracy that America stands for. "I believe if the law is not respected by the highest authority, a revolution or chaos will come to this land and destroy everything the American people treasure!"

I also stated that the public had the right to know the kind of genius we have in the White House, and again I told them that what I was planning to publish would not hurt the national security of this country.

On September 15, 1986, the Justice Department sent a letter to my lawyers demanding that I turn over my manuscript. The letter also included the following:

> For his [Mansur Rafizadeh's] part, we ask that you and your client provide us with assurance that no copies of the original manuscript remain in the hands of third parties at the time of submission and agree not to distribute any version of the manuscript different from that finally approved.

I tried to analyze my options and realized that I was faced with an agonizing dilemma. The Justice Department wanted to silence me and wouldn't hesitate to take whatever steps it deemed necessary to prevent the publication of my book, though, I hoped, short of murder.

Was I willing to take the consequences? After all, I knew that President Reagan was selling arms to Iran and negotiating for hostages, that Robert C. MacFarlane, representing President Reagan, had made a historical trip to Iran in May 1986, carrying a special message, and that there had been a misappropriation of funds from these arms sales. Didn't I want the public to know the truth? Adding to my frustration was the fear that my phone might be tapped and therefore create problems for whomever I called. I was forced to make all of my phone calls from outside of my home.

When I met with my attorneys Melvin Gittleman and Raymond Durr they got right to the point. "Are you going to give them the manuscript, Mansur?" I replied with an emphatic "No!" Pleased, they then said, "Now we know where you stand." Most curious, I asked, "Are you going to defend me?" Without a moment's hesitation, they answered, "Yes! The first thing we will do is consult with the Civil Liberties Union and find out the best way to defend your constitutional rights." I embraced them tearfully and thanked them. This was the *other* side of American justice.

Three years of work on my manuscript, added to the CIA's and the Justice Department's prolonged harassment, made me so physically and emotionally drained that I became hospitalized with a severely perforated ulcer.

During my convalescence in October, in a final act of desperation, I even attempted to call ABC-TV correspondent Ted Koppel. When informed he was out of town and asked to leave my name, I told his office that I would call again.

A few days later, a source called from Tehran and reported that Ayatollah A. H. Montazeri's faction was preparing a newsletter that would make public facts about the "secret" American arms-hostage negotiations.

The first week of November the arms scandal splashed across the front pages of newspapers around the world. I was vindicated. The Justice Department hasn't communicated with me since.

CHAPTER FORTY-TWO

When the Hostages Didn't Come Home

By the time Jimmy Carter became president, the shortsightedness and mistakes of other administrations had allowed the shah to arouse the furious animosity of the Iranian people against both himself and the United States. Carter correctly perceived the need to champion the cause of human rights and political reform in Iran, but unfortunately the shah and his predecessors had antagonized the citizenry beyond reconciliation.

In a world drowning in cynicism, President Carter was a man of principle who courageously tried to reconcile his personal beliefs and diplomacy. He stood firm and refused to sacrifice his values in the name of political expediency. As a result, he subsequently lost the presidency in the next election.

In line with his strong and unwavering position on human rights, President Carter pressured the shah into releasing vast numbers of political prisoners. Once freed, these very same people caused the shah's downfall.

President Carter's deeply ingrained sense of morality foreclosed any possibility of trading the ailing shah for the American hostages, and therefore he desperately sought alternative solutions. The ultimate one, the military attempt to rescue the hostages, was doomed from the start because, in addition to all of the problems inherent in an operation of such complexity, President Carter was handicapped by several inherited factors.

One of the most damaging was the rigid Republican loyalty of the CIA officers in charge of the Iran desk. These men wanted war. General Oveissi and I had had several meetings with these CIA officers during that period, and I was astounded by their callous remarks. One agent said to me, "What do fifty-two American lives mean? Every Thanksgiving, hundreds of Americans die on the highways. What's the big deal, Mansur?"

I came upon further proof of the strong anti-Carter sentiment in the CIA when I learned that it was allowing misinformation about the hostages to get to Carter, such as: they were being forced to play Russian roulette, were kept bound in handcuffs on the floor, and were often beaten up severely and left bleeding. The Agency wanted President Carter to believe the hostages were brutally treated, when in fact the Iranian captors took great care to keep their prisoners in as good health as possible.

The CIA gave President Carter these false reports because it hoped to get him to abandon his nonviolent stance and go after Khomeini with guns blasting. But I discovered the most damning example of this anti-Carter sentiment when I surreptitiously discovered that Khomeini had planned to release the hostages the moment President Reagan was elected.

Khomeini was completely ignorant of American political procedures. He believed that immediately after his victory, President Reagan would have a dossier prepared on President Carter and subsequently have him arrested. After all, this was customary procedure in many Middle Eastern countries. Khomeini's lack of knowledge about Western culture and history was a constant problem for his aides. For the longest time, Khomeini even believed that the word "Carter" was a synonym for head of state, and, much to the embarrassment of his countrymen, would publicly refer to the Carter of England, the Carter of France, etc.

Because his aides had made a point of telling Khomeini about President Carter's nonviolent protests—his use of a candlelight vigil, symbolic yellow ribbons, and church services to demonstrate his approach to free the hostages, Khomeini had absolutely no fear of this nonaggressive leader.

Conversely, Khomeini's aides painted a very different picture of Ronald Reagan, telling him that Reagan was a warmonger and the second that he took office he would bomb Tehran.

Fearing this new American leader, Khomeini wanted to free the hostages immediately after the November 4 election. In fact, George

Bush had been director of the CIA during the Nixon administration and still had friends in the Agency. When the Republican party nominated the Reagan-Bush ticket, it was supported by the CIA. Upon their election on November 4, 1980, the CIA's Iran desk considered the president-elect and vice-president-elect as their chief executives, and Jimmy Carter as a lame duck. Therefore, some CIA agents, one of them Sadegh Ghotbzadeh, were briefed by Agency officers to persuade Khomeini not to release his prisoners until Ronald Reagan was sworn in. The CIA, consistently hostile to Carter, told Khomeini not to bother giving Carter the credit when he would no longer have any power. Thus, the CIA, who had tried to manipulate President Carter into aggressive behavior by using false reports about "brutal hostage treatment," now sentenced the American hostages to seventy-six more days of imprisonment.

On January 20, 1981, the hostages boarded a waiting jet at Tehran Airport. As they sat trembling in their seats, still unsure of their next destination and their ultimate fate, a guard stood outside the aircraft with a radio pressed to his ear and a walkie-talkie clutched in his hand. Only after the very moment that Ronald Reagan was sworn in as president did the guard signal the pilot. As Reagan delivered his inaugural address, they were airborne to freedom.

During the period of indecision and chaos that followed the return of the hostages immediately after President Reagan's inauguration in 1981, Reagan and the director of the CIA, William Casey, secretly ordered the Agency to give money and other support to Khomeini's strongest opposition groups. The CIA sought out the leaders, and soon had liaisons with Shahpur Bakhtiar, based in France, General Gholam Ali Oveissi, based in the United States, Dr. Ali Amini, based in France, Admiral A. Madani, based in Germany, General F. Jam, based in England and the shah's son, Reza Pahlavi, based in Morocco.

The CIA was able to convince these groups to accept their cooperation and trust by focusing on the purity of their motives: America had experienced deep humiliation at the hands of the Khomeini regime, the American pro–human-rights position was well known, and Iran's emergence as a terrorist training ground was making the headlines.

Hence, the CIA officers in charge made it very clear that they would not participate in this anti-Khomeini operation without the president's first issuing an executive order. In September 1981 such an executive order was issued with a one-year limitation. This precaution was taken so that if the CIA could not promote the overthrow of

Khomeini within this period, it would have to go back to the president for another such order. Privately, we informants were all told by the CIA that if during this time no one group proved dominant, the United States would have no choice but to make peace with Khomeini. The CIA recognized a major problem with these groups: They were so diverse philosophically that they were too busy fighting each other to be really productive.

In 1982 word leaked out to the Iranians that the president, the CIA, and other American officials were divided as to whether post-Khomeini Iran should become a republic or return to a monarchy. The various opposing factions were delighted, as now each believed that it had someone in the CIA supporting its own particular cause.

The CIA continued to foster this impression by assigning an officer to each group, someone who would give the illusion that he was sympathetic only to it. He would meet with the group's leader and gain his trust by promising to bolster his position if he could show proof of his faction's strength in Iran. "Washington is under the impression that Khomeini's opposition is made up of all chiefs and no Indians," he might say. "If you want to strengthen your leadership position, you must provide us with as many specifics as possible about your network in Iran. You must give us the names of your people."

All the leaders of these opposition groups fell for this ploy—hook, line, and sinker. During the next few months, they desperately vied with each other to provide as much information about their support people in Iran as they could.

Shortly after they had all dutifully handed over the information, their CIA contacts startled them by disclosing that a single Iranian official had been listed as a primary supporter by no fewer than five different opposition groups. Each CIA contact then asked, "How can you prove that he is yours? You must give us more precise information." Desperate to prove the man theirs alone, they eagerly offered all the minute details of the man's *modus operandi.*

Throughout this period, George Cave, the CIA liaison, operating under a pseudonym, carried the liaison officers' promises one step further by assuring each group that it was the American government's favorite, destined to wear the mantle of Iran's leadership.

General Oveissi, like the rest of the opposition leaders, was a victim of this deception. At a meeting in Hamburg with a CIA liaison officer, the general, and me, we discussed various civil servants, religious leaders, and businessmen in Iran who were supporting General Oveissi. Then the CIA agent matter-of-factly produced a chart depicting the entire Iranian Army structure, including names and ranks. He casually told General Oveissi, "Tell me which ones are yours. I'll take this to Washington and discredit all the other opposition and prove once and for all that you should be the leader. This," he continued cheerfully, "will prove that you are the strongest. If you want to be shah—we'll make you shah!"

General Oveissi slammed the chart closed and said, "No more! I don't trust you people!"

The CIA officer became angry. He appealed to me. "We try to help and look what he says! I want to make him the shah and he doesn't trust us!"

I tried to calm Oveissi down and quickly ushered him into an adjacent room. "If you have more information," I pleaded with him, "give it to them! They are telling the truth. They only want to help restore human rights to Iran. They are tired of having the American government humiliated and are tired of having a terrorist government in power. The American government wants only to help."

Eyes blazing, General Oveissi pounded on the table and said, "You are naïve. I will be wrong in God's eyes." His rage escalating, he added, "I did it but I'm going to stop it now. They are devious liars!"

I smiled. "You are a cynic," I told him.

"I don't care what you call me," he responded. "All I know is that God wouldn't forgive me if something happened to these men."

We returned to the other room and I apologized to the CIA officer for General Oveissi's behavior.

The officer commented calmly, "I understand. He's frustrated. Let's put this chart together. I'll take it to Washington and then we will be able to provide him with all our support."

During the entire flight to Paris from Hamburg, Oveissi tried to convince me that I was wrong, but I held fast to my belief that the administration and the CIA were too ethical ever to cooperate with Khomeini's government.

After a few weeks I learned that the CIA had extracted similar intelligence from all of the opposition groups with the same promises of support. But still unwilling to believe that the CIA would be so deceptive, I continued to justify its behavior.

Four months later I was summoned to Oveissi's apartment in Paris. As we walked to a nearby park on Avenue Foch, I asked him what was so urgent. Turning to him, I was stunned to see this tough soldier with tears streaming down his cheeks.

He looked at me and said, "I just received intelligence from Iran that Khomeini got the whole list of officers that I gave to the CIA. They'll all be killed."

I was shattered. It was inconceivable to me that the CIA would do such a thing.

"They only wanted to trick us from the beginning," he continued. "Reagan's administration only wanted to get on Khomeini's good side. This is what they really wanted—to gain *his* trust. We were duped."

I still couldn't accept this. "Your intelligence must be wrong!" I insisted. "It can't be true!"

After hashing these events over and over, the general despairing and I disbelieving, we decided to confront the CIA liaison officer. He denied providing the list to Khomeini or having any complicity in the matter. Instead, he tried to shift the blame to General Oveissi.

"It's you who have given interviews to reporters from *The New York Times* and *The Washington Post*," he accused. "You know they are loaded with Communists! Maybe you leaked the information."

"I never gave them any names!" Oveissi responded angrily.

The CIA officer attacked again. "It is you who have been meeting with members of the House and the Senate. I warned you to be careful. They all come from the same breed of asshole. *You* must have dropped the information."

Superficially it appeared that the United States was funding the opposition groups operating in exile in order to develop and maintain networks in Iran to overthrow Khomeini's regime. When Khomeini became aware of the CIA's role in this matter, he was extremely angry. Attempting to smooth his ruffled feathers and prove the United States' good intentions, the CIA passed the word through intermediaries that they were not really helping the opposition but merely using them as intelligence resources to strengthen the Khomeini government. In order to show its sincerity and hoping that this would prove its true motives, the CIA compiled a detailed list of intelligence information and attached an anonymous letter explaining its intentions. The CIA then placed the information in a large manila envelope and left it in front of the Tehran home of Dr. Mohammad Beheshti, one of Khomeini's top aides.

In a few days Oveissi discovered conclusively through his sources in Iran that the American government had indeed supplied the list of Iranians to Khomeini. Horrified by his role in betraying their identities, Oveissi futilely attempted to warn as many people as possible in the hope that some might still be able to escape.

Unfortunately, only some survived. In all, over one thousand names had been provided by the leaders of the opposition groups. Some of these people were killed, some were imprisoned, and others placed under house arrest.

Over the next few months the media gave saturation coverage of these poor victims' trials and executions. I was numbed by the knowledge that I was partly responsible for their deaths. Throughout the trials I met periodically with General Oveissi. Humbly, I apologized to him for having been so completely stupid. I had been blinded by wishful thinking. At one of these meetings, Oveissi said to me, "I forgive you, but I don't know if God is going to forgive either of us." Crying, General Oveissi raised his hands toward the sky and implored God— "You will take care of President Reagan and William Casey! I had good faith when I gave names to them!"

Still troubled by what he regarded as the CIA's betrayal, General Oveissi met once again with the agents. At this meeting, the CIA continued to deny any responsibility, and this time tried to shift the blame to the State Department.

Before leaving, the CIA officer in charge asked Oveissi, "Is there anything I can do for you?"

After a long, thoughtful pause, Oveissi stared at him and said, "Can you free me?"

Puzzled, the CIA man asked, "What do you mean?"

General Oveissi begged, "Free me! Free me! Send me to Khomeini so he can kill me—then I won't have these nightmares every night!"

The agent stared at him coldly and responded, "General, you're too emotional."

Why did the Reagan administration allow itself to be involved in such unethical behavior? Because it believed that its actions were justified. It felt it was the most expeditious way to reach its long-range objective—stop the spread of communism. The Reagan administration was interested in maintaining a fundamentalist government in Iran at any cost, even if it meant supporting a cruel dictator, disregarding people's basic human rights, returning Iran to a seventh-century mentality, or taking hostages. It fit in with its ultimate goals—to keep fundamentalism in power and put a "Green Belt" (referring to the color green, which appears in most flags of Muslim countries) around the southern border of the Soviet Union, thus preventing the Soviet Union from ever controlling the warm waters of the Indian Ocean.

The Reagan administration truly believed that Muslim fundamentalism was its most effective weapon against communism in the area, and wouldn't take the risk of allowing a moderate or liberal to come to power in Iran. Unfortunately, this was not the only disastrous example of the administration's desperate and misguided pursuit of Khomeini's "good side."

In 1982 a high-ranking KGB officer, who had worked in Tehran as a Soviet diplomat but who was actually in charge of the KGB's Iran desk, defected to the West. After being extensively interrogated by both British and American intelligence, he provided a wealth of accurate information about the Tudeh party's (the Iranian Communist party) officers, members, long-range plans, and other connections.

Although the British were also in possession of this information, they didn't choose to use it.

But in 1984 the CIA felt it expedient to hand over the names of the Iranian Communists to Khomeini's regime. Khomeini had them all immediately arrested. Hundreds were brutally killed and hundreds are still in jail.

I tried to sort out my own feelings and put these events into some kind of perspective.

For 444 days, Khomeini had kept the American diplomats hostage. Then fifty-two volumes of top-secret documents found in the American embassy were published, and America was debased further when copies of the documents were sold on Iranian street corners for ten cents a copy.

As I've indicated, a few months before the shah's hasty departure from Iran, I and other concerned Iranians repeatedly urged the CIA to remove the embassy's documents from Iran. Iran was a country in which the shah felt even his father's bones were not safe, and we knew just how vulnerable classified documents would be when Khomeini took over. The CIA refused to heed our warnings. Now secret United States information was available to the Soviet Union or anyone else who wanted it.

It was uncanny. Iran had consistently humiliated the U.S. government by burning American presidents in effigy and openly praying for America's downfall. Every public gathering (including the deliberations of Parliament) was punctuated with rousing shouts of "Down with America!"

When Khomeini received the news that the United States had supplied his aides with information about opposition forces in Iran, he laughed and said, "So that's the United States's position on human rights."

How could the American government constantly talk about championing human rights while so flagrantly ignoring them in its own actions? Was its position always a sham?

CHAPTER FORTY-THREE

First Arms Shipment to Iran

During the shah's reign, the great preponderance of Iranian arms had been bought from the United States. The shah needed the United States in order to maintain his sophisticated, costly equipment. Obviously this offered the United States an almost foolproof method of controlling the shah's army. When Khomeini toppled the shah's regime, he inherited therefore not only an outstanding military arsenal but also a built-in dependency on American industry.

As the Iranian war with Iraq escalated, the United States was confident that Iran could not sustain the hostilities for longer than two years without refurbishing its major weapons. This was America's trump card—Iran would collapse without American replacement parts. The United States seized this opportunity to influence the outcome of the Iran-Iraq conflict and make inroads with Khomeini's government.

In the spring of 1982, General Oveissi received intelligence from sources close to Khomeini that in 1981 the United States government had offered arms to Khomeini's regime. The Reagan administration via the CIA had made several overtures in hopes of developing a relationship. Khomeini, however, had turned them down, saying that he didn't need to get any arms from the United States "Satan." Privately, he said, "The Americans would sell their mother for one dollar. We can get arms from all over. Why should we deal with them?"

Undaunted by this rebuff, the Americans made another offer through the CIA again, but this time it carried a stern warning. "If you try to buy arms from alternative American sources [private arms dealers], the people you deal with will be punished to the full extent of American law."

The Iranians responded, "That's your affair. You take care of it any way you want to!"

In 1982 Oveissi was disgusted and dejected. At a meeting with the CIA he confronted his Agency liaison. "You say that you are helping us. At the same time you offer Khomeini arms! I know what your game is. You are using us as bait to lure Khomeini to the bargaining table. If the American people find out about this deal, they are going to be furious. They will never accept this after all Khomeini has done to humiliate their country. I'm going to tell."

Unmoved, the CIA officer pleaded ignorance of any arms offer and, without missing a beat, shifted the blame this time to the State Department. "Trust me," he said. "We are not involved in any arms negotiations with Khomeini. If what you say happened, it must have come from the State Department. They have a lot of assholes loose all over the Middle East making all kinds of deals."

When Oveissi then pressed the CIA agent, the latter allowed that he felt the arms offer really wasn't such a bad idea. "Selling arms to Iran," he said, "might accomplish several objectives. The United States would be able to discover what arms the Iranians needed and, therefore, which areas were weak. Also, it would facilitate direct contacts with current Iranian Army officers, and it would best serve America's interests to bolster the Iranian Army's spirit by seeing to it that Iran was well supplied and strong enough to win against Iraq, a Communist camp."

Oveissi then said, "It sounds as though you believe the same thing the State Department does. Why do you deny it? Aren't these also your true objectives?"

"Yes," the agent admitted. "These are our objectives, but we have not offered the Iranians arms. The State Department is always in a race with us, so perhaps they offered them."

Oveissi, frustrated and beside himself with anger, shot back, "The international credibility of the United States would be finished if Khomeini were to receive arms. I'm going to write the president and the secretary of state and tell them what the consequences will be!" He held up his fingers and said, "You don't soak your fingers in honey and then put them into someone's mouth who will surely bite them off."

The CIA officer, secure in his role, said offhandedly, "First of all, I shouldn't have told you this and, second of all, I'd never deliver such a letter. But if you ever do send such a letter, the State Department wouldn't hesitate to revoke your political-asylum status and have you and your whole family placed in jeopardy. Those bastards would send you right back to Khomeini."

The next day when I was alone with the same CIA officer, I took the opportunity to speak from my heart. "I want to believe you, but all the evidence seems to indicate that something fishy is going on. I've known you for many years and can read in your eyes that you're not telling us the truth. If I'm right, can you imagine how many Iranians and Iraqis will be killed? This foolish strategy will cripple peace in the Middle East for years. The Saudi Arabians will be furious when they discover that you are arming Khomeini."

He smiled and said, "On that last point you are wrong. The Saudis don't move without waiting for the green light from Washington. If Washington tells the Saudis to give money to Khomeini's opposition, they do it in a flash. If they tell them to buy arms for Khomeini—they do that, too." I stared at him in disbelief. He added, "They *are* the world's best businessmen."

Shocked by his candor, I asked, "How can you allow this to happen when you know that right now there are central terrorist training camps in Iran and that their primary targets are American citizens? How can you arm this crazy man? Look, I have no concrete proof that you plan to give Khomeini arms, but if you do, can you even begin to appreciate the grief this action will bring down on the American people?"

At that he became enraged. "Mansur!" he shouted. "You are not a policymaker and I am not a policymaker. If President Reagan does it, he does it!"

Later, in the winter of 1982, the same CIA officer insisted that I arrange a meeting with General Oveissi in Paris. Oveissi initially refused, saying, "It's a waste of time. They're too busy having a love affair with Khomeini." Then, ruefully, he added, "You know, we've done this all wrong. It seems the best way to deal with the Americans is to abuse them—then they'll help you." But shortly he relented. "Pick a good restaurant," Oveissi said.

When we met the CIA man at a four-star restaurant, where we ordered drinks and Oveissi had his usual glass of orange juice, the general began to act very strangely. "I don't want to talk politics today," he announced immediately. "I want to cry. But a restaurant is not an appropriate place to cry, so I will laugh." Throughout the meal, whenever the CIA man mentioned anything related to politics, Oveissi erupted into boisterous laughter.

The CIA man, unnerved by Oveissi's outbursts, was at a total loss. "Why doesn't he want to talk to me?" he said in consternation. "What's wrong with him?"

I glared at the general. "Say something!" I hissed in Farsi, which the CIA man did not understand.

"No," the general replied furiously. "My answer today is to laugh."

"I am terribly sorry about the way the office has been treating you." The CIA man apologized in English.

General Oveissi laughed uproariously.

The CIA man, quite distressed, tried again. "You must be very hurt and angry about what happened," he said. "We didn't give the names of your network to Khomeini. There are Communists in your group as well as the other opposition groups. How many times have I warned you all? Those Communists reported to Moscow. Moscow supplied them to Khomeini."

Again General Oveissi exploded in laughter. By now everyone in the restaurant was staring at us. Despite the CIA man's desperate attempts to convince General Oveissi that the CIA held him in high esteem, the general's only response was gales of laughter. This went on for more than two hours.

As we left the restaurant, General Oveissi turned to the CIA man and, much to my relief, finally spoke to him in a normal manner. "You are a good friend of mine," he said. "I enjoy seeing you. I hope the next time you are in Paris you will come to see me again."

We got a cab for the CIA man, then the general took my arm and we started walking down the street to his apartment. That was the last contact General Oveissi had with the CIA. Two years later, on February 8, 1984, he and his brother were both assassinated while walking on the same street near their apartment in Paris. I have wondered ever since whether Oveissi was the target of Khomeini or of the CIA.

On April 18, 1983, two months after I severed my services with the CIA, the American embassy in Beirut was bombed and forty-six people were killed and eighty were wounded.

In August 1983 Oveissi told me that arms continued to be shipped to Iran through third countries, with Washington giving the green light. He was outraged. He said, "I'm done with politics. I'm finished. When they play dirty games, they will become its victims and pay the price. Let me give you just one example," he continued. He mentioned the name of a senior CIA officer who had actively supported sending Khomeini arms and who had been killed at the American embassy in Beirut. He then told me that Khomeini, just prior to the explosion, had

sent a substantial amount of money to Shiite Muslims in Beirut specifically to support terrorist activity against American targets.

"Just how involved is he?" I asked, referring to Khomeini. "How
much money did he send?"

"At least one million dollars," he replied. "And I'm sure there will
be more." He hesitated. "Their main target was the embassy but what
will be next? Fate has vindicated me," the general said.

CHAPTER FORTY-FOUR

The Brotherhood of Assassins: From Hasan ibn al-Sabah to Khomeini

In the eleventh century, Persia's secret sect of assassins gave the world a new word for political murder—assassination.

Perhaps some readers are unaware of the origin of the word "assassin" and may think that it derives from French or Latin. It does not. It is of Persian derivation.

Hashashin, or addicts of the drug hashish (hemp), a secret order of religious fanatics, originated in the Isma'ili branch of the Shiite sect. Founded in Iran by Hasan ibn al-Sabah, a Persian Fatamid missionary (died in 1124), the movement was dedicated to propaganda with little regard for spiritual values. Hasan ibn al-Sabah, known to the Crusaders as Shaykh al-Jabal, the "old man of the mountains," was chief of operations. He was aided by two groups of subordinates, the grand priors, and below them, contingents of desperadoes ready to do or die in blind obedience to the command of their chief.

From Alamut, a mountain stronghold in Kazvin in Iran, Hasan presided over a network of terrorists, directing activities and pursuing a policy of secret assassination against the order's enemies. There are many legends about Hasan, one of the most mysterious figures in Persian history. Two stories that best describe his power and charisma involve his conquest of Alamut Castle in A.D. 1090.

The shah, angered by Hasan's bloody rampages, sent one of his most trusted and important envoys to demand that he cease and desist at once or else deal with his wrath. Hasan, who had an enormous network of spies throughout the land, was forewarned and prepared for the envoy's arrival. Hasan, along with his chief of protocol, greeted the shah's envoy with great pomp, but before offering him the customary refreshments suggested that he show him the view from the castle's tower.

Hasan immediately led the envoy to Alamut tower, and no sooner were they on top than Hasan summoned one of his followers and asked him, "How much faith do you have in me?" The man immediately responded, "Your will is my command!" Hasan then told the man to plunge his dagger into his own heart. The envoy was stunned as he watched the man obey without any hesitation and in a flash fall dead at their feet. Without missing a beat, Hasan summoned another man and asked him, "How much do you believe in me?" The man quickly replied, "With all of my soul!" Hasan then signaled him to leap off the parapet. An instant later the man lay dead at the bottom of the tower.

Very calmly Hasan led the trembling envoy to his room. Even though he was still shaking, the envoy couldn't help noticing how plain and unadorned this powerful leader's room was in contrast to the shah's magnificent surroundings. Once they were seated, Hasan spoke in deep, forceful tones, "This is my answer to the message that you were sent to deliver to me. Tell your shah," he continued, "that I have seventy thousand more of the same kind of loyal followers that you saw today!"

One morning shortly thereafter when Sanjar Shah woke up, he was horrified to discover a sword pierced through his pillows and jammed into the floor. A note placed next to the sword read "Your Majesty— if I didn't respect you, the sword would have been pushed into your heart. The same person who is capable of pushing a sword into the hard floor, can easily push it through your soft flesh." It was signed "Hasan." Henceforth, even the king of Persia accepted his vulnerability and lived in fear of Hasan.

The Crusaders returned to Europe bringing with them tales of Hasan's vicious exploits. His men were charged with being responsible for the deaths of many statesmen, including some in Egypt and Syria.

The point for today's history is that Hasan was able to maintain absolute control over his minions because he was a charismatic religious leader who had convinced his followers that all of his enemies were God's enemies and therefore deserved to die. After giving them hashish and delivering powerful rhetoric, he used their blind obedience to rid himself of all his political foes.

From the eleventh through the twentieth centuries, many other Persian religious leaders and kings were able to manipulate their followers, but I can't help noticing that Persian history has unfortunately begun to repeat itself in an extremely curious way.

In 1963 Shah Mohammad Reza Pahlavi sent a secret message through General Hassan Pakravan, then chief of SAVAK, to Ayatollah Khomeini, who was living in Qom, the leading Shiite religious center. The note read "If you don't stop criticizing and agitating against my government, I am going to wear my father's boots [meaning "I am going to resort to my father's repressive methods"]."

Khomeini, a brilliant dramatic orator, didn't answer immediately, but waited until after he had gone to the mosque later that day. There he repeated the shah's message and then, in his most scathing manner, replied, "My answer to him is—your father's boots are too big for you!"

The next day, on June 5, 1963, Tehran was shaken by huge riots in which hundreds of people were killed. The shah reacted by having Khomeini jailed and then exiled to Turkey. Over the next years, Khomeini would be forced into a lengthy exile that would take him from Turkey to Iraq and from Iraq to Paris. He refused to return to Iran until the shah had left the country. He made his triumphant return to Tehran in 1979.

There are many similarities between Khomeini and Hasan. Like his prototype, Khomeini lives modestly in a humble room, where, in a country famous for luxurious carpets, he sleeps on a shabby rug and eats peasant food; like his famous forebear, he hides behind the banner of religion, labels all of his opponents God's enemies, and uses his believers to destroy them; like Hasan, Khomeini is a crafty and charismatic orator capable of swaying vast crowds.

While Hasan fortified his believers before battle with hashish, Khomeini uses just a gimmick. He issues them special "keys to heaven" —key-shaped plastic medallions that have been blessed by him and inscribed with Allah's name. Whoever martyrs himself for Khomeini while wearing his "key" is guaranteed entrance to heaven and welcomed into Allah's arms. Iran's mullahs, Shiite Muslim clerics, extol martyrdom, promising direct entry into paradise to all the fallen. Khomeini's believers, wearing their keys around their necks, fearlessly attempt the most suicidal missions. Children without proper weapons are routinely sent off to war against Iraq wearing the keys and shirts proclaiming GOD IS GREAT as their only protection.

Khomeini has a perfect sense of theater and uses it shrewdly. Before speaking to a large crowd, he will often stand silently with an outstretched hand for a few minutes. Then he will suddenly reach out and touch one of his disciples, who in turn will touch the person next to him, who in turn will touch the next one, and the chain is continued until everyone present has been touched. The entire mob becomes charged with excitement as if an electric current had surged through it. The people really feel as if they had been touched by Khomeini himself, and, therefore, touched by God.

When drama alone isn't enough to manipulate his followers, Khomeini stoops to outright trickery and deception.

Many thousands of boys went to war and died wearing Khomeini's keys. As a result, the government's casualty stipend that went to their families was creating a drain on the national treasury. In order to meliorate this economic problem, a clergyman, with great fanfare, announced that he had had a dream about the young martyrs. He vividly described how happy the kids were in heaven, but how embarrassed they were that their families had been paid for their ecstasy. Many parents were so moved by the mullah's subterfuge that they returned the money to the government.

Another example of Khomeini's trickery, how he plays on people's superstitions, was his resort to the "angel of the battlefield." After an especially horrible battle, in which thousands of boys were left dead or maimed and awaiting medical attention, a helicopter secretly landed a well-trained actor wearing flowing white robes and a turban ingeniously wired with lights and batteries to create a halo effect around his head. Thus illuminated, he crossed the field of battle and, in resonant tones, exhorted the wounded to continue their privileged mission. "My children," he declared, "we sent you Khomeini to bring you to Islam. You are God's servants and will go to heaven. All who die here will go to heaven, and roses and tulips will spring up from this earth."

In sophisticated Western countries like the United States and France, there are often stories about religious paintings that cry real tears, and of statues with stigmata, so it is easy to understand why weary, uneducated Iranian boys are so willing to accept religious myths.

Khomeini always gave the appearance of rewarding his loyal followers. He often held special gatherings for young men who had returned crippled from war, and he proudly spoke to them: "Some of our brothers are lucky—they are already in heaven. Some like you are luckier, you have seen the 'angel of God,' and brought the message back. I was moved when I heard it, but I send a special message to the women of Iran. Sisters, you will be blessed if you marry these men."

Subsequently, many of these unfortunate wretches, some of whom could not perform their husbandly duty, acquired several wives to care for them, and therefore didn't need to live in state-funded rehabilitation centers.

In these and similar ways, Khomeini created an arsenal of human weapons and used them against anyone who opposed him. He even disposed of enemies by sending men into mosques with TNT strapped to their bodies—in effect, walking bombs.

Above all, Khomeini constantly rallied his people to destroy God's worst enemy, America—at any cost. Over the years he targeted many enemies, but his favorite target was always the United States. The United States was synonymous with evil, and in his tirades he liked to demonstrate just how evil, by pointing out the many instances of God's wrath against the United States and, in contrast, how God had always supported him.

Had not God after all chased the evil shah out of the palace in spite of American support? During the aborted rescue mission, had He not made the red sand rise up from the desert and destroy the American helicopters? And hadn't the evil Jimmy Carter lost his election? Khomeini constantly reinforced the notion that his wishes were identical with God's, and therefore he, representing goodness, had to triumph over evil America at any cost.

Because of Khomeini's determination to shatter America's image and knowing that Beirut was filled with Shiite extremists financed by him, I realized that the American embassy in Beirut was an obvious terrorist target and tried to warn the CIA. The agents dismissed the idea. "Don't be silly," they said. "We have barricades, platoons of guards, radio control. It's impossible to penetrate. You give Khomeini too much credit." They refused to believe me. We continued to argue back and forth. I was adamant. "You don't understand," I said. "They don't care about their lives. They don't mind dying. They'll do it." Finally, in desperation, I told them another cautionary tale. They were relieved that I was going to amuse them. At least they could eat and drink.

"A man came out of his house one day dressed for hunting, carrying his gun, wearing a cartridge belt with extra ammunition, carrying food and water. He was well equipped. His neighbor came out and asked, 'Where are you going?'
'Lion hunting.'
'Oh? How much ammunition do you have?'
'Fifty or sixty rounds.'
'What will you do when you see a lion?'
'Shoot it.'

'What if two come at you from the same direction?'

'Kill them both.'

'What if you are then attacked by two coming from the left and two from the right at the same time?'

'I'll climb a tree.'

'What if there is a lion guarding the base of the tree?'

'I'll shoot it, and then climb the tree.'

'What if more come and climb atop the body to reach you?'

'I'll shoot them, too.'

'And if you run out of ammunition?'

'I'll use my bayonet to kill them.'

'And if it bends?'

'What! Why are you giving me such a hard time? Whose side are you on—the lion's or mine?' "

They laughed, but they did not see how the story applied to them.

Then, on April 18, 1983, a dozen men, wired with explosives and mesmerized by their fanaticism, shot their way through the embassy's checkpoints, stormed the compound buildings, and blew up both the buildings and themselves.

On October 23, 1983, as if one horrible lesson in Beirut was not enough, the CIA tragically learned that it had underestimated the enemy again. The barracks near Beirut's airport that had become home to several hundred U.S. Marines, Ronald Reagan's token of earnestness to the status quo in war-torn Lebanon, and which the CIA had believed to be even more secure than the embassy, was blown up and 253 Americans were killed and 75 were wounded. The terrorists had used an almost identical *modus operandi:* Young guerrillas in a truck loaded with explosives penetrated the checkpoints and, smiling triumphantly, hit the target.

I was baffled by American behavior even though I understood they wanted to keep religious fundamentalists ("Green Belts") in power against communism. "How could [you] give arms to this maniac, Khomeini?" I asked. "When you arm Khomeini," I told the CIA, "you are not just arming Iran against Iraq or American citizens, you are arming him against humanity."

From 1982 to 1986, the United States' behavior toward Iran became extremely schizoid. The Reagan administration was supplying Iraq with anti-Khomeini intelligence and demanding that the FBI arrest anyone in the United States discovered selling arms to Iran. Simultaneously, the government was covertly arming Khomeini's regime. In addition, it was supplying these arms knowing that Khomeini was developing sophisticated terrorist training camps throughout Iran.

In this instance, as in others I know of, the CIA always blamed incompetence on other countries but never did it admit to its own. Whenever the Agency's competence was questioned, or when it was confronted with defeat, it hid behind an elaborate smokescreen by saying it couldn't give further information because of national security.

The CIA's past was filled with anomalies. Had the CIA foreseen that the shah would fall? It did not: In 1978 the CIA's Department of Analysis predicted that the shah would stay in power another twenty years. The CIA was so consistently ineffective that it could not protect William Buckley, its own station chief in Beirut, who was kidnapped on March 16, 1984, by Shiite extremists and later murdered.

William Buckley was subjected to unbelievable torture and untold agony for many months. He was forced to tell everything he knew about the CIA, its structure and operation. One of the instruments of torture they used was an electric samovar. The samovar was bound by a belt across the small of his back. When he refused to talk, they heated the samovar and when he began to talk, they would remove it. There was no way Buckley could keep from speaking. His photograph, which was periodically distributed at various intervals during his captivity, is the portrait of a man in hell.

One of his tormentors reported to Khomeini that after a prolonged session with the samovar, Buckley was thrown into a dark, dank basement where he was left whimpering in pain to die alone like an animal. It took two and a half days.

Buckley was a direct victim of CIA misjudgment and incompetence. This raises important security questions. As chief of station, Buckley was in charge of other CIA agents, who worked under him as case officers, code experts, and otherwise. But far more significant was the fact that he knew the names of all the Lebanese agents and spies, and he knew the identities of his colleagues throughout the Middle East. In addition to knowing their identities, he was also privy to their policies, needs, and goals, and to the CIA's chief objectives in the Middle East.

When a man in Buckley's position is kidnapped, tortured, and then dies, one can only imagine how much information may have fallen into enemy hands. If the press had been responsible for leaking even a small part of what this man undoubtedly was forced to tell, it would have been pilloried for a breach of security of such enormous proportions that anyone connected with the disclosure would have gone to jail. This episode was especially humiliating for the CIA because, after all the major inroads the agents had claimed to have made into the Khomeini regime with arms sales, they were unable to secure Buckley's release.

In September 1981, eight months after the American hostages were freed in Tehran, William J. Casey, the director of the CIA, met with President Reagan and proposed selling arms to Iran. The reasons Casey gave were that this would enable the United States to gather intelligence inside of Iran, to initiate contact with the Iranian Army, and to discover Iran's military deficiencies.

It was at the same meeting that Casey also proposed the plan that would later bring General Oveissi and me such personal grief. Casey would fund the opposition groups in exile and determine their capabilities. He would request the names of their network members in Iran and offer this information to Khomeini in order to instigate a relationship. President Reagan agreed and signed an executive order in September 1981. Thereafter, the arms were taken from Israel's stockpile, sent to Iran, and later replaced by the United States.

But in spite of this, Reagan failed to make any inroads with fundamentalist Iran. By 1984 there were new hostages in Beirut.

In 1985, when Reagan was savoring his election to a second term and enjoying the height of his popularity, he turned again to his friends in the CIA. President Reagan, with his White House cronies Meese, Bush, Casey, and McFarlane, decided to take a more direct approach. They bypassed the House and the Senate and, trusting the CIA, offered Khomeini a more straightforward deal—arms for hostages. Reagan's stance, however, for the benefit of the American public was quite different from his secret position.

In his January 20, 1981, inauguration speech, he stated:

Let terrorists beware that when the rules of international behavior are violated, our policies will be one of swift and effective retribution. We hear it said we live in an era of limit to our powers. Well, let it be understood, there are limits to our patience.

Throughout the 1981 to 1986 negotiations with Khomeini, and from 1985 to 1986 during the arms-hostage negotiations, the White House never sought Middle Eastern advice from America's vast pool of scholars and political strategists, nor did it go to the State Department. Secretary of State George P. Shultz was kept unaware of Reagan's secret negotiations, but his department was dragged unwittingly into the scheme because the CIA never represented itself to Iran as such. Instead, the agents masqueraded as officers of the State Department throughout their dealings with the Iranians.

In December 1986, at the public congressional hearings, Shultz disclosed that the United States ambassador to Lebanon, John Kelly, had bypassed the secretary of state to conduct negotiations for the release of American hostages in Beirut. Ambassador Kelly had reported only to the White House through a CIA channel—namely, George Cave, his CIA contact, who reported to Chief of Staff Donald Regan.

CHAPTER FORTY-FIVE

Unholy Deals

On December 12, 1983, members of the Iranian Hezbollah (Party of God), Khomeini's only official political party in Iran, followed a familiar pattern. They piled one-quarter ton of explosives into a truck and crashed into the United States embassy compound in Kuwait. Shortly thereafter, five other bombs also exploded at United States, French, and Kuwaiti targets around the city. In all, six people were killed and sixty-three were wounded. Seventeen Shiites were arrested and put in Kuwaiti prisons.

Khomeini was frustrated by his inability to obtain their release, but instead of retaliating directly against the Kuwaitis, who were Muslim, he decided to take seventeen hostages from the international community. The initial plan was to use these hostages to obtain the freedom of the seventeen Shiite terrorists, but that was never accomplished.

Since 1984 Khomeini has never allowed the number of his hostages kept in Beirut to fall below seventeen. A careful examination of how many hostages have been taken would show that although sometimes there have been more than seventeen at one time, there have never been less than seventeen. Periodically, the Khomeini government would barter one or more of the hostages for arms, but it would always make sure additional people were immediately taken as replacements. It is no coincidence that in June 1985, when a TWA plane was hijacked to Beirut, the hijackers made sure that they held their captives for exactly seventeen days. After seventeen days, the terrorists released their hostages; they never meant to keep them longer. By releasing them exactly after seventeen days, they were sending a hopeful message to the Shiite terrorists' inner circles in Iran and Lebanon, and especially to the seventeen prisoners in Kuwait, that they were not forgotten.

The most shocking thing about this whole episode is that the CIA, the head of an entire intelligence community of some 100,000 individuals, and with a billion-dollar budget, failed to discover this correlation. It is the CIA's function to gather reliable intelligence and offer it as an aid to America's policymakers. If the CIA had been diligent and discovered Khomeini's true motives for taking hostages after March 1984, perhaps President Reagan might have chosen to take a different direction in his negotiations.

In 1985, because new American hostages had been taken in Beirut, President Reagan again turned to his trusted friends in the CIA. William Casey continued to present the CIA's case to the president's closest White House aides. They were the only ones privy to the proposed Iranian strategy. These included Chief of Staff Donald Regan, Vice-President George Bush, Attorney General Edwin Meese III, and the head of the National Security Council, Robert C. McFarlane. The bulk of the cadre was made up of retired men such as former CIA officer George Cave and retired Air Force Major General Richard V. Secord.

The reason ex-officials were in the cadre was that in the event of disclosure, the administration would be able to say that these men were not currently in the employ of the United States government. In this manner, the White House would be able to conduct foreign policy privately. With no official standing, this team answered to no one but President Reagan, Donald Regan, and William Casey.

Donald Regan personally briefed President Reagan regularly and brought the other members of the cadre to see him frequently. This was very unusual because the group was composed of members of the lower echelons of government, and Regan, therefore, was bypassing their superiors by arranging direct access to the president. This unorthodox procedure enabled the cadre to tell the Iranians, "We have direct contact with the president."

In essence, the Reagan/Bush/Regan/Casey cadre had carte blanche to use government services and operational money without restraint. These men were entrusted with setting up secret negotiations with Iran in order to provide that country with arms in its war with Iraq. This way it was hoped to establish a dialogue and position of trust with Iran, and thereby to negotiate release of the hostages in Beirut.

From January 1985 through the summer, the president's cadre

sought intermediary links to Khomeini's command, among them several known arms dealers who claimed to be well connected to the Khomeini government. Up to this time the CIA had very few, if any, useful contacts with members of Khomeini's regime.

In July 1985 McFarlane discussed with President Reagan the sale of weapons to Iran through arms dealers in exchange for the release of American hostages. The president's cadre was faced with a dilemma. Each of these dealers had sold arms to Iran in the past. Each claimed to have connections with the most powerful people in the regime.

In 1980 Manucher Ghorbanifar, an Iranian arms dealer, had approached the CIA claiming that he could buy the fifty-two hostages' freedom. The CIA contacted me to establish his credibility. I knew Ghorbanifar and believed him to be bad news. In Persian Ghorbanifar means "glorious sacrifice," and I firmly advised them, "As his name implies, Ghorbanifar would sacrifice anything for money. Stay away from him!"

In 1985, in spite of earlier warnings from other sources as well as from me, Ghorbanifar was selected. He and his group promised the cadre that they would be put in touch with authorities in Khomeini's regime.

Who were these authorities? They were high government officials and businessmen, Ghorbanifar assured the cadre.

At a meeting in the summer of 1985 with the president's cadre, Ghorbanifar's group arrogantly pointed out that since 1980 the United States' efforts to negotiate with Iran, directly and indirectly, through Middle Eastern and European countries as well as through Japanese and Chinese channels, had proved futile. The CIA officers were indignant and interpreted these remarks as an assault on their competence.

The dealers then offered to demonstrate their credibility. They would provide the most powerful and influential members of the revolutionary government, as opposed to the ineffectual underlings the CIA had dealt with previously, to meet with the cadre in several European capitals.

The CIA representatives said sarcastically, "Then do it!"

Subsequently, in London and other European capitals, several dozen Iranian officials and businessmen were lavishly entertained at the arms dealers' expense.

How did the death merchants effect these informal negotiations? At the outset, they contacted influential friends in Tehran, many of them mullahs in Khomeini's theocratic regime, and suggested that they plead illness or other personal reasons for going to Europe. This all-expenses-paid holiday to Europe was a welcome respite from the austerities of the Khomeini era. Thereafter, some mullahs dressed in flowing robes were observed departing Tehran aboard an intercontinental jet, and, later still, arriving in Europe dressed in well-tailored suits, bereft of any hint of their fundamentalist religious vocation.

There they were pampered by the arms dealers, at first spending a few nights with high-priced prostitutes and enjoying themselves. After all, there was nothing wrong with buying non-Muslim women with non-Muslim money. One of the clergymen even asked if the girl he was with had a brother. Instantly, a boy was presented for his pleasure.

Meanwhile, the mullahs and other Khomeini allies had been coached by their friends, the arms dealers, on how to behave. They were to indicate to the cadre's representatives that they had overriding influence with the Khomeini regime. They were to make promises of cooperation with the Reagan administration and also make it "crystal clear" that they were doing this out of friendship with Ghorbanifar and would work only through him.

For several months these negotiations and indulgences went on, solely to effect a connection between Washington and Tehran. Bit by bit, the door seemed to open. But this apparent success became the source of endless bickering among the various cadre members. The CIA representative, George Cave, took credit for the CIA, the NSC representative, Robert McFarlane, took credit for the White House, and on top of it all, the military hero of the piece, a young marine lieutenant colonel, Oliver L. North, an NSC member, took credit for himself. Even Ghorbanifar took credit. But where was the proof of their success? Finally, who was going to bell the cat and travel to Tehran?

Notwithstanding advice from all members of the cadre that no one should go to Tehran alone, for fear of being taken hostage, Colonel North volunteered to travel solo to Tehran. In December 1985 he flew there with Ghorbanifar and was received with great hospitality by his new friends, his companions at the arms dealers' European parties. For several days he was introduced to important people in the Khomeini government. Indeed, so earnest were his friends' efforts to make him happy and comfortable that specially prepared Western-style foods were served to him in his personal suite at the former Tehran Hilton.

And on his safe return—everyone being relieved that he had not been taken hostage on his unauthorized mission—Colonel North reported directly to the president.

The president, Chief of Staff Donald Regan, and William Casey received North at the White House, where the colonel had an office. They were delighted with North's account of his progress. Nothing loath to accept the plaudits due him, Colonel North pointed out that up to this time the administration had negotiated with the Khomeini regime only through third countries, and with unsatisfactory results, yet this mission, the first direct one with Tehran since 1980, had been a signal success.

Colonel North was smug about his success and frequently bragged to his new Iranian friends and other cadre members about how highly President Reagan regarded him. It was reported to me that North went so far as to tell the Iranian contacts, who knew the CIA did not like him and feared its interference, not to worry because he could go see the president anytime he wanted. To my knowledge North met privately with President Reagan at least nineteen times. North's arrogant attitude left him open to CIA jealousy and hostility.

Several additional solo trips were made by Colonel North and Ghorbanifar. Acting on North's intelligence, without further consultation, the president and all the members of his cadre decided to deal directly with the Khomeini regime through Ghorbanifar and eliminate third-country intermediaries.

Although numerous shipments, including 508 TOW antitank missiles, had been shipped from Israel's stockpile to Tehran, only one hostage, the Reverend Benjamin Weir, was released on September 14, 1985. The Iranians always contended that the shipments were incorrect, incomplete, or composed of inferior materials. Complying with their requirements, the United States tried to rectify the problems by correcting the inaccuracies.

On December 4, 1985, Robert C. McFarlane resigned from his post as head of the National Security Council, and was succeeded by Vice-Admiral John M. Poindexter.

McFarlane immediately became the president's secret representative in the arms deals, now ensuring, since McFarlane was no longer an official of the Reagan administration, the privatization of this mission.

On December 8, in his new role, McFarlane traveled to London with Colonel North and delivered the last order to the intermediaries brokering weapons sales to Iran. He announced to David Kimche, the director general of Israel's Foreign Ministry, Manucher Ghorbanifar, and Yaacov Nimrodi, an Israeli arms dealer, that "by presidential decree, the weapons shipments are finished." With this untrue statement, McFarlane eliminated Israel and Ghorbanifar from the arms deals, thereby clearing the way for private negotiations between the White House and Khomeini's regime.

Later in December, Amiram Nir, an Israeli government counterterrorist expert, went to Washington and said, "The Iranians had sweetened the terms. Just one more shipment and they would release the five hostages in Lebanon and open ties to moderates in Tehran."

By January 1986 the National Security Council was composed mostly of military men. The CIA was constantly looking for flaws in their operations and had never trusted Ghorbanifar. When the entire cadre, along with Ghorbanifar, came to Washington in January to discuss and evaluate the Iranian situation, a senior CIA officer insisted that Ghorbanifar take a polygraph test. Ghorbanifar submitted to the test but failed. The CIA reported, "He lied about everything but his name."

Anxious to make North look bad and get rid of Ghorbanifar once and for all, the CIA informed Casey that Ghorbanifar had failed the polygraph test. Casey told the president of the test results and its possible ramifications. He warned the president that "Ghorbanifar's information could be a deception to impress us." According to intelligence regulations, anyone who fails this test can no longer be considered suitable to serve in the intelligence community. At the same time, North had promised Ghorbanifar that he would go to the president and bail him out. The end result was that the president told Casey to waive the results. This further infuriated the CIA.

On January 7, 1986, President Reagan met in the Oval Office with Bush, Shultz, Weinberger, Casey, Regan, Meese, and Poindexter. Shultz and Weinberger argued strongly against selling arms to Iran, but Casey and Poindexter argued in favor of resuming the program with direct arms shipments. The president decided to keep the channels open.

On January 17, 1986, at the urging of Vice-President George Bush, Casey, and Poindexter, President Reagan signed a secret intelligence "Finding"[16] that authorized the United States to sell arms directly to Iran. This document was designed to legitimize retroactively previous arms shipments. The president's executive order for an intelligence Finding only authorized the CIA to engage in that particular covert action. Therefore, any National Security Council involvement was illegal. However, the NSC not only played a major role in the Iran initiative, it also usurped the CIA's power. In reality, the cadre, headed by Donald Regan, was running this operation and keeping Shultz and Weinberger in the dark.

Later in January in London, the president's men informed their Iranian contacts of the president's decision to sell arms directly to Iran. These direct shipments, although having been approved by executive order, were still to be made in the utmost secrecy because Congress had not been informed. The cadre representatives briefed Ghorbanifar and his associates about the executive order, and demanded their assurances that this information would be known only to them. Their reason: Communists were all over—in the Senate, in the House, in the press. The group insisted that if word got out, the whole deal would be damaged. And they added a warning to the Iranian contacts—if they leaked the information they would kill them.

When Khomeini was told the story of "Communists all over . . .," he said mockingly, "So that's how a real democracy works!" He then instructed his government: "Get the arms, we will defeat Iraq and then we'll chase the Americans out of the Middle East with their own weapons." He also instructed his aides to release hostages in return for the arms. "But," he added, "take two new hostages for every one released."

In the first direct shipment of weapons on February 16, 1986, to Iran, the Pentagon transferred one thousand TOW antitank missiles, more than the United States' entire yearly production. The CIA flew them to Tel Aviv, and the Israelis flew them to Tehran.

In Tehran meanwhile, cadre representatives, in return for promises of friendlier relations, agreed to furnish Khomeini additional sophisticated American arms to use in Iran's long war with Iraq. This was done at a time when the United States was providing satellite spy intelligence to Iraq concerning the military movements of Iran.

By 1986 the Americans had worn a path to Prime Minister Mir Hossein Mousavi's door and were now involved in direct negotiations with the Iranian government. They believed that they were making inroads by telling Prime Minister Mousavi that America was prepared to recognize the Islamic Republic of Iran, and that the United States was not going to interfere with Iran's internal affairs. The White House cadre representatives kept trying to reassure the prime minister that all President Reagan was interested in was aiding the Iranian government in its war with Iraq and protecting it from communism.

A secondary purpose of these contacts, later much publicized, was to establish better communications between Washington and moderate elements in Tehran, the better to facilitate friendly relations between the two countries in the event of Khomeini's demise or downfall. But in fact, not one of the factions contacted was moderate.

In addition to negotiations with the office of the prime minister, Robert McFarlane, Lieutenant Colonel Oliver North, and George Cave with Ghorbanifar, helped develop a contingency plan. Ghorbanifar was responsible for initiating contact with Ayatollah H. A. Montazeri's faction. Montazeri, a supposed moderate, is Khomeini's second-in-command and heir apparent, by the will of the Supreme Jurist, Khomeini, who has been mandated to rule not only Iran and Muslims but the whole world.

In several meetings inside and outside Iran, the administration emissaries assured Montazeri's aides that they would approve of his succession because of his popularity and powerful position, and they wanted to be friends. They promised that the United States would recognize his government and continue to support it directly with money and arms. They explained that the United States had no choice but to do so, as at that point Iran would be bankrupt and still mired in an endless war with Iraq.

The individual members of the cadre emphasized that America was most concerned about Iran's precarious borders. At one point, they even went so far as to feed the Iranians deliberate misinformation about Soviet intelligence, saying that the Soviets had imminent plans to invade Iran. Above all, they approved of Montazeri as Iran's best defense against Communist subversion.

When all of the cajoling and friendly overtures ended, the administration representatives got down to their real motives, and said, "This is what our president wants. We have proven our sincerity. You have received the arms. Now prove your sincerity—free the remaining hostages!"

In return, Montazeri's aides, with some members of the cadre as well as Ghorbanifar, expressed friendship toward America and its president. They also appealed to President Reagan for emergency assistance for the nation's leading theological school in Qom, which they described as a vital bastion against internal communism. This assistance was paid over on the spot by Ghorbanifar.

At this level, the cadre assumed that Prime Minister Mousavi, always loyal to Khomeini, was keeping him informed about what was transpiring between the two nations. But the members of the cadre miscalculated their relationship with Montazeri when they told him to keep *their* contact with him secret.

Montazeri, Khomeini's heir apparent, was not going to risk his standing and play with fire. Knowing that the Israelis were helping the United States in efforts to release the hostages, he said to an aide,

"When a cake is baked by America and decorated by Israel—I'm certainly not going to eat it!" Montazeri did not hesitate to report all of his dealings with the president's secret group to Khomeini.

During this same period, the CIA members of the cadre, led by George Cave, privately wanted to oust Ghorbanifar and overshadow North. They told their fellow members that they should not take any chances by supporting only Montazeri, but pursue another powerful Iranian leader as well—Speaker of the House A. H. Rafsanjani. Even though there was some dissension among them over the issue, George Cave went ahead with this plan. The CIA immediately began to negotiate with Rafsanjani's aides, and through them, made what they believed to be great headway with none other than Rafsanjani's son, Mehdi.

The CIA assured Rafsanjani that the United States government regarded him as the best possible successor to Khomeini. They also advised him that they would seek to develop Rafsanjani as a hero to the Iranian people in their struggle with Iraq. They would do so by providing American arms to win the war against Iraq. Rafsanjani's son was invited to Washington, where he was promised that the United States would send Iran an additional five hundred TOW missiles.

The idea was for the Americans to capitalize on their knowledge that Rafsanjani wanted to usurp Montazeri's position. They assured Rafsanjani that they would do everything in their power to get rid of Montazeri.

Rafsanjani shrewdly mistrusted the CIA cadre's intentions and dutifully reported all of their meetings to Khomeini. Khomeini, always the master puppeteer, didn't tell Rafsanjani that Montazeri had also been in touch with the Americans and, conversely, he didn't inform Montazeri that Rafsanjani had also had meetings with the Americans. When my source told me this, I knew Khomeini was playing a Persian game.

In April 1986 the president's secret emissaries, with Ghorbanifar's help, began what they believed to be successful negotiations directly with the Iranian government. On May 15, 1986, President Reagan approved a mission to Iran, sending his representative, Robert McFarlane, to get four hostages released and bring William Buckley's body home. But the Iranians did not go along with the release of all four hostages at once. They proposed that when the United States sent them the sophisticated arms they had requested, they would then release two hostages. If these arms were satisfactory, they would renegotiate for the remaining two hostages and Buckley's body.

McFarlane and Ghorbanifar agreed. Before heading for Tehran,

McFarlane had asked Ghorbanifar to guarantee that two of the hostages be released shortly after they landed. He felt this would give the Iranians ample time to check the arms that McFarlane's airplane carried. Meanwhile, CIA representative George Cave, who spoke a little Persian, made a secret call to Prime Minister Mousavi from the United States. In a coded conversation in Persian, Cave told him, "I am calling from the bank and the president sends his regards. We will be happy if you send us one promissory note right away." George Cave had deliberately undermined McFarlane and Ghorbanifar's deal calling for *two* hostages. At this point Ghorbanifar's relations with Mousavi began to deteriorate.

The prime minister called Ghorbanifar in a rage. "Now I want you to tell me," he screamed, "what are you trying to pull? The Americans want one hostage released and you want two. Aren't you tired of suckering up to them?"

On July 8, 1986, President Reagan said:

There can be no place on earth left where it is safe for these monsters to rest, or train, or practice their cruel and deadly skills. We must act together or unilaterally if necessary to insure that terrorists have no sanctuary anywhere.

On May 23, 1986, only forty-six days before this statement was made, McFarlane, North, and other members of the presidential cadre boarded a plane loaded with spare parts for Hawk antiaircraft-missile batteries, and took off for Tehran—the world's primary sanctuary for international terrorism. This was destined to become a history-making journey.

In addition to a cargo of sophisticated weapons, they brought with them special presents from President Reagan destined for Khomeini—a cake, a verse, a verbal message, an autographed Bible, and two Colt pistols. The cake was not only decorated with a chocolate key, an exact replica of the key-shaped medallions that Khomeini's men wear into battle, but it was also meant to represent the American government's desire to open up the door for direct negotiation with Iran. The verbal message from President Reagan stated that he swore on the enclosed Bible that he should be trusted, that the United States now understood how genuine the revolution was, and how eagerly we sought the Iranian people's friendship.

The verses from the Koran were from Sura Jumu'a LXII:

Verse 6.

Say: "O ye that
Stand on Judaism!
If ye think that ye
Are friends to God,
To the exclusion of
[Other] men, then express
Your desire for Death,
If ye are truthful!"

Verse 7.

But never will they
Express their desire
[For Death], because of
The [deeds] their hands
Have sent on before them!
And God knows well
Those that do wrong!

The Iranian officials who received this odd assortment of gifts sent on behalf of the president of the United States were taken aback by what they could only interpret as his insensitivity or stupidity.

The autographed Bible was considered most offensive by the Muslims, who viewed the defacing of a holy book (be it the Old Testament, the New Testament, or the Torah, etc.) as sacrilegious. And because Persian literature had always portrayed Jesus as a prophet who advocated "the turning of the other cheek" and nonviolence, they were baffled by the contradiction of a Christian president sending both a Bible and Colt pistols. But they felt the most ludicrous aspect of these gifts was the selection of verses from the Koran that admonished the Jews for calling themselves chosen to the exclusion of other men. How could the White House send this quotation as a message to Khomeini and simultaneously honor U.S. friendship with Israel? The end result of the cadre's "gift bearing" was that Iranian officials now believed that President Reagan was either a fool or trying to fool them.

Instead of using their own identities and nationalities, the president's men traveled with Irish passports created by the Forging Office of the CIA. For instance, the forged passport of Robert C. McFarlane showed he had been traveling under the name of Sean Devlin. If these men were truly attempting to open the door for direct Iranian-American negotiations, why did they fear using their own passports? It seems as if almost all of their behavior was unique. It is possibly the first time in American history that representatives of the president of the United States have gone on a mission using illegal passports without the knowledge of the State Department or Congress.

Upon their arrival in Tehran, McFarlane, North, Cave, and the rest went to their suites on the fifteenth floor of the former Tehran Hilton. McFarlane began to listen to his radio for news of the freed hostages. Since there was no announcement, he believed that the Iranians might have needed more time to check the weapons. He kept listening, but no news of their release was reported.

"What am I supposed to tell President Reagan?" McFarlane queried. "Two hostages were supposed to be released the minute we landed."

Ghorbanifar's men replied, "Don't get so excited. Wait a little longer. Don't get your blood pressure up. They need time to check the arms!"

McFarlane said loudly, "I have explicit instructions from the president that if the four hostages and William Buckley's body are not released, we are to leave immediately."

(The Khomeini government had taken advantage of the extremely elaborate surveillance equipment that the shah installed throughout the fifteenth floor of the hotel. Every room was bugged.)

After realizing their mission had failed and believing the suite was bugged, the Americans went out on the balcony—which, unbeknownst to them, was also bugged—and commiserated with one another. McFarlane, very upset, was still listening to the radio in the futile hope that the other hostages would be released. North was weeping. Cave was philosophical. He said, "I don't need this. I have money in the stock market."

After the Americans had cooled their heels in Tehran for four and a half days, McFarlane was furious. He stated that they had delivered the arms, brought the cake and other symbols of America's good intentions; they had been promised the release of at least two hostages upon delivery of the arms. So, since the hostages hadn't been freed, they were leaving immediately.

The president's emissaries took off on an empty plane. They couldn't very well demand the return of their arms delivery because the

Iranians had already unloaded the plane; but they did leave behind a hefty telephone tab at the hotel amounting to $4,800. When the Iranian government was informed of this, they said, "Don't worry. They'll be back."

The primary reason they had made this trip was to ensure the hostages' release before the November 1986 election. McFarlane didn't realize that the hostages' fate was controlled only by Khomeini, who would never permit the number of people taken to fall below seventeen.

In addition to continuing the courtship of the Khomeini-Montazeri groups from May 1986 to October 1986, the president's men intensified their concentration on wooing Rafsanjani through his son, Mehdi. They briefed Mehdi's and Rafsanjani's aides about attempts made by an Iranian-Soviet network to prevent Rafsanjani from gaining leadership. They told them about the United States' plans to do everything possible to squelch the Soviets' efforts and make Rafsanjani Khomeini's successor. In return for its support, America wanted only the hostages' freedom.

In their desire to keep the channels open for additional arms shipments, the Iranians released the Reverend Lawrence Martin Jenco, a Roman Catholic priest, on July 26, 1986. He had been held captive for more than eighteen months.

Between July 1986 and October 1986, Cave and McFarlane continued to negotiate with Rafsanjani for the rest of the hostages' freedom. In return, the Americans assured Rafsanjani that a final shipment of five hundred TOW antitank missiles would be sent to the government of Iran. They also reiterated their pleas that all of the hostages be released before the November 1986 election. "It means a lot to the president," they said.

A shipment of arms was sent on October 29, the last to go via Israel; and immediately after that, another hostage, David Jacobsen, was released. However, the American government, in a futile hope that it would be able to announce the freedom of all the hostages, delayed making Jacobsen's release public for five days until November 2. When word leaked out that he had been freed earlier, the White House said it had held back the news for "security reasons."

In the summer of 1986, George Cave and his CIA colleagues decided to terminate Ghorbanifar's services and negotiate future arms contracts directly with the Iranian government. In this way they could get even with Ghorbanifar, who had slighted them and tarnished the CIA's image. In spite of vehement opposition from Colonel North and from Ghorbanifar himself, who had been principally responsible for the negotiations with Ayatollah Montazeri, the CIA representatives informed A. H. Rafsanjani, speaker of the house, that Ghorbanifar was out.

By this time, of course, the CIA men had placed themselves in opposition to North, whom they had regarded all along as a self-serving soldier of fortune. In particular, they resented North's direct access to President Reagan, who in fact eventually pronounced Lieutenant Colonel North "our national hero."

Washington, deep down, wanted to help Montazeri. The CIA representatives of the cadre were not specifically opposed to Montazeri, but they were opposed to Colonel North, Montazeri's man. And as the consensus in Washington formed around Montazeri, the CIA members decided to torpedo the negotiations rather than see North get the credit. In order to do so, they counseled dismissing Ghorbanifar with whom North had worked so closely and apparently successfully, charging that Ghorbanifar had been a double agent.

In the fall of 1986, everyone was happy. Montazeri and Rafsanjani each had a piece of the arms deal, the arms dealers continued to do a brisk business, the other members of the presidential cadre, as well as the Iranians involved, were all receiving money under the table, and the president's men were stashing funds in numerous secret accounts in Switzerland, Ireland, and other countries. Money was the lubricant that kept it all in motion and there was plenty of it.

In August 1986, while I was trying to extricate myself from CIA and Justice Department harassment, a source reported to me that the rumor mills in Iranian government circles were buzzing and churning out story after story about the arms dealings. So many different astronomical numbers were being bandied about—thousands of millions of dollars—that they had become meaningless—this Swiss bank account, that Swiss bank, secret missions!

My curiosity aroused, I asked, "What are these rumors?"

He answered, "This White House secret mission to Iran has turned into an octopus. Rumor is, the arms dealers have been grossly overcharging the Iranian government and the dealers are claiming that the United States government is marking up the arms to begin with." He elaborated. "Those fools in the White House are funneling these profits to the contras in Central America and the Republican campaign fund."

I said to him, "At least the money didn't wind up in their pockets." "Who knows?" my source said. "Of all the money that the Saudi government and the other heads of states have contributed for the contras—most of it—millions, has disappeared." He continued. "The arms that were earmarked for Afghanistan are being sent to the contras. The funds for Afghanistan and the money from the Iran arms sales are commingled. Who on earth can separate these funds? To top it off, your president, who has launched such a massive antidrug campaign with his wife, Nancy, leading off all the fanfare, doesn't know that the planes that delivered the arms carried loads of drugs back from Central America."

"You must be joking!" I said. "How are they shipping drugs on United States Air Force planes?"

He derided me. "You have been there too long! You have begun to think like one of them. Am I speaking Greek? I didn't say the air force. The drug runners have their own airline. It is called Southern Air Transport and is based in Miami. It used to be entirely owned by the CIA, but now it is also owned by General Secord, Albert Hakim, and others. Both of these men are part of the president's mission." Exasperated, he said, "If the president's men ever tell the truth, about how much wrong has been done and how often the law has been broken, the doorpost will shudder."

After I hung up, I tried to digest what he had just reported. I was again being accused of being naïve, not devious enough, and too Westernized. I thought about all of the allegations against the Reagan government. The cadre members had flagrantly overcharged Iran, sent money to the contras when Congress had voted against it, put money in secret bank accounts, and engaged in South American drug smuggling. If such extensive corruption and illegal activities were indeed being committed by President Reagan's "private government," then these crimes would hang like an albatross around President Reagan's neck.

The accusations that my source reported to me in August 1986 were confirmed in November and December 1986 by various United States authorities, including the Justice Department. The money is in the Swiss bank accounts of the president's men—Secord, North, and others whose names are still unknown. The arms-dealing cadre claim some of the money went to the contras. When Southern Air, owned by General Secord, Albert Hakim, and the CIA, delivered arms to the contras in Nicaragua, my source said that the empty planes stopped in Panama and loaded up on drugs before heading to the United States. Despite my incredulity at my source's information, he was justified again when *The New York Times,* on January 20 and 30, 1987, featured articles on the contras in which it found that "American flight crews covertly ferrying arms to the rebels returned to the United States by way of

Panama, a major drug transshipment center, to pick up cocaine and marijuana." *The New York Times* quoted a drug-enforcement official as saying, "It was not one of the big smuggling rings anyway." It was like saying, "She's a little bit pregnant."

The American people have been faced with layers of lies. As of this writing in February 1987, the Justice Department is investigating the money that went to the Republican campaign fund. During all of their illegal acts, the president's men traveled on forged passports. Though President Reagan ordered a swift investigation of the scandal, his most trusted colleagues have taken the Fifth Amendment.

When it was disclosed that President Reagan had sent a Bible to Khomeini, the White House denied it. Later on, the White House stated if the Bible was sent, the president was unaware of it. On January 28, 1987, when Tehran showed the press the handwritten verse and signature of the president on the Bible, dated October 3, 1986, the White House said it was not the president's idea but Colonel North's to send the Bible.

In February 1987, as reported by *The New York Times,* McFarlane said that he didn't know Ghorbanifar's background, and if he had known what he knows now, he would never have suggested the United States get involved with him. McFarlane apparently had forgotten a great deal, including the fact that in January 1986 Ghorbanifar went under the polygraph and failed. The president waived the results, even though the CIA was against it.

This all reminds me of a Persian story:

A thief was caught in a garden with a big sack of pumpkins. The owner saw him and asked what he was doing in his garden. The thief said, "You won't believe it but a strong wind came and blew me here. I'm not lying." The owner said, "Granted. But who picked all the pumpkins?" The thief said because the wind was so strong and was going to carry him off to some other place, he had to hold on to the pumpkins and they came off. "I'm not lying," he said. The owner again said, "Granted. But can you tell me how the pumpkins got into your sack?" The thief cried, "I have the very same question! How *did* the pumpkins get into my sack?"

What happened to the money? This is a question that the whole world is asking, and perhaps that is why Secord, North, and Poindexter are taking the Fifth Amendment.

*   *   *

In the summer of 1986, Reagan's emissaries were congratulating themselves that their mission had been an unalloyed success—Iran was theirs. The proof was the return of some of the hostages taken in Lebanon. In a mood to celebrate, they got together for a party in Western Europe, and euphorically laid down their plans for future adventures. With Iran now in America's pocket, they would move farther east—to Afghanistan to solve that country's problems, too, and with the leftover, laundered proceeds of their Middle East operations, finally they would heat up America's secret war in Central America.

But the CIA, angered and disgusted by Ghorbanifar from the very beginning of their relationship, decided to depict the Ghorbanifar group as crooks, incompetents or both. In the fall of 1986, the CIA members of the cadre moved independently to sell to the Iranian government, through Rafsanjani, arms for up to 60 percent less than previous weapons sold by Ghorbanifar and other dealers.

The damage was done. Back in Tehran, the government accused all the arms dealers, especially Ghorbanifar, of gross overcharging. The arms dealers had lied to the government and it wanted its money back.

Ghorbanifar's colleagues were furious at having been betrayed by their American collaborators. Among themselves, the dealers spoke of revenge and said, "Hadn't we freed some of the hostages before their damn election? Opened the door for negotiations? Made them money and even pimped for them? We are the ones who actually put the American hand in the Iranian hand, and this is the end result! How right Colonel North was. He always said the CIA would screw us in the end. Let's give it to them!"

Ghorbanifar's group retaliated by blowing the cover of President Reagan's cadre. First, they contacted Montazeri's aides and told them that the Americans had been in touch with Rafsanjani all along, and were against him and Khomeini. They advised Montazeri's aides to move quickly and go public. The aides issued a press release, describing in detail negotiations between the Americans and Rafsanjani—announcing to the world that the United States was exchanging arms for American hostages. This was picked up by the Beirut weekly magazine *Al Shiraa,* and ultimately by all the news services.

It was a bombshell! In an instant, Colonel North's personal triumph exploded into an international disaster whose reverberations were felt around the world. Colonel North emerged as a controversial and mysterious figure. He was at once summarily fired and praised as a hero by President Reagan.

Khomeini, ever the sly fox, seized the moment to reiterate his old warning. "How many times have I said, 'Don't get involved with the

"Great Satan"—the evil United States?'" Khomeini's government demanded immediate retribution. Montazeri's aides were disgusted by America's behavior, Rafsanjani arrested close to five hundred of Montazeri's followers and put them in jail, and Rafsanjani's son, Mehdi, was forced to flee the country. The arms dealers demanded payment in full for their services.

The Reagan administration, hounded by the press, was forced to confront an incipient crisis.

When the United States began flirting with Ayatollah Khomeini, it had hostages only in Lebanon and none in Iran. In February 1987 three have been released, one has died; there are new hostages in Iran and more in Lebanon than at the beginning of the White House-Khomeini romance.

Reagan's administration claimed that it sought a dialogue with moderates in the Khomeini government, but unfortunately there are few moderate voices in the Khomeini regime. Even so, if there was a possibility of establishing contact with moderates, the cadre was too inept and amateurish to discover who they were, or to deal successfully with them. As soon as Khomeini took control, he methodically eliminated all the moderate political and religious voices and subjected Iran to the most barbaric aspects of Islamic judicial practices. The only people the cadre was ever in contact with were Khomeini's prime minister, Mousavi, Rafsanjani, his speaker of the House, and Montazeri, his second-in-command. Certainly none of them represents a moderate point of view.

These "moderates" were disciples of a man who, after several sophisticated arms shipments reached Iran for which the CIA demanded William Buckley's return, asked his aides, "Did you receive the whole order?" When an aide answered, "No, just a part of it," Khomeini replied, laughing, "Well, send them a portion of William Buckley—one arm and one leg."

Above all, Vice-President Bush was officially informed while in Israel in the summer of 1986 that arms were sent to Iran for the radical groups, not the moderates, if there were any. If the vice-president informed the president of the nonexistence of moderates what logical reason did the president have to continue the arms? If Bush did not inform the president, what logical reason did Bush have? But the naked truth is that the president, the vice-president, and their men were aware that they were sending arms to the disciples of Khomeini.

In early November 1986 a source reported that Khomeini was very angry about the picture the world press was being given of his regime, and felt that the remarks made by the American government about Iran were insulting and degrading. Khomeini's aides threatened the president's men that they would go public and reveal the incriminating details of America's clandestine dealings unless Ronald Reagan made the following statements to the American people:

1. There was never an exchange between Iran and the United States government of arms for hostages.

2. The Iranian revolution was a genuine one.

3. The Iranian government is not a part of world terrorist activity.

As I listened in amazement, my source went on to say that White House intermediaries had replied to these threats by assuring the Iranians that they would pass the message along to the president.

I was astounded. I couldn't believe that the White House would even listen to this obvious blackmail, just to mollify Khomeini's newly wounded sensibilities. Khomeini was like a wise serpent—he struck at just the right time.

On November 13, 1986, President Reagan addressed the nation in a live broadcast from the Oval Office. His talk included the following statements:

I know you've been reading, seeing and hearing a lot of stories the past several days attributed to Danish sailors, unnamed observers at Italian ports. . . . Well, now you're going to hear the facts from a White House source, and you know my name. . . .

For 18 months now we have had underway a secret diplomatic initiative with Iran. . . .

The United States has not made concessions to those who hold our people captive in Lebanon. And we will not. The United States has not swapped boatloads or planeloads of American weapons for the return of American hostages. And we will not. . . .

During the course of our secret discussions, I authorized the transfer of small amounts of defensive weapons and spare parts for defensive systems to Iran. . . .

These modest deliveries, taken together, could easily fit into a single cargo plane. . . .

Some progress has already been made. Since U.S. Government contact began with Iran, there's been no evidence of Iranian Government complicity in acts of terrorism against the United States. . . .

The Iranian revolution is a fact of history, but between American and Iranian basic national interests there need be no permanent conflict. . . .

To summarize. Our government has a firm policy not to capitulate to terrorist demands. That no concessions policy remains in force, in spite of the wildly speculative and false stories about arms for hostages and alleged ransom payments. We did not—repeat—did not trade weapons or anything else for hostages nor will we. . . .

We have not, nor will we capitulate to terrorists. . . .

As President, I've always operated on the belief that, given the facts, the American people will make the right decision. . . .

So angered was I by what I had just heard in my own living room that I had to suppress an urge to throw something at the TV screen.
The American people, alas, have been given everything *but* the facts.

> O thou who will be king after me,
> Do your best to abstain from lying,
> If you think of what you must do to save your country,
> Annihilate the liars.

> —DARIUS I, THE GREAT
> Reigned c. 552–486 B.C.

THE END OF A ROAD

From my student days I had worked toward one goal, a rule of justice and human rights for my oppressed country. The shah became monstrous, growing more and more cruel and tyrannous throughout his reign. I was to learn that the CIA, unbridled by accountability to the American public, cared little for justice and humanity, but cared a great deal for power, which it used arrogantly and dangerously.

I believe in the essential goodness of people, and I believe that goodness can prevail if the truth is known. Through my book I hope to shed whatever light I can on a very dark period of history. The truth is my last weapon. My father's words echo: "A lie has a short life. Soon it decays and the decay is the fertilizer from which a truth will grow and blossom, a truth that will last forever."

AFTERWORD

Persia, once the cradle of civilization, carrying the torch of humanity in poetry, literature, and art, has been cursed. Historians only note that it is a country that has consistently destroyed the fruits of its creation.

After 2,500 years of Persian monarchy, after the reigns of approximately 350 shahs, there was not, nor is there now, one existing statue of a shah. Each shah obliterated every vestige of his predecessor. Nowhere in the history of any other country has the number of kings killed at the hands of his people been so great. The shortest rule was one day —and the longest, sixty-eight years.

Iran's bloody history could be an endless source of inspiration for students of political intrigue and regicide.

Of 350 kings:

85 were killed, poisoned or blinded by their own father, son, wife, brother or uncle;

128 were killed by their own subjects;

62 were killed in battle;

67 died while hunting, while in jail, while escaping from Iran, while being sent into exile; some committed suicide and a few died of natural causes;

8 were deposed.

The first king to be deposed lost his throne in A.D. 40. The last shah to be deposed was Mohammad Reza Pahlavi, who ruled for thirty-seven and one half years, and was ousted by Khomeini's referendum in 1979.

The Persian pattern is ageless.

Khomeini, man and memory, cannot escape the Persian fate.

NOTES

1. General Oveissi had been one of the most powerful Iranian generals while serving as the former commander of the ground forces in Iran and the last commander of martial law in the final days of the shah, and he was in exile and trying to overthrow Khomeini's government.

2. Sufism was founded in the tenth century as a protest against the formalism of all religion. It gradually developed into a rebellion against the decadence, corruption, and tyranny of a materialistic society. Sufism is the antithesis of arrogance, intolerance, hypocrisy, and inhumanity. The Sufi's goal is to create a renaissance of man's spirit in which he might live a simple life, at peace with himself and his Creator.

3. *Language and Modernization: A Comparative Analysis of Persian and English Texts,* Raymond D. Gastil, Center for International Affairs, Harvard University, Cambridge, Mass., July 1959.

4. SAVAK was established in Iran in 1957 on the joint advice of the CIA, the British intelligence service, and Mossad, the Secret Service of Israel. The name SAVAK is an acronym for Sazeman Ettelaat va Amniyat Kashvar (National Security and Information Organization). By consent of the three foreign intelligence groups, Britain had no active involvement in SAVAK's operations. Mossad was involved in textbook teaching—instructing Iranian members of SAVAK in such things as preparation of reports and keeping of files—and it provided instructors who introduced themselves as European "professors."

The CIA, on the other hand, went all out. It took charge and became deeply involved in every aspect of SAVAK's daily operations. It instructed

Iranians on how to set up SAVAK's divisions, to organize and choose its personnel, to select and operate its equipment, to run its agents and double agents—hands on. The CIA was deeply enmeshed from day one. The Iranians, although past masters at brutality, at beatings and torture, were innocents in the field of espionage. They accepted any aid that was offered. The shah, anxious to protect himself, welcomed the establishment of SAVAK.

The government of Iran was highly compartmentalized and there was no provision in the law or room in the administration for the new infant, SAVAK. Existing police, army intelligence, and the gendarmerie were considered sufficient under the law for the country's protection. Therefore, because of the sensitive nature of the organization, and to avoid conflict, SAVAK was placed within the office of the prime minister, and the chief of SAVAK was a deputy prime minister, thereby occupying the second highest position in the nation.

Under the nine provisions of the National Security Act, established by then Premier Dr. Mossadegh, and in particular under Article 5 of the Act, all human rights were taken away from the subjects of the shah. It was a magnificent piece of legal theft. It left not a single loophole, not a single right; it permitted the government, in the interests of national security, to arrest anyone without charges, without the necessity to inform either the accused or the Department of Justice of his or her whereabouts, or to specify the time for which the accused could or would be jailed. It was later modified slightly by General Zahedi, who, although a military man and a dictator in his own right, was all too aware of the law's fearsome potential. At the time that Dr. Mossadegh, with his plenary powers, wrote the law, it was subject to furious questioning and opposition in Parliament. Dr. Baghai challenged Dr. Karim Sanjabi, a professor at the law school in Tehran University, an associate of Dr. Mossadegh's, and a former member of the delegation to the International Court in The Hague and to the Security Council of the United Nations, stating that the National Security Act legalized torture.

"Well," Sanjabi answered, "if you don't torture the accused, no one will ever reveal anything."

The Act, the antithesis of Article 5 of the Charter of Human Rights of the United Nations (which states that torture is contrary to any and all human rights), was signed by Dr. Mossadegh. Torture was legalized, and the path was cleared for the inevitable offspring of the National Security Act—SAVAK.

5. At the end of 1978, just before the shah fell, I had, at most, 120 agents in the United States, their pay scale ranging from a minimum of one hundred dollars per month to a maximum of one thousand per month. There were approximately twenty Iranian "diplomats"; about twenty relatives of SAVAK people (these agents did absolutely nothing); twenty-five disabled people who were kept on the payroll for humanitarian reasons; forty agents who were all talk, no action; ten (three of whom were excellent) who had succeeded in infiltrating the activists; and five—three of whom were very good and two

whom I never completely trusted—who had broken into the Communist circle.

6. My resolution paid dividends. After the revolution, many activists returned to Tehran and read their SAVAK files. Many of those who had cursed me and considered me their enemy when I was chief of SAVAK later became my friends.

7. In 1984 a report of the closed hearing disclosed the following comments made by the three members: (Humphrey) "This crowd [the ruling elite in Iran] are dead—they just don't know it"; (Fulbright) [We] have encouraged [Iran] to enlarge their military beyond their capacity to support it . . . this is one of the causes of the bankruptcy of the regime . . ."; (Church) "All I know about history says that [the shah] is not long for this world, nor his system. And when he goes down, boom, we go with him."

8. KOOK, designated as the Center Attached to Civilian Employees of the Country. This organization was not listed in any branch of government in which SAVAK was listed. The shah found it both a wise and necessary course to offset SAVAK's power by forming a separate organization of his own men. Although it was limited in its membership, anyone who qualified, according to the shah's specifications, could become a member—army officers, government employees, even SAVAK employees—as long as their highest loyalty was to the shah and their reports went directly to him.

9. Bakhtiar's mission was to convince the CIA to topple the shah and change the monarchy to a republic. Bakhtiar, as previously mentioned, wanted to be the first president of the new republic of Iran.

10. *Department of State Bulletin,* Vol. 57, September 18, 1967, p. 360.

11. Later I would learn that after Khomeini's arrival in Iran, General Khowsrodad, who was then in hiding, called the authorities and disclosed his whereabouts. He may have felt that it was dishonorable for a man in his position to be in hiding. In any case, he was promptly arrested, tried, and on February 16, 1979, executed by the Revolutionary Guards.

12. Ibrahim Yazdi, M.D., Muslim fanatic, American citizen, doing cancer research in Houston, Texas, was one of Khomeini's foreign ministers. Sadegh Ghotbzadeh, an Iranian student in the United States until he was deported, later became foreign minister in Khomeini's regime and was later executed by him.

13. Shahpur Bakhtiar was the last prime minister under the shah, and Mehdi Bazargan was the first prime minister of the revolutionary government.

14. The soldier later was shot by the revolutionary government for his loyalty.

15. Radical opposition leaders pressed for outright confrontation with the

government and called a general strike. The government imposed martial law on the evening of September 7. By the following morning, over twenty thousand people congregated in Jaleh Square in Tehran for a religious rally. Troops ordered the crowd to disperse. When they refused, the soldiers opened fire on the crowd. Estimates of casualties varied enormously—from three hundred to two thousand killed and a greater number wounded.

16. Congress has enacted a number of statutory requirements for the Executive Branch to inform it when new covert actions are initiated. The most important of these requirements are the Hughes-Ryan Amendment of 1974 (Section 662 of the Foreign Assistance Act of 1961), which requires a Presidential Finding before the CIA can spend any money on a covert activity, and the Intelligence Oversight Act of 1980 (Title V of the National Security Act of 1947), which requires notice of those Findings.